I0818496

IMPULSE REMBRANDT

TEACHER, STRATEGIST, BESTSELLER

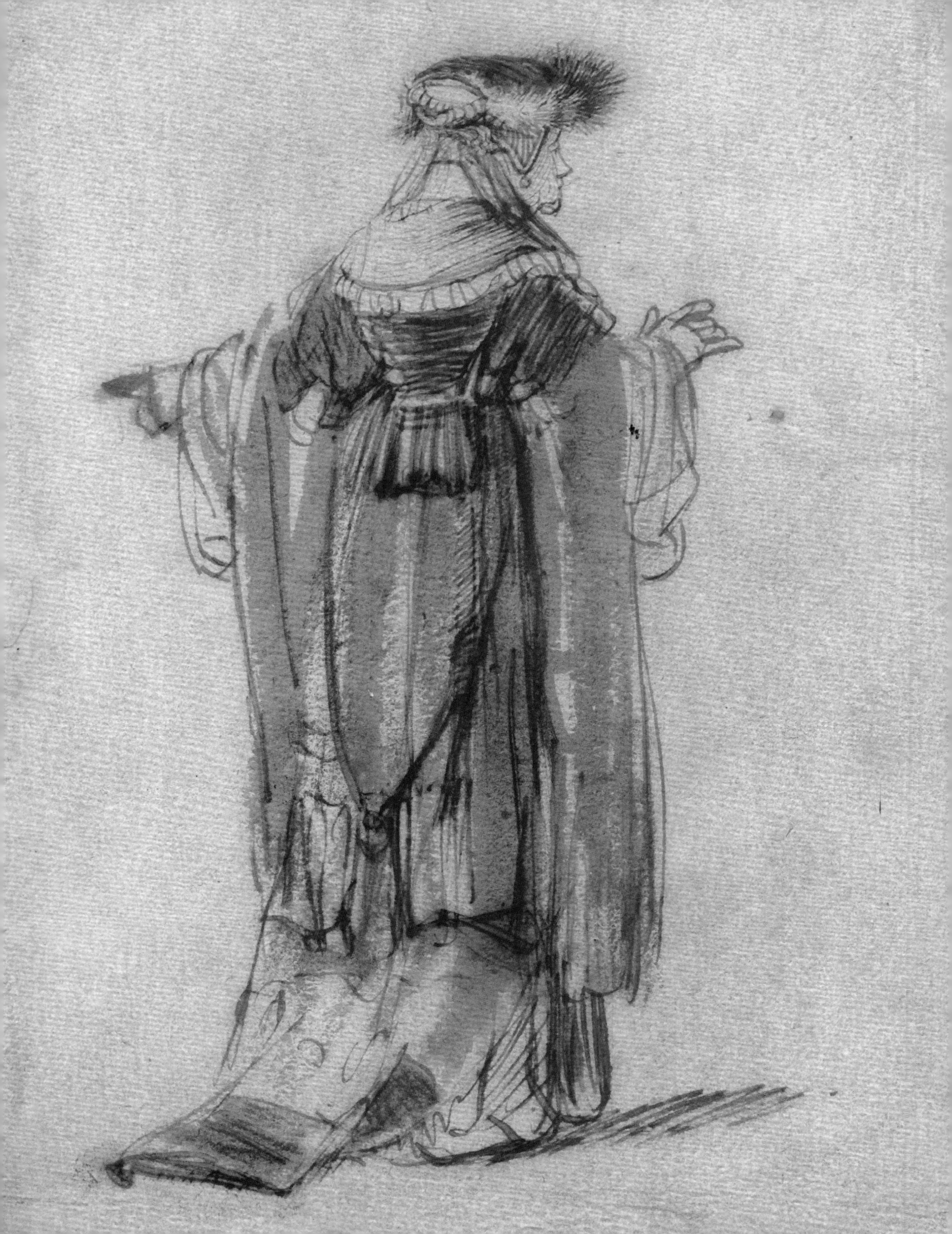

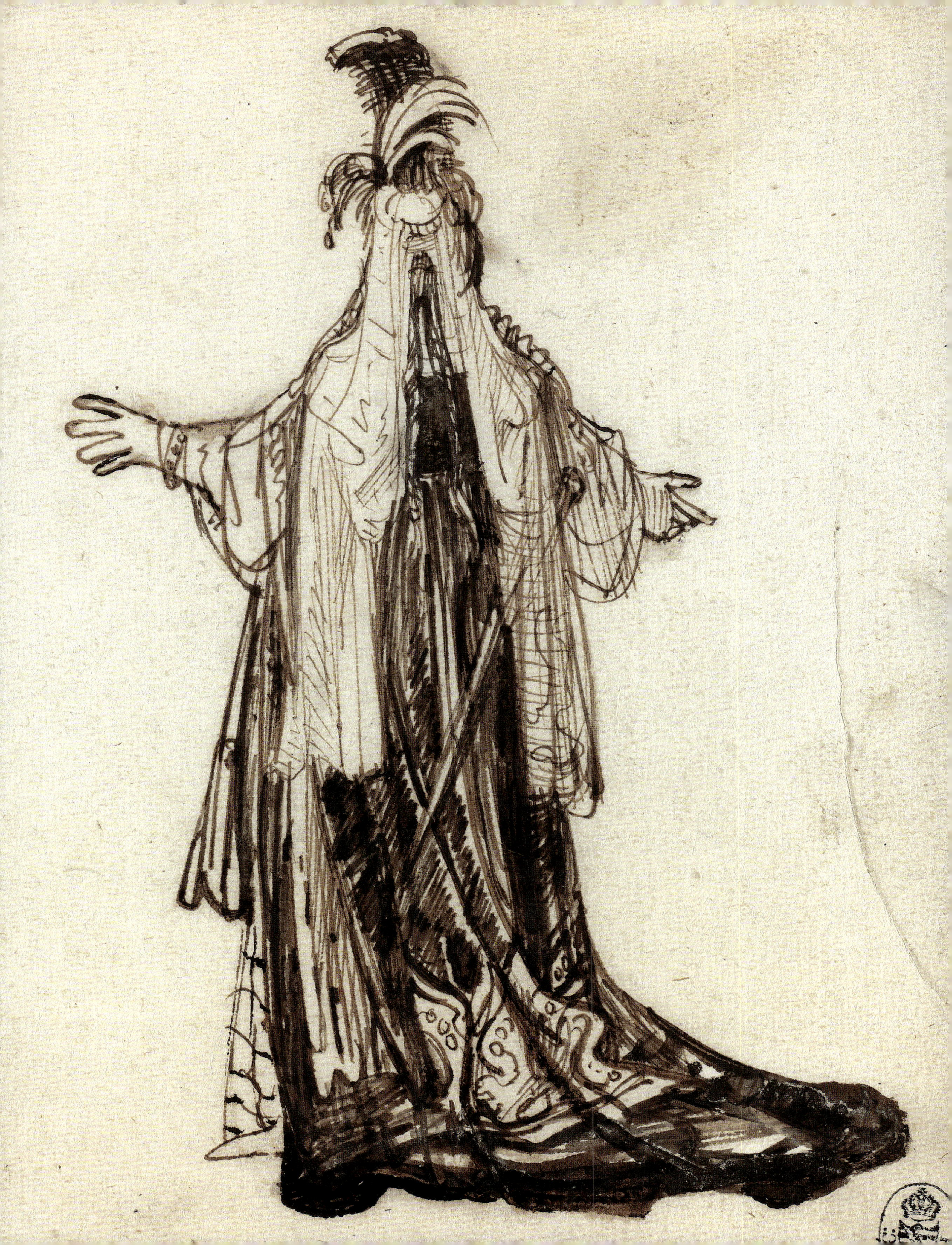

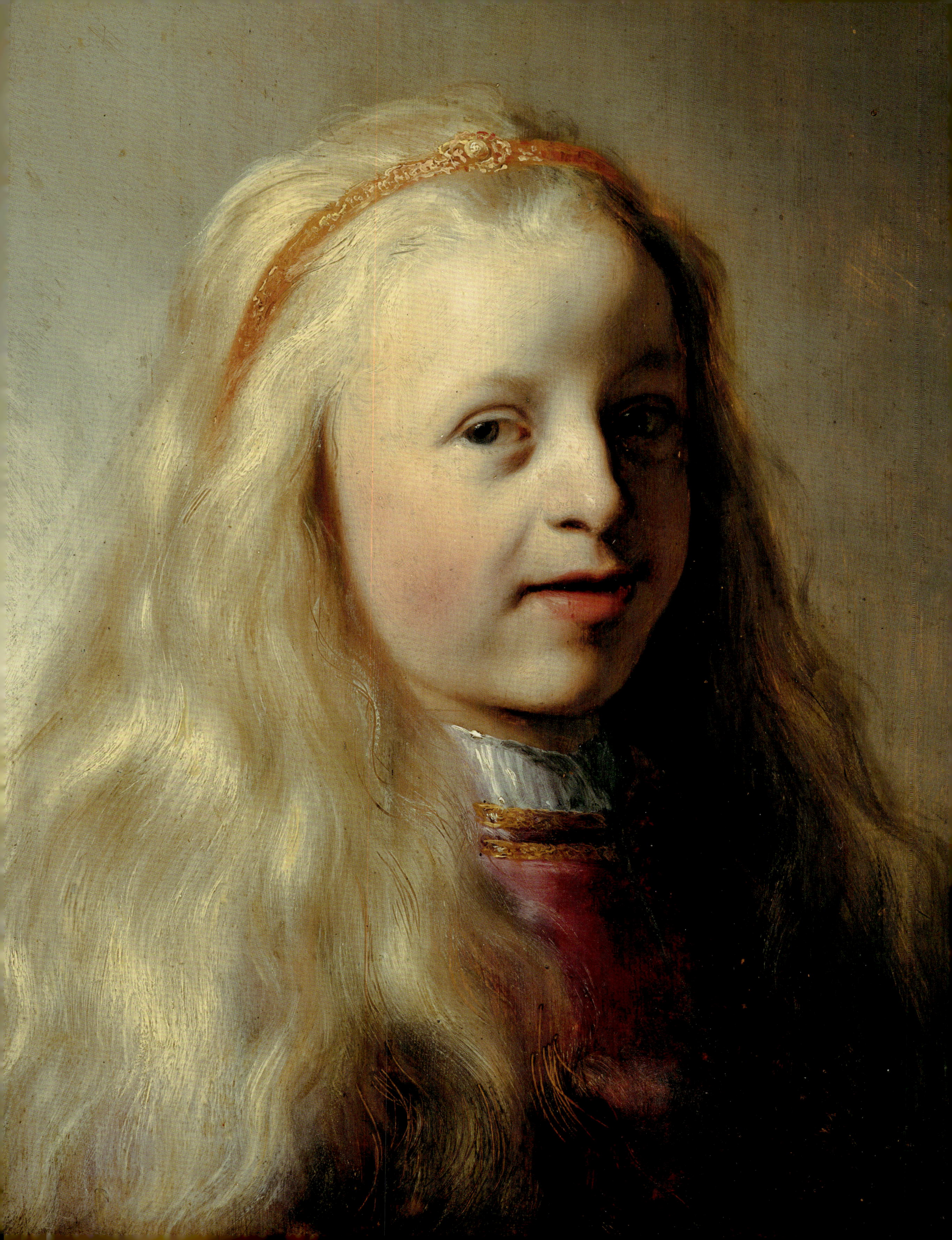

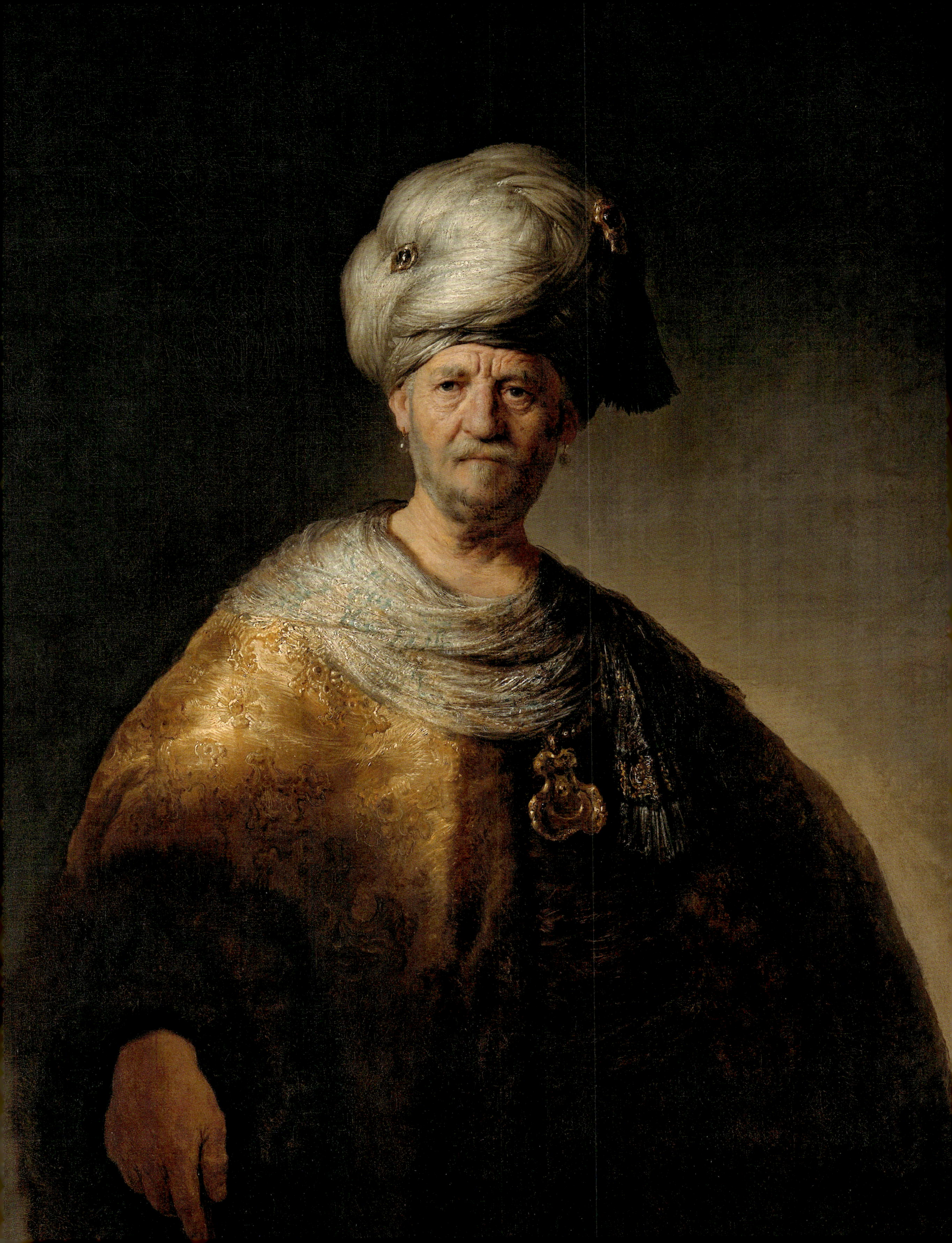

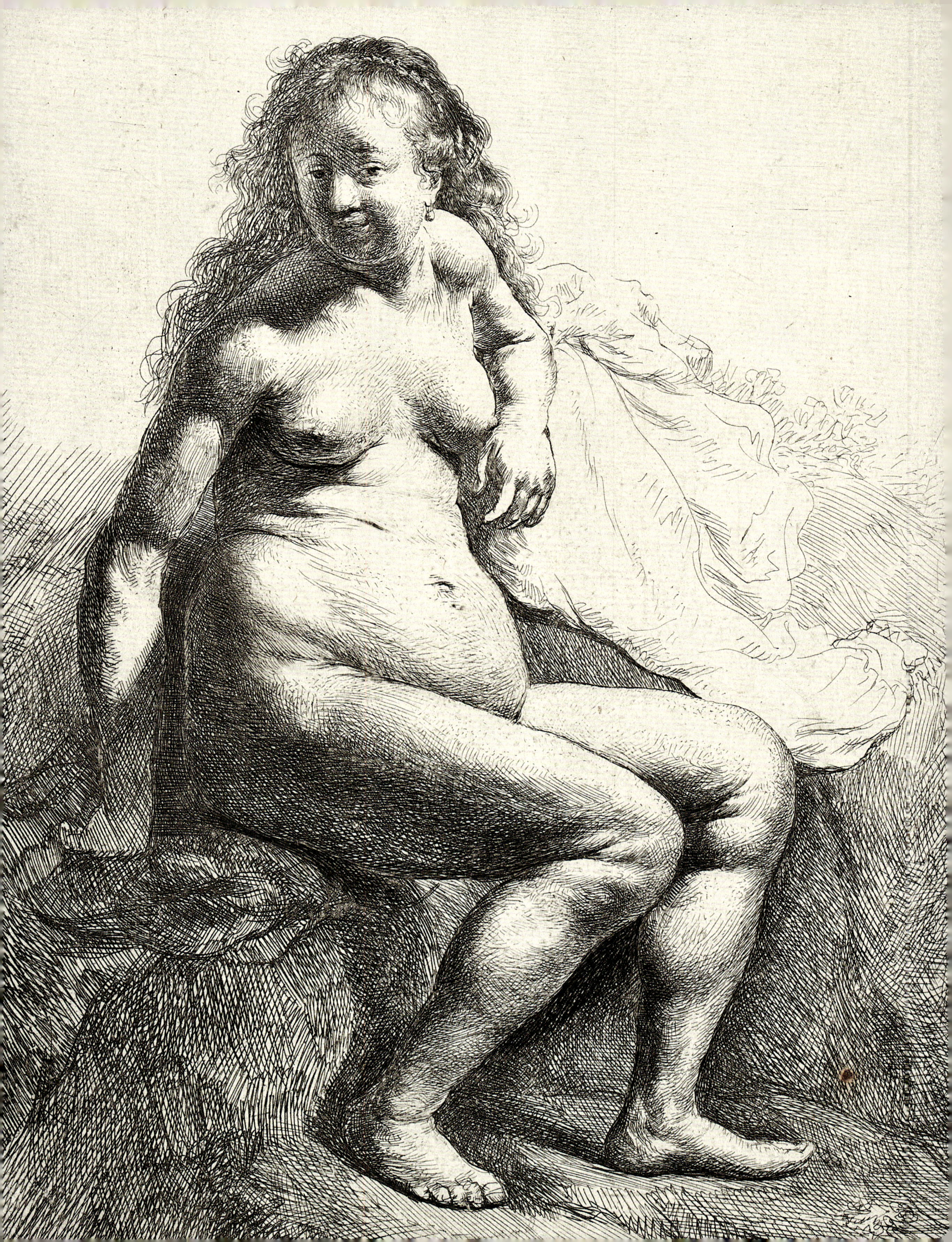

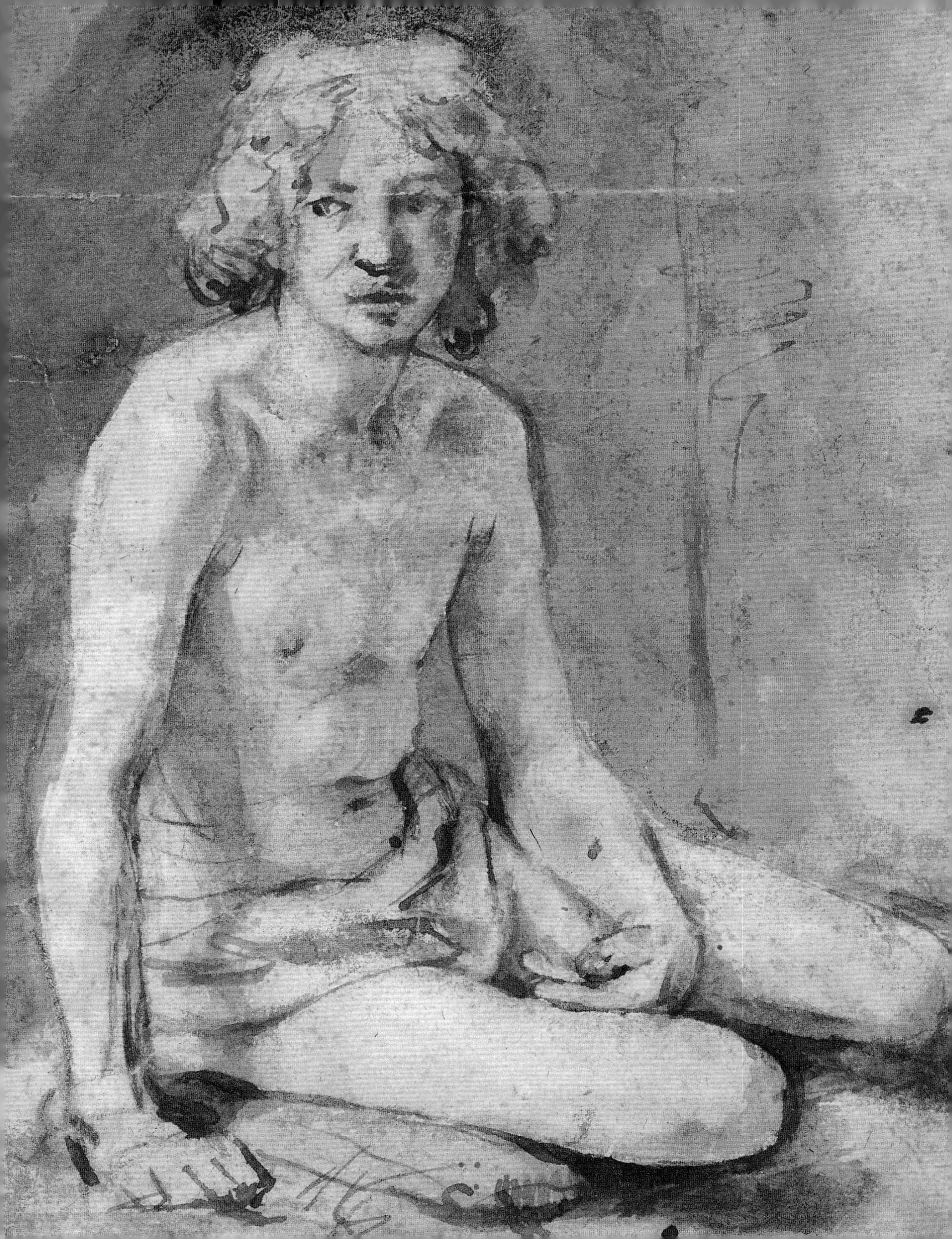

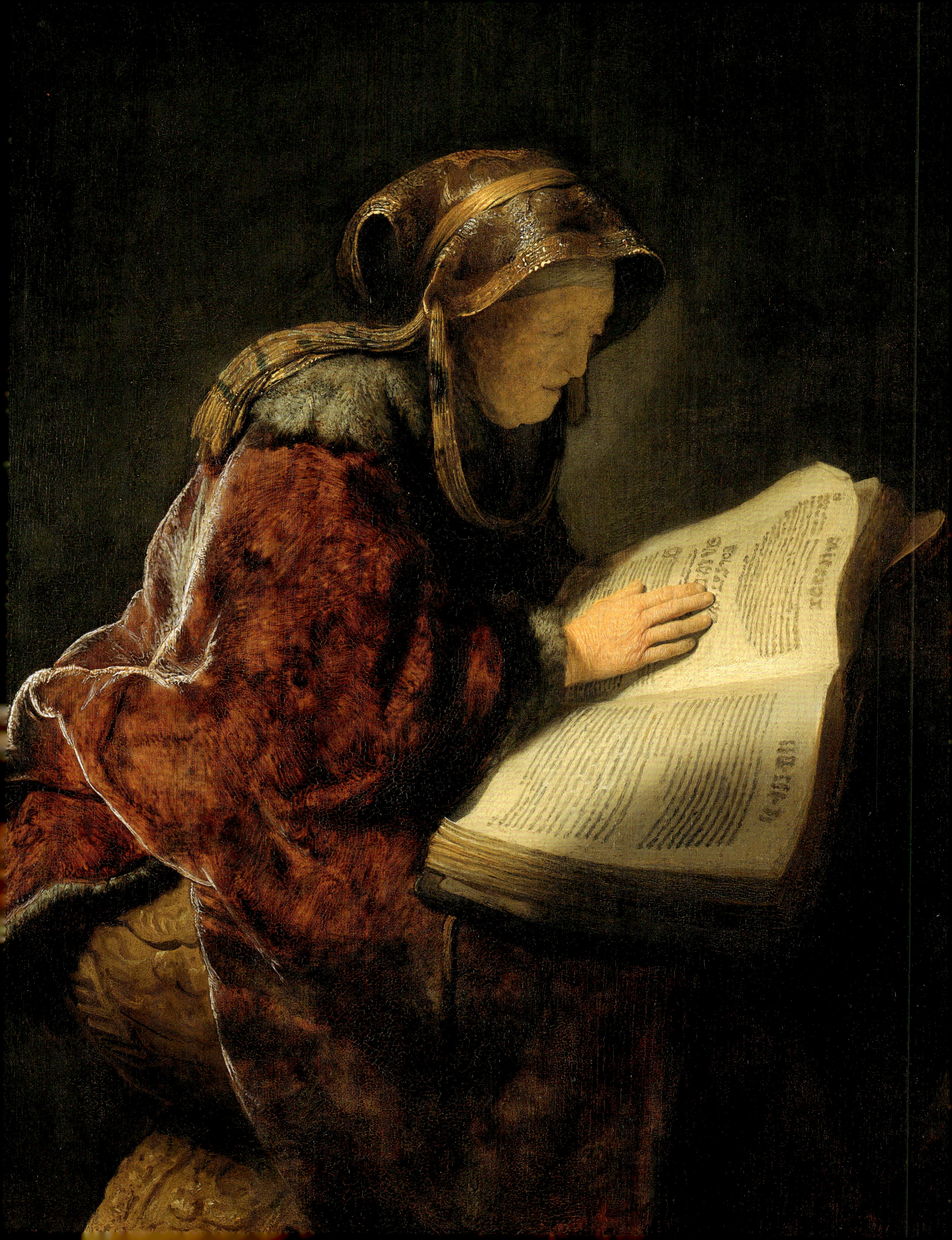

LENDERS

Germany
Berlin, Staatliche Museen zu Berlin Preußischer Kulturbesitz, Gemäldegalerie
Berlin, Staatliche Museen zu Berlin Preußischer Kulturbesitz, Kupferstichkabinett
Braunschweig, Herzog Anton Ulrich-Museum
Bremen, Kunsthalle Bremen
Coburg, Kunstsammlungen der Veste Coburg, Kupferstichkabinett
Cologne, LETTER Foundation
Cologne, Wallraf-Richartz-Museum & Fondation Corboud
Darmstadt, Hessisches Landesmuseum Darmstadt
Dresden, Staatliche Kunstsammlungen Dresden, Gemäldegalerie Alte Meister
Dresden, Staatliche Kunstsammlungen Dresden, Kupferstich-Kabinett
Frankfurt am Main, Städel Museum/ Städelsches Kunstinstitut and Städtische Galerie
Gotha, Friedenstein Stiftung Gotha, Herzogliches Museum
Hamburg, Hamburger Kunsthalle
Karlsruhe, Staatliche Kunsthalle Karlsruhe
Kassel, Museumslandschaft Hessen, Gemäldegalerie Alte Meister
Kiel, Kunsthalle zu Kiel der Christian-Albrechts-Universität
Leipzig, Stadtgeschichtliches Museum Leipzig
Munich, Bayerische Staatsgemäldesammlungen, Alte Pinakothek
Munich, Staatliche Graphische Sammlung München
Nuremberg, Germanisches Nationalmuseum
Stuttgart, Staatsgalerie Stuttgart
Weimar, Klassik Stiftung Weimar

Austria
Vienna, Albertina Museum

Belgium
Brussels, Private collection, Courtesy Lempertz

France
Paris, Fondation Custodia/Collection Frits Lugt
Paris, Musée du Louvre, Département des Peintures
Paris, Musée du Louvre, Département des Arts graphiques

Great Britain
London, The National Gallery

The Netherlands
Amsterdam, Museum Het Rembrandthuis
Amsterdam, Rijksmuseum
Dordrecht, Dordrechts Museum
Rotterdam, Museum Boijmans Van Beuningen
The Hague, Mauritshuis

Sweden
Stockholm, Nationalmuseum

USA
New York, The Metropolitan Museum of Art

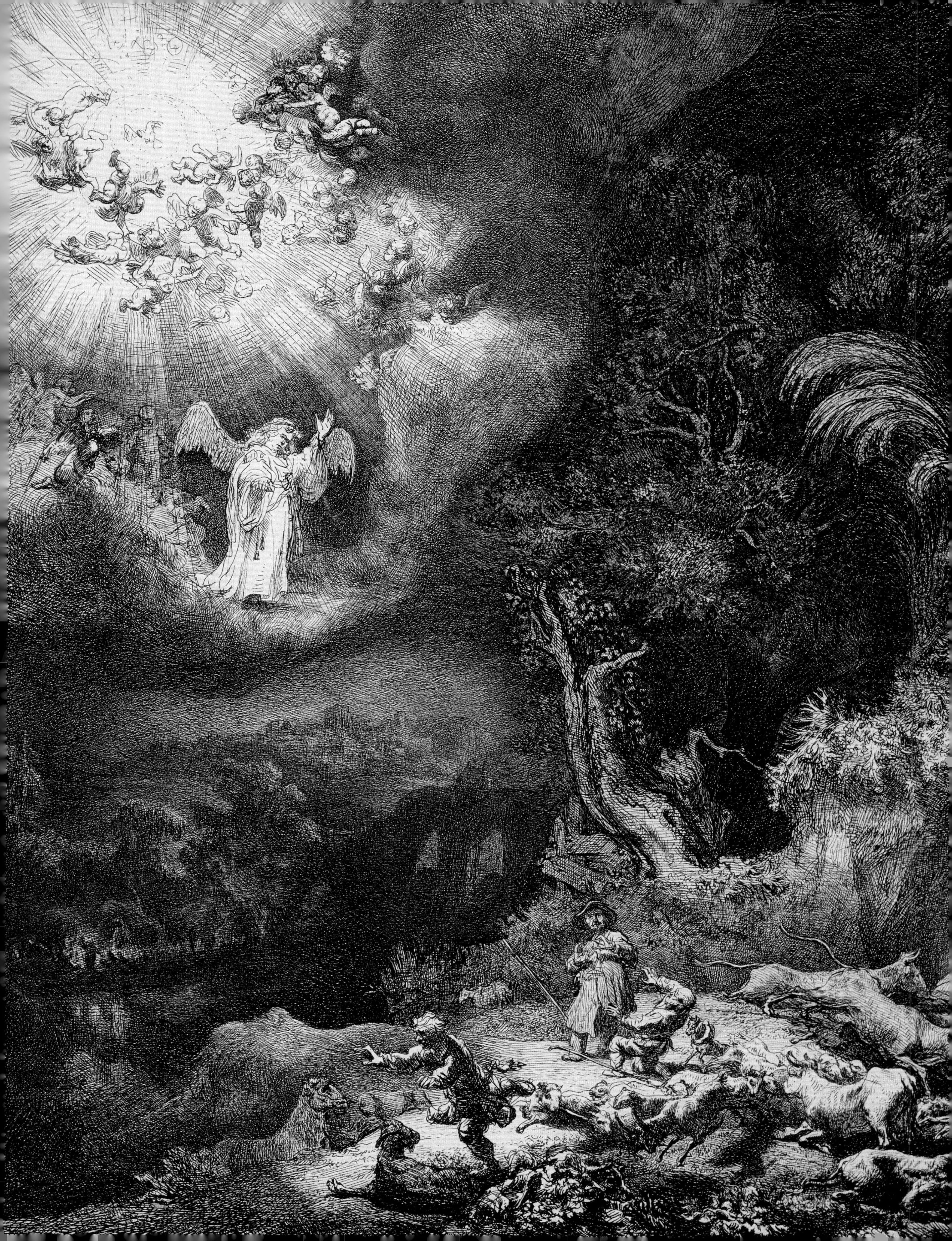

REMBRANDT'S WORKSHOP: BETWEEN PRODUCTION FACILITY AND SCHOOL OF SEEING

Jan Nicolaisen

What distinguished Rembrandt's workshop from those of other Dutch painters of the seventeenth century? What was the appeal of this artist that drew young talents from Holland and Europe to Amsterdam over a period of four decades? Is it possible to identify special teaching contents and methods? Rembrandt's rapid rise to fame – already as a 23-year-old he received visits from high-ranking figures such as Constantijn Huygens, secretary to Stadtholder Frederik Hendrik, in his studio – was no doubt an important factor. A key aspect was the extraordinary quality of his art: the realism of his paintings; their vividness and power of illusion, achieved through the use of colour and application of paint; his renewal of portrait and religious history painting in the early 1630s and 40s; the dramatic quality and persuasive power of his pictorial narratives, which involved a hitherto unknown expression of feelings and passions; the touching humanity of his works; and, last but not least, his great success due to these very characteristics of his work – this was what drew pupils from beyond the region.

From the beginning of his career, moreover, Rembrandt not only sought to explore new formal and thematic possibilities in his art, but also pursued economic expansion. He did not fear experimentation or risk, certainly not in art, but also not in economic matters. In 1631, at the age of 24, he invested the considerable sum of 1,000 guilders in the art dealer's shop of Hendrick Uylenburgh, for whom he worked until 1635.[1] It was there that Rembrandt created his first portraits, mainly of the wealthy (Mennonite) Amsterdam upper class (which the art dealer sold in his own name after arranging the commissions), and taught pupils who made copies of paintings for Uylenburgh to sell.[2] It was also during this period that Rembrandt created his large-scale orientalising tronie (New York), an attention-drawing painting illustrative of the young painter's enterprising attitude (cat. 35). The organisational structure of the workshop under art dealer Uylenburgh was probably a business model that deeply inspired Rembrandt. When in 1635, a year after joining the Guild of St Luke in Amsterdam, he set up his own workshop in Amsterdam where he could paint *and* have pictures painted exclusively on his own account, this was a step towards greater economic independence. But it was not automatically accompanied by good economic sense. For one thing, the flow of portrait commissions slowed after the end of his collaboration with Uylenburgh. In the second half of the 1630s, Rembrandt initially concentrated on history painting, for which there was a competitive market in Amsterdam.[3]

A telling example of Rembrandt's willingness to take financial risks was his art collection, on which he spent vast sums throughout his life (more than he could afford); another was the purchase of the enormously expensive house on Sint Antoniesbreestraat in 1639, which cost him 13,000 guilders. Rembrandt's income from art sales over the next two decades was never enough to repay his debts in full. Given this, his bankruptcy in 1656 was virtually preordained.

For the miller's son from Leiden, the purchase of the house (now home to the Rembrandthuis Museum), which had been renovated by Jacob van Campen, the star architect of the day, served the purpose of social self-aggrandizement. He resided there in style, not far from the homes of his teacher Pieter Lastman and Hendrick Uylenburgh. The house was spacious enough to accommodate several pupils in separate rooms in the attic, for whose tuition Rembrandt demanded a steep fee (100 guilders per pupil per year, excluding board and lodging). However, other painters such as Honthorst, Dou, Lievens and Sandrart charged an equally high tuition fee.[4] In addition, Rembrandt is said to have earned 2,000 to 2,500 guilders a year from the sale of pupils' works. The German painter, art historian and Rembrandt rival Joachim von Sandrart wrote about this in a slightly mocking tone in his *Teutsche Academie*, albeit thirty years after Rembrandt's time in Amsterdam. Sandrart states that Rembrandt's house had been 'filled with almost innumerable genteel children for instruction and teaching',[5] thereby pointing to the social status of the parents who could afford such an expensive education for their children.[6]

The employment of some 40 to 50 pupils and assistants over a period of five decades was probably a combination of a useful source of income, a strategy to increase artistic productivity and the ethos of wanting to pass on his own experience and artistic views as a teacher. According to Arnold Houbraken, Rembrandt rented studio space in a warehouse on Bloemgracht for pupils to learn to draw nudes.[7] Rembrandt's on the whole rather rare large-scale commissions (such as *The Night Watch*, completed in 1642) do not suffice to explain the presumed workshop operation. A certain number of pupils and assistants was probably part of his idea of a successful painter-entrepreneur, much like the art collection and the large house. This was connected to his strategy to market his specific style (which was constantly changing), i.e., to popularise and capitalise on it.[8] It may be assumed that Rembrandt took on pupils in Amsterdam only starting in 1635, after he had finished working for Uylenburgh and moved into a house on Nieuw Doelenstraat with his young wife, Saskia van Uylenburgh (a cousin of the art dealer, whom he had met through the latter), four years before moving into the stately house on Sint Antoniesbreestraat.[9] After the forced sale of the latter house in 1658 and his subsequent move to Rozengracht, he no longer had enough space to accommodate a large number of pupils.

Between Gerrit Dou, his first pupil in Leiden in the second half of the 1620s, and Aert de Gelder, a pupil from the 1660s who carried Rembrandt's late style well into the eighteenth century, there was a string of young artists of different talents who worked in Rembrandt's workshop, usually for two to three years. This complex practice has been a frequent subject of scholarship and exhibitions.[10] Yet we still do not know how many pupils actually worked for him, partly because some of them, such as the Danish painter Bernhard Keil who is said to have worked in Rembrandt's workshop from 1642 to 1644, are mentioned in written sources but have left no other traces from the period.[11] A large group of works in Rembrandt's style were created not by putative workshop assistants, but by contemporary and later imitators of the artist (cf. cat. 19). They, too, contributed to the image of the large workshop. Among those who came to Rembrandt were aspiring artists who pursued a professional career – and subsequently practised – as painters, as well as amateurs and art dilettantes such as Constantijn van Renesse, who merely took drawing lessons from the famous master.

While the focus of art historical research in the 1980s and 90s was on the critical stylistic distinction of hands between works by Rembrandt and those by his pupils and followers, interest has more recently shifted to Rembrandt's teaching content and methods. The many years of research by Ernst van de Wetering and numerous others as part of the Rembrandt Research Project (RRP), as well as recent exhibitions at the Museum Het Rembrandthuis in Amsterdam, have made a significant contribution in this regard. Van de Wetering has emphasised the imparting not only of practical, but also of theoretical knowledge by Rembrandt.[12] The following discussion draws on this research and enquires into a specific aspect of Rembrandt's teaching: the pictorial narrative as a subject of teaching, i.e., his ambition and ability as a teacher to convey a typical Rembrandtesque narrative style, which was especially important for history painting.

Rembrandt's career can be roughly divided into three phases: the early period in Leiden with his first pupils (second half of the 1620s), his establishment and success as an innovator of portrait and history painting in Amsterdam (1630s–40s) and his late period (1650s–60s). In each of these phases, different pupils and assistants were active in his workshop. Gerrit Dou was the most important pupil in the 1620s, while Govert Flinck, Ferdinand Bol and Gerbrand van den Eeckhout were Rembrandt's principal assistants in the 1630s. In the 1640s, Carel Fabritius and Samuel van Hoogstraten were among his most talented pupils. In the 1650s, Willem Drost and Nicolaes Maes were Rembrandt's top pupils, followed by Abraham Dijck and, in the 1660s, Aert de Gelder. Other artists such as Heyman Dullaert, Barent Fabritius, Hinrich Jansen,

Isaack Jouderville, Godfrey Kneller, Jacobus Leveck, Johann Ulrich Mayr, Jürgen Ovens, Christopher Paudiß, Constantijn van Renesse and many others should also be mentioned.

THE USEFULNESS OF PUPILS

Fundamentally, Rembrandt not only gave to his pupils, but also profited from his workshop – one need only think of his collaboration with the likewise highly talented young Jan Lievens in his early career. Lievens, who was two years older, was not a pupil, but a fellow painter in Leiden and a later competitor with whom Rembrandt may have shared a studio in their hometown.[13] Lievens preceded Rembrandt in developing the tronie into a distinct type of work (cat. 34.1–4) and influenced him through his painterly technique of suggesting three-dimensionality through the impasto application of paint. Samuel van Hoogstraten and Nicolaes Maes were only around 14 and 12 years old respectively when they joined Rembrandt's workshop, but already possessed basic skills.[14] Contrary to Sandrart's suggestion, in the 1630s and 40s, at least, there was an above-average number of assistants in Rembrandt's workshop who had already learnt the basic skills of painting from another teacher and were therefore considerably older than the usual 12 to 15 years – specifically between 18 and 22 – such as Flinck (18), Bol (20) and Carel (c. 19) and Barent Fabritius (22). They probably did not all have to pay the expensive apprentices' dues, since they could be called upon to assist him to a greater extent. Their main objective was to round off their training under Rembrandt, whose style was novel and popular in the 1630s.[15] After his three-year apprenticeship with the Leiden painter Isaack van Swanenburg, even Rembrandt himself had tacked on another six months of studies under history painter Pieter Lastman in Amsterdam, which were decisive for his artistic development. Lastman's narrative style and the colour schemes of his paintings strongly influenced him (cf. cat. 2). The stylistic closeness to a successful painter also promised success on the art market, which in turn explains why his pupils at least temporarily adopted his style.[16] This is still observable in the national and international art market today when the signature style of a successful artist becomes a model. Style was and is also an economic factor.

Teaching contracts of the period specifically stipulated the teacher's obligation to not withhold any knowledge from his pupils.[17] Teaching and running the workshop forced Rembrandt to continually reflect on both the practical and theoretical foundations of his art in order to impart them to his pupils. Precisely because learning his personal style through imitation was a central subject of instruction – as was common practice in the seventeenth century – the copies and variations of his pupils and assistants held up a mirror to him, which at the same time sharpened his perception and judgement of this signature style. This constant 'corrective' may have helped shape Rembrandt's power of innovation, since he was confronted with it in the form of pupils' works, including their many drawings, which he collected in albums.

It has often been discussed that the young Rembrandt competed with Peter Paul Rubens (cat. 1), his admired predecessor whose painting *Hero and Leander* (New Haven, Yale University Gallery) he acquired in 1637 for over 420 guilders.[18] For all the differences in organisation and commission flow, the Flemish Baroque painter's workshop may initially have functioned, at least to some extent, as a model from afar. In any case, at the beginning of the 1630s, Rembrandt also intended to reproduce his paintings by means of prints, like Rubens, who incidentally used Dutch engravers for this purpose. One of them was Willem van Swanenburg, the brother of Rembrandt's first teacher, Jacob Isaacz. van Swanenburg. To this end, Rembrandt hired the Leiden engraver Jan van Vliet, who ultimately did not meet Rembrandt's expectations.[19] During this period, Rembrandt was also commissioned with a Passion series by Stadtholder Frederik Hendrik, which took many years to complete (1632–46). Because he was late in delivering the paintings – and probably also because of the exorbitant remuneration he expected – Rembrandt did not receive any major commissions in the immediately subsequent period, for which he could have made use of workshop assistants.[20]

What, then, remained for the pupils and assistants in his workshop to do? A question that arises in this context is whether there are any paintings by Rembrandt's own hand that recognizably involved the collaboration of pupils. The joint work of master and assistants on a painting, it seems, was not the rule. Van de Wetering lists a group of paintings – a manageable number, in fact – where both Rembrandt's hand and the involvement of workshop collaborators may be assumed: primarily portraits from the 1630s, which were produced according to an established compositional scheme (for the positioning of hands, figures and clothing motifs) that assistants could follow.[21] However, these paintings date from the period when Rembrandt worked for Uylenburgh, i.e., before he set up his own studio in Amsterdam.[22] This means that the bulk of his verified painterly oeuvre was largely done by his own hand. Hence, one of his pupils' principal tasks would have been to make copies and variants of Rembrandt's paintings, as can be seen in a number of paintings and drawings in the exhibition (cats. 21.1–3).[23]

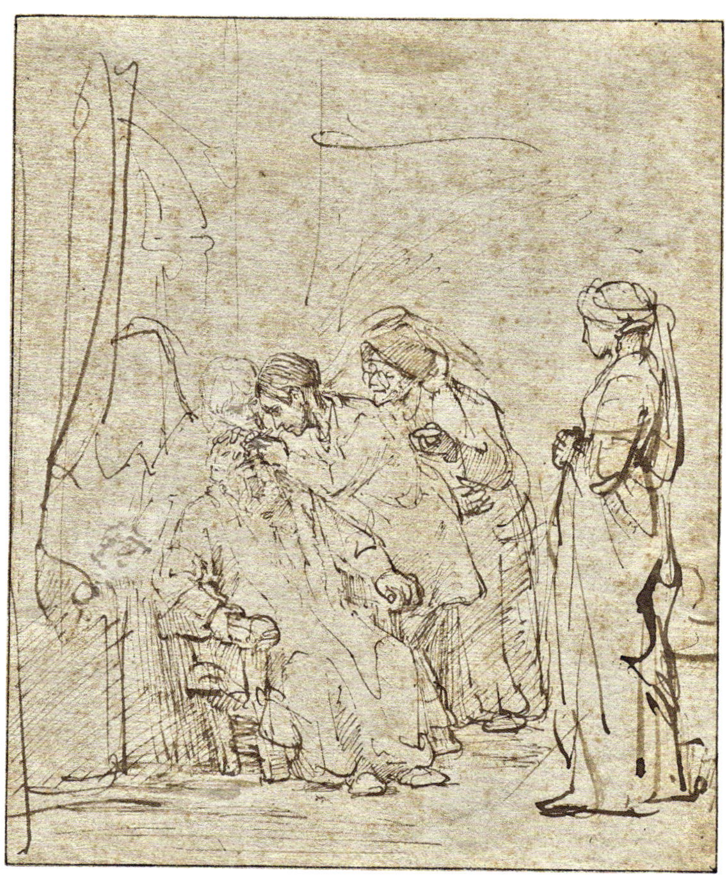

Fig. 1: Rembrandt, *Tobias Healing his Father's Blindness*, c. 1641. Pen and brown ink, touched with white gouache, 21 × 17.7 cm. Cleveland, Ohio, The Cleveland Museum of Art, J. H. Wade Fund

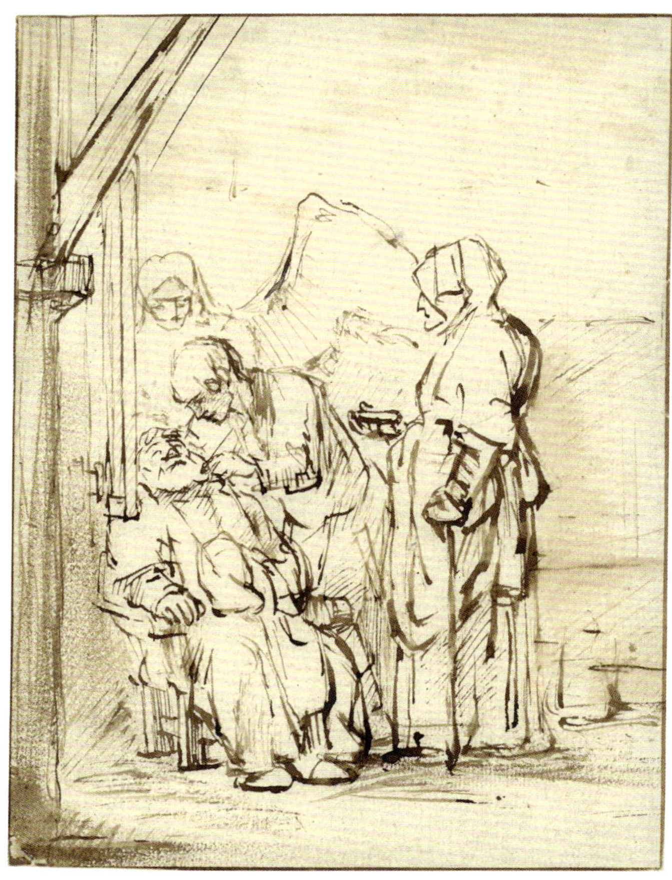

Fig. 2: Rembrandt pupil, *Tobias Healing his Father's Blindness*. Pen and brown ink, brush in brown wash, 17.3 x 13.3 cm. Staatliche Museen zu Berlin, Kupferstichkabinett

BETWEEN IMITATION AND INDEPENDENCE

To copy a painting, one first had to be able to create a drawing of it. An example of this is the drawing by the young Ferdinand Bol after Rembrandt's *Minerva* dated 1635 (New York, The Leiden Collection; cat. 9), which he probably made during the first year he worked in Rembrandt's workshop. Bol studied the painting in the studio. Transferring the large format (138 × 116.5 cm) into a small 25 × 20 cm drawing and converting the colour values into monochrome grey-scale values was in itself already a demanding task that required an advanced draughtsman.[24] In the process, the young artist from Dordrecht sharpened his own perception as he studied elements of the painting such as composition, lighting, differentiation between delicately and cursorily painted areas and the rendering of different materials and reproduced them using grey and black chalk and wash in a painterly and tonal manner. The drawing, which probably remained in the workshop for later use after the sale of the painting, was not solely a practice piece, but also served as an aide-mémoire and as documentation, much like a photograph does today for an artist's image archive.

In principle, Rembrandt sold works by his pupils, both paintings and drawings, for his own personal gain.[25] Around 1636, for example, he noted on the reverse of a drawing after Pieter Lastman (*Susanna in the Bath*, Berlin, Kupferstichkabinett, KdZ 5296) the proceeds from the sale of works by two pupils, Leendert Cornelisz van Beyeren (who would bid on behalf of Rembrandt at auctions) and 'Fardynandus', i.e., Ferdinand Bol.[26] According to Willem Goeree (1635–1711), the author of an internationally successful drawing manual from 1668, pupils used such copies to acquire basic skills relating to 'de schikkinge, vaste omtrek, actie, dag en schaduwe, enz.' (the composition, firm outline, action, light and shade, etc.).[27]

LEARNING FROM THE DIRECTOR OF EMOTIONS

Bol's drawing *Joseph Interprets the Dreams of his Fellow Prisoners*, created around ten years later and long

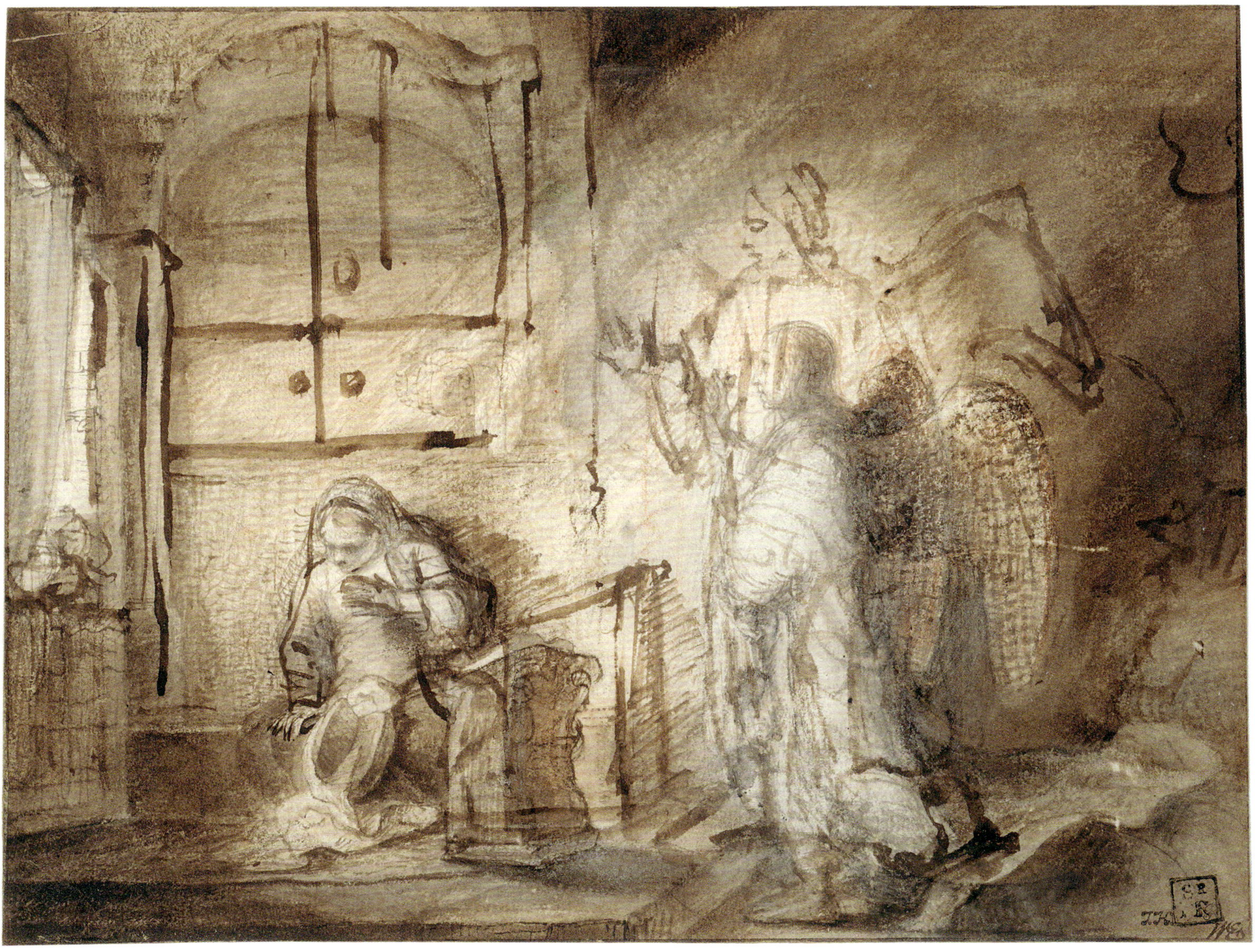

Fig. 4: Constantijn van Renesse, with corrections by Rembrandt, *The Annunciation to Mary*. Black and red chalk, pen and brown ink, brush and brown wash, heightened with white, 17.4 × 23.1 cm. Staatliche Museen zu Berlin, Kupferstichkabinett

freedom of the graphic technique. Because of their sketch-like character, his etchings were well suited to practising his specific way of drawing. The concentration on the expressiveness of the line, on the varied grouping and arrangement of figures in space, as well as the expressive, often high-contrast lighting – characteristic features of many of Rembrandt's etchings – made them instructive visual examples. The basic principles of painting described by Karel van Mander and Samuel van Hoogstraten in their seventeenth-century painting treatises, such as *ordinantie* (composition), *houding* (tonal organisation of pictorial space), *sprong* (varied, rhythmic arrangement in space), *schickschaduw* (shadow as a compositional element) and the like, are more easily comprehensible especially in the etchings, reduced as they are to the expression of light and dark.[61] And etchings are viewed up close. This allowed the pupils to discern the harmony of figures, pictorial space, architecture, mood, emotional expression, composition and lighting as well as the depicted subject.

Surely also significant was the etcher's typical way of merely hinting at certain passages and figures in his images, causing them to appear unfinished, while other parts of the composition are carefully worked out. Given their reduction to outlines, the etched figures were relatively easy to copy. Many pupils therefore repeatedly

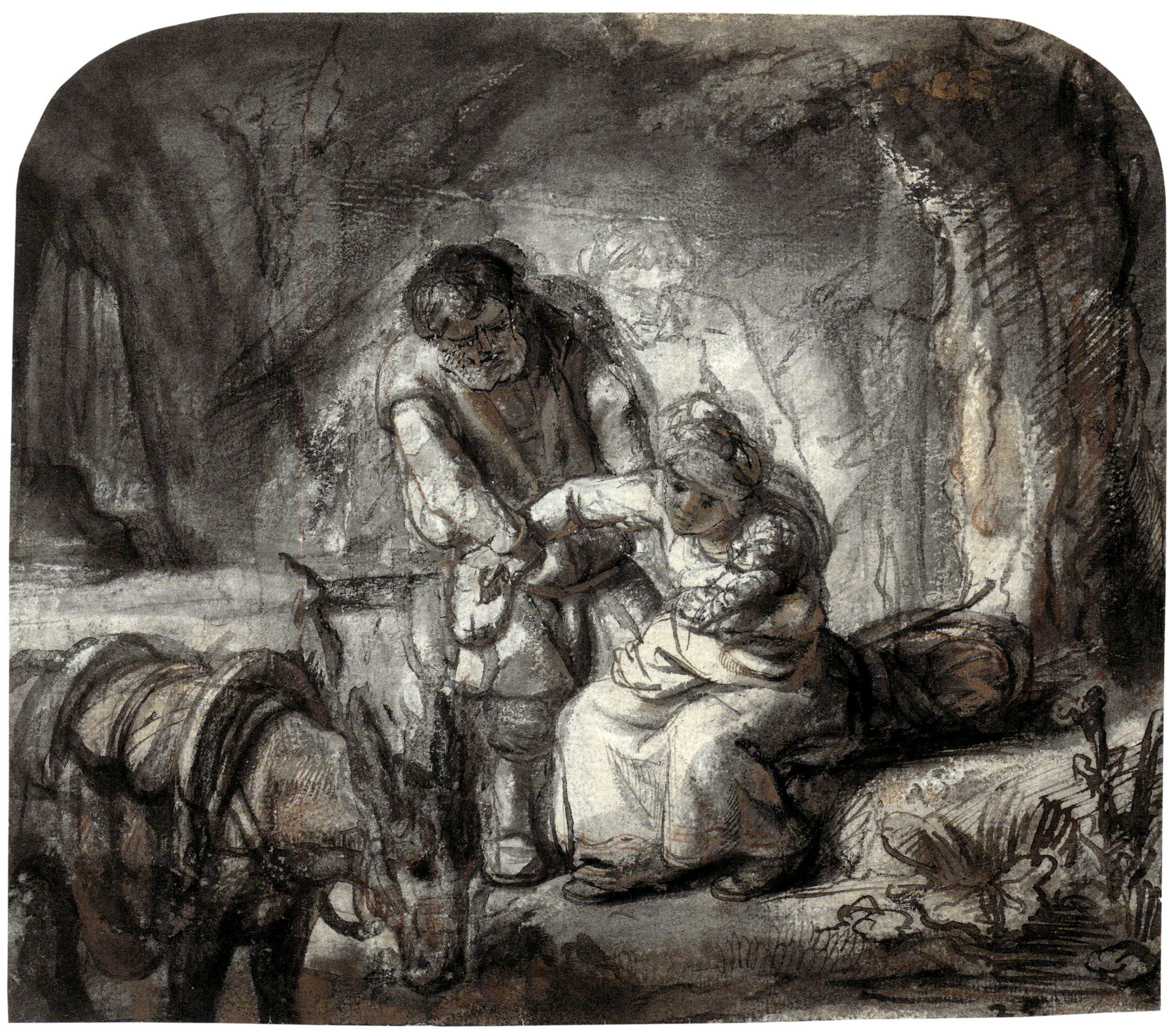

Fig. 5: Constantijn van Renesse, *The Return of the Holy Family from Egypt*. Black and red chalk, pen and brown and grey ink, brush and grey wash, heightened with white, 19.5 × 22.3 cm. Staatliche Kunstsammlungen Dresden, Kupferstich-Kabinett

borrowed individual figures from Rembrandt's etchings and inserted them into their compositions. Govert Flinck, for example, copied *The Apostle Paul at his Desk* in a red chalk drawing (Staatliche Museen zu Berlin, Kupferstichkabinett, KdZ 12001) after the corresponding etching by Rembrandt (Bartsch 149).[62] Ferdinand Bol took the striking rear figure on the far left in Rembrandt's *Hundred Guilder Print*, which has recently been interpreted as a variant of the figure of Amsterdam actor Willem Ruyter, and repeatedly varied it in drawings and paintings, including in the Braunschweig oil study, many years after his apprenticeship in Rembrandt's workshop (cats. 17.2, 45).[63] Flinck's large-scale painting of the *Annunciation to the Shepherds* from 1639 (Paris, Musée du Louvre) is a variation on Rembrandt's 1634 etching of the same name (figs. 7, 8). These are just a few examples from the vast and growing collection of etchings on which the pupils in the workshop could draw.

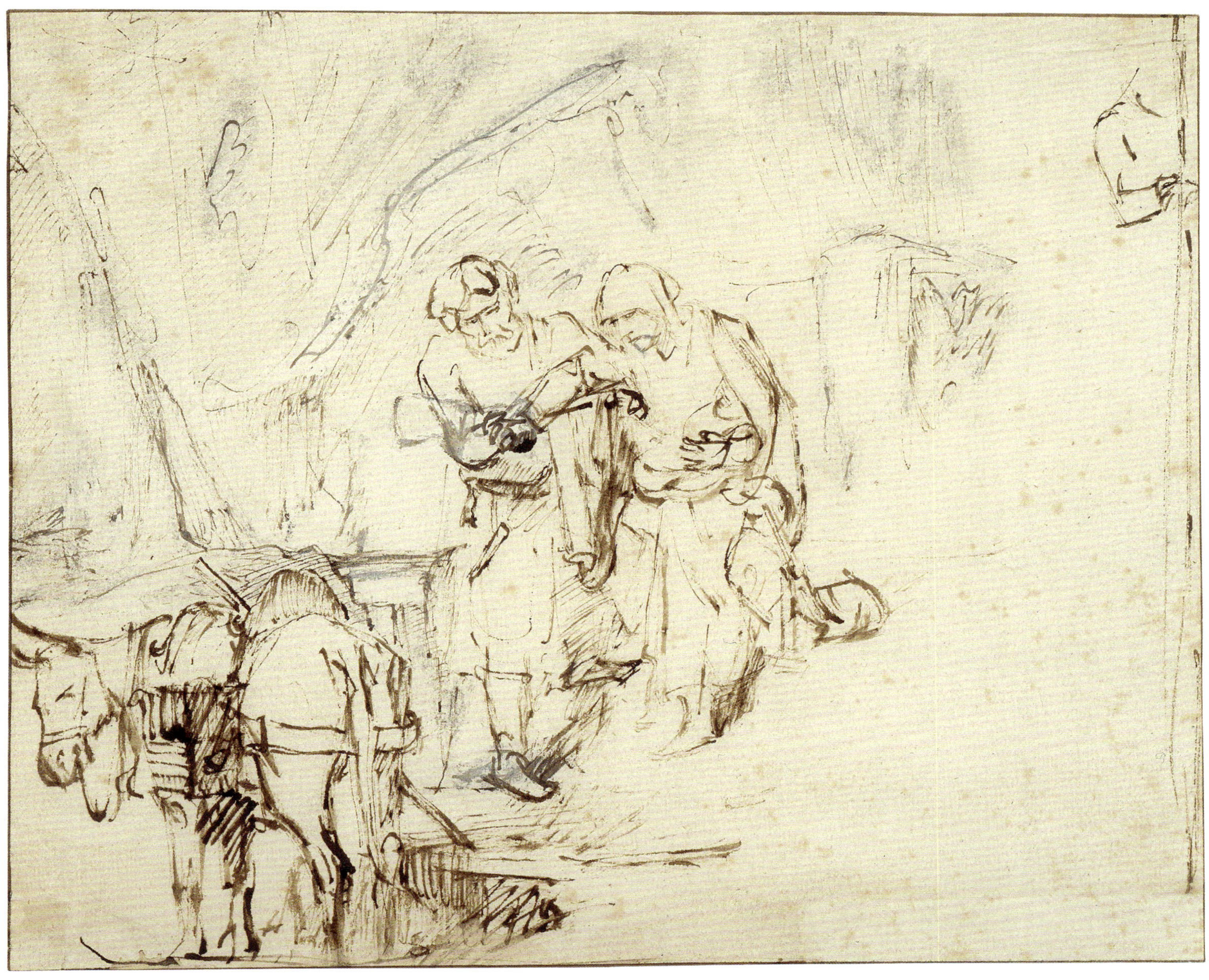

Fig. 6: Rembrandt, *The Return of the Holy Family from Egypt*. Pen and brown ink, slightly washed, corrections in white, 19.4 × 24.2 cm. Staatliche Museen zu Berlin, Kupferstichkabinett

'FALSE' SELF-PORTRAITS BY REMBRANDT

In learning the master's painterly style, pupils could also practice using copies and variants of his self-portraits, in which Rembrandt tended to take even more artistic liberties than in official portrait commissions.[64] The boldness of Rembrandt's brushwork can be clearly seen in his early, tronie-like self-portraits from around 1630, which are also studies in light. These small-scale paintings apparently remained in the workshop for a long time. In any case, the Kassel copy of the early Amsterdam self-portrait was probably painted a few years after the original (cat. 21.1, figs. 9, 10). The Leipzig *Self-Portrait* is also presumably a copy or variant by an assistant after a somewhat older, lost self-portrait (cat. 21.2). The unfinished and unsigned painting was certainly not intended for sale in this condition.[65]

Similarly, the self-portrait in Stuttgart is in all probability not an autograph work, but rather a very free variant of the self-portrait in the Frick Collection (cat. 21.3).[66] The painting's controversial attribution history extends back to the 1990s, and in the fourth volume on Rembrandt's self-portraits published in 2005, the authors of the RRP still expressed uncertainty in the

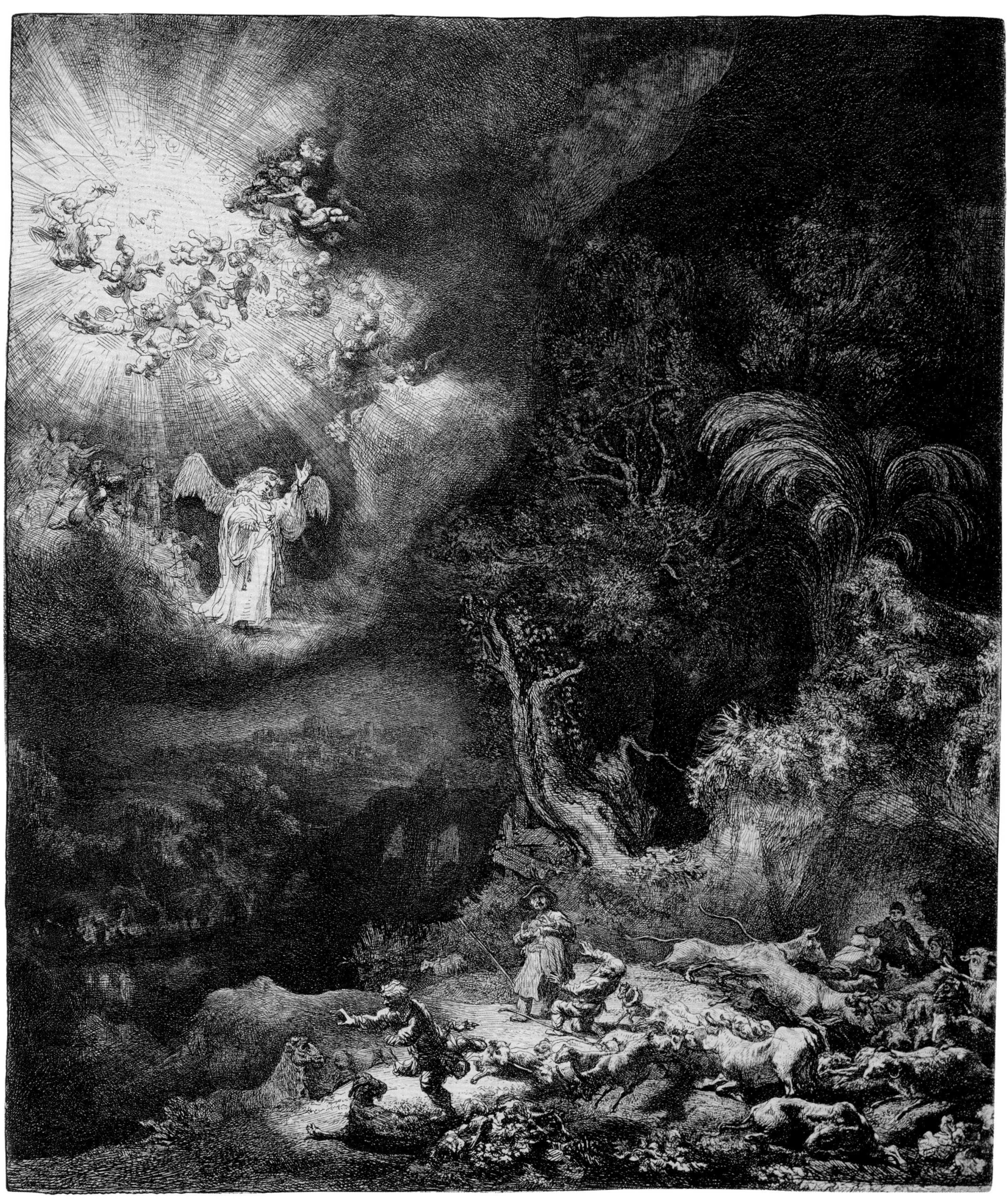

Fig. 7: Rembrandt, *The Annunciation to the Shepherds*, 1634. Etching, etching needle and drypoint, 26.6 × 22.3 cm (sheet). Frankfurt a. M., Städel Museum, Graphische Sammlung

TRONIES IN REMBRANDT'S WORKSHOP PRACTICE AND IN THE EARLY WORK OF HIS PUPILS

Dagmar Hirschfelder

Among the many innovations characterising Rembrandt's œuvre is the invention of a new type of painting, the so-called tronies. Taken from contemporary sources, this term meant 'face', 'head' or 'facial expression'.[1] Together with fellow artist Jan Lievens, Rembrandt introduced tronies into seventeenth-century Dutch painting as a product to be sold on the open market during his time in Leiden in the 1620s.[2] This did not happen out of the blue. Art historians consider Flemish study heads by masters like Peter Paul Rubens, Anton von Dyck and Jacob Jordaens to be precursors of the Dutch tronie.[3] Such studies were created in preparation for heads in larger compositions and were therefore, unlike the Dutch paintings, linked to a larger work context.

The production of tronies played a central role in Rembrandt's workshop and training practice. Consequently, such works make up a significant part of the œuvre of many of Rembrandt's pupils who were already independent. Tronies served a variety of purposes in the master's workshop. Before examining these connections in more detail, we should briefly outline how tronies ought to be defined according to the current state of research.[4]

TRONIES AS AN INDEPENDENT ART FORM

Seventeenth-century tronies are paintings featuring heads, busts or half-length figures depicted in isolation against a mostly neutral background. The sitters' clothing resembles the garb of the figures in genre and history paintings. Based on their often decidedly portrait-like conception, the paintings may be understood as 'fantasy portraits'. They are not, however, representative portraits with a memorial function: Rather than patrons who were eager to be recognised in a portrait painting and were depicted in accord with their social status, the works show fictitious figures who represent certain types of people, such as the type of the old man, the oriental person, the soldier or the shepherdess.

In adding accoutrements to their tronies, artists often avoided any attributes or symbols with a specific meaning. As a result, the figures are not iconographically fixed. They cannot be identified as particular biblical, historical, mythological or literary figures. Nor can such tronies be linked to the kind of meanings common in genre painting at the time, which were indicated by attributes. In fact, tronies were usually distinguished by their openness to different interpretations and associations on the part of the viewer.[5] A fundamental feature of the tronies that were widespread in the Northern Netherlands in the seventeenth century is their lifelike mode of representation – they were usually painted from the living model.[6] For this reason, the sitters can occasionally be identified. For example, it was especially common for artists to base tronies on their own facial features, without the pictures thereby becoming official self-portraits. Another important characteristic of tronies is the emphasis placed on the artistic means employed, such as a particularly free, sketch-like, coarse, often impasto manner of painting or an extremely smooth style that impresses for its fine

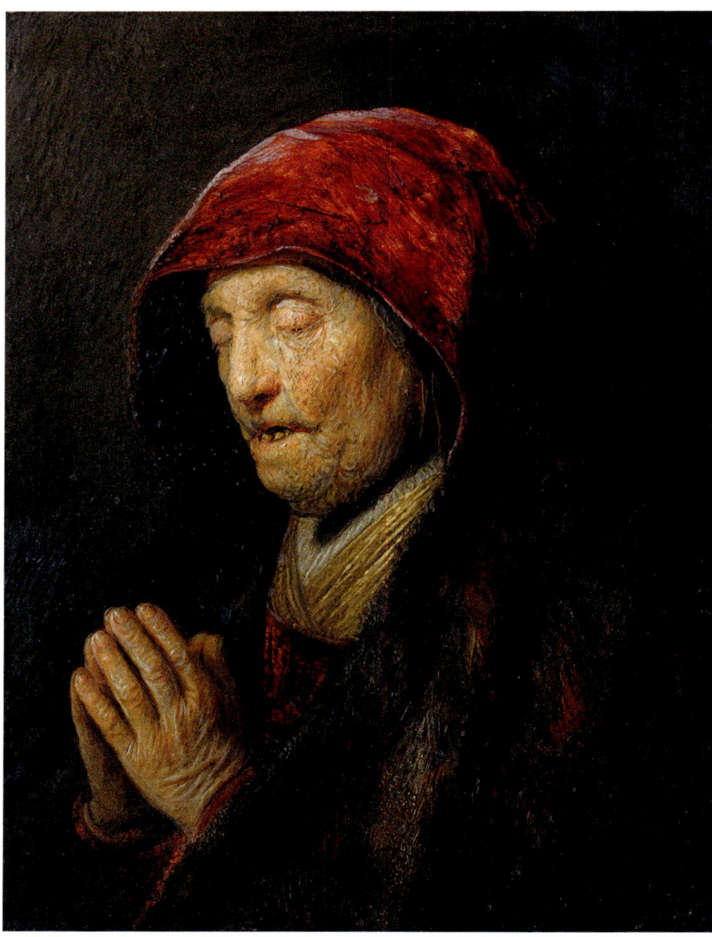

Fig. 1: Rembrandt, *Old Woman in Prayer*, c. 1629–30. Copper, 15.5 × 12.2 cm. Salzburger Landessammlungen, Residenzgalerie

painterly qualities, high-contrast, effective use of light and very nuanced or unusual colour scheme. Tronies served as showpieces demonstrating the painterly skills and individual style of their creators.[7] Already in the seventeenth century, one of the main reasons for the popularity of such works was the quality of their artistic expression.

In the 1620s, Jan Lievens, Rembrandt and Frans Hals established tronies as an independent art form involving specific representational intentions, which at the same time gave rise to distinct pictorial traditions. This type of painting was subsequently widely disseminated in the Northern Netherlands, not least thanks to the significant contribution of Rembrandt's pupils. Not constituting a genre in their own right, tronies are to be situated within history and genre painting and were created by painters working in these fields.[8] Accordingly, the boundaries to other image categories are porous, since many history and genre painters composed their bust or half-length figure paintings with attributes in a similar way to their tronies. As a result, it is difficult to make a clear-cut distinction between the various types of reduced single-figure paintings, nor does such a differentiation correspond to contemporary artistic practice or the reception of the works by buyers.[9] On the contrary, the boundaries were blurred as the different types of painting fertilised one another.

TRONIES IN THE EARLY WORK OF REMBRANDT'S PUPILS

Tronies were an important subject in the work of Rembrandt and that of most of his pupils and assistants.[10] For about half of the documented pupils with surviving works, this type of picture was a main pursuit.[11] Many well-known Rembrandt pupils created a striking number of tronies, especially at the beginning of their careers. This is true for, among others, Gerrit Dou (1613–1675), Govert Flinck (1615–1660), Samuel van Hoogstraten (1627–1678), Carel Fabritius (1622–1654) and Willem Drost (1633–1659).[12] In creating their tronies, they drew closely on the works of their master, imitating his style of composition and painting.

Adopting a 'manner' that was in demand among seventeenth-century Dutch art lovers and buyers and thereby emulating the painting style of a successful master was seen as an important training objective for young painters.[13] Arnold Houbraken relates that following his apprenticeship with Lambert Jakobsz, Govert Flinck spent a year as an apprentice to Rembrandt in order to learn his 'treatment of colour and manner of painting'.[14] Flinck reportedly was able to imitate Rembrandt's works so skilfully that some of his paintings were mistaken for originals by the master and sold as such. Houbraken says of Rembrandt's pupil Samuel van Hoogstraten that 'he adhered to [Rembrandt's] way of painting for some time but gradually weaned himself away from it and in the end adopted an entirely different way of painting'.[15] According to Houbraken, Hoogstraten's pupil Aert de Gelder (1645–1727) still went to Amsterdam to learn Rembrandt's painting style.[16] Many of Rembrandt's pupils, such as Gerrit Dou, Govert Flinck and Aert de Gelder, had already completed an apprenticeship under other masters by the time they began their training with him.[17] They were therefore more advanced and are not necessarily to be regarded as apprentices, since some may already have had the status of journeymen or assistants.[18] The early tronies of Rembrandt's pupils clearly show the young painters striving to emulate the works of their master as closely as possible.

Gerrit Dou's tronie of an *Old Woman with Spectacles, Reading a Newspaper* in Dresden (cat. 33.2), for example, revisits the type of the pious old woman in rich fur clothing with gold and other jewellery that Rembrandt had established in Leiden and for which the master had used the model known as his mother.[19]

STAGING REMBRANDT: A NARRATIVE OF GERMAN HISTORY AND GHOSTS

Stefan Weppelmann

OPACITY AND POPULARITY

A painting long associated with Rembrandt in the Gemäldegalerie at the Kulturforum in Berlin shows the bust of an elderly man with a helmet and gorget (fig.1; cf. cat. 40). The image derives its dramatic tension from the darkness shrouding the figure, while the helmet gleams in the light. The interplay between the figure, the twilight and the reflections lends the canvas its fascinating power.

Upon closer inspection, a further contrast emerges: The man's face is painted in blunt, blended colour tones with thin, transparent layers of paint using short, hatching brushstrokes. The helmet, on the other hand, is executed in loose brushwork with a pronounced impasto. As a result, the head and headdress look like elements of different realities; the helmet even appears to be hovering above the head. And compared to the man's shoulders, the head is too small, causing the figure as a whole to appear inorganic. The figure is not conceived as a body, but seems pieced together from individual parts – torso, head and helmet.[1]

Despite these obvious flaws, the work is probably the most widely travelled Old Master painting in the western hemisphere.[2] As such, it has a Wikipedia entry that suggests facts, and it can be found reproduced in children's books[3] and schoolbooks,[4] comics[5] and catalogues, occasionally even as their cover.[6] Collectible coins,[7] postcards, refrigerator magnets, socks or wall plates also feature the image of the old man. And then there are the countless artistic references, including Matthias Weischer's painting *Innenraum* (Interior) at the Museum der bildenden Künste in Leipzig, where it appears in the background (fig. 2).

Astonishingly enough, very little is known about the object itself – by whom and when it was painted, what it originally looked like and who it depicts; all this is largely uncertain. The composition has been altered several times over the years. Early commentators saw it as a self-portrait or a portrait of Rembrandt's father[8] or brother.[9] At times, it was believed that the sitter could be identified as the Dutch commander William of Orange.[10]

Eventually, the face was consigned to anonymity and came to be seen as an allegorical image depicting anything from ancient deities (Mars, Saturn) and Christian heroes (St Longinus)[11] to the 'image of old age'.[12] Other authors, in turn, discussed it as a study of a helmet.[13] For some, this helmet was understood as a precious showpiece of 'pure, glistening gold',[14] while others felt it was more likely to be intended to represent bronze.[15] Some even identified figural elements on the

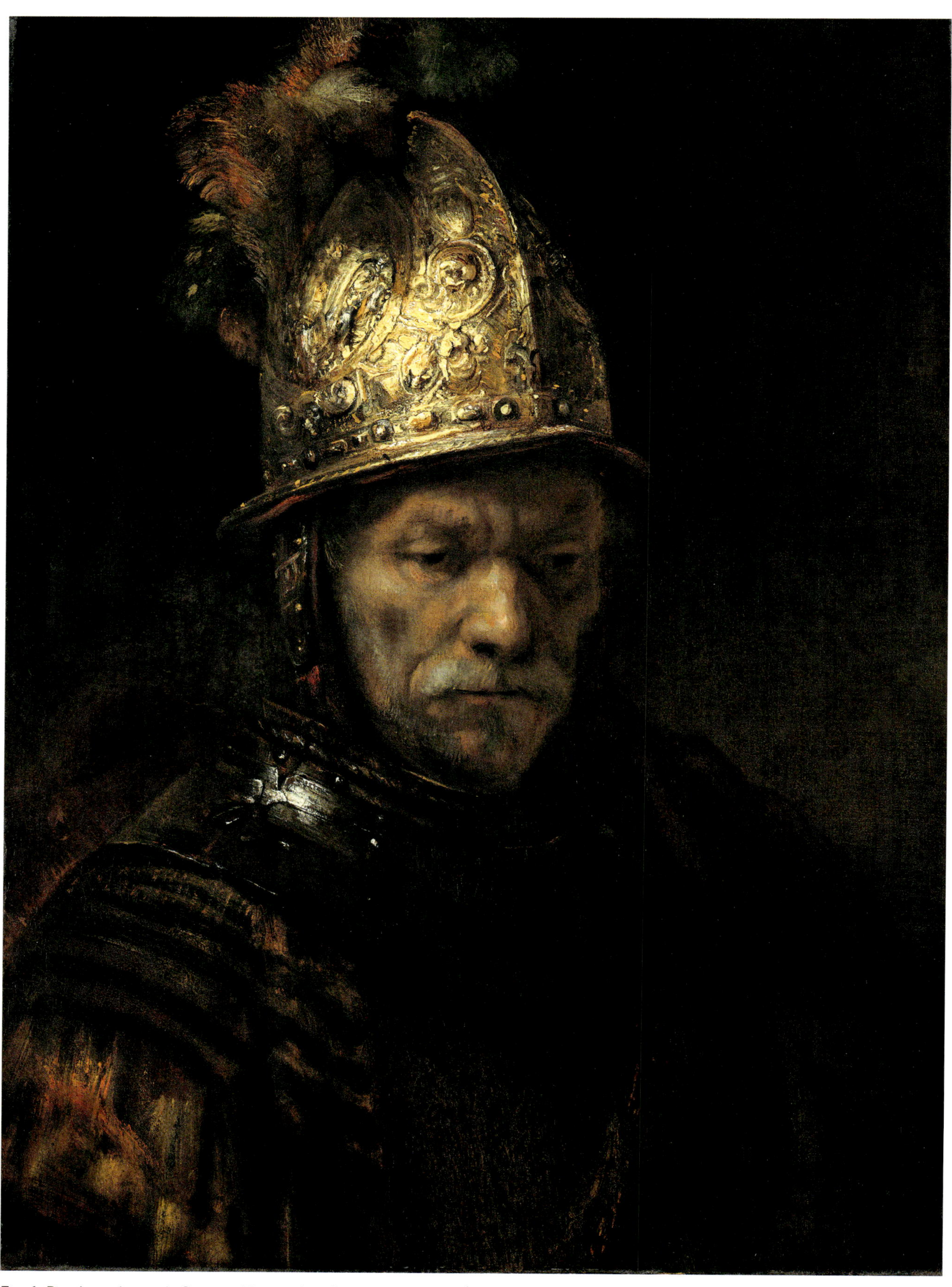

Fig. 1: Rembrandt pupil, *Costume Tronie of an Old Man in Armour* (so-called *Man with the Golden Helmet*), c. 1650–5.
Canvas, 67.5 x 50.7 cm. Staatliche Museen zu Berlin, Gemäldegalerie (cf. cat. 40)

the scene, opens the curtains to create the lighting that would become the painting's distinctive feature and announces: 'This is how I will paint you'.[69] Steinhoff seized upon not only Bode's styling of the sitter as the painter's brother, but also the idea of the artist whose work represents lifelikeness and truth as typical German qualities – in contrast to the imagined and expressively 'degenerate'.

The painting had become a national icon, though the canvas itself was no longer on view after 1939. Due to the ongoing war, it initially ended up in the vault of the Reich mint and later, together with other works from the Gemäldegalerie, in the anti-aircraft bunker in Berlin-Friedrichshain.[70] At the same time, the image was widely disseminated through reproduction. By styling the introverted man in armour as the embodiment of the heroic and the soldierly – as the 'Rembrandt-German' – the barbarism of war could be perfidiously ennobled.

'WEIGHED DOWN BY THE GOLDEN HELMET'

For the painting, the years that followed were turbulent: In March–April 1945, the Berlin museums organised several evacuation transports, during which more than 1,200 paintings were taken to the Kaiseroda salt mine near Merkers in the Wartburg district of Thuringia. In mid-April, American troops transferred these collections first to Frankfurt am Main and then to Wiesbaden,[71] where the United States used the Landesmuseum as a central collecting point for works of art secured by the US Army.

In November of that same year, the US Army shipped the half-length image of the old man, along with 202 other paintings, to Washington, DC, where the works were initially stored. Not until 1948 were they presented to the public in an exhibition. Eventually, a show featuring 150 paintings toured 12 major cities in the United States.[72] The absolute highlights of this presentation were Rembrandt and Vermeer. After almost ten years of not having been on view at all, the painting of the old man in armour was finally exhibited again. Not insignificantly, it was shown together with a painting by Jan Vermeer whose title was similarly inspired by an accessory, in this case a pearl necklace. The exhibition was unprecedented in bringing together the two most important artists of seventeenth-century Dutch painting. The *Man with the Golden Helmet* and the *Young Lady with a Pearl Necklace* (fig. 5) thrilled an audience of millions, likely reinforcing each other's popularity. The Berlin painting was accordingly insured for a high sum, and visitors began to inquire after the 'three-million-dollar painting'.[73]

Ultimately, the painting not only drew tremendous attention, but was also subjected to a radical revaluation of its subject, with the sitter now being read as a

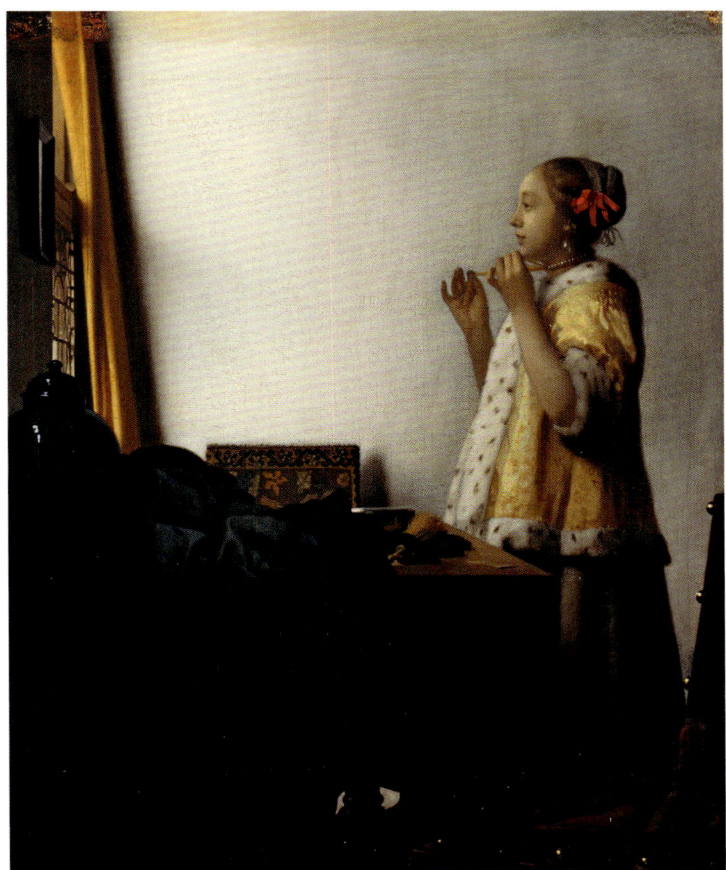

Fig. 5: Jan Vermeer, *Young Lady with a Pearl Necklace*, 1662–5. Canvas, 55 x 45 cm, Staatliche Museen zu Berlin, Gemäldegalerie

melancholic character, a figure that expressed awareness of the horrors of the recent war. The old condottiere was believed to be 'weighed down by the golden helmet, a symbol of splendour, robbed of his humanity'.[74]

In the widely read Rembrandt monograph by Jacob Rosenberg, published in New York in 1948, the author even effusively characterised the sitter as filled with an 'inner glow' and described the work in terms more related to music than to fine art. In the end, he stated that 'the old warrior of this portrait might almost be taken for the pious Roman captain of the Crucifixion scene'.[75] With this view, Rosenberg, who had worked at the Berlin Kupferstichkabinett before the war but had been dismissed because of his Jewish faith, was instrumental in helping to rehabilitate the painting. From an emblem of nationalism it had become an image of deeply felt humanity.

This revaluation dovetailed with the enlistment of the Berlin paintings in the service of the idea of a rescued civilised nation and, by extension, a restoration of European culture. In this sense, it is not surprising that the painting of the old man, in which Hitler had seen the Aryan par excellence, now served to raise

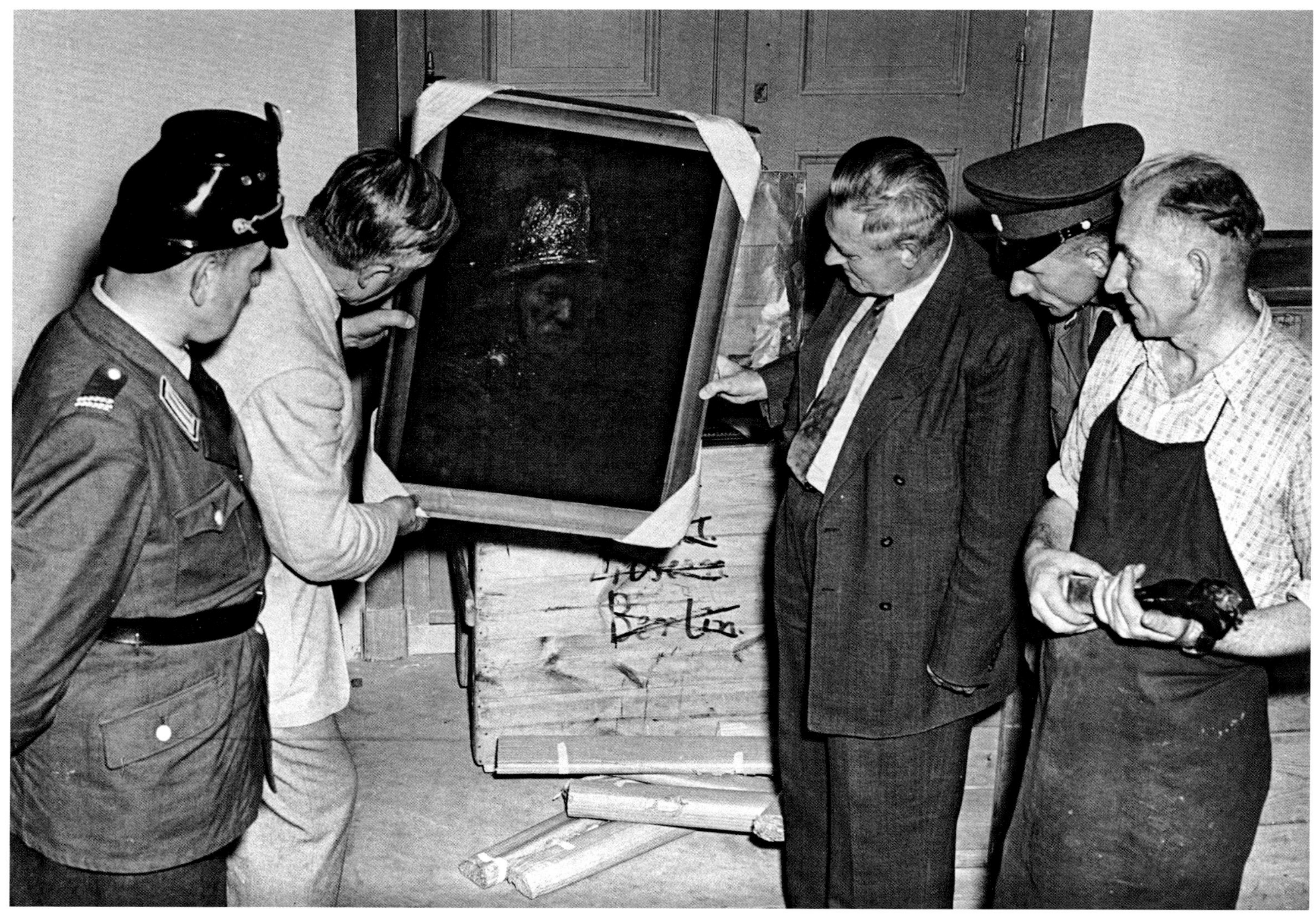

Fig. 6: Return of the artworks of the Kaiser Friedrich Museum Association from the Wiesbaden depot, 1953: arrival of the *Old Man in Armour*. Left: Ernst-Heinrich Zimmermann, director of the Berlin Gemäldegalerie

money for German war orphans, the charity to which the proceeds from the touring exhibition went.[76]

After travelling 20,000 kilometres, the tour ended on 31 March 1949 in Toledo, Ohio,[77] and on 22 April the painting, along with the other works, was sent back to Germany on board an army transport ship.[78] In the summer of 1949, it was shown in Wiesbaden[79] and reintroduced to the German public for the first time, as if turning over a new page.

REMBRANDT WEST AND EAST OF THE WALL

In 1951, the Berlin attorney Anna von Schönbeck, secretary of the Kaiser Friedrich Museum Association, began campaigning for the return of all the association's artworks remaining in Wiesbaden. To this end, she filed a lawsuit against the state of Hesse. In this dispute, the association focussed specifically upon the alleged Rembrandt painting, which also took centre stage in the whole media coverage of the trial.[80] When the association finally received its works back (fig. 6), they were at the core of a presentation that reopened on 11 September 1953 in the former Asian Museum in Berlin-Dahlem.[81]

In keeping with its status as a masterpiece, the painting of the old man in armour was given its own darkened, square room on the second floor, at the end of the corresponding wing of the building.[82] There it was displayed as the 'showpiece of the exhibition',[83] at eye level and in a new frame. This impressive presentation on a low plinth against a draped wall resembled the display of a sacred image on an altar (fig. 7). The spatial setting was consistent with the quasi-religious veneration the work now inspired.

COLLECTING REMBRANDT: WORKS BY THE MASTER IN SAXON COLLECTIONS OF THE EIGHTEENTH AND NINETEENTH CENTURIES

Sven Pabstmann

INTRODUCTION

In the course of the early modern period, European courts competing with each other at various levels established large painting galleries. In eighteenth-century Germany, above all Dresden, Braunschweig, Kassel, Düsseldorf, Mannheim, Munich and Berlin developed into outstanding centres of princely collecting. The pioneers were leading collectors in Paris who, contrary to prevailing academic art doctrine, began collecting seventeenth-century Dutch genre and landscape paintings at the beginning of the century. Collecting Rembrandt paintings was also popular in France in the early eighteenth century. However, it was the small, often finely painted cabinet pieces by masters such as Gerrit Dou, Frans van Mieris, Gabriel Metsu, Gerard ter Borch, Godfried Schalcken, Caspar Netscher, Paulus Potter, Cornelis van Poelenburgh, Bartholomeus Breenbergh, Adriaen van Ostade and Philips Wouwerman – some of the most popular artists in the eighteenth century – that initially aroused enthusiasm. Although they always remained subordinate to the Italian masters, they became obligatory for aristocratic collectors, so that the princely galleries of the time were basically similar.[1] One of the most important collectors of Dutch paintings of the Golden Age was undoubtedly William VIII, Landgrave of Hesse-Kassel (1682–1760), who was among the few people to own a large number of works by Rembrandt. Between about 1730 and 1760, he amassed one of the largest collections of the painter's work in Europe, with 34 paintings attributed to Rembrandt at the time.

The eighteenth-century enthusiasm for Rembrandt that gripped wealthy collectors, particularly in Germany, Austria and England, was fuelled in no small part by the abundant supply on the art market: in the 1730s, some of the large Rembrandt collections in Holland and the southern Netherlands were liquidated and sold at auction in places such as Amsterdam, The Hague and Brussels. Moreover, the purchase prices – especially for his portraits and tronies with a coarser, looser painting style – were still significantly lower than those of other painters.[2] In the early eighteenth century, many French, English, Italian and German painting enthusiasts outside of the Netherlands, including Augustus II the Strong, elector of Saxony (1670–1733), already had large numbers of Rembrandt paintings in their collections.[3]

But even more than Rembrandt's paintings, it was his etchings that made him famous far beyond the borders of the Netherlands. Despite the limited size of the editions, they made the painter's artistic achievements known throughout Europe. Largely independent of the stylistic trends of the day, Rembrandt's etchings were sought-after – and expensive – collector's items even during his lifetime.[4] In the early 1640s, both Christian IV of Denmark (1577–1648) and the Polish statesman and writer Count Krzysztof Opaliński (1611–1655) of Sieraków owned a collection of Rembrandt etchings. They could also be found in Paris at that time: the art dealer François Langlois (1598–1647) sold four small prints to the Italian etcher Stefano della Bella (1610–1664) on 28 March 1642, and Pierre Mariette (1634–1716), a member of the famous Parisian family of art dealers, already owned a print of *Student at a Table by Candlelight* (1642) in 1646. In 1667, the French clergyman Michel de Marolles (1600–1681) sold his important collection of engravings, including no fewer than 224 etchings by Rembrandt, to the library of Louis XIV.[5] Alongside princely and private cabinets of prints and drawings, the galleries in Kassel and Dresden were the most important sources of knowledge of Rembrandt in eighteenth-century Germany.[6] The Dresden painting gallery in particular was considered exemplary and set the standard for the development of aristocratic collections.[7]

The great popularity and growing demand for Dutch art among collectors throughout Europe from the eighteenth century onwards – in France, there was talk of a 'Hollandomania' – could not fail to have an impact on artistic production. Around 1750, many German artists made more or less obvious references to seventeenth-century Dutch painting and graphic art, especially to paintings and etchings by Rembrandt.[8] Along with Frankfurt am Main, Dresden in particular established itself as a centre of 'Rembrandtism' in the second half of the century – despite the increasingly classicistic tastes of educated circles under the strong influence of Winckelmann's art theory.[9] One of the most important 'Rembrandtists' was the Saxon court painter Christian Wilhelm Ernst Dietrich (1712–1774), known as Dietricy, who was extremely influential in the reception of Dutch art in Dresden, especially Rembrandt's paintings and prints.[10] Last but not least, the Rembrandt fashion also influenced local acquisition policy, reflected in the targeted purchase of works by contemporary artists 'in the manner of Rembrandt'.[11]

THE ELECTORAL ROYAL COLLECTIONS IN DRESDEN

As early as 1700, Augustus II, elector of Saxony and king of Poland, had begun to expand the nascent painting gallery through strategic purchases of works by renowned artists. Augustus the Strong's collecting interests focused on the works of the Dutch 'fijnschilders' and above all the paintings of Philips Wouwerman, but paintings by Rembrandt or 'in the manner of Rembrandt', preferably small portraits, character heads and tronies, were also among the focal points of collecting in Dresden at the time.[12] Thanks to this targeted collecting policy, supported by numerous agents in European art centres, by 1722 the electoral royal collection already possessed an astonishingly large group of works by Rembrandt and his students.[13] As early as 1718, the majority of new acquisitions, which within a few years had increased the collection to some 3,500 individual works, were brought together in a first gallery in the residential palace.[14]

The interest in acquiring works by Rembrandt and Dutch painting continued unabated under Augustus III, despite a general preference for Italian art and culture at the royal court. During his reign, art purchases in Europe reached unprecedented levels, making the Dresden collection the leading gallery north of the Alps alongside Paris. In the 1740s, at the behest of Prime Minister Heinrich, Count von Brühl (1700–1763), further works by Rembrandt came to Dresden from famous French private collections via art agents working in Paris.[15] Many of the most important works in the Dresden Rembrandt collection arrived there around 1750, including the portrait *Saskia with a Red Flower* of 1641 and *The Bittern Hunter* of 1639.[16] The Seven Years' War and the inevitably enormous burdens it imposed led to massive cuts in public prestige spending, which also halted the growth of the Dresden collections for a long time.

The last purchase of a Rembrandt original in the eighteenth century was the then-famous 1635 painting *Ganymede in the Clutches of the Eagle*. Karl Heinrich von Heinecken (1707–1791), head of all royal painting acquisitions from 1739 and inspector of the royal collection of prints and drawings from 1746, probably acquired it at the Leipzig Michaelmas Fair (or in Hamburg) in 1751.[17] A preliminary drawing by Rembrandt's own hand had entered the Dresden collection of prints and drawings some twenty years earlier, when Augustus the Strong acquired the collection of the Leipzig master builder Gottfried Wagner in 1728 (fig. 1).[18]

By the mid-eighteenth century, the Dresden Rembrandt collection had grown to 17 'originals' and a further eight paintings 'after the school of Rembrandt'. The Dresden painting gallery thus housed one of the largest Rembrandt collections in Europe outside the Netherlands, although the attribution of the works changed several times over the centuries and many of the paintings still in the Dresden collection are now considered to be works by followers or copies after Rembrandt's originals.[19]

After the public was granted access early on to individual collections, such as the Green Vault, during the reign of Augustus the Strong, from 1747 visitors could view the royal collection of paintings in the converted former stable building on Dresden's Neumarkt for a gratuity.[20] The gallery was probably open to artists free of charge, and others, such as Johann Joachim

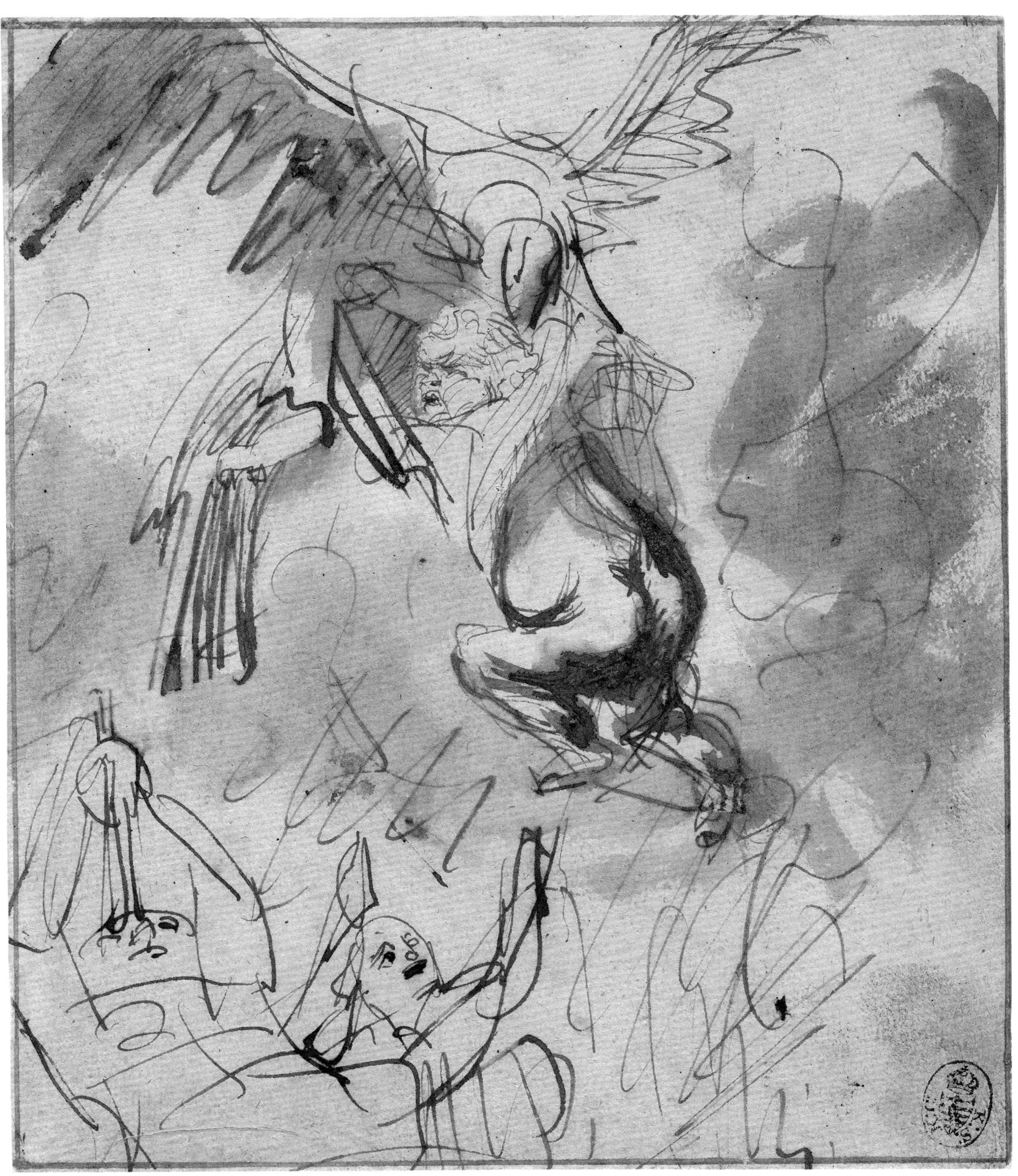

Fig. 1: Rembrandt, *Ganymede in the Clutches of the Eagle*, c. 1635. Pen and brown ink, brush and brown wash, 18.6 × 16.1 cm. Staatliche Kunstsammlungen Dresden, Kupferstich-Kabinett

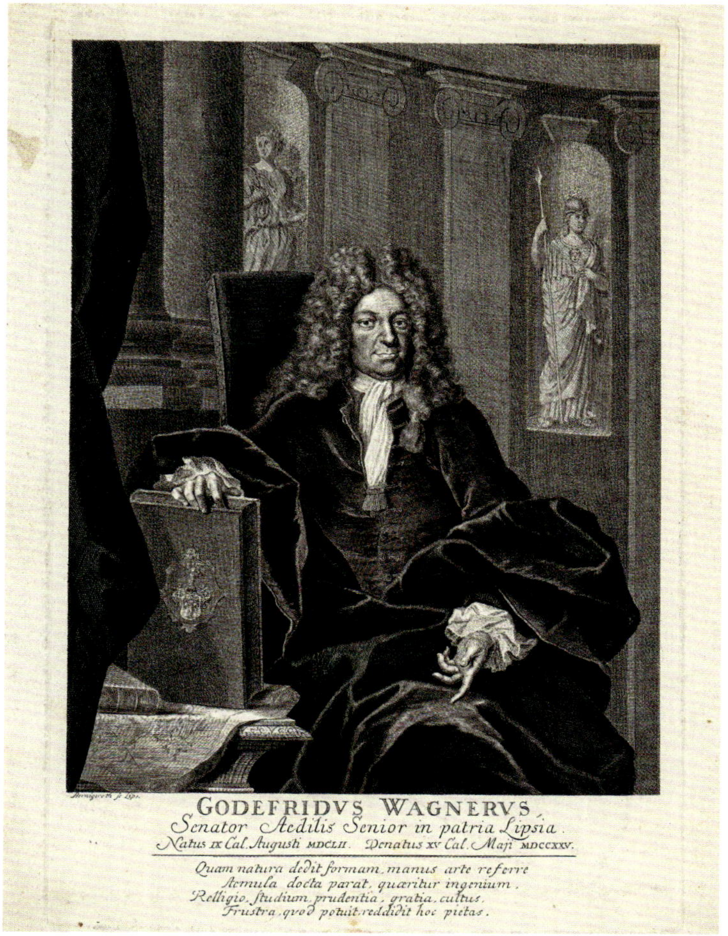

Fig. 2: Johann Martin Bernigeroth, *Portrait of the Master Builder, Councillor, Art Collector and Philologist Gottfried Wagner*. Engraving, 44.5 × 33.1 cm (sheet). Staatliche Kunstsammlungen Dresden, Kupferstich-Kabinett

Winckelmann (1717–1768), were even allowed to spend as much time there as they wished. Surviving guest lists in which the gallery's custodians recorded the date of a visit as well as the name, place of origin, status and occupation of each visitor show that the collection was frequented by people from a wide range of social and geographical backgrounds.[21] A number of art collectors and connoisseurs appear in the lists, including the Leipzig merchant and banker Gottfried Winckler (1731–1795), who visited the gallery on 25 January 1755.[22]

Rembrandt's *Ganymede* and a large portion of his works that had already arrived in Dresden were thus accessible to the public early on, as the first art-theoretical reactions to the work in the 1750s and 1760s suggest.[23] For example, the painting was the only one of the Rembrandts in Dresden to which Christian Ludwig von Hagedorn (1712–1780), who was also in charge of the painting gallery from 1764, devoted a separate section in his *Lettre à un Amateur de la Peinture*, published in 1755; in his *Betrachtungen über die Mahlerey* published seven years later, he chose it as the starting point for an extensive discussion of the 'character of happy imitators'.[24] Hagedorn not only collected works by 'Rembrandt', he even occasionally practised etching character heads as well as genre and landscape scenes 'in the manner of Rembrandt'. Around the same time, Heinecken began work on the *Recueil d'Estampes d'après les plus célèbres Tableaux de la Galerie Royale de Dresde*, a lavishly designed publication with a descriptive introduction and plates with large engravings of the most important works; as the first art historical publication on the Dresden painting gallery, it was initially published in two volumes in 1753 and 1757 by Christian Heinrich Hagenmüller.[25]

Along with the two elector kings, the prime minister Heinrich, Count von Brühl was by far the most important private collector in Dresden during the 'Augustan' period. As head of the royal electoral collections, he maintained a dense network of art agents and royal envoys at home and abroad. His secretary Karl Heinrich von Heinecken, who also published a comprehensive catalogue with engravings of works from the Brühl painting collection in 1754, coordinated the development of his wide-ranging collections.[26] The collection contained over a thousand paintings, mainly by seventeenth-century Dutch and Flemish genre and landscape painters, including several paintings attributed to Rembrandt.[27] In 1768, the Russian empress Catherine II acquired from the Brühl collections some 600 paintings for the collection of the Hermitage in St Petersburg, as well as around 300 albums containing approximately 30,000 engravings and some 1,000 drawings, including Rembrandt's *Winter Landscape* of around 1650–4 (St Petersburg, Hermitage) and a separate album containing numerous Rembrandt etchings.

THE DRESDEN KUPFERSTICH-KABINETT AND THE WAGNER COLLECTION

The Kupferstich-Kabinett (Cabinet of Prints and Drawings), founded in 1720 as an institution for the collection and study of graphic art following the dissolution of the Dresden Kunstkammer under Augustus the Strong, acquired a large number of drawings and etchings by Rembrandt in the eighteenth century through purchases made by its then director, Johann Heinrich von Heucher (1677–1747).[28] Many of these works were acquired together with more than 300 drawings, mainly by Flemish and Dutch masters of the sixteenth and seventeenth centuries such as Rubens, Jordaens, Lievens, Van Ostade, Lairesse and Schalcken. The drawings were purchased in three bound volumes between 1723 and 1726 from the Leipzig bookseller and publisher Moritz Georg Weidmann the Younger (1686–1743), owner of the famous Weidmann bookshop.[29]
It is not known where Weidmann, who had extensive

the study of the Winckler collection. More recently, Dieter Gleisberg (2011) has conducted extensive research on the subject in his search for the provenance and whereabouts of former 'Winckler paintings'. As a result of this research, approximately 200 paintings from the Winckler Collection have been identified and located. Despite these detailed, specialised studies, the provenance of the works in the collection (paintings, drawings, prints) and the exact sources of Winckler's acquisitions are still largely unknown.

Many acquisitions came from German private collections, such as the Heinecken (Dresden) and Böttcher (Leipzig) cabinets; the latter probably contained more than 200 paintings, mainly by seventeenth-century Dutch and Flemish painters, 40 of which were acquired by Winckler alone. Margravine Karoline Luise von Baden (1723–1783) also acquired 11 paintings from the Böttcher cabinet around 1760 to form the basis of her own collection.[58] Auctions in the Netherlands and on the Paris art market were also important sources for Winckler's purchases. Some 40 of the high-quality and sometimes very expensive paintings in his collection were acquired at Dutch auctions between 1760 and 1766.[59] In Paris, Winckler maintained contacts with the banker and art agent Johann Heinrich Eberts (1726–1793) and above all with the engraver Johann Georg Wille (1715–1808), who had been based in the French metropolis since 1736 and who procured for him paintings by Greuze and Chardin as well as a large number of drawings.[60]

Some of the collections from which Winckler acquired paintings already enjoyed an excellent reputation due to their aristocratic provenance, such as the extensive collection of paintings belonging to the Roman cardinal Silvio Valenti Gonzaga (1690–1756), parts of which were auctioned in Amsterdam in 1763, as well as paintings owned by 'Prince Trivulze', probably the Milanese prince Antonio Tolomeo Gallio Trivulzio (1692–1767), and by Claude-Alexandre de Villeneuve, Comte de Vence (1702–1760), in Paris.[61] Winckler also acquired works from lesser-known German collections, such as a 1646 landscape by Nicolaes Berchem (Leipzig 1768, no. 267) and a 1636 church interior by Peeter Neeffs the Elder with painted staffage by Frans Francken the Younger from the 'small collection' of Lorenz Poppe (1692–1760), as well as a portrait by Balthasar Denner (Leipzig 1768, no. 85) from the holdings of the Hamburg mayor Cornelius Poppe (1691–1768).

Interestingly, in his travel diary the Berlin engraver Daniel Chodowiecki (1726–1801) mentions 'a very beautiful cabinet' belonging to a 'Hamburg merchant Popel [!]' in Dresden.[62] This was the collection of paintings left behind by Franz Poppe (1716–1771), which must have arrived in Dresden in the early 1770s via his widow, Anna Christiane (née Dinglinger), granddaughter of the famous court jeweller and goldsmith Johann Melchior Dinglinger. Chodowiecki had seen this cabinet during his stay in Dresden on 5 November 1773, when he visited the miniature and pastel painter Sophia Friederika Dinglinger, sister of the aforementioned and a former pupil of Oeser, and had also come across a 'head by Rembrandt' alongside works by Wouwerman, Ruisdael, Van Goyen, Ostade, Teniers, Poelenburgh, Van der Meulen, Dietrich and Van der Neer.

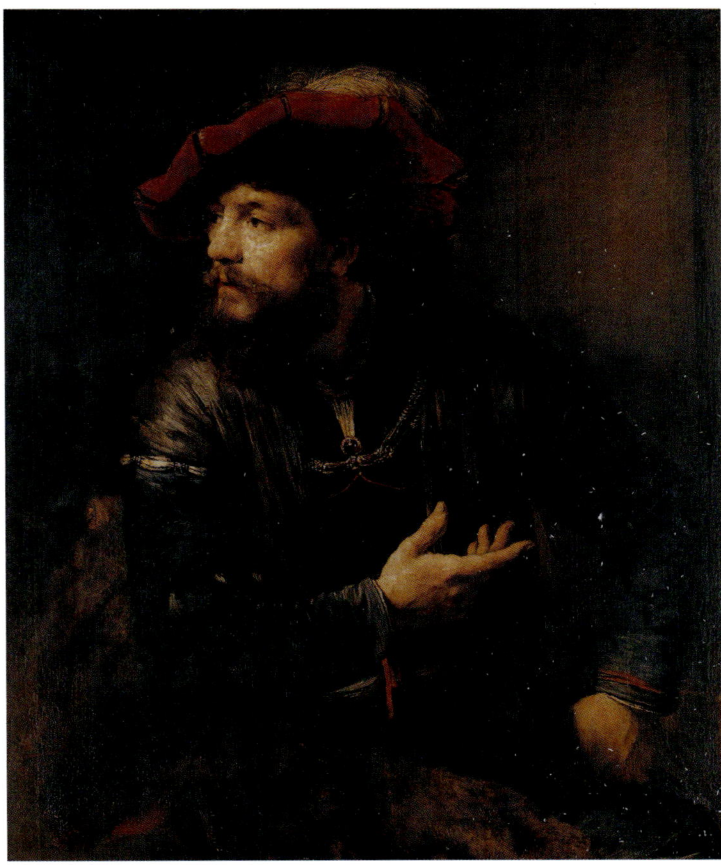

Fig. 10: Willem Dros-, *Man with a Plumed Red Beret*, 1654. Canvas, 102.9 × 92.1 cm. Location unknown

PAINTINGS BY REMBRANDT AND HIS CIRCLE IN THE WINCKLER COLLECTION

A painting attributed to Rembrandt, *Portrait of a Devout Young Man* (Leipzig 1768, no. 493), later often interpreted as a portrait of Rembrandt's son Titus, was acquired by Winckler in 1760 at the beginning of his collecting activities for only 84 guilders from the cabinet of Gerard Hoet (1698–1760) in The Hague.[63] The painting later became part of the collection of the industrial magnate Fritz Thyssen (1873–1951) and has been downgraded by recent scholarship as the work of an unknown Rembrandt imitator.[64]

Winckler also owned a *Raising of Lazarus* from 1632, which after stations in St Petersburg, Geneva, London, Paris, New York and Philadelphia has been in the Los Angeles County Museum of Art since 1972 and which then, as now, was regarded as an original work by Rembrandt (fig. 7, cat. 49.2).[65] Other works from the Winckler collection attributed to the Dutch master in the eighteenth century are now ascribed to artists from Rembrandt's circle, followers or imitators, including the small painting *Head of an Old Woman* (fig. 8; Leipzig 1768, no. 495) in the National Gallery of Art in Washington, DC, which Winckler later combined with the study of the head of an 'old man with a broad nose' (Leipzig 1768, no. 496), formerly attributed to Rembrandt, to form a pair of paintings (pendants), or the painting *Rembrandt as a Young Man* in The Metropolitan Museum of Art in New York (fig. 9).[66] Winckler's paintings by Rembrandt also included *Old Woman Reading (The Prophetess Anna?)* (Leipzig 1768, no. 494), now attributed to his student Abraham van Dijck (cat. 41.1).[67] Winckler's great interest in Rembrandt's art also encouraged him to acquire works by various of the latter's students including Ferdinand Bol, Salomon de Bray, Gerbrand van den Eeckhout, Govert Flinck, Aert de Gelder, Jan Victors, Philips and Salomon Koninck and Gerrit Dou, as well as Willem Drost (fig. 10, cf. cat. 49).[68]

Winckler's cabinet also contained pieces by eighteenth-century artists who produced works in 'Rembrandt's taste'. In addition to numerous Rembrandtesque works by the then highly regarded Christian Ernst Wilhelm Dietrich, these included several study heads 'in the manner of Rembrandt' by the Frankfurt painter Johann Georg Trautmann and a replica of Oeser's painting *Saul and the Witch of Endor* (now in the Stadtgeschichtliches Museum Leipzig), commissioned in 1767 and based on Rembrandt's much admired chiaroscuro painting.[69]

It is also likely that Winckler's cabinet, like many other collections of the time, contained a number of copies of works by great masters. Despite the high esteem in which the Winckler collection was held in the eighteenth century, visitors sometimes took offence at this, as can be seen from several contemporary travel accounts. Others were irritated by the overcrowding and lack of order in the picture cabinet. Among the critical voices was Pierre Jacques Onésyme Bergeret de Grancourt (1715–1785) of Paris, who became famous as a wealthy patron and supporter of Jean-Honoré Fragonard. From October 1773 to September 1774, he accompanied Fragonard on a Grand Tour through France, Italy, Austria and finally Germany. On their return journey from Dresden, where they had spent about two weeks, they made a brief stop in Leipzig on 3 September 1774 to view Winckler's collection of paintings. Bergeret wrote succinctly of the two-hour visit in his travel diary: 'After Dresden, I stopped in Leipzig for only a few hours to view a cabinet of paintings belonging to the merchant Gottfried Winckler... There are many paintings in this merchant's cabinet, but also many copies; one can count about thirty beautiful and genuine paintings there, and that is quite a lot. This gave us great pleasure and kept us busy for about two hours.'[70]

In his posthumously published notes, Johann Heinrich Jugler (1758–1812), who as a young medical student at the university in Leipzig between 1777 and 1779 had familiarised himself with the sights of the city, gave not only practical tips for visiting the 'Winklerisches Malereycabinet', but also some interesting impressions of the state of the collection: 'But it is a pity that there is not a somewhat better order in the cabinet, for the rooms do not seem spacious enough for all these paintings, and that there are so many newly added works which have not yet been hung, numbered or described.'[71]

THE WINCKLER COLLECTION IN THE CONTEXT OF REMBRANDT'S RECEPTION

The opening of Winckler's cabinet eventually led to the collection being frequented by aspiring artists from the Academy of Fine Arts, founded in 1764, which was reflected in the numerous engravings and drawings regularly shown at the academy exhibitions in Dresden.[72] The director of the academy, Adam Friedrich Oeser, was particularly appreciated by patrons in Leipzig for his Rembrandt imitations, although he himself said that he had no great liking for Rembrandt. Rather, he represented the Italian artistic tradition favoured at the academies of the time, especially seventeenth-century Italian painting.[73] Oeser's preference for Italian Baroque painting is reflected in his own private collection of around 100 works of art: in addition to a large number of Dutch works, including drawings and etchings by 'Rembrandt', it included works by Cagnacci, Carpioni (whom Oeser particularly admired), Cortona, Domenichino, Guercino, Magnasco, Maratta and Spagnoletto.[74]

Nevertheless, Oeser yielded to the bourgeois taste of the time and, in a letter to Hagedorn dated 7 February 1772, justified his tendency toward Rembrandtesque design by pointing to the good sales prospects for such works:

'I myself have made an imitation of Rembrandt for an etching. But you must not suspect me of wanting to live and die for Rembrandt. It is only to help poor aspiring artists to make some money quickly. But I know of no good master whose taste is so loved as Rembrandt's. So the young artist hides his inability and gets money for his efforts. It could easily happen that the world would be inconvenienced with a number of sheets after Rembrandt's original drawings from the Leipzig Academy, merely with the intention of filling empty stomachs a little.'[75]

Four etchings by Oeser after alleged compositions by Rembrandt are known: an undated depiction of Christ in the Temple, in which Oeser may have used motifs from

Rembrandt's drypoint etching *The Presentation in the Temple in the Dark Manner* (c. 1654); from 1765, *Saul and the Witch of Endor* after an unknown painting by 'Rembrandt' from the collection of Heinrich Wilhelm Bachmann (1737–1776) in Magdeburg; the undated *Christ Blessing the Children*; and finally *The Angel Leaves the House of the Old Tobias* (cat. 18.3).[76] The drawing on which the latter etching is based, now in the Graphische Sammlung of the Albertina in Vienna, was once attributed to Rembrandt and is now ascribed to his student Abraham van Dijck (cat. 18.1). Oeser, who already during his time in Dresden had been one of the draughtsmen preparing the engravings for the 'Galeriewerk' of Augustus III, closely followed the original in his etching, but covered the entire composition with the 'sfumato'[77] that was typical of his work and was demanded by Hagedorn in particular. In doing so, he weakened the dramatic effect of the original in favour of a more harmonious pictorial expression. Oeser's students also followed this style, including his son, the engraver Johann Friedrich Ludwig Oeser (1751–1792), whose undated etching *Christ Breaking Bread at Emmaus* clearly refers to the Rembrandt painting *Christ at Emmaus* of 1648 in the Louvre, Paris.[78]

Around 1770 under Oeser's direction, artists at the Leipzig academy including the architect Johann Carl Friedrich Dauthe, the painter Ernst Gottlob and the engraver Johann Friedrich Bause intensively studied the various printing techniques for reproducing drawings and watercolours. As a result, from 1770 onwards numerous attempts were made to reproduce ink drawings from the Winckler collection, such as the sheet *Ruines d'Italie* by Dauthe after a wash drawing by Bartholomeus Breenbergh. At the same time, Gottlob published a very similar aquatint reproduction of a composition then still attributed to Rembrandt under the title *The Prophet of Bethel*, which later came to the Museum der bildenden Künste Leipzig with the Speck von Sternburg collection (cat. 30.2). Both prints bear a dedication in the caption to the French painter and official inventor of the aquatint technique, Jean-Baptiste Le Prince.[79]

WINCKLER'S COLLECTION OF PRINTS

In addition to the paintings in Winckler's cabinet attributed to Rembrandt, his collection of engravings, which he is said to have kept in over 800 albums or portfolios, included almost all of Rembrandt's etchings. Together with the various state prints and Rembrandt copies sought by connoisseurs, the auction catalogue of his Dutch prints (1805) lists some 820 sheets under Rembrandt's name, 339 of which are listed as original Rembrandt prints according to Adam von Bartsch's (1757–1821) *Catalogue raisonné* of 1797, including the *Hundred Guilder Print*.[80] Thus it is not surprising that Winckler made no secret of his passion for collecting, and in 1756 had himself portrayed by Johann Heinrich Tischbein the Elder with a 'Rembrandt copper [engraving]' (Leipzig 1768, no. 232).[81] It is not known which print this was, perhaps a sheet etched 'in Rembrandt's taste'.[82] When Winckler's collection of engravings was liquidated in a series of auctions between 1801 and 1810, one of the purchasers was Francis, Duke of Saxe-Coburg-Saalfeld (1750–1806), who bought some 130 sheets from the extensive Rembrandt collection, which are still in the holdings of the Kupferstichkabinett of the Kunstsammlungen der Veste Coburg which he founded.[83]

WINCKLER'S COLLECTION OF DRAWINGS

Since the study of drawings and the drawing styles of the great masters played a central role in eighteenth-century connoisseurship training, Winckler – 'in earlier times advised by Gotthold Ephraim Lessing, Adam Friedrich Oeser, Michael Huber and other excellent men' – also collected drawings on a large scale. According to the preface to the auction catalogue of his drawing collection, he was so 'attracted by Rembrandt and his bold, ingenious frivolity' that he bought 'several complete collections of his drawings in Holland'.[84] In the course of his collecting activities, Winckler amassed a considerable number of drawings attributed to Rembrandt, of which sheets in Dresden, Hamburg, Weimar and Vienna are still considered to be by the artist.[85]

At the estate auction of Winckler's collection of drawings on 16 October 1815, which, according to the attributions of the time, included master drawings from all schools from the Renaissance to Rococo and Classicism, 108 drawings were auctioned under Rembrandt's name.[86] A total of some 3,500 drawings were for sale, but these probably represented only the remainder of the collection, which was originally estimated at 8,000 sheets. A considerable part of Winckler's collection of drawings, including works by Lucas Cranach the Elder, Matthias Grünewald and Rembrandt, remained in the possession of Gottfried Winckler's descendants – some of them until the twentieth century.[87] In addition, significant parts of the collection had already been sold by private treaty in the run-up to the auction. For example, Duke Albert of Saxony-Teschen, who had already bid generously at the auctions of Winckler's engraving collection, acquired some 750 drawings, including works by Parmigianino, Rembrandt, Rubens and Tiepolo, which are now also in the Albertina in Vienna, which he founded and is named after him (see cats. 12.1, 14.1, 18.1).[88]

LEIPZIG ART COLLECTIONS AFTER 1800

In addition to European and regional buyers, important private collectors in Leipzig took advantage of the liquidation of Winckler's drawing collection to build up their own collections of important drawings, including the municipal and criminal court judge August Otto Gehler (1762–1822) as well as the merchants and tradesmen Ernst Peter Otto (1724–1799), Heinrich Wilhelm Campe (1770–1862) and the aforementioned Johann Caspar Lampe. This circle also included the music critic and Weimar court counsellor Johann Friedrich Rochlitz (1769–1842), who played an important role in the sale of the Winckler collection. He had married Henriette Friedericke Winckler (née Hansen, 1770–1834), the widow of Gottfried Winckler's eldest son Friedrich Daniel Winckler (1760–1809), and thus came into possession of part of the collection (cat. 41.2).[89] In 1861, Gustav Moritz Clauß (1796–1871) donated a total of 68 oil paintings from the collection of Ernst Peter Otto to the Städtisches Museum Leipzig, mainly by seventeenth-century Dutch masters, including a *'Self-Portrait'* of Rembrandt originally thought to be by Rembrandt, but now attributed to his workshop (cat. 21.2).[90]

The merchant Maximilian Speck, who belonged to the Leipzig circle of collectors and has already been mentioned several times, was elevated to Knight von Speck in 1825 and Baron von Sternburg in 1828. Contrary to the changing taste in art, which set new trends in collecting in the first half of the nineteenth century, Speck had placed seventeenth- and eighteenth-century Dutch and Flemish art, which had temporarily fallen out of fashion, at the centre of his collection, thus deliberately linking himself to the bourgeois collecting tradition in Leipzig.[91] Works by 'Rembrandt' and his students therefore played an important role in his collection. Among these was the *Head of an Old Man* (cat. 32.4), dated to around 1650–2, which Maximilian Speck acquired as a work by Rembrandt from the collection of Ludwig Puttrich in Leipzig in 1817 for 100 thalers. In 1809, he had already purchased the painting *Old Woman Reading (The Prophetess Anna?)* by Abraham van Dijck of around 1655 (cat. 41.1), still attributed to Rembrandt at the time, from the collection of the painter Johann Gottlieb Glume (1711–1778), a member of the important Berlin sculptor family, for the considerable sum of 1,840 thalers.[92] While many of the local private collections have long since disappeared or have been absorbed into various museums, the Speck von Sternburg collection, essentially amassed between 1807 and 1832, has remained intact and almost unchanged as one of the few bourgeois collections of the Goethe era, despite several major sales in 1820 and 1857.[93]

PRIVATE COLLECTIONS IN LEIPZIG AROUND 1900

The 1870s saw another significant upsurge in collecting in Leipzig, in which art collectors such as Alfred Thieme (1830–1906) and Julius Otto Gottschald (1841–1903) played a key role. Unlike their eighteenth- and nineteenth-century predecessors, however, both concentrated almost exclusively on Dutch landscape and genre painting.

The entrepreneur and consul general Alfred Thieme was the owner of the traditional Leipzig iron wholesaler 'C. F. Weithas Nachfolger' and had begun collecting Dutch art in the 1860s. He was advised by Wilhelm von Bode (1845–1929), who made purchases on behalf of Thieme and many other private collectors on the art market and at auctions in Germany and abroad. Hundreds of surviving letters from Thieme to Bode document the development of his collection and bear witness to the close and intensive dialogue between the two men over a period of some forty years.[94]

In 1886–9, on the occasion of the completion of the extension to the Städtisches Museum on Augustplatz, Thieme donated 66 paintings, for which Bode compiled a catalogue.[95] Thieme subsequently amassed a second collection of Dutch paintings, which is described in detail in a lavish catalogue, again compiled by Bode, entitled *Galerie Alfred Thieme in Leipzig* and published in 1900 by his son, the art historian Ulrich Thieme (1865–1922).[96] In 1916, the city of Leipzig acquired the collection of 98 paintings. Among them was the *Portrait of Rembrandt's Sister* (Museum der bildenden Künste Leipzig, inv. G 1054), supposedly by Rembrandt, which Bode had acquired for Thieme in London in 1895.[97] Bode's vehement defence of the painting's authenticity caused controversy in specialist circles even then. The painting is now considered to be a copy of a picture by Jacob Adriaensz. Backer in the National Gallery in Stockholm.[98] In December 1905, on the occasion of Bode's sixtieth birthday, Thieme gave Bode the oil sketch *The Good Samaritan* (Staatliche Museen zu Berlin, Gemäldegalerie, cat. 812B), which he had acquired in 1892 from the Parisian art dealer Charles Sedelmeyer (1837–1925) as a work by Rembrandt and which is now regarded as the work of a Rembrandt follower from around 1648.[99]

Bode also helped the independently wealthy Julius Otto Gottschald to develop his collection. In addition to buying paintings at auctions and from art dealers in Berlin, Amsterdam, London and Paris, he acquired important works by Barend Avercamp, Claes Pietersz. Berchem, Salomon van Ruysdael, Abraham Stalbemt and Dirk Stoop from older Leipzig collections.[100] Following Thieme's example, a catalogue of his collection was published in 1901.[101] In 1903, the Museum der bildenden Künste received 50 paintings as a bequest from Gottschald. The painting *Bearded Old Man* (cat. 32.2), originally acquired on the London art market and at the time attributed to Rembrandt as an early work, also came into the museum's possession.[102]

The Thieme and Gottschald collections are the last vestiges of a two-hundred-year bourgeois collecting culture devoted to seventeenth-century Dutch art and in particular to the art of Rembrandt, his students and his followers.

1 Koch 2014, p. 23.
2 Altes 2006, p. 40.
3 Ibid., p. 28.
4 Märker 1993, p. 5.
5 Weimar 2011, p. 17.
6 Heiland/Lüdecke 1960, p. 11.
7 Koch 2009, p. 119.
8 Heiland/Lüdecke 1960, p. 12; Röver 1986, p. 52.
9 Neidhardt 2005, p. 241.
10 Keller 1981, pp. 9f., 57f.; Röver 1986, pp. 56–8; Hausler 2002, pp. 164–71; Neidhardt 2005, p. 247.
11 Neidhardt 2005, p. 248 [translated].
12 Ibid., pp. 244f.
13 Ibid., p. 242.
14 Laabs 2001.
15 See Spenlé 2001.
16 Dittrich 2004, p. 33; Neidhardt 2005, p. 245.
17 Neidhardt 2005, p. 247.
18 Ketelsen 2006.
19 Neidhardt 2005, pp. 243, 247.
20 By around 1700, several German residences such as Salzdahlum and Düsseldorf had built their own galleries to house their collections of paintings, which were open to the public.
21 In 1754–5, an average of 20 to 30 people visited the Dresden painting gallery each month.
22 Spenlé 2005, pp. 107f. Whether Winckler visited the gallery in the company of his wife, as Spenlé claims, is doubtful; Winckler married Johanna Henriette (née Schmidt, 1738–1829), only in 1758.
23 Neidhardt 2006, pp. 7, 18, note 2.
24 Ibid., p. 7 [translated].
25 Dittrich 2004, p. 34; Neidhardt 2006, p. 7. The first printed catalogue of the painting gallery was published in 1765.
26 Dittrich 2004, p. 35; Koch 2009, p. 104. See also the essays by Alexei Larionov (on the collection of drawings) and Dimitri Ozerkov (on Heinrich von Brühl's cabinet of prints and drawings) in the same volume as Koch 2009.
27 See Loewinson-Lessing 1975.
28 Dittrich 1978; Dittrich 2004, pp. 26–8.
29 Dittrich 2004, pp. 28f.; Melzer 2010, pp. 453f.
30 The first two volumes were associated with the Wagner collection as provenance, but according to Dittrich they could also have come from a Dutch collection. Dittrich attributed the third volume to Weidmann; see Dittrich 2004, p. 29; Melzer 2010, p. 454.
31 Dittrich 2004, pp. 31–3; Melzer 2010, p. 471.
32 Dittrich 1978, p. 20; Dittrich 1987, p. 8; Dittrich 2004, pp. 29–31; Melzer 2010, pp. 451–6, 463–70.
33 Dittrich 2004, pp. 31–3; Melzer 2010, pp. 463–6; Wätjen 2021, p. 28.
34 Dittrich 1987, p. 12; Wätjen 2021, p. 36.
35 Melzer 2010, pp. 465f.; Ketelsen/Melzer 2011, pp. 45, 50.
36 Dittrich 1987, p. 15; Dittrich 2004, p. 30; Melzer 2010, pp. 468f.; Berlin/Amsterdam/London 1991, pp. 48–50. For more on the owners of Rembrandt drawings in the seventeenth century, see Gelder 1973, pp. 197f.
37 Czok 1989, p. 41.
38 Vienna 1989, p. 17.
39 Ibid., p. 213.
40 Stockhausen 2002, p. 105.
41 See Hommel 2018.
42 Mehnert 1972, p. 290; Leipzig 1990, p. 11–13; Melzer 2010, pp. 463f.
43 Vienna 1989, no. V/1/12; Leipzig 1999; Leipzig 2014, pp. 64–99.
44 Vienna 1989, p. 214.
45 Trautscholdt 1957, pp. 226–8; Heiland 1989.
46 Heiland 1976–7; Leipzig 2012, no. 284.
47 Kreuchauff 1776, p. 307.
48 Ibid., p. 312.
49 Stefes 2011.
50 Kreuchauff 1776, pp. 312–21; Heiland 1989, p. 141.
51 Kreuchauff 1776, p. 308.
52 Universitätsbibliothek Leipzig, Rep. VI 25n.
53 Goeckingk 1778, p. 468 [translated].
54 Vienna 1989, p. 214; Gleisberg 2005, p. 79.
55 Gleisberg 2011–12, pp. 148f. Perhaps the hanging plans were also intended for a never-realised illustrated and expanded new edition of the painting catalogue, such as already existed for other major collections.
56 Ibid., p. 122.
57 Ibid., pp. 157f.
58 Trautscholdt 1957, pp. 221f.; Gleisberg 2011–12, pp. 139–43.
59 Trautscholdt 1957, pp. 222f.
60 Ibid., p. 223; Gleisberg 2011–12, pp. 142f.
61 Gleisberg 2011–12, pp. 145f.
62 Stübel 1920, p. 67 [translated]. Chodowiecki also visited Winckler's collection in 1773 and again in 1789.
63 Trautscholdt 1957, p. 223. The painting is also documented in one of C. F. Wiegand's watercolours of the hanging in Winckler's garden house (Stadtgeschichtliches Museum Leipzig). Valentiner 1920, pp. 132, 136.
64 Gleisberg 2011–12, pp. 128f., 163.
65 Ibid., pp. 129, 162.
66 Ibid., pp. 130, 188.
67 Trautscholdt 1957, p. 250, note 29; Gleisberg 2011–12, p. 130.
68 Gleisberg 2011–12, pp. 131f.
69 Ibid., p. 133.
70 In the original wording: 'Comme je ne me suis arrêté à Leypsick, après Dresden, qu'une couple d'heures pour voir un cabinet de tableaux de M. Godefroy Vinkler, négotiant... Il y a nombre de tableaux dans ce cabinet de négotiant, mais il y a beaucoup de copies; on y peut compter une trentaine de beaux et vrais tableaux et c'est beaucoup. Cela nous a fait très grand plaisir et nous a occupé environ deux heures.'; quoted in Tornézy 1895, pp. 417f.
71 Quoted in Zarncke 1909, p. 72 [translated].
72 Gleisberg 2011–12, p. 133.
73 Heiland/Lüdecke 1960, p. 9.
74 Ibid., p. 51; see also the auction catalogue of Oeser's estate, Rost'sche Buchhandlung, Leipzig, 9 February 1800.
75 Quoted in Baden 1797, p. 288 [translated].
76 Heiland/Lüdecke 1960, pp. 50f.
77 Quoted in Hagedorn 1762, p. 555.
78 The etching is mentioned in *Neue Bibliothek*, vol. 18, 1776, under the title *Christus mit den Emauntischen Jüngern, wie er bei einem Licht das Brot bricht* (Christ with the Disciples in Emmaus Breaking Bread by a Light).
79 Rebel 1981, pp. 69–72; Coburg/Aachen 2007, pp. 247–53.
80 Leipzig 1805, pp. 646–822, lots 3672–4490; the *Hundred Guilder Print* is listed under lot 3806.
81 Kassel/Leipzig 2005, no. 47, pp. 162f.
82 Gleisberg 2011–12, p. 133.
83 Ibid., p. 129; see also Coburg/Freiburg 2017, pp. 36–47 (S. Knöll). The collection of engravings put up for auction comprised a total of 23,318 lots, including a whole series of engravings bound together in larger groups.
84 Quoted in Leipzig 1815, p. XLV [translated].
85 Gleisberg 2011–12, p. 129.
86 Leipzig 1815, lots 1393–1500, 2074 (addendum).
87 In November 1920, 818 Old Master drawings 'From the famous Winckler Collection founded in the eighteenth century' were auctioned by F. A. C. Prestel in Frankfurt am Main.
88 Gleisberg 2011–12, pp. 150–3. Cf. Mehnert 2013–14, pp. 235–67; Mehnert 1986.
89 Gleisberg 2011–12, pp. 155–7.
90 Leipzig 2012, no. 269, p. 254.
91 Gleisberg 1998, pp. 23, 28.
92 Ibid., p. 32, no. I/118, pp. 342f.; Leipzig 2012, no. 68.
93 Leipzig/Munich 1998.
94 Leipzig 2012, p. 16.
95 Leipzig 1886; cf. Leipzig 2012, p. 17.
96 See Leipzig 1900.
97 Ibid., pp. 23–5, 70, no. 66, pl. III.
98 Leipzig 2012, no. 5.
99 Leipzig 1900, no. 67.
100 Vienna 1989, p. 216; Leipzig 2012, pp. 16–18.
101 See Leipzig 1901.
102 Leipzig 2012, no. 270.

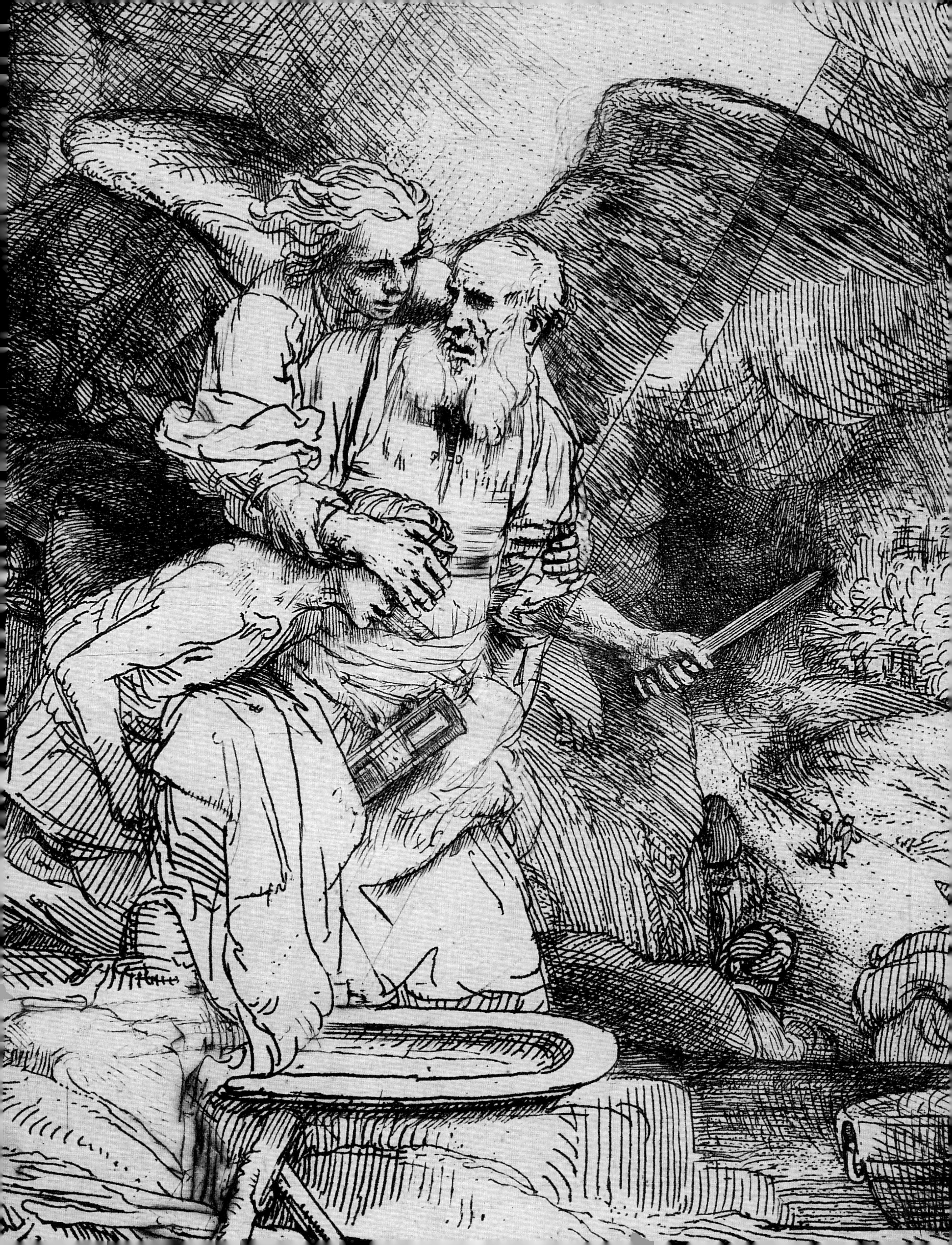

REMBRANDT AS VISUAL DIRECTOR

Jan Nicolaisen JN
Louise Charlotte Schmidt LCS
Julian Galla JG

1 PETER PAUL RUBENS

(Siegen 1577–1640 Antwerp)

The Miracle of St Walburga

c. 1611
Panel, 75.2 × 98.5 cm
Maximilian Speck von Sternburg Foundation in the Museum der bildenden Künste Leipzig, inv. 1589
Lit.: Leipzig/Munich 1998, no. I/56; Braunschweig 2004, pp. 209–11, no. 39; Leipzig 2012, no. 284.

The waves pound against the overcrowded sailing boat, which seems lost like a nutshell in the raging sea. With her hands raised in prayer, Walburga stands among the boat's crew, whose faces express despair and panic. Walburga's calm, upright form contrasts with the agitated figures around her. According to legend, Walburga, a Benedictine nun, was caught in a violent storm on her way from England to the European mainland to convert the pagans there. Walburga continued to pray until the storm subsided.

Rubens chose the most dramatic moment for his painting. With their muscles strained to the limit, the rowers try to battle the raging masses of water. Their athletic bodies were inspired by classical models, particularly Michelangelo's frescoes in the Sistine Chapel, which Rubens had seen during his travels in Italy (1600–8).[1]

The Miracle of St Walburga was the left of three predella panels on the high altar in the St Walburga Church in Antwerp, with a depiction of the Raising of the Cross as its centrepiece, which Rubens was commissioned to paint in June 1610. Rembrandt, who never left Holland, was unable to see the altarpiece with his own eyes, but was familiar with graphic reproductions of the centre panel. His paintings of the *Elevation of the Cross* from the early 1630s

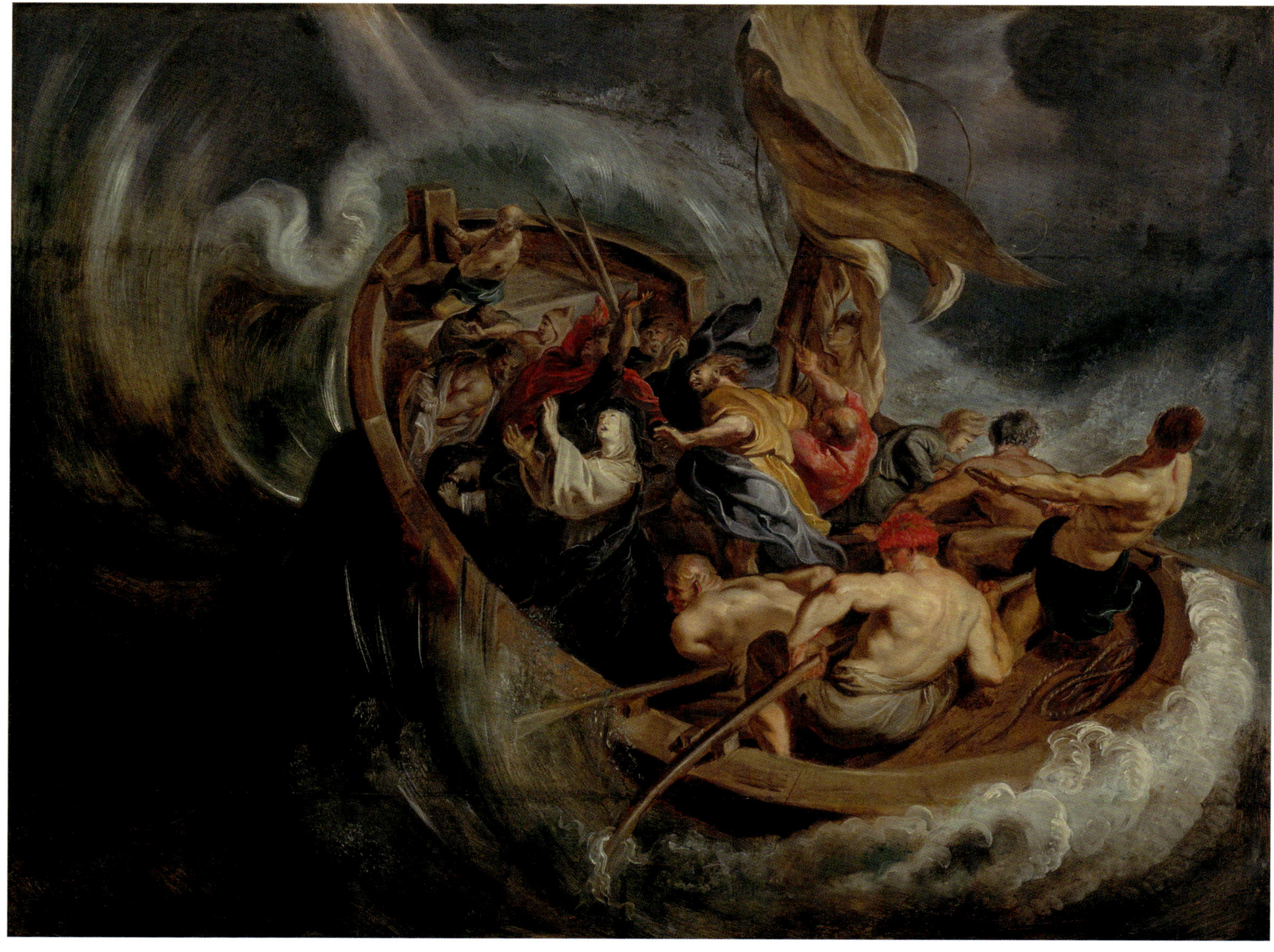

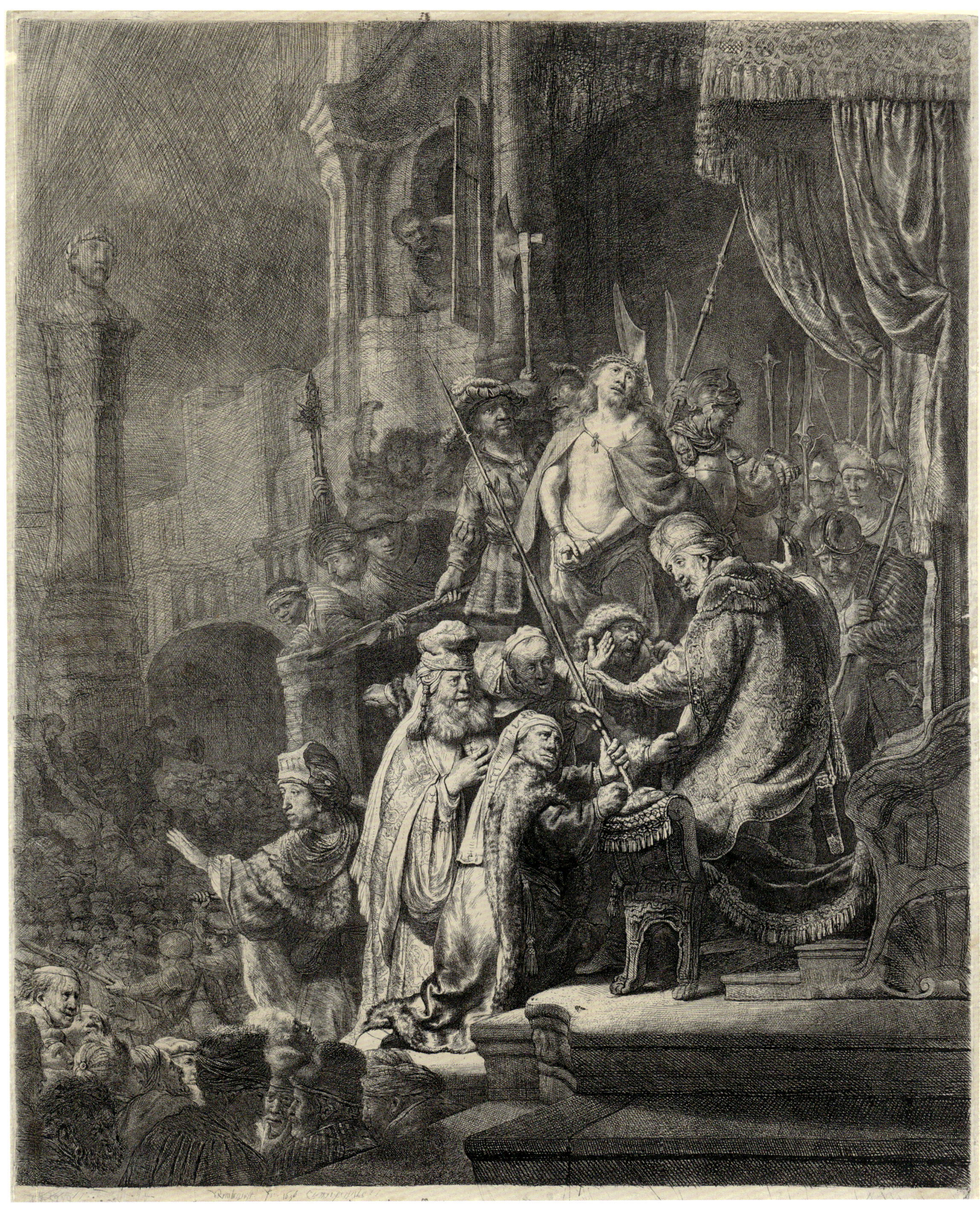

3.3

1 Schnackenburg 2016, pp. 71f.
2 *Isaac and Esau*, c. 1633–5; *Susanna and the Elders*, c. 1634; see Amsterdam 1996, nos. 34, 35; Schnackenburg 2016, nos. 62f.
3 Amsterdam 1991, pp. 58f.
4 Amsterdam 1996, p. 44.
5 Ibid., p. 45.
6 Weimar 2011, p. 62.
7 Ibid., p. 63.
8 For more on the cycle, see Van de Wetering, 'Remarks on Rembrandt's oil-sketches for etchings', in Amsterdam/London 2000, pp. 39–57; Hinterding 2006, vol. 2, pp. 92–6.
9 Weimar 2011, p. 63; Leiden/Oxford 2019, nos. 113, 114.
10 Corpus 1982–2015, vol. 5, p. 178.
11 Amsterdam/London 2000, pp. 139f.
12 Sumowski 1983–94, vol. 2, no. 935.

4.1 REMBRANDT

Simeon and Anna in the Temple

c. 1627–8
Panel, 55.5 × 44 cm
Hamburger Kunsthalle, inv. HK-88
Lit.: Bauch 1960, p. 122; Corpus 1982–2015, vol. 1, A 12; Melbourne/Canberra 1997, no. 2; Kassel/Amsterdam 2001, no. 30; Leiden 2005, pp. 112f.; Schwartz 2019, p. 97; Corpus 1982–2015, vol. 6, p. 486, no. 16; Leiden/Oxford 2019, pp. 41f.

4.2 REMBRANDT (?)

Circumcision of Christ

c. 1646 (or 1650s?)
Pen and brown ink, brush and brown and grey wash, opaque white (touches of red chalk), 23.4 × 20.4 cm
Arched upper edge
Staatliche Graphische Sammlung Munich, inv. 1385
Lit.: Benesch 581; Munich/Amsterdam 2001, no. 58; Munich 2003, pp. 95–114 (Th. Ketelsen), pp. 115–24 (V. Manuth); Corpus 1982–2015, vol. 5, pp. 226, 431–4; Schatborn/Hinterding 2019, Z 82; Royalton-Kisch online, Benesch 581.

4.3 JÜRGEN OVENS

(Tönning 1629–1678 Friedrichstadt)

Simeon and the Child Jesus (Simeon's Song of Praise)

1651
Canvas, 113 × 100 cm
Kunsthalle zu Kiel, inv. CG 4
Lit.: Sumowski 1983–94, vol. 3, no. 1483; Köster 2017, pp. 33–6, no. G 11.

4.4 REMBRANDT

Simeon and the Child Jesus (Simeon's Song of Praise)

1669
Canvas, 98.5 × 79.5 cm
Stockholm, Nationalmuseum, inv. NM 4567
Lit.: Stockholm 2005, no. 419; Corpus 1982–2015, vol. 6, no. 324; London/Amsterdam 2014, pp. 265–8.

In accord with Jewish law, Mary and Joseph took their first-born son to the Temple to consecrate him to God and to sacrifice two turtledoves. There, the aged Simeon, whom God had promised that he would not die until he had seen the Messiah, recognised him in the child and prophesied to Mary: 'Behold, this child is destined for the fall and rise of many in Israel, and to be a sign that will be contradicted (and you yourself a sword will pierce) so that the thoughts of many hearts may be revealed' (Luke 2:22–40). In the Hamburg painting, Rembrandt places Simeon at the centre of the group of figures (cat. 4.1). He turns to the praying figure of Mary with the child in his arms and blesses her. The prophetess Anna stands above him, arms outstretched in praise of God. Joseph is kneeling in the foreground, only visible from the rear, with a straw hat in his hands.

Characteristic of Rembrandt's early period is the dense, slightly asymmetrical concentration of the figures in the left half of the picture, while the right side is empty.[1] Here, the extinguished candle in the darkness contrasts with the radiant light streaming in from the left, probably a sign of the new covenant between God and man. Different states of mind – the visible emotion of the old prophet and prophetess and Mary's pensive surrender to her fate – are condensed into one scene. The 21-year-old Rembrandt was already striving to capture emotion. Originally, Simeon was shown looking up with his head raised in praise of God, as X-ray examinations have revealed.[2]

The young artist paid particular attention to the realistic depiction of materiality. The fur trim on Simeon's and Anna's robes is rendered in detail with individual brushstrokes. On the whitewashed wall, the incidence of light is realistically represented by the shadows cast by the window frame – an innovation in Dutch painting at the time. At the same time, the visionary aspect of the knowledge of God is emphasised by the pointed direction of the light, an echo of Utrecht Caravaggism. Simeon speaks as he holds the child in his arms: 'for my eyes have seen your salvation...a light for revelation to the Gentiles' (Luke 2:30–2). A slightly later version of Rembrandt's *Simeon's Song of Praise* from 1631 (The Hague, Mauritshuis) is also characterised by accentuated contrasts of light and dark.

The theme of the Presentation in the Temple, along with the related theme of Simeon's Song of Praise, preoccupied Rembrandt throughout his life, since it involves the demonstration of an inner revelation and thus the visualisation of strong emotions. The artist treated the subject in several paintings, etchings and drawings (e.g. Bartsch 49, 50, 51; Benesch 373, 486; Corpus 1982–2015 A 34). When Rembrandt died in 1669, the unfinished painting

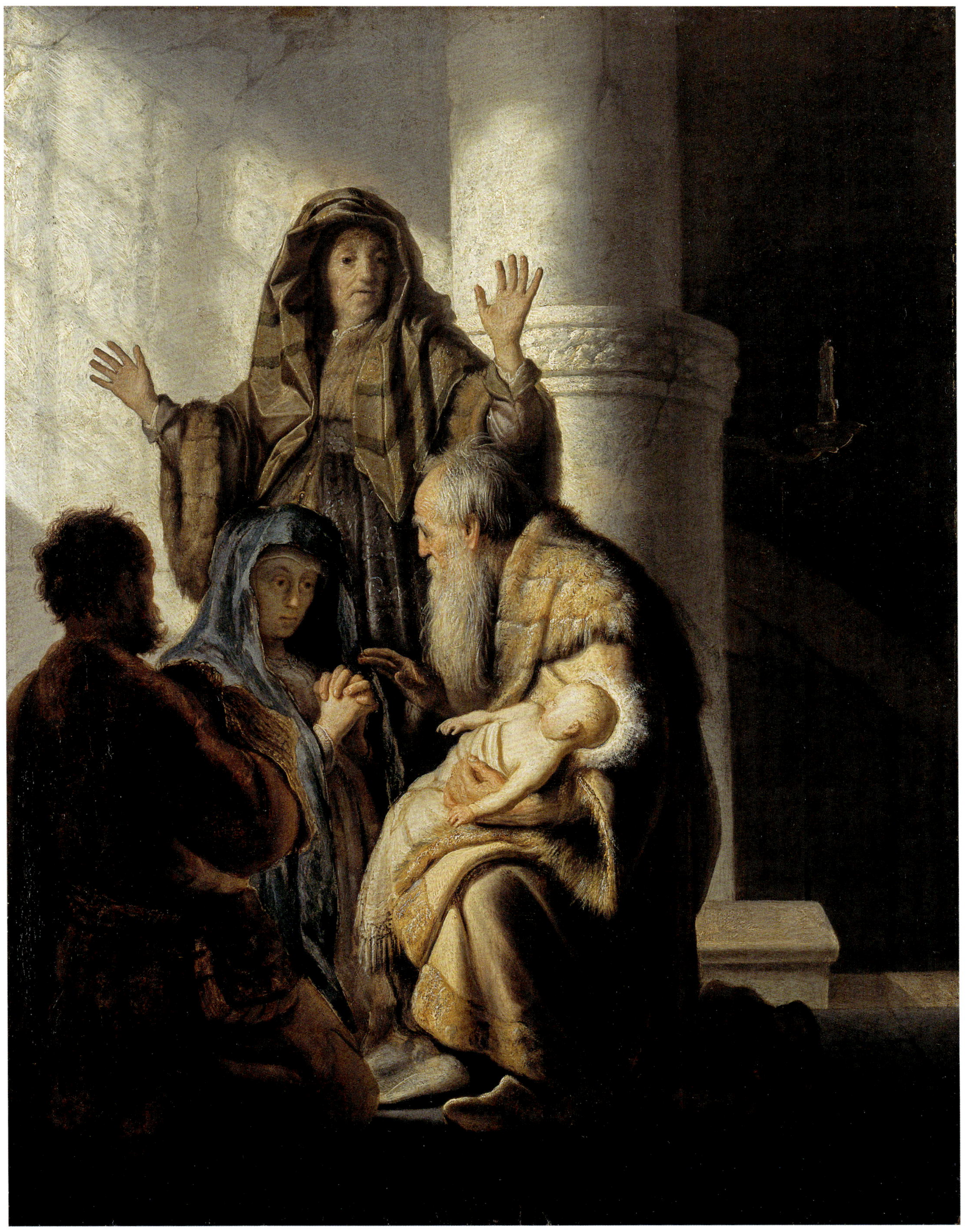

4.1

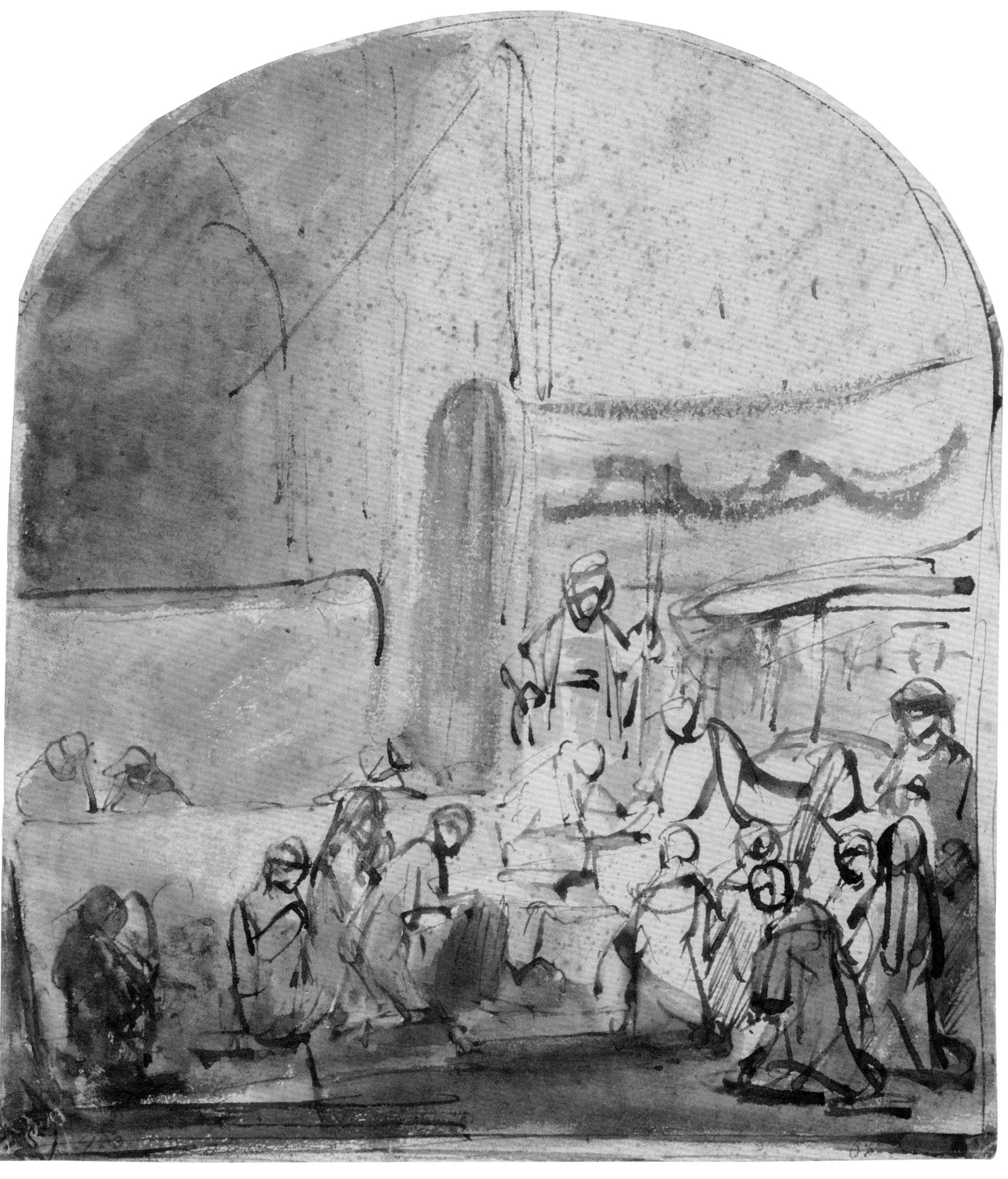

4.2

Simeon and the Child Jesus was on the easel (cat. 4.4). A notarised statement from 1671 records that the two painters Allaert and Cornelis van Everdingen saw the painting in Rembrandt's studio during its creation and discussed it with him.[3] It was commissioned and paid for in advance by the art dealer and collector Dirk van Cattenburgh.

In this painting, Rembrandt emphasises the contrast between old age and infancy, as well as between the outer and inner worlds. Every element of action is reduced in favour of the introspection of the almost blind old man with the child in his arms. The infant Jesus gazes into the world with open eyes, while Simeon's half-closed eyes testify to his spiritual contemplation.[4] The application of paint shows the characteristic manner of the late work: rough, with juxtaposed, partially unblended colours, which may have been applied to the canvas with a palette knife.[5] The warm colours of Simeon's robe, his skin tones, and those of the infant Jesus shimmer brightly against the dark background.

This tendency to reduce the external action also characterises the 1651 painting created in Amsterdam by the northern German painter Jürgen Ovens, who had studied under Rembrandt in the 1640s (cat. 4.3).[6] The influence of Rembrandt and Lievens is clearly evident in the striking chiaroscuro and the shimmer of the golden cloak (cf. cat. 5). As in the earlier painting in Hamburg, the child's alert eyes shine in the heavenly light.

The treatment of light was a central theme of Rembrandt's painting and consequently of his teaching, as the Munich drawing (cat. 4.2) makes clear. The authorship, function, and dating of this exquisite drawing are disputed among scholars. What is certain is that in 1646, in the context of the commissions for a cycle of the Passion, Rembrandt delivered a painting of the *Circumcision of Christ* to the stadtholder Frederik Hendrik, which was then lost in the first half of the eighteenth century. Some authors consider the Munich drawing to be a sketch by Rembrandt in preparation for the lost painting of the *Circumcision of Christ*, a copy of which has survived (Braunschweig, Herzog Anton Ulrich-Museum, inv. 241). Others see a student at work here, who created a copy after the lost original. Dating also varies between 'circa 1646' and the 1650s, with the watermark suggesting the 1640s.[7] Volker Manuth has pointed out that Rembrandt's inventory of 1656 apparently included a copy after the lost painting.[8] This could be one of the variants that Rembrandt had his students make for commercial purposes in accordance with his workshop practice. The draughtsman could therefore have produced the sheet in Rembrandt's workshop in front of a modified version of the now lost painting. Rembrandt's authorship cannot be ruled out with certainty. The interweaving of the figures into a lively group in a coherent composition, as if on a

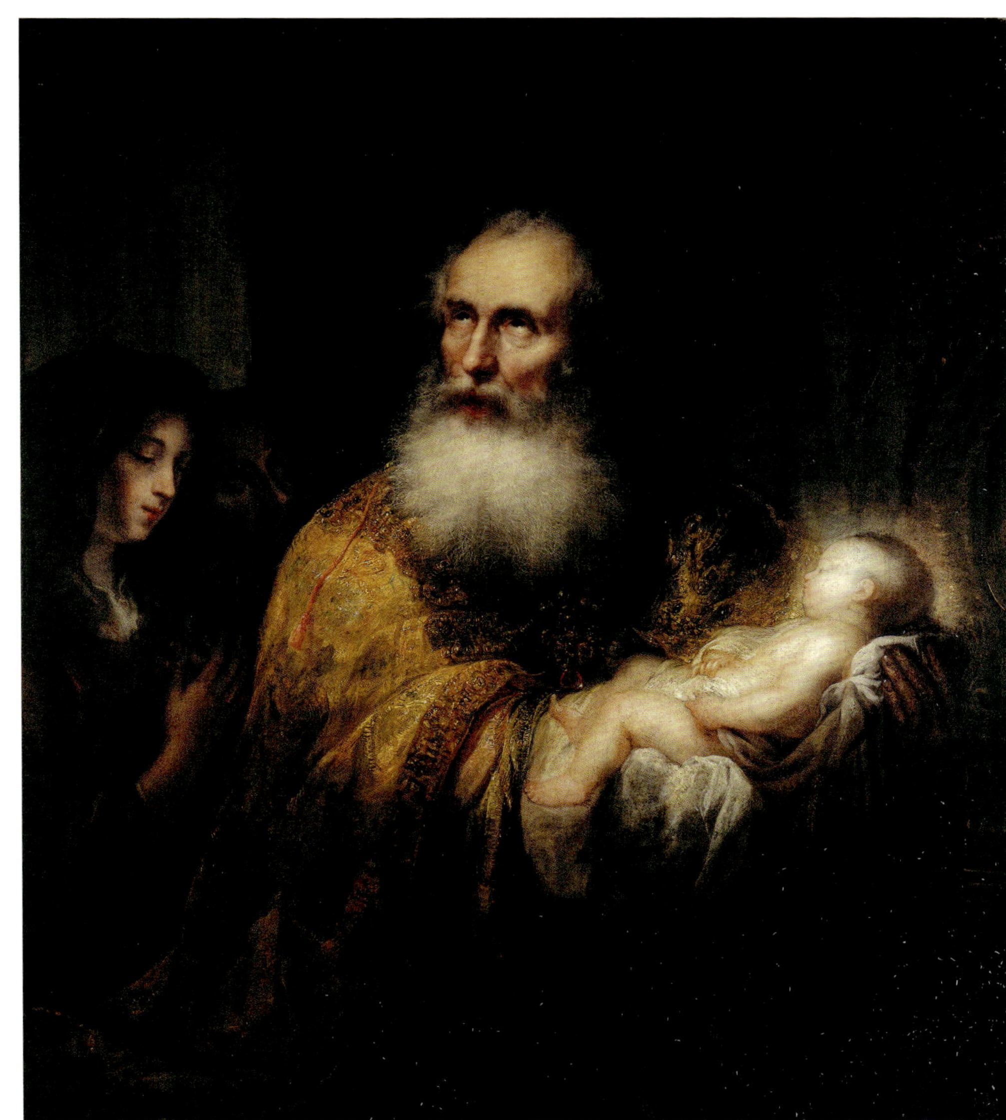

4.3

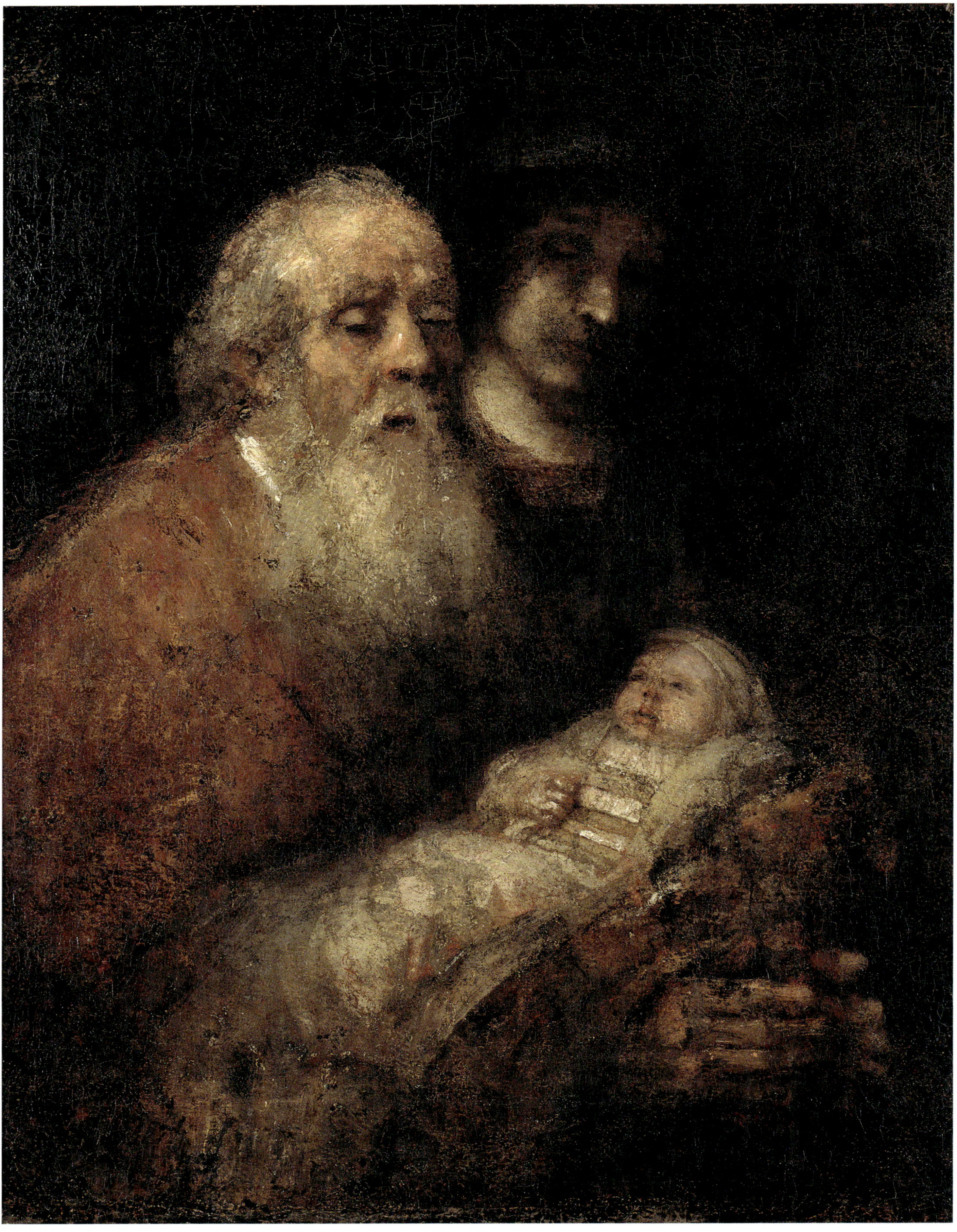

4.4

stage, as well as the pointed direction of the light and the style of drawing seem to speak in favour of an attribution to him.

It is noteworthy that the draughtsman was primarily concerned with the lighting, while the arrangement of the figures is only sketched with geometrising abbreviations. The central circumcision scene is accentuated by the blank paper, as if illuminated against the semi-darkness of the temple. The drawing thus demonstrates an awareness of the importance of the nuances of lighting in the shadow effects of the half-tones and mid-tones. The lighting is captured even before details of physiognomy or costume. Rembrandt's students learnt this 'storytelling with light' in his workshop while copying and sketching biblical stories. JN

1 Bauch 1960, p. 122.
2 Melbourne/Canberra 1997, p. 86.
3 Stockholm 2005, p. 415.
4 London/Amsterdam 2014, p. 267.
5 The painted surface was badly damaged by inexpert restoration work in the first half of the twentieth century. The female figure, possibly conceived by Rembrandt, is a later addition. See Stockholm 2005, p. 413.
6 Köster 2017, p. 33.
7 Munich/Amsterdam 2001, p. 224, note 10.
8 Munich 2003, p. 119.

5 JAN LIEVENS

(Leiden 1607–1674 Amsterdam)

A Priest Writing

1631–2
Panel, 56.3 × 47.5 cm
Brussels, Private collection, courtesy Lempertz
Lit.: Sumowski 1983–94, vol. 3, no. 1241a; Schnackenburg 2016, no. 191; Cologne/Prague 2019, no. 16; Leiden/Oxford 2019, no. 108.

A priest in ornate liturgical vestments writes with a pen in a book held open in his left hand. His gaze is fixed on the page illuminated by the light. Two tall candles burn in the semi-darkness, within which another open book can be glimpsed on the table in the left background. An engraving hangs over the front edge of the table. At the front left, another heavy tome lies on the table, suggesting the elderly clergyman's erudition.

From the tronie of an old man with a book, Lievens uses costume, décor and lighting to develop a religious story whose meaning, as Anja Sevcic notes, remains 'iconographically indeterminate'.[1] The act of writing may allude to the priest Zechariah, to whom an angel announced the birth of his son, the future John the Baptist (Luke 1:12–17). Because of his lack of faith, he was struck mute. Later, at the circumcision of his son, Zechariah was only able to write the child's name on a tablet (Luke 1:62–3).[2] However, it is doubtful whether this secures the identification of the figure. A high priest and a church father have also been considered.

The popularity of the painting, of which ten versions have survived, is probably due not to the specific subject matter, but rather to the aesthetic of the image. Lievens transforms the scene into an opulent sacred still life through the lustre and shimmer of the textiles: the brocaded coverlet, the gold-embroidered robe, the silken sheen of the cloak and the priest's embroidered cap. The cool tones of gold and yellow sparkle in the darkness of the vaguely indicated room and are reflected in the wooden floorboards. The old man's face, absorbed in the process of writing, shines out of the darkness. The brilliance of the rendering of textiles also characterises Rembrandt's painting *Old Woman Reading (Prophetess Anna)* from the same period (cat. 7), underlining the proximity of the two artists, whose paintings could be mistaken for each other.[3]

The physiognomy of the man with a long, slightly curved nose recurs in modified form in several paintings and etchings by Rembrandt and Lievens, as well as in works by Gerrit Dou. It was thus part of the studio's stock of tronies from which both older and younger male heads could be modelled in painting by working out the corresponding physiognomic details. According to a document by the Leiden city historian Jan Orlers from 1641, the model was the steward of an almshouse in Leiden.[4] Schnackenburg considers four of the ten versions to be works by Lievens himself, and this painting (cat. 5) to be a copy of the original by his own hand.[5] According to the inventory of his bankruptcy estate of 1656, Rembrandt owned the painting 'A Priest after Jan Lievens', which could have been one of these versions.[6] JN

1 Cologne/Prague 2019, p. 102.
2 Ibid.; cf. Schnackenburg 2016, p. 354.
3 See the essay by Jan Nicolaisen in this catalogue, pp. 32–3.
4 Cologne/Prague 2019, p. 130; Washington/Milwaukee/Amsterdam 2008, p. 118.
5 Schnackenburg 2016, pp. 354–6.
6 Radboud Universität Nijmegen, RemDoc 1956/12.

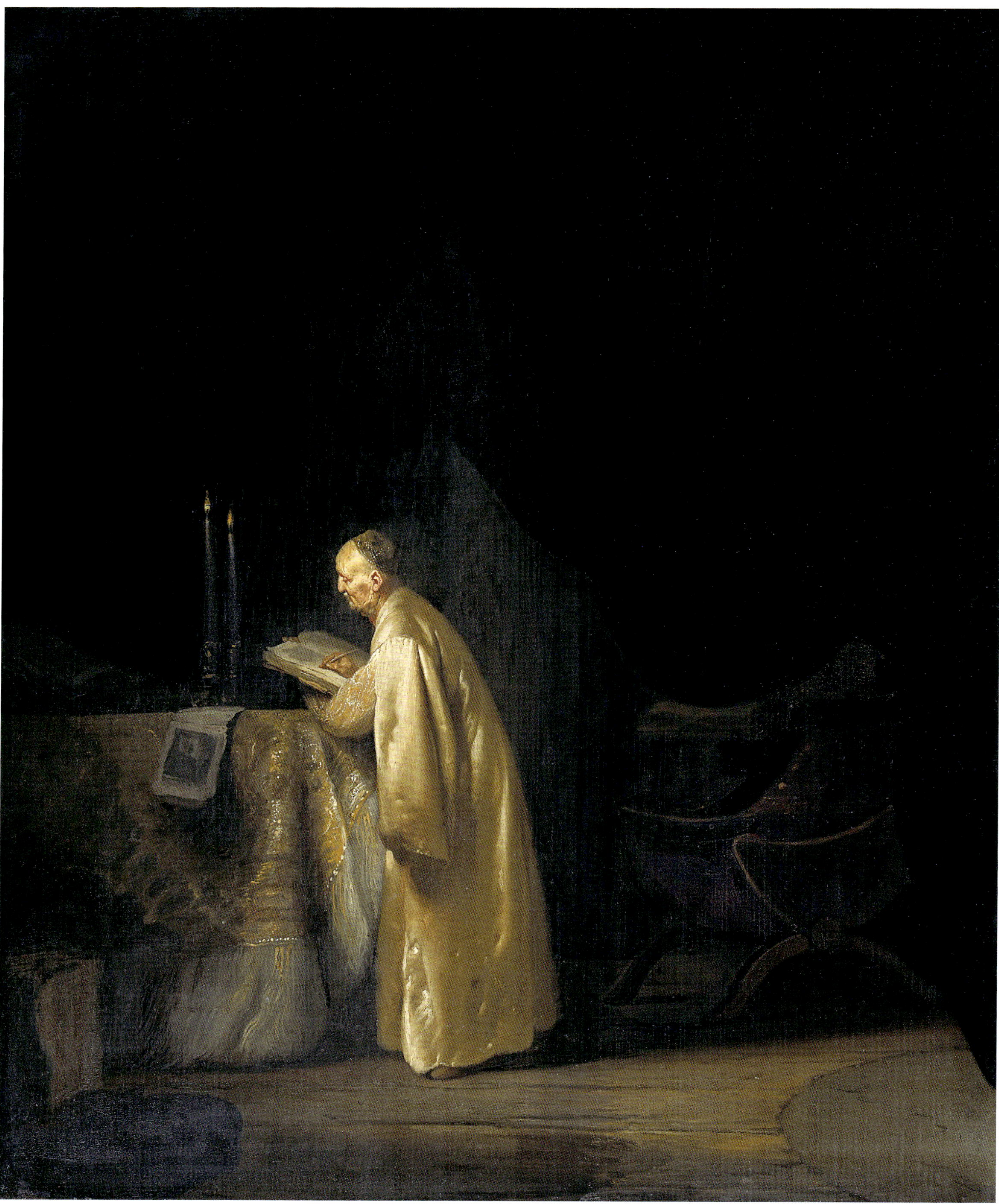

5

8 REMBRANDT

Minerva in Her Study

c. 1631
Panel, 60.5 × 49 cm
Signed (centre right): R (no longer visible)
Staatliche Museen zu Berlin, Gemäldegalerie, cat. 828C
Lit.: Corpus 1982–2015, vol. 1, A38; Berlin/Amsterdam 2006, no. 12; Corpus 1982–2015, vol. 6, no. 54; Manuth/Winkel/Leeuwen 2019, no. 95.

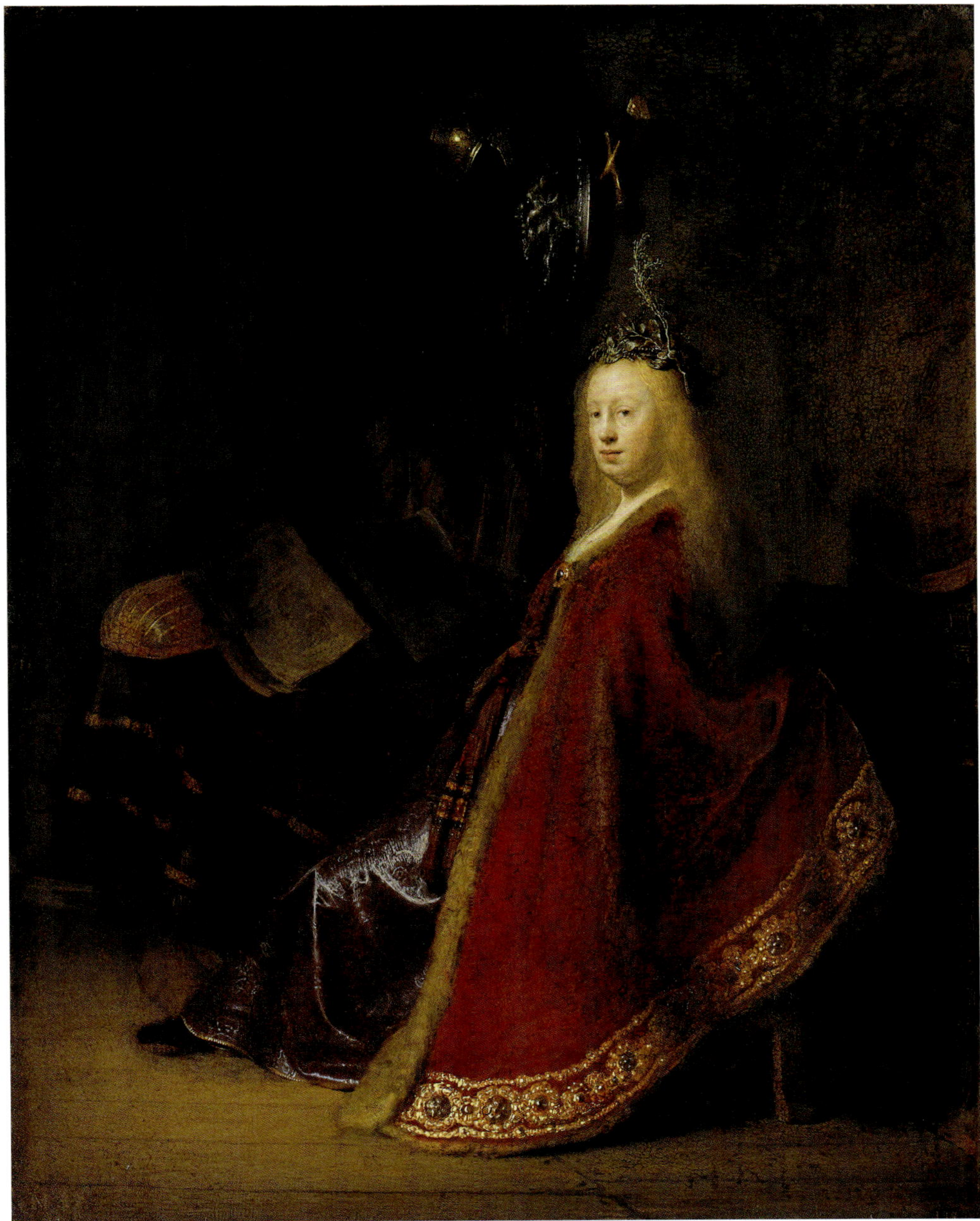

8

In *Minerva in Her Study*, Rembrandt develops the pictorial narrative from the tronie of a young woman, whom he identifies as the patron goddess of the arts and wisdom as well as of the art of war through her elaborate costume and still life-like accessories. In the tradition of Leiden still life painting, a lute, books and a globe are placed on a table in the background. The open book shows a spoked wheel, probably a reference to a scientific illustration that researchers have associated with the Flemish mathematician and engineer Simon Stevin (1548/49–1620).[1] The motif underlines the artist's intention to depict Minerva not only as the goddess of war, but also as the polymath goddess of science. Hanging above her are a gilded helmet and sword, as well as a shield with the head of Medusa. This blonde, very Dutch-looking goddess of war wears a laurel wreath on her head. Her costume is sumptuous and colouristically delicate, with a purple dress and a red fur-trimmed cloak with a gold hem. The costume stands out dramatically against the rough floorboards with nailed planks, which lend the scene a domestic simplicity. The warm colours glisten from the interior, which is shadowed in umber tones against which the bright complexion of the face stands out in striking luminosity.[2]

Researchers generally assume that the Berlin painting is identical with the one mentioned in a 1632 inventory of the stadtholder Frederik Hendrik, 'depicting Melancholy, a woman sitting on a chair at a table with books, a lute, and other instruments, by Jan Lievens'.[3] This provenance is not entirely convincing, as there is no clear attribute of Melancholy, nor are there any other musical instruments other than the lute. It is possible, however, that the term 'instrument' refers to the globe, and in any case, paintings by Lievens and Rembrandt were occasionally mistaken for each other at this time due to their stylistic similarities. The serious expression on the face and the dark tone of the room may have favoured an interpretation as 'Melancholy'.

The subject of Minerva was painted several times in Rembrandt's circle around 1630. Two paintings in Denver and The Hague, for example, show a very similar composition.[4] Interestingly, in the version preserved in The Hague, which is similar in format to the Berlin painting, the goddess Minerva rests her head in her hand on the table in a classic gesture of melancholy.

A few years later, Rembrandt painted the large-scale *Minerva in Her Study*, also depicting her as the goddess of wisdom with the attribute of an open tome. Researchers have suggested that this iconographic accent may be linked to Rembrandt's desire to reach an academic clientele in Amsterdam associated with the Athenaeum, the forerunner of the University of Amsterdam.[5] JN/JG

1 Manuth/Winkel/Leeuwen 2019, p. 557.
2 The work's current poor state of preservation weakens the former effect of these painterly means; see Corpus 1982–2015, vol. 1, pp. 360–2.
3 Ibid., pp. 362f.; Berlin/Amsterdam 2006, p. 262.
4 Isaac de Jouderville, *Minerva in Her Study*, c. 1631, 43.9 × 35.6 cm, The Denver Art Museum, inv. 1959.114; Rembrandt's Workshop, *Minerva in Her Study*, 1630, 61.7 × 53.5 cm, The Hague, Mauritshuis, inv. 626. Jouderville was one of Rembrandt's first students in the early 1630s.
5 Rembrandt, *Minerva in Her Study*, 1635, 137.2 × 116 cm, New York, The Leiden Collection, inv. RR-107; Manuth/Winkel/Leeuwen 2019, p. 563.

9 FERDINAND BOL

(Dordrecht 1616–1680 Amsterdam)

Minerva Reading

1636
Black chalk, pen and black ink, brush and grey wash and opaque white, 25.6 × 20.1 cm
Signed (upper left): F:bol.ft.
Amsterdam, Rijksprentenkabinet, inv. RP-T-1975-85
Lit.: Sumowski 1979–92, vol. 1, no. 126x; Bruyn 1989, pp. 12–16; Amsterdam 2017, pp. 40–53, no. 97; V. Manuth, 'Minerva in Her Study' (2017), in *The Leiden Collection*, https://theleidencollection.com/artwork/minerva-in-her-study/; Schatborn 2017, pp. 184f.

Ferdinand Bol was about twenty years old and already a professional painter when he joined Rembrandt's workshop.[1] In order to study the master's painting style, the students copied his works. Bol copied Rembrandt's large painting *Minerva Reading* of 1635 (New York, The Leiden Collection), which he was able to view in the studio. Rembrandt's Minerva wears a dress of heavy, shimmering fabric and a cloak of gold brocade as well as pearl jewellery. A magnificent tapestry is spread out on the table. The delicate colour chords of blue-silver and gold enhance the impression of warm, radiant lighting. Copying trained the eye for brightness values, since the colours had to be converted into shades of grey.[2] Bol also honed his sense of proportion by transferring the 138 × 116 cm painting to the small format of a drawing.

The contours, rendered with a pen, are very delicate and in places dissolve into the washes. In their nuanced gradations they correspond exactly to the chiaroscuro values of Rembrandt's painting. The execution of the washes convincingly depicts the materiality of the textiles and objects. Bol captures the shimmer of the garment with an emphatically fluid brushstroke, which contrasts with the areas painted with a drier brush, such as the hair, the book and the pile of the woven tapestry. These areas are also underlaid with black chalk and therefore have a rougher texture. The reflection of light on her face and shoulder makes Minerva stand out from the dark surroundings of the room and gives the figure greater plasticity. Comparing the composition of the drawing with that of the painting, the sheet appears to have been cropped on both sides.[3]

Bol also made drawings after Rembrandt's *Flora* of 1635 (London, National Gallery) and the *Standard Bearer* of 1636 (Amsterdam, Rijksmuseum), which was also copied by Govert Flinck. Together with the Amsterdam drawings, these works form a stylistically related group. Bonny van Sighem and Ilona van Tuinen note that the ink colour of the signature matches some details of the drawing (the clasp of the cloak and the contours of the Gorgon's head). They put forward the plausible hypothesis that here, Bol was already developing his later signature.[4] JN/JG

1 See Blankert 1982, pp. 17, 71; Amsterdam 2017, p. 42.
2 Franken 2006, pp. 160f.
3 B. van Sighem, 2000/I. van Tuinen, 2018, Ferdinand Bol, *Minerva in her Study*, Amsterdam, c. 1636, in Turner online.
4 Ibid.

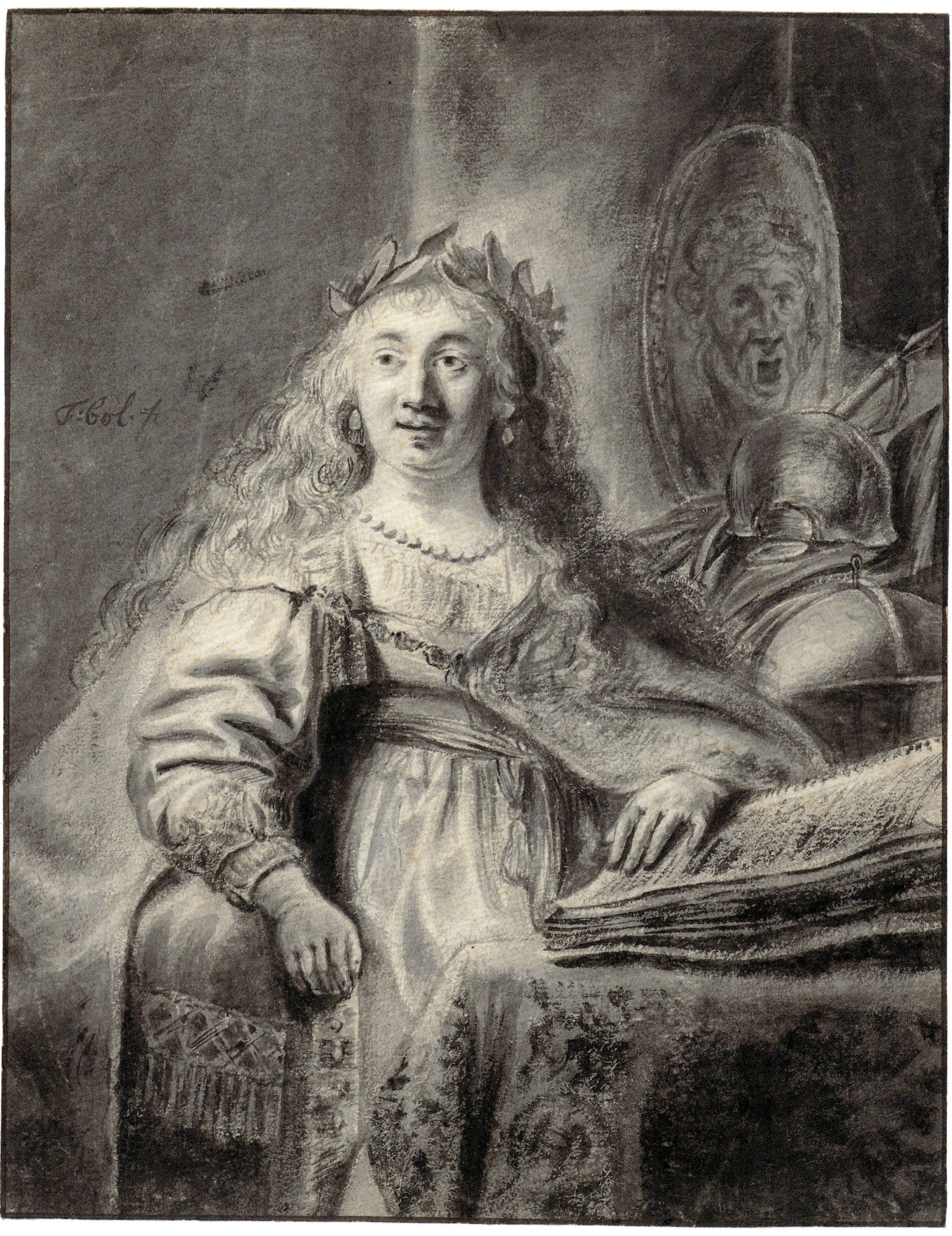

9

10.1 REMBRANDT

Actor or Study of a Woman in an Elaborate Costume

c. 1638
Pen and brown ink, brush and brown wash on red-brown prepared paper, 19.8 × 13.1 cm
Museum der bildenden Künste Leipzig, Graphische Sammlung, inv. NI. 470
Lit.: Benesch 321; Leipzig 1990, no. 43; Winkel 2006, pp. 245f.; Los Angeles 2009, no. 16.1; Royalton-Kisch online, Benesch 321; Amsterdam 2024, pp. 53–5.

10.2 GERBRAND VAN DEN EECKHOUT

(Amsterdam 1621–1674 Amsterdam)

Actor or Study of a Woman in an Elaborate Costume

c. 1638
Pen and brown ink, 19.4 × 15.5 cm
Staatliche Kunstsammlungen Dresden, Kupferstich-Kabinett, inv. C 1980-494
Lit.: Benesch 319; Dresden 2004, no. 107; Bevers 2010, p. 63; Amsterdam 2024, pp. 53–5.

10.3 GERBRAND VAN DEN EECKHOUT (?)

Gijsbrecht van Amstel before Bishop Gozewijn

c. 1638
Pen and brown ink, brown wash, opaque white, 20.9 × 16.5 cm
Braunschweig, Herzog Anton Ulrich-Museum, Kupferstichkabinett, inv. Z 552
Lit.: Benesch 122; Braunschweig 2006, no. 40; Bevers 2010, pp. 63–5; Amsterdam 2024, p. 53.

10.4 REMBRANDT

Medea (The Marriage of Jason and Creusa)

1648
Etching and drypoint, IV (of V), 24 × 17.6 cm (plate)
Signed and dated: Rembrandt f. 1648
Hamburger Kunsthalle, Kupferstichkabinett, inv. 6232
Lit.: Bartsch 112; NH 241; Marieke de Winkel, 'Medea: Rembrandt versus Jan Six', in Amsterdam 2024, pp. 64f.

For a history painter who, like Rembrandt, was fascinated by the expression of emotion through body language, the opening of the 'Schouwburg' theatre in Amsterdam in the new building designed by the architect Jacob van Campen in January 1638 must have been an attraction. There is some evidence that Rembrandt attended not only theatre performances there, but also rehearsals, and drew during them.[1] The fact that some of these drawings were made not by Rembrandt but by his students may indicate that he took them to the theatre for practice.[2]

Ever since the interpretation of the Leipzig costume study as a depiction of Badeloch, the wife of the eponymous hero Gijsbrecht van Amstel in the tragedy of the same name by Joost van den Vondel (1587–1679) – which opened in the newly built Schouwburg – the drawing from the collection of Johann August Otto Gehler (1762–1822; cat. 10.1) has been discussed in connection with Rembrandt's interest in the theatre.[3] In a group of drawings now attributed partly to Rembrandt but mainly to students, he seems to have explored this drama. However, scholars have also interpreted the drawings as costume studies, possibly based on historical costume books from the sixteenth century.[4] The drawings have also been understood as the result of joint exercises by Rembrandt and his students from costumed models in the studio.[5]

A woman in an elaborate costume – or a male actor in women's clothes – stands before us with an outstretched, strongly foreshortened left arm and a gesture of the raised right hand that demands attention. It was not until 1655 that actresses were allowed to perform in Holland, before which female roles had to be played by men.[6] As the figure is shown from behind, the physiognomy can only be guessed at, making it difficult to determine whether it is a man in women's clothing (i.e., a male actor) or a woman. Leonore van Sloten suggests that actors may have worn gloves – as in the Leipzig sheet – in order to appear more feminine.[7] Rembrandt was not interested in the facial expression, but in the imposing posture, body language and historicising costume, which is characterised by great delicacy in its materiality.[8] The shimmering velvet shows regular but sweeping parallel layers. The fur trim of the bonnet is rendered in detail with bristly, diverging strokes. The model wears a light, almost transparent veil around her neck and over her arms, which contrasts with the heaviness of her clothes. The washes are carefully but vigorously applied, giving the costume plasticity and a certain monumentality through nuanced gradations of light and dark. Because of these qualities, the Leipzig drawing is now considered the only costume study that can be securely attributed to Rembrandt and is discussed in the context of comparable studies of women in elaborate dress from the late 1630s.[9] It seems doubtful that Rembrandt could have drawn such a detailed study during a rehearsal, as the actor would not have stood still long enough.

Compared with the Dresden drawing (cat. 10.2), the differences are striking: both actors are lit from the left, but the lighting in the Leipzig drawing is noticeably more subtle. The body language and gestures of the hands also seem less

a poisoned goblet. The jealous Medea will use them to kill the children of her marriage to Jason, who had abandoned her for the king's daughter Creusa, to whom she will now send a poisoned dress. A text added in the fourth state describes Medea not only as an avenger but also, with a certain degree of understanding, as a betrayed wife.[15] Marijke de Winkel has pointed to Rembrandt's careful reading of Ovid's *Metamorphoses* (Book 7), in which Medea is described as the granddaughter of the sun god Helios: the painter indicates this by the sun she wears as a pendant on a necklace.[16] It is clear that he carried out detailed research in order to give his pictorial narratives historical veracity. In her pose and historicising clothing, the tragic figure of Medea resembles the female costume figures of Rembrandt and his students. JN

1 Amsterdam 2024, p. 53.
2 Martin Royalton-Kisch suspects that Govert Flinck and Gerbrand van den Eeckhout attended theatre performances together with Rembrandt, since he recognises their handwriting in corresponding drawings; see Royalton Kisch online, Benesch 120; Amsterdam 2024, p. 53.
3 Henri van de Waal, 'Rembrandt at Vondel's Tragedy *Gijsbrecht van Aemstel*', in *Miscellana I. Q. van Regteren Altena 16/V/1969*, Amsterdam, 1969, pp. 145–9; Ben Albach, 'Rembrandt en het toneel', in *Kroniek van het Rembrandthuis*, 31 February 1979, pp. 2–32. In Act 3, Badeloch delivers a monologue in which she recounts how she was told in a dream that Amsterdam, besieged by enemies, would fall and was advised to flee. However, she decides to stay with her husband and children and die a heroine's death. By divine providence, the family is saved in the end by fleeing. Older scholars saw this monologue depicted on the Leipzig sheet.
4 Winkel 2006, pp. 244–52.
5 Berlin 2018, p. 122.
6 Amsterdam 2024, p. 57.
7 Ibid.
8 The same artistic interest in the realistic reproduction of materiality can be seen in the paintings of the 1630s; cf. cats. 7–8.
9 Bevers 2010, pp. 60–3.
10 Ibid., p. 63.
11 Ibid.; Martin Royalton-Kisch online, Benesch 319.
12 Braunschweig 2006, p. 106.
13 Ibid., pp. 108f.; Bevers 2010, pp. 63–5; Royalton-Kisch online, Benesch 122.
14 Weimar 2011, p. 118.
15 Dickey 2004, pp. 112f.
16 Amsterdam 2024, p. 64.

11 FERDINAND BOL

(Dordrecht 1616–1680 Amsterdam)

Joseph Interpreting the Dreams of His Fellow Prisoners

c. 1640
Pen and brown ink, brush and brown wash, 16.6 × 22.9 cm
Hamburger Kunsthalle, Kupferstichkabinett, inv. 22412
Lit.: Sumowski 1979–92, vol. 1, no. 101; Bremen 2000, no. 3; Jan L. Leja, Ferdinand Bol and Rembrandt: Authorship and Iconography in Drawings of Biblical Subjects, c. 1636–1650, PhD diss., New York University, Institute of Fine Arts, 2004, pp. 160–7; Amsterdam 2017, p. 192; Hamburger Kunsthalle online (A. Stefes).

In many of his works, Rembrandt depicted episodes from the novel-like story of Joseph (Genesis 37–50), which was already popular in the circle of the Pre-Rembrandtists.[1] He was probably interested in the story because of its rich psychological content. The story of Joseph's interpretation of dreams during his imprisonment (Genesis 40:1–22) was treated in several drawings by Rembrandt and by students such as Ferdinand Bol, Govert Flinck, Gerbrand van den Eeckhout, Willem Drost, and Jan Victors.

Joseph, who was unjustly imprisoned in Egypt, interprets the dreams of his fellow prisoners, the baker and the cupbearer, who have also fallen out of favour as officials at Pharaoh's court. He prophesies the release and rehabilitation of the cupbearer and the death by hanging of the baker within three days.

In Bol's drawing, the despairing baker, for whom Joseph has just predicted death, wrings his hands. This gesture and the tilt of the head are largely copied from Rembrandt's repentant Judas, which Jan van Vliet had etched as a single figure in 1634. This figure, based on a painting by Rembrandt (*Judas Repentant, Returning the Pieces of Silver*, 1629, private collection), had already been praised by Constantijn Huygens the year of its execution for its emotional expressiveness.[2] Bol took the figure of the cupbearer to the right from a drawing by Rembrandt on the same subject.[3] It is remarkable how skilfully the young painter combined motifs available in his workshop into a coherent composition.[4] Bol had already treated the subject in a drawing from the late 1630s, which was probably corrected by Rembrandt.[5]

Rembrandt dealt with the subject in several drawings around 1638–9 (London, British Museum; Benesch 423 verso/Los Angeles, J. Paul Getty Museum, inv. 95. GA.18)[6] and again around 1650 (Amsterdam, Rijksprentenkabinet; Benesch 912).[7] He was inspired by a 1512 engraving by Lucas van Leyden, whom he greatly admired as a graphic storyteller and from whom he borrowed details of the costumes and above all the composition with the fellow prisoners reclining on the floor in conversation.[8]

On the right, steps lead up from the cell, the massive walls of which are only hinted at by a pillar. The focus is not on the décor but on the emotional content of the scene. The tonal washes in the background bring out the characters in the biblical story. With such drawings, students and other members of the workshop practised developing and recombining motifs from Rembrandt's pictorial narratives. Holm Bevers suggests that they may have produced drawings of the same subject in a kind of competition with each other, similar to the practice at Carracci's academy in Bologna.[9] While Joseph and the cupbearer, as those favoured by fate, are depicted close together and captured in bold outlines, the unfortunate baker appears isolated and fragile in the light, emphasised by fine pen strokes.[10]

The Hamburg drawing served as a sketch for a painting.[11] Rembrandt explored the subject of Joseph as

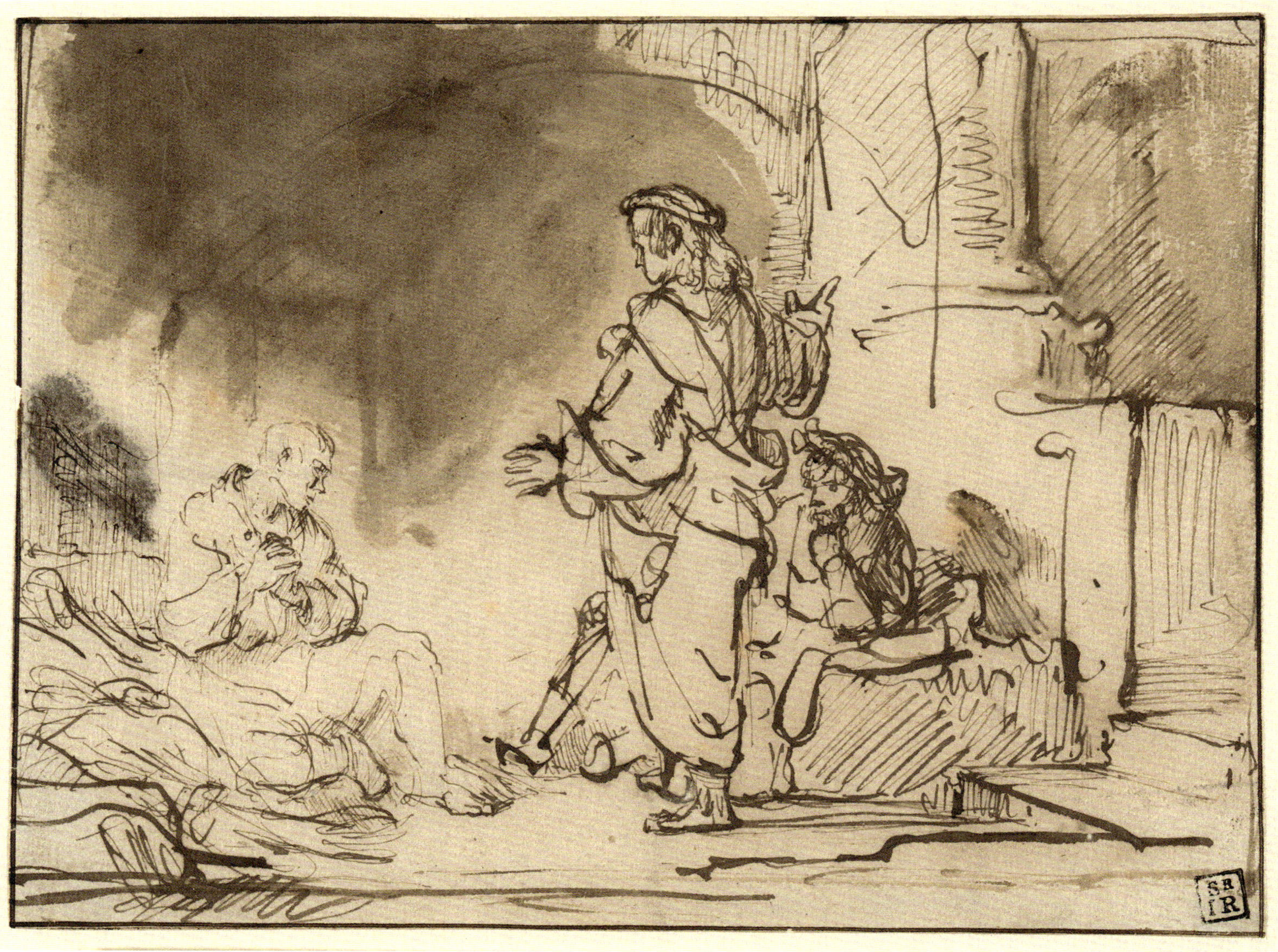

11

the interpreter of dreams on several occasions.[12] The motif probably appealed to him in its combination of introspection, dialogue, and reaction to what is heard. JN

1 See Münster/Amsterdam/Jerusalem 1994, p. 42.
2 See the essay by Jan Nicolaisen in this catalogue, p. 22.
3 Amsterdam, Rijksprentenkabinet, inv. RP-T-1901-A-451; cf. Leja 2004, pp. 164f.
4 It is possible that Bol was familiar with a drawing by Govert Flinck of the same subject, which was probably included in a volume of student drawings that Rembrandt made for teaching purposes; see Los Angeles 2009, nos. 4.2, 7.2.
5 Staatliche Kunstsammlungen Dresden, Kupferstich-Kabinett, inv. C 1300; cf. Dresden 2004, no. 72.
6 https://www.getty.edu/art/collection/object/103R78#full-artwork-details.
7 https://www.rijksmuseum.nl/en/collection/RP-T-1901-A-4529/catalogue-entry.
8 Lucas van Leyden, *Joseph Interpreting the Dreams in Prison*, B. 22; cf. Bremen 2000, p. 36, fig. 3a.
9 Los Angeles 2009, pp. 20, 78f., nos. 7.1, 7.2.
10 See Hamburger Kunsthalle online (A. Stefes).
11 *Joseph Interpreting the Dreams of His Fellow Prisoners*, canvas, 165 × 212 cm, Staatliches Museum Schwerin, inv. G 65.
12 See Rembrandt's 1638 etching *Joseph Telling His Dreams* (B. 37) and the 1633 grisaille of the same subject (Cologne/Prague 2019, no. 14).

12.1 FERDINAND BOL
(Dordrecht 1616–1680 Amsterdam)

Jacob's Dream

c. 1642
Canvas, 128.5 × 97 cm
Inscribed (lower right): f. Bol. fecit
Staatliche Kunstsammlungen Dresden, Gemäldegalerie Alte Meister, gal. no. 1604
Lit.: Blankert 1982, no 5; Sluijter 2015, pp. 336–8.

12.2 REMBRANDT'S WORKSHOP (?)

The Liberation of Peter

1640s
Pen and brown ink, brush and light grey-brown wash, small corrections in white, 19.5 × 22.2 cm
Frankfurt a. M., Städel Museum, Graphische Sammlung, inv. 858
Lit.: Benesch 616; Frankfurt 1994, Z 59; Frankfurt 2000, no. 59.

12.3 FERDINAND BOL

Abraham Meeting the Three Angels

Second half of the 1640s
Pen and brown ink, brush and brown wash, 17.6 × 20.3 cm
Vienna, Albertina, inv. 8764
Lit.: Sumowski 1979–92, vol. 1, no. 259*.

12.4 REMBRANDT

Abraham's Sacrifice

1655
Etching and drypoint (only state), 15.4 × 13 cm
Signed: Rembrandt f 1655
Museum der bildenden Künste Leipzig, Graphische Sammlung, inv. NI. 2045
Lit.: Bartsch 35; NH 287.

12.1

Angels play a special role in Rembrandt's pictorial world: through their appearance, God reveals himself.[1] Since Rembrandt's angels are always coherently integrated into a composition in which they interact with other figures, they appear not only as the exaltation, but also as the plausible visualisation of an action.

A prime example from Rembrandt's late period is his 1655 etching *Abraham's Sacrifice* (cat. 12.4). Based on Genesis 22:1–13, the artist shows the angel using both hands to prevent Abraham, who has already covered the child's eyes, from carrying out the deed. The expression on the old man's face reflects the inner anguish that this

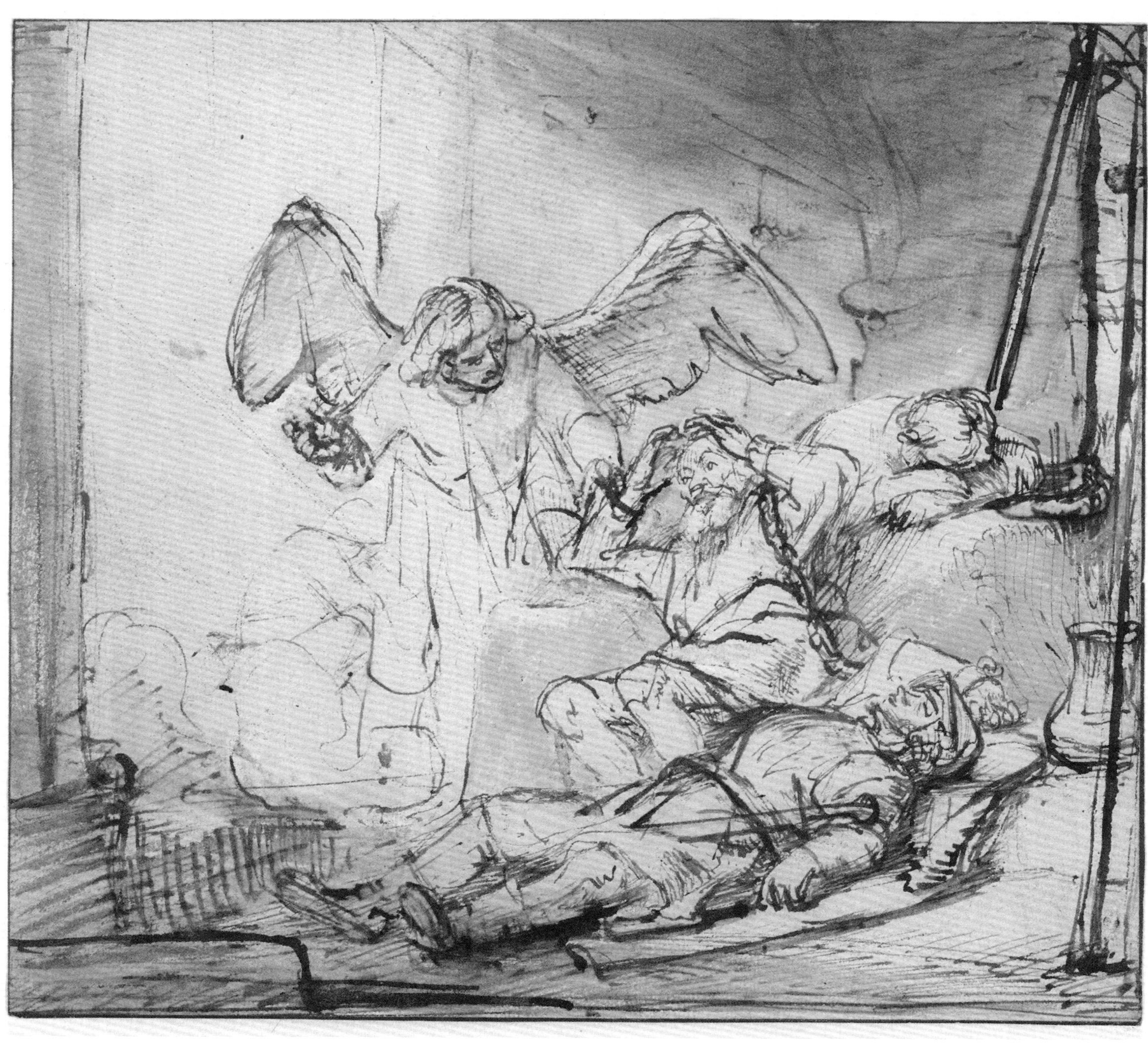

12.2

action requires of him.[2] The head is reminiscent of the early tronies of old men by Lievens and Rembrandt (cat. 31.3). The angel's gentle facial expression contrasts with the drama of the moment.

Rembrandt had already depicted this theme in a painting from 1635.[3] In contrast to the dramatic, action-filled works of the early period, the action in the later etching is internalised, with the drama centred on the emotional experience of Abraham. Rembrandt uses the motif of the angel to illustrate the *self-stryt*, the inner conflict of faith, and its conciliatory resolution.[4]

Rembrandt's students also learned to depict the divine sphere as manifested in angelic form.[5] Shortly after establishing himself as an independent painter, Ferdinand Bol created the large-scale painting *Jacob's Dream* (cat. 12.1). Fleeing Esau, whose vengeance he fears, the sleeping Jacob has a vision of

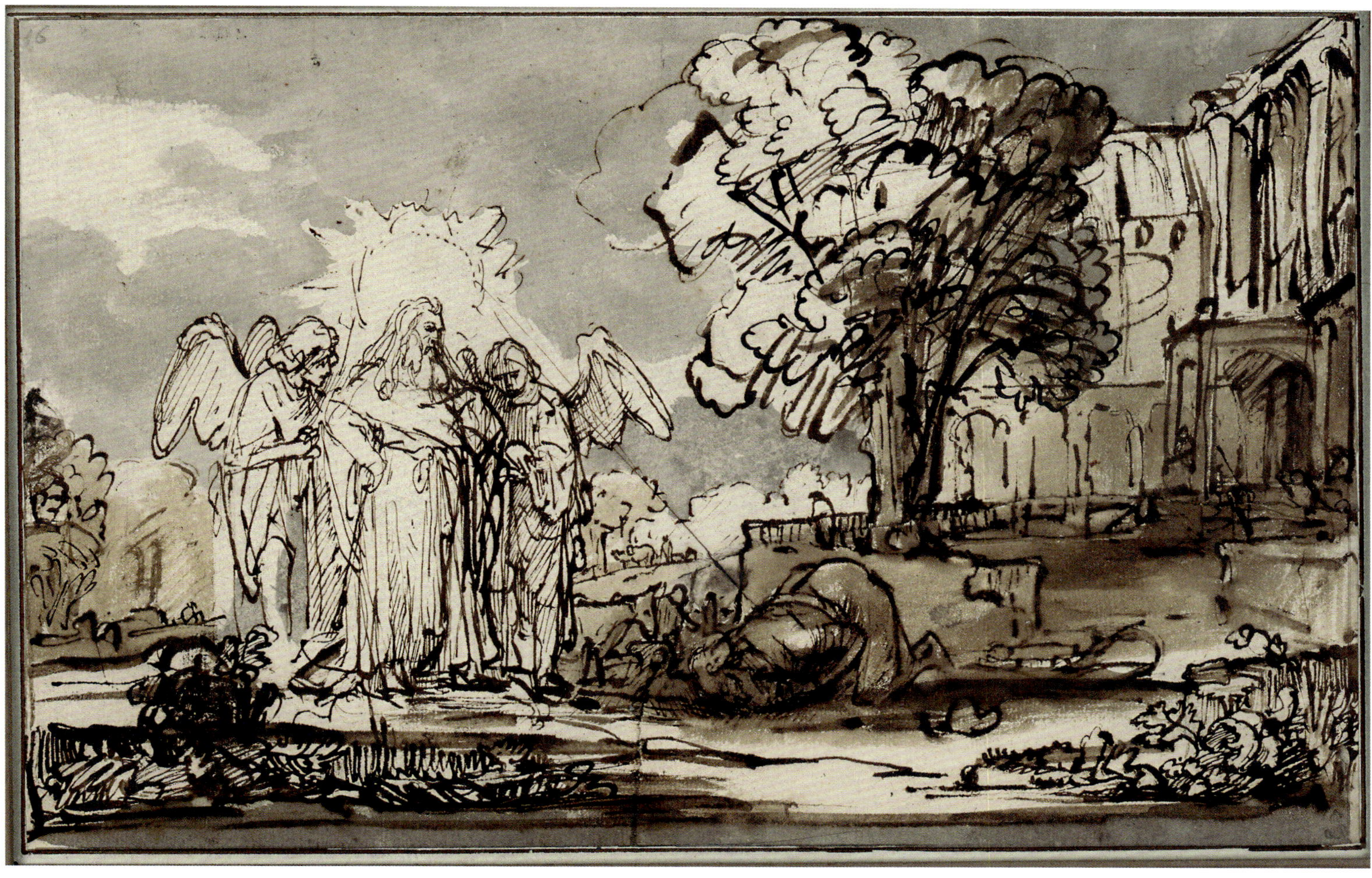

12.3

a ladder reaching to heaven with angels ascending and descending (Genesis 28:10–22). As almost always, Bol based his composition closely on models by Rembrandt as well as on a painting by Gerbrand van den Eeckhout, who was active in the workshop at the same time as Bol and produced at least three depictions of the subject.

Rembrandt's small etching *The Raising of Lazarus* (B. 72) from 1642 was probably the inspiration for the majestic standing angel with outstretched hand.[6] The angel in Rembrandt's etching of *The Annunciation to the Shepherds* (B. 4) has also been cited by Peter Schatborn as a model.[7] The process by which the Dresden picture was created thus illustrates how students and other artists in the workshop viewed Rembrandt's pictorial inventions in terms of their reusability.

Bol probably also modelled the angel as a figure of light on Rembrandt's 1636 painting *The Ascension* (Munich, Alte Pinakothek).[8] Sluijter points out that, in comparison with Rembrandt, the emotionality of Bol's scene is muted, expressed in the warm colours and soft transitions between light and dark.[9] In the medium of drawing, however, he was far more expressive, as a lively preparatory drawing for the painting shows (Besançon, Musée des Beaux-Arts, inv. D 2626; Sumowski 1979–92, vol. 1, no. 92).

The drawing *Abraham Meeting the Angels* (cat. 12.3) in Vienna comes from the Leipzig collection of Gottfried Winckler (1731–1795), where it was thought to be by Rembrandt. It is now attributed to Ferdinand Bol, who used washes of dark ink to create striking contrasts of light and dark. Abraham prostrates himself before the three men the moment he recognises them as God and angels (Genesis 18:2). Bol used light to dramatise the moment of this apprehension of the divine. A single ray of light falls on the kneeling Abraham, symbolising the touch of faith.

In the Frankfurt drawing of *The Liberation of Peter* (cat. 12.2), probably by a student of Rembrandt, we see the angel awakening the sleeping apostle and – despite his chains – urging him to rise.[10] The

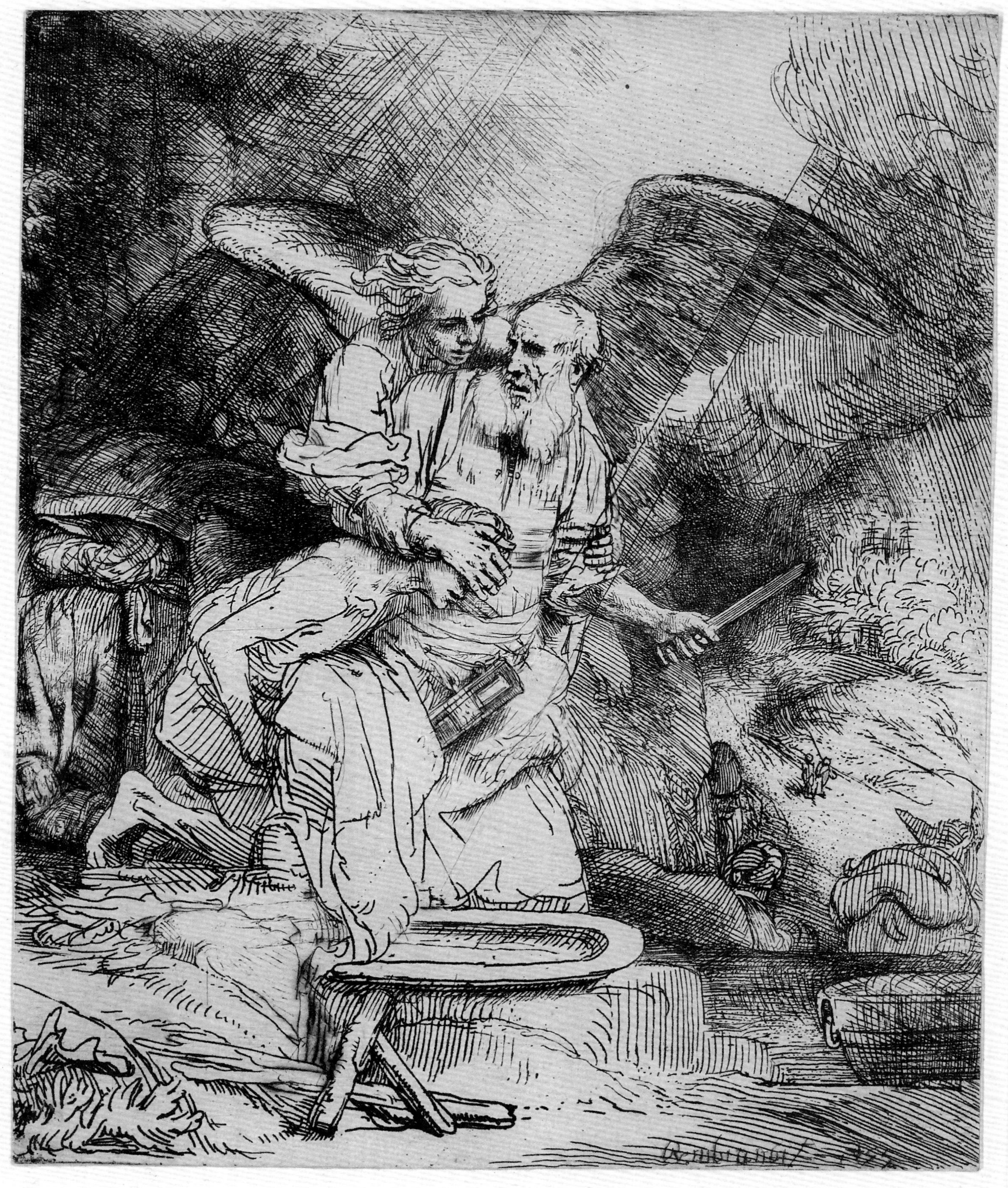

12.4

subject was treated several times in the workshop, as can be seen from a drawing in Amsterdam, now attributed to Carel Fabritius, in which the posture of the angel and Peter is prefigured.[11] Here, too, the draughtsman has incorporated the dramatic incidence of light as a narrative impulse. In the Frankfurt drawing, Peter holds his arms above his head in fright, blinded by the light coming through the door with the angel, while the guard and a fellow prisoner remain asleep (Acts 12:5–7). The artist focuses the action on an emotional moment, namely the intrusion of divine power into the reality of the cell. We can see that certain motifs, such as the sword of the sleeping guard or the chains with which Peter is bound, have been traced with broad strokes of the pen over finer lines. These are probably not corrections by the master, but an independent attempt by the draughtsman to give expression and spatial presence to the figures and the action. JN

1 See Dresden 2004, p. 15 (Thomas Ketelsen).
2 Münster/Amsterdam/Jerusalem 1994, p. 159.
3 St Petersburg, Hermitage, inv. 92. A version of the painting by a student, presumably Govert Flinck, is in Munich, Alte Pinakothek, inv. 438; cf. Dekiert 2004; London/Amsterdam 2014, pp. 253f.
4 London/Amsterdam 2014, pp. 250, 253–7.
5 For example, a well-known correction by Rembrandt on the drawing of the *Annunciation* by his student Constantijn van Renesse aims to visualise the appearance of the angel as a supernatural phenomenon through the monumentality of the figure. See the essay by Jan Nicolaisen in this catalogue, pp. 25–6.
6 Blankert 1982, p. 18.
7 Amsterdam 2017, p. 189.
8 Sluijter 2015, pp. 336–8.
9 Govert Flinck also distanced himself early on from the expressiveness of Rembrandt's colours and lighting; cf. ibid., p. 338.
10 https://sammlung.staedelmuseum.de/de/werk/die-befreiung-petri.
11 Amsterdam, Rijksprentenkabinet, RP-T-1930-31; cf. Los Angeles 2009, p. 138; Bevers 2022, p. 56.

13.1 REMBRANDT

The Triumph of Mordecai

c. 1641
Etching and drypoint, III (of IV), 17.4 × 21.5 cm (sheet)
Museum der bildenden Künste Leipzig, Graphische Sammlung, inv. NI. 2044
Lit.: B. 40; NH 185; Schwerin 1995, no. 18; Amsterdam/London 2000, no. 44; Weimar 2011, no. 33.

13.2 AERT DE GELDER

(Dordrecht 1645–1727 Dordrecht)

Ahasuerus with Mordecai and Esther

c. 1685
Canvas, 108.3 × 134.3 cm
Maximilian Speck von Sternburg Foundation in the Museum der bildenden Künste Leipzig, inv. G 1634
Lit.: Leipzig 1996, no. 2; Leipzig/Munich 1998, no. I/119; Leipzig 2012, no. 99.

The Book of Esther was a popular theme in the seventeenth-century Netherlands, as was also reflected in several contemporary plays.[1] The dramatic story of the beautiful heroine Esther who succeeded in saving her people was adapted by many artists. Rembrandt and his students Jan Victors, Philips Koninck and Gerbrand van den Eeckhout took up the theme several times. No other painter, however, dealt with the subject as extensively as Aert de Gelder.[2] During his apprenticeship with Rembrandt from about 1661 to 1663, he probably saw relevant models such as Rembrandt's 1660 painting of the *Feast of Esther*.[3]

Unlike many of Rembrandt's pupils, Aert de Gelder remained faithful to the master's late style throughout his life. Arnold Houbraken, a student of De Gelder who had observed him in the studio, wrote of his working method: 'Sometimes, for example, when he wanted to paint fringes or embroidery on a piece of fabric, he would smear the paint on the panel or canvas with a broad palette knife and scratch the pattern of the embroidery or the threads of the fringes out of the layer of paint with the handle of his brush.'[4] Rembrandt was also known for his coarse painting style in which he applied the paint impasto with a palette knife.

Aert de Gelder's *Ahasuerus with Mordecai and Esther*, painted around 1685, shows the formative influence of his teacher (cat. 13.2). It depicts the scene from the Book of Esther (8:2) in which the Persian king Ahasuerus gives his signet ring to Esther's uncle Mordecai. In doing so, he confers royal authority on the hero and heroine, and the threatened destruction of the Jewish people is averted. The warm palette of soft browns and golden yellows and the brightly painted faces standing out against the dark background show the artist's proximity to Rembrandt.[5] The beauty of the young Esther, positioned in the centre, is enhanced by the detailed rendering of her elaborate garments. The golden threads of her dress and the pearls of her precious jewellery shimmer in the light. De Gelder followed his teacher in depicting Old Testament figures in oriental dress. Such subjects greatly fascinated Rembrandt and his circle.

Rembrandt's ability to express human emotion is also impressively demonstrated in his etching *The Triumph of Mordecai* from around 1641 (cat. 13.1). An earlier episode from the Book of Esther (6:7–12) served as the literary model. The scene shows Ahasuerus thanking Mordecai for uncovering a plot against him. The king instructs his assistant Haman to lead Mordecai in triumph through the city like a king. Haman, however, hates the Jews, especially Mordecai, who has refused to pay homage to him.

Like his students, Rembrandt used a variation on older compositions

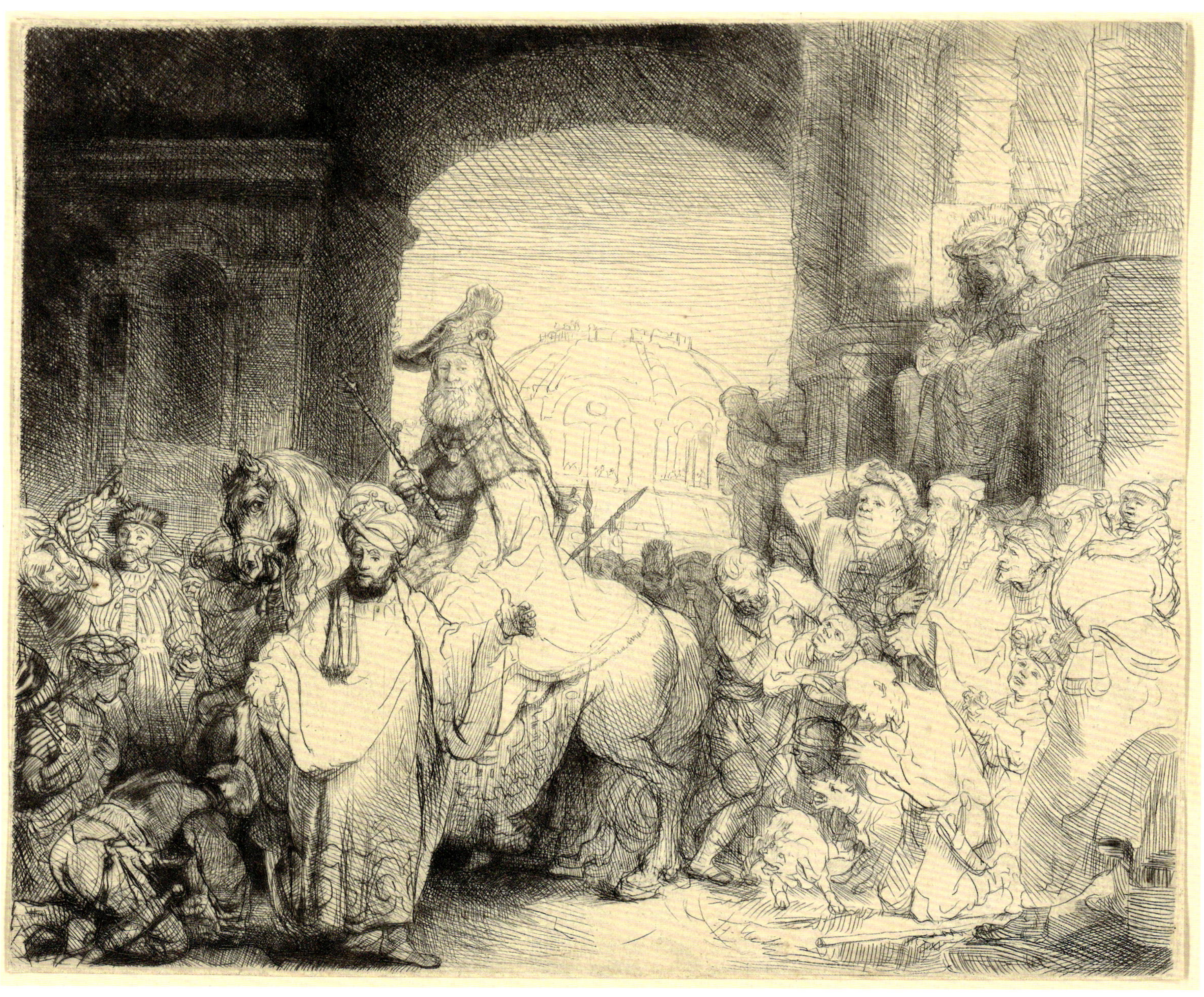

13.1

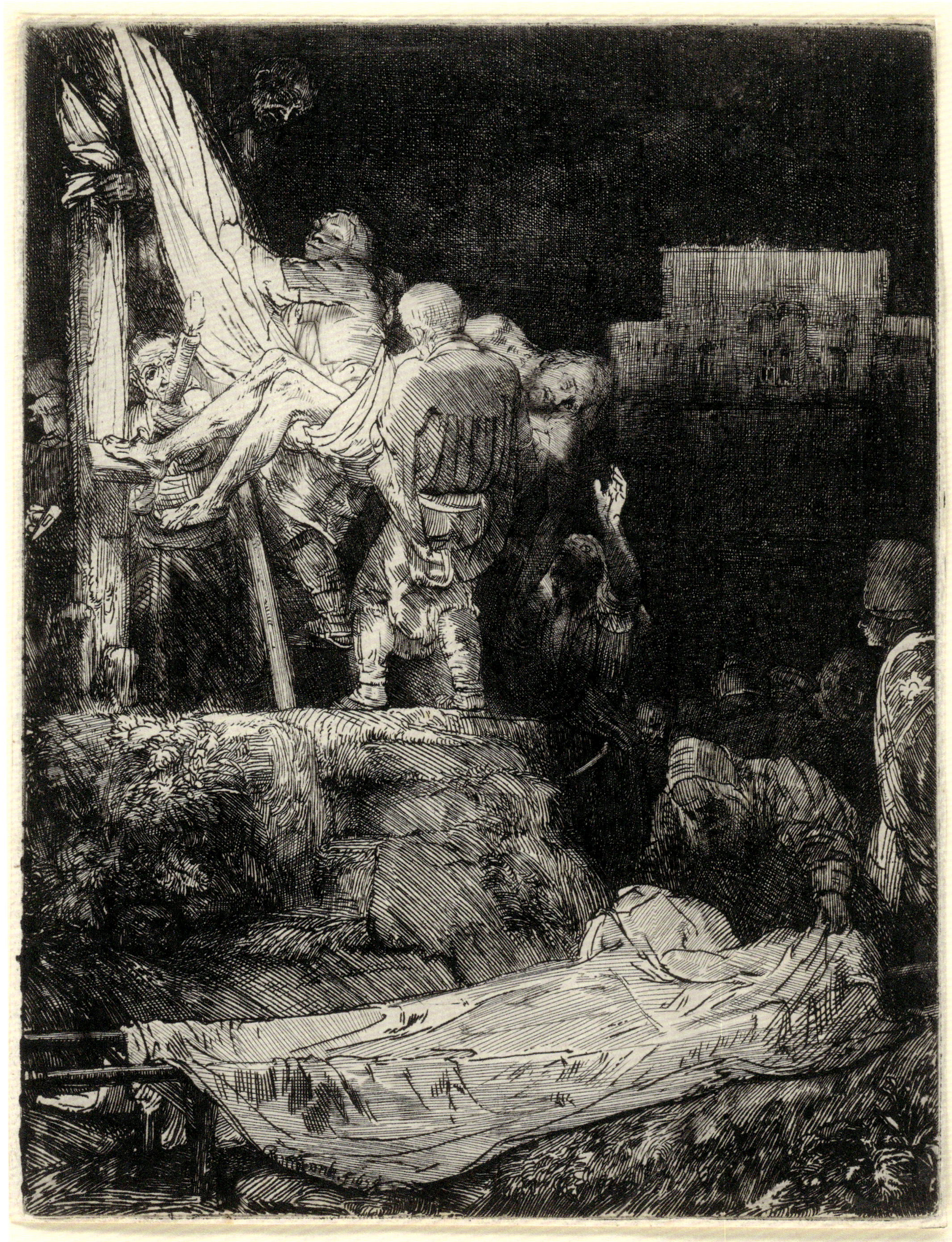

16.3

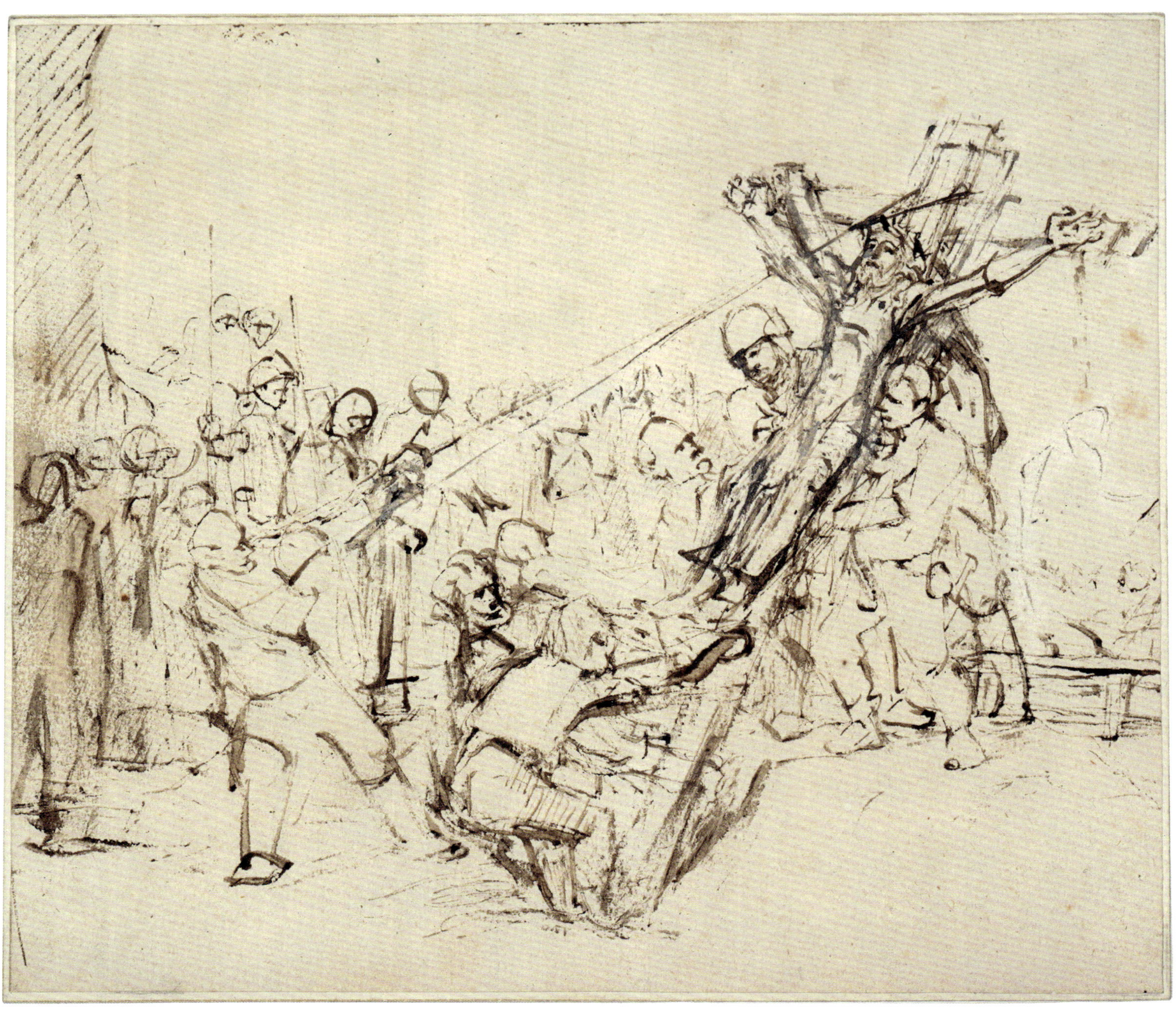

16.4

The descent from the cross takes place in total darkness. The only source of light is a torch held by a man standing beneath the cross. Rembrandt combined the motifs of the Descent from the Cross and the Entombment to create a novel pictorial narrative.

Rembrandt's ability to depict episodes from the life of Christ in a realistic manner is also evident in his drawing *The Raising of the Cross* from 1655–8 (cat. 16.4). The lifting of the cross is depicted as an act of great effort, requiring about half a dozen men. A crowd of onlookers, including Roman soldiers with lances, is gathered in the background. A taut rope is attached to the upper crossbeam, and one of the men has wrapped it around his torso. He uses all his weight to pull the cross, which leans at an angle, towards him. Although the pen strokes are quick and sketchy, the tense facial expressions show great effort and the stooped postures testify to full physical exertion.

The drawing shows clear parallels with Rubens, who had treated the theme of the Raising of the Cross in 1609–10 in the three-winged high altarpiece for the St Walburga

Church in Antwerp. Rembrandt was probably familiar with the corresponding three-part engraving by Hans Witdoeck.[5] In particular, he seems to have adopted the detail of the taut rope, although he modified the depiction to show the rope tied around the henchman's body for maximum traction.

A later copy after Rembrandt's *Raising of the Cross* reveals that the right edge of the picture has been cropped. In the Turin version, there is a figure of a rider on the right, and in the Berlin Rembrandt drawing, part of the figure holding the reins of the original horse can still be seen. This finding provides further evidence that Rembrandt also oriented himself compositionally to Rubens's altarpiece, where a similar equestrian figure appears in the right-hand panel.[6] LCS

1 One pictorial element already hints at the further course of the biblical story: in the lower right-hand corner, the rock tomb in which Christ will be buried appears in the form of a stone cave.
2 Berlin/Amsterdam/London 1991, no. 35.
3 The late dating is supported by the close resemblance of the added horseman to a figure from Rembrandt's Stockholm painting *The Conspiracy of Claudius Civilis*, c. 1661–2. However, Erik Hinterding's examination of the watermarks has shown that all four states of *The Three Crosses* were printed on the same paper, with the exception of the vellum proofs, suggesting that the fourth state may have been created much earlier than previously thought – perhaps even as early as 1653; Weimar 2011, no. 54; Hinterding 2006, vol. 2, pp. 402f., no. 82.
4 Rembrandt, *Descent from the Cross*, c. 1633, panel, 89.4 × 65.2 cm, Munich, Alte Pinakothek, inv. 395; Peter Paul Rubens, *Descent from the Cross*, 1611–14, panel, 421 × 311 cm, Antwerp, Cathedral of Our Lady. The central panel shows Christ's descent from the cross and was reproduced in a 1620 engraving by Lucas Vorsterman, whom Rembrandt probably knew: Lucas Vorsterman after Peter Paul Rubens, *Descent from the Cross*, 1620, engraving, 58.2 × 43.5 cm, London, British Museum, inv. R,3.79; Boston/Chicago 2003, nos. 40–6.
5 Hans Witdoeck after Peter Paul Rubens, *Raising of the Cross*, 1638, engraving, 61.4 × 46.4 cm (centre plate), Amsterdam, Rijksmuseum, inv. RP-P-OB-70.361.
6 Unknown artist after Rembrandt, *Raising of the Cross*, after 1655–8, pen and brown ink, Turin, Biblioteca Reale; Berlin 2006, no. 419.

17.1 FERDINAND BOL

(Dordrecht 1616–1680 Amsterdam)

The Fearlessness of Gaius Fabricius Luscinus

1652–5
Pen and brown ink over black chalk, brush and brown and grey wash, 39.4 × 33.2 cm
Staatliche Graphische Sammlung Munich, inv. 1749
Lit.: Munich/Amsterdam 2001, no. 41; Munich 2003, pp. 83–93 (A. Golahny).

17.2 FERDINAND BOL

The Fearlessness of Gaius Fabricius Luscinus

1655–6
Canvas, 81 × 65 cm
Braunschweig, Herzog Anton Ulrich-Museum, inv. 248
Lit.: Blankert 1982, pp. 42f., no. 56; Amsterdam 2017, no. 107; Eric Jan Sluijter, 'Govert Flinck en Ferdinand Bol in het Burgermeestersvertrek', in Amsterdam 2017, pp. 132–41.

Two former students and collaborators of Rembrandt, Ferdinand Bol and Govert Flinck, received the prestigious commissions to decorate the Burgemeesterskamer (mayors' chamber) in the newly built Amsterdam city hall, the Stadhuis, which opened in 1655. Like no other, the palatial, classicistic building by the architect Jacob van Campen embodied the economic prosperity and power of Holland and of the metropolis of Amsterdam in the mid-seventeenth century. The mayor's chamber was decorated with two monumental paintings by Flinck and Bol, which still hang above the fireplace. Bol's painting *The Fearlessness of Gaius Fabricius Luscinus* measures 485 × 350 cm. Two of the artist's drawings illustrating the design process for this painting have survived in Munich.[1]

The earlier of the two Munich drawings, shown here (cat. 17.1), dates from the beginning of Bol's work on the project, which lasted several years. The scene from ancient history depicts the meeting of King Pyrrhus, who is at war with the Romans, with the consul Fabricius during peace negotiations in 284 BC. Pyrrhus, who in Bol's work is characterised by his turban as an ancient oriental ruler, attempts to bribe the Roman negotiator. According to Plutarch, when he fails, he shows Fabricius an elephant to intimidate him. The Roman consul, however, proves to be not only incorruptible but also fearless.[2] This virtuous behaviour was intended to serve as a moral example to the mayors gathered in the chamber. The fact that incorruptibility and courage are addressed here can also be seen as an indication that corruption in high office was not unknown in seventeenth-century Amsterdam.

Bol's drawing shows the two rulers in conversation in a palace, while the elephant approaches from the right. The action takes place on a stage-like level, enlivened by other figures and above all by the light streaming in from the left. Stylistically, Bol borrows from Rembrandt in his historicising costumes and design of the lighting. The horizontally oriented action was only partially suited to the vertical format of the painting; in a second step, therefore, Bol radically altered the composition.

In the Braunschweig oil study (cat. 17.2), which reflects the later large-scale painting in detail, the action is monumentalised and dramatised by the strong view from below. Here, the light falls from the right, corresponding to the actual presentation of the painting in the Burgemeesterskamer. King Pyrrhus, in profile, looks angrily at the visibly unimpressed consul Fabricius, who points to the trumpeting elephant appearing behind the curtain.

Inspired by engravings after Rubens, Bol placed the two main

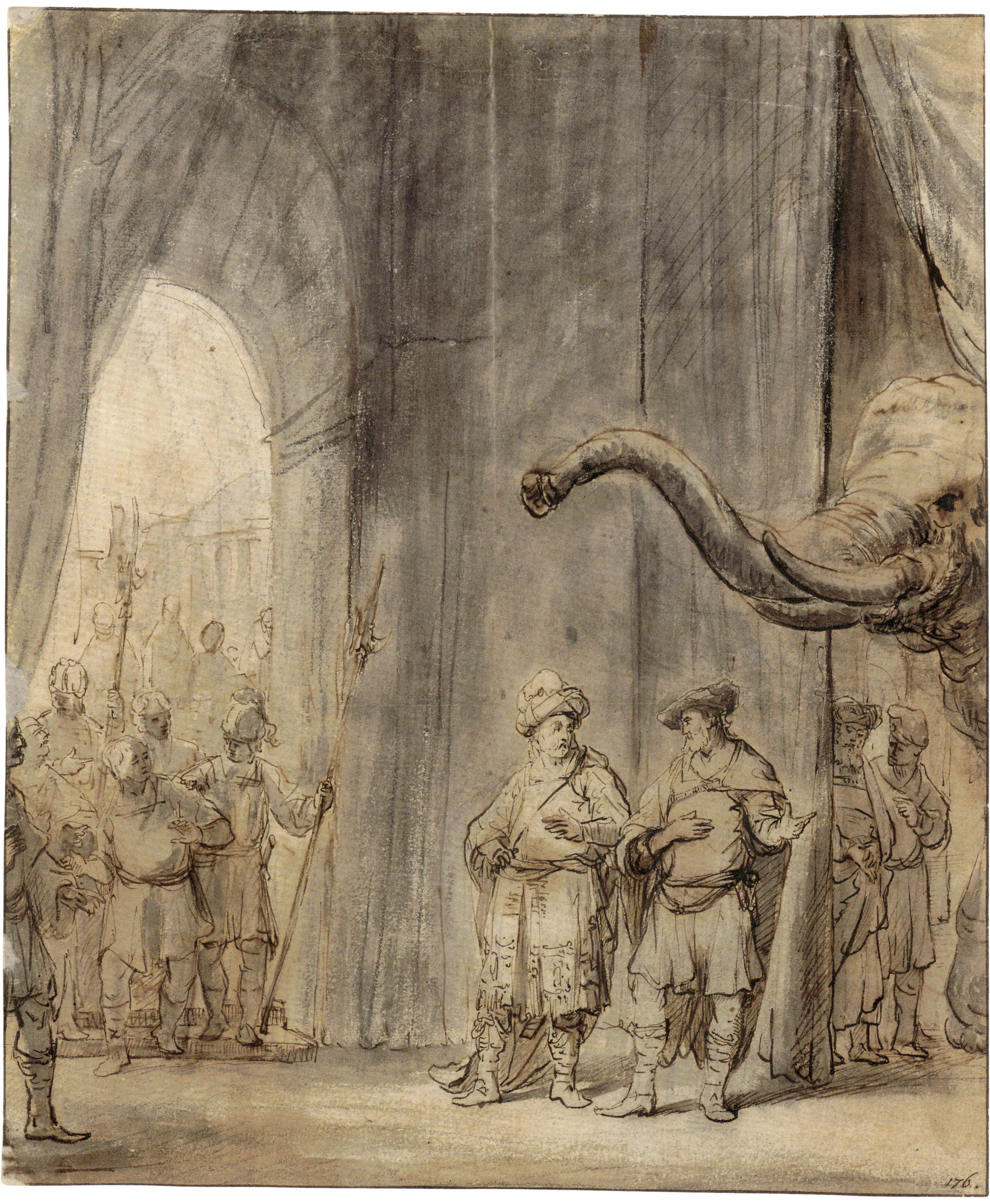

17.1

IN THE STUDIO

BETWEEN ARTISTIC TRAINING AND SELF-REPRESENTATION

20.1 REMBRANDT

Self-Portrait with Open Mouth

1630
Etching, III (of III),
7.5 × 6.5 cm (sheet)
Museum der bildenden Künste
Leipzig, Graphische Sammlung,
inv. NI. 2063
Lit.: B. 13; NH 67; London/The Hague
1999, no. 23; Corpus 1982–2015,
vol. 4, pp. 165–71.

20.2 REMBRANDT

Self-Portrait with Angry Expression

1630
Etching, III (of III),
7.4 × 6.3 cm (sheet)
Museum der bildenden Künste
Leipzig, Graphische Sammlung,
inv. NI. 5804
Lit.: B. 10; NH 68; London/The Hague
1999, no. 21; Corpus 1982–2015, vol.
4, pp. 165–71.

20.3 REMBRANDT

Self-Portrait with Beret

1633
Etching, V (of V),
14.3 × 10.5 cm (sheet)
Signed and dated (lower left):
Rembrandt f. 1633
Museum der bildenden Künste
Leipzig, Graphische Sammlung,
inv. NI 5799
Lit.: B. 17; NH 120; London/The
Hague 1999, no. 38.

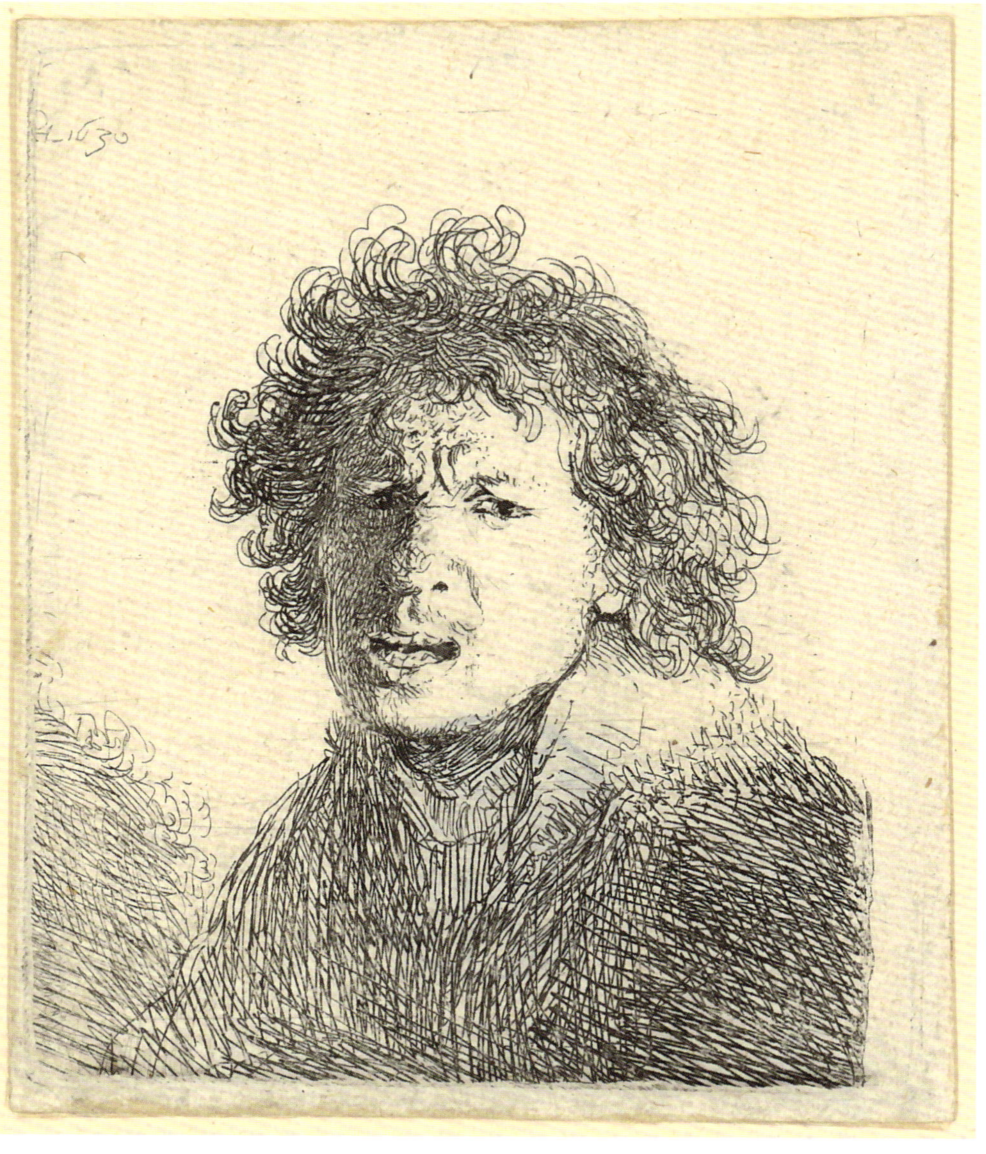

20.1

20.4 REMBRANDT

Self-Portrait with Beret

c. 1634–5
Etching (only state),
4 × 3.4 cm (sheet)
Museum der bildenden Künste
Leipzig, Graphische Sammlung,
inv. NI. 2065
Lit.: B. 2; NH 133; London/The Hague
1999, no. 44; Corpus 1982–2015,
vol. 4, pp. 198f.

20.5 REMBRANDT

Study Sheet with Self-Portrait

c. 1631–2
Etching, II (of II),
10.6 × 10.9 cm (sheet)
Museum der bildenden Künste
Leipzig, Graphische Sammlung,
inv. NI. 2069
Lit.: B. 363; NH 115; London/
The Hague 1999, no. 31; Corpus
1982–2015, vol. 4, pp. 192f.

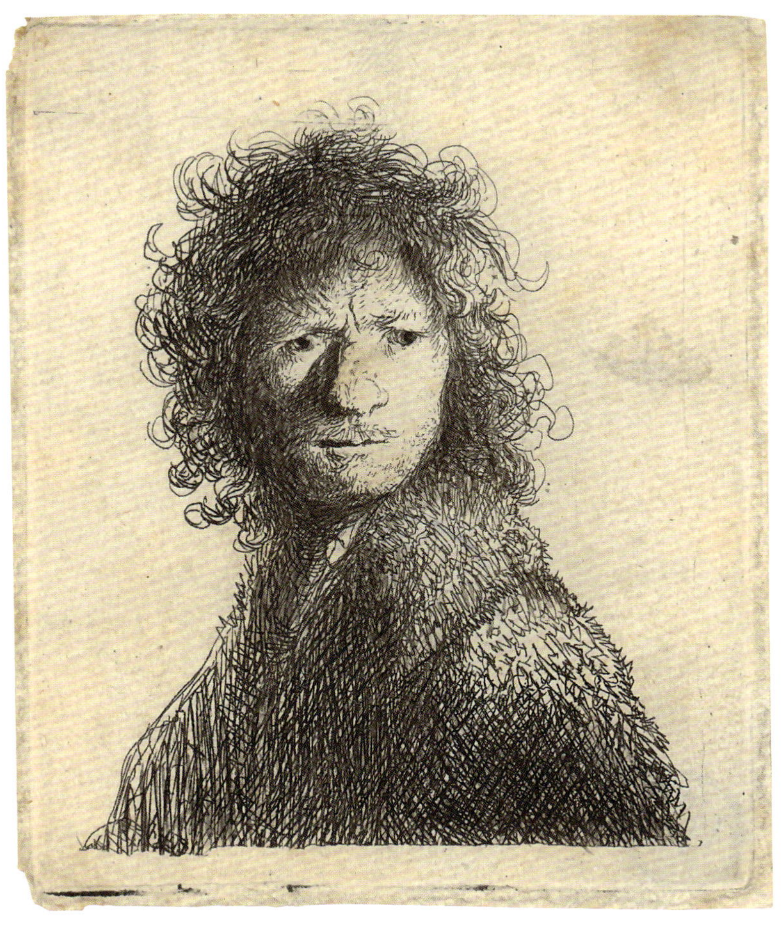

20.2

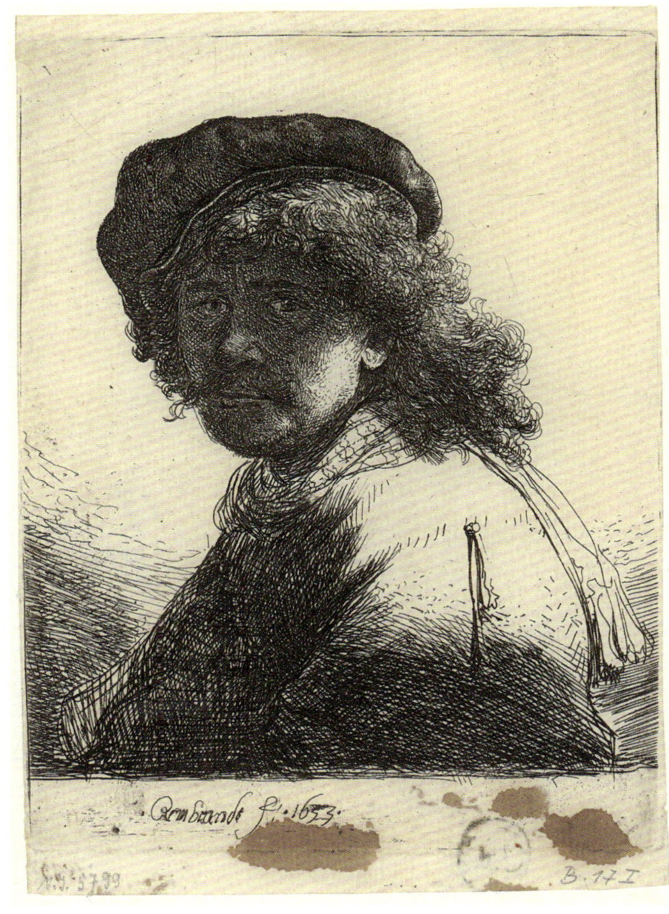

20.3

20.6 REMBRANDT

Self-Portrait as an Oriental Potentate with a Kris

1634
Etching and engraving, II (of II), 12.7 × 10.5 cm (sheet)
Signed and dated (upper left): Rembrandt f. / 1634
Museum der bildenden Künste Leipzig, Graphische Sammlung, inv. NI. 5798
Lit.: B. 18; NH 134; London/The Hague 1999, no. 41; Corpus 1982–2015, vol. 4, p. 190.

20.7 REMBRANDT

Self-Portrait at a Window, Drawing on an Etching Plate

1648
Etching, drypoint and engraving, IV (of IX), 15.5 × 13 cm (plate)
Signed and dated (upper left): Rembrandt. f. 1648
Kunstsammlungen der Veste Coburg, Kupferstichkabinett, inv. VII,375,23
Lit.: B. 22; NH 220; London/The Hague 1999, no. 62; Corpus 1982–2015, vol. 4, pp. 187–9; Coburg/Freiburg 2017, no. 6.

For twenty years, from about 1628 to 1648, Rembrandt depicted himself in etched self-portraits, many of which are not formal self-portraits in the strict sense, but rather tronies for which he used his own face. As his fame grew in the 1630s, the play of the recognisable physiognomy of one of Amsterdam's most successful portraitists and the eccentric roles he assumed must have given these etchings special appeal. Such is the case, for example, with the *Self-Portrait as an Oriental Potentate with a Kris* (cat. 20.6) of 1634. By this time, Rembrandt had attracted the interest of the highest social circles in Holland with his history paintings and had also produced the sensational painting *Anatomy*

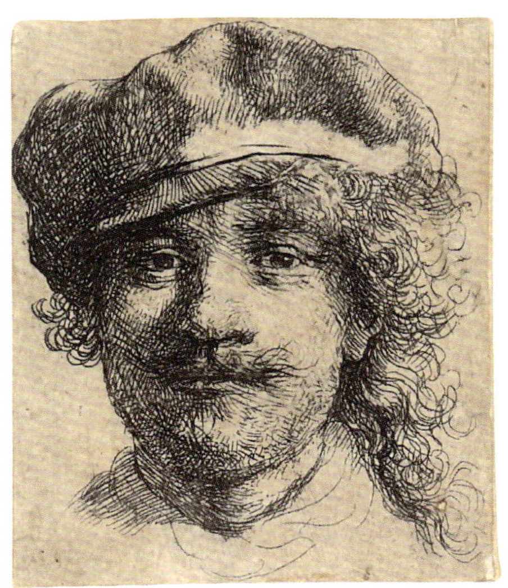

20.4

Lesson of Dr Nicolaes Tulp of 1632 (The Hague, Mauritshuis), in which he renewed the genre of the group portrait, which was otherwise characterised by a tendency to stiffness. The painting *The Shipbuilder Jan Rijcksen and His Wife* (London, Buckingham Palace) of 1633, for example, shows the scenic animation of a couple portrait. A dramatising self-portrait in orientalising costume could therefore have served as a kind of advertisement for his special skills as both a history *and* a portrait painter.

In any case, Rembrandt did not shy away from popularising his own likeness on the art market through eye-catching self-dramatisation, for which the medium of print was particularly suited. The early self-portraits from the Leiden period are evidence of this. In 1630, for example, he etched a group of small sheets that look as if he had drawn himself laughing, angry or in pain in front of a mirror (cats. 20.1–2). As informal and scribbled as the sheets may appear, they document the young artist's claim to be able to reproduce emotions and passions in a lifelike manner. Older treatises had already noted this ability as a prerequisite for history painting: the history painter had to be able to express the inner emotional life of the figures in order to create convincing pictures. In his influential treatise on painting, *Grondt der edel vry schilder-const* of 1604, the painter and art theorist Karel van Mander wrote that 'wrinkles and deep lines there [on the forehead] show that a sorrowful soul is hidden within us, oppressed and full of worries'[1] and asserted that the history painter should empathetically slip into the roles of figures who are characterised by a certain mood. Samuel van Hoogstraten, Rembrandt's student for several years, maintained that 'one must completely transform oneself… by being both actor and spectator in front of a mirror'.[2]

Another of Rembrandt's self-portraits can be seen in an etching with several figure studies that looks as if Rembrandt had torn a page from a sketchbook (cat. 20.5). At right angles to the self-portrait there appear, among others, a peasant couple and the faces of an old woman and an old man, motifs that often preoccupied the artist at this time. Rembrandt may have reproduced a sketchbook page that served as a model for his students' exercises. These etchings may also have sensitised them to the depiction of emotions and the art of self-dramatisation.

The 1633 etching *Self-Portrait with Beret* (cat. 20.3) strongly recalls Rembrandt's *Self-Portrait* in the Rijksmuseum, Amsterdam, painted some five years earlier and copied by a student in the workshop (cat. 21.1, cf. fig. p. 32). Once again, the figure is illuminated mainly from behind and thus appears backlit. A cord hangs from Rembrandt's shoulder to fasten a gorget, a metal breastplate that was also worn as a fashion accessory in the 1630s. The painter seems to have been more interested in the eccentric lighting of the sheet than in capturing a particular mood.

In the smallest of all Rembrandt's self-portraits (cat. 20.4), the artist depicted himself wearing a beret and a fashionable lock of hair known as a cadenette or lovelock, which was usually reserved for members of the aristocracy.[3] The artist, who in the 1630s was driven by the ambition of social advancement, portrayed himself in this way in several self-portraits from that decade. This tiny etching was probably the result of an unfinished project for a larger etching.[4] For example, a strip on the otherwise detailed cap has not yet been hatched and therefore appears white.

Rembrandt's final etched self-portrait from 1648 is also his most sober: the artist shows himself at work in a simple painter's jacket (cat. 20.7). He wears the same hat in a drawing now attributed to Willem Drost (cat. 22.2). He is working with an etching needle on a plate supported by two books. Light falls through the window opening onto the drawing hand, which is brightly lit in contrast to the heavily darkened interior, from which the artist's eyes shine as he gazes into the mirror. A cloth hangs down from the window to soften the harsh light – a common feature in painters' studios of the period, including Rembrandt's. In the fourth state, shown here, Rembrandt added a hilly landscape with foreign architecture visible through the window. In the 1640s, he had to cope with the death of his wife Saskia and with economic difficulties that led to the disillusionment this portrait seems to show.[5] Artists' self-portraits, however, were not psychological self-interrogations as we have come to know them since the nineteenth century. Rather, they served as sophisticated self-depictions – aimed in particular at art collectors – that emphasised the artists' own abilities.[6] Here, for example, Rembrandt shines with a self-portrait between light and dark to demonstrate his virtuoso handling of light and shadow. His scrutinising gaze demonstrates that looking closely and drawing 'naer het leven'

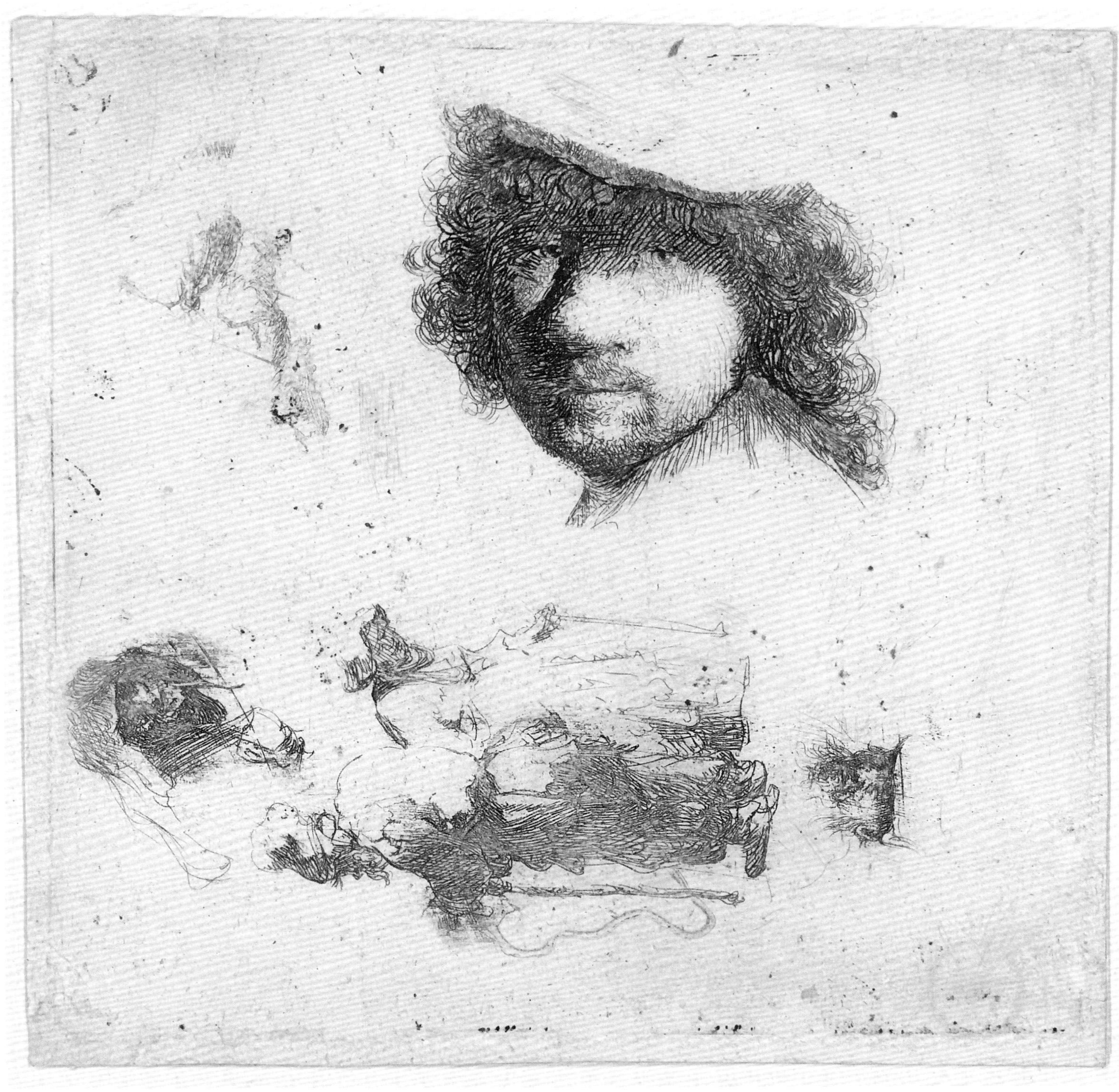

20.5

(from life) was a prerequisite for the striking realism of his art.

The same year, 1648, the Rembrandt pupil Hinrich Jansen (1625–1667) of Flensburg, freshly returned from Amsterdam, painted the figure of Joseph of Arimathea on an epitaph in his hometown using Rembrandt's features, which had become a trademark.[7] JN

1 Quoted in Mander/Miedema 1973, vol. 1, pp. 166f. [translated].
2 Hoogstraten 1678, pp. 109f.; quoted in London/The Hague 1999, p. 21 [translated].
3 London/The Hague 1999, p. 160.
4 Corpus 1982–2015, vol. 4, pp. 198f.
5 Cf. Chapman 1990, p. 79; Corpus 1982–2015, vol. 4, pp. 188f.
6 Raupp 1984; Corpus 1982–2015, vol. 4, pp. 78–80.
7 Hinrich Jansen, *The Entombment*, 1648, Flensburg, St Marien, epitaph of the merchant Niels Hacke; Sumowski 1983–94, vol. 2, no. 928.

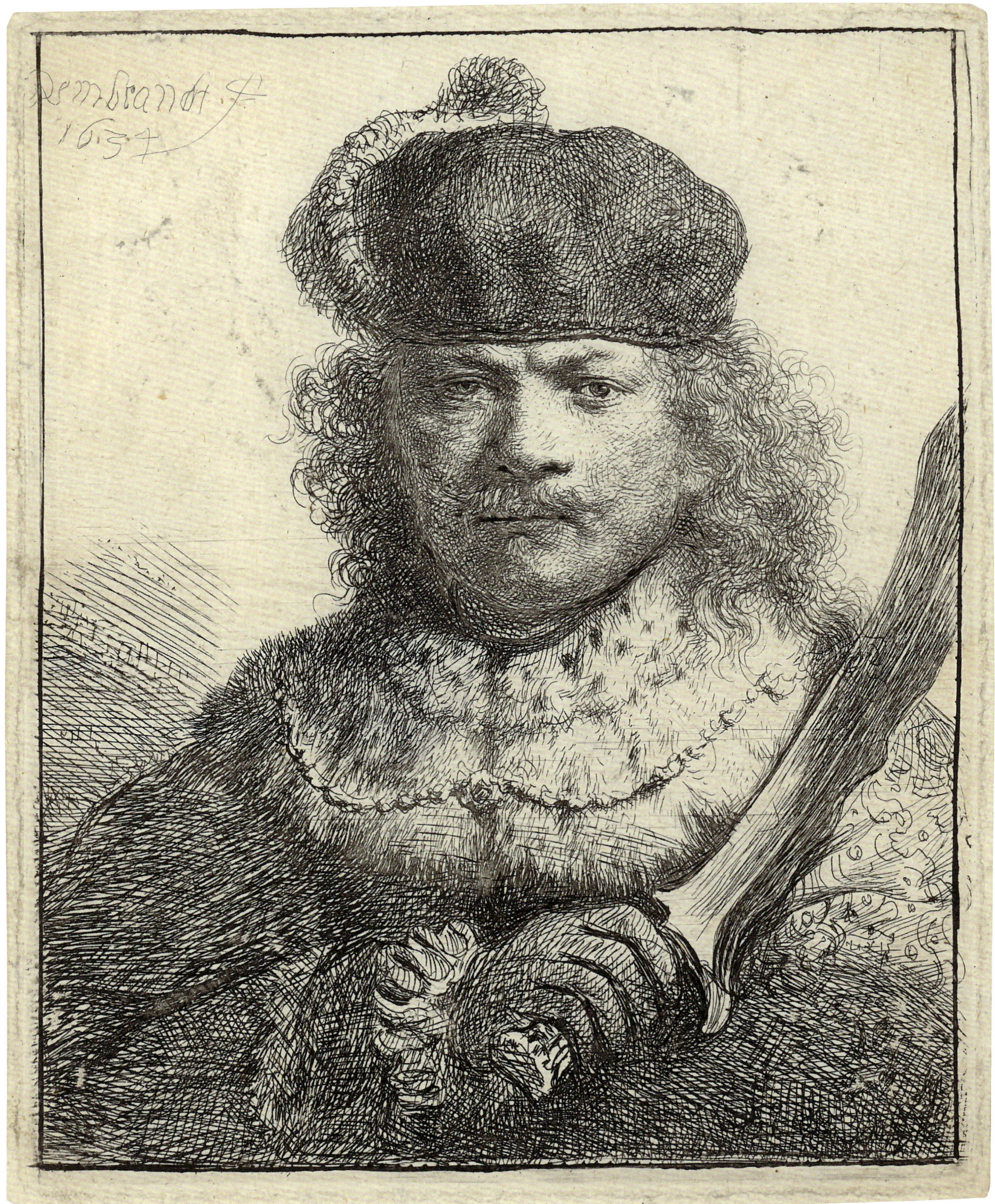

20.6

stage in their training, as Jaap van der Veen has illustrated with a series of student self-portraits.[6] Among these is the self-portrait of the young Nicolaes Maes, about 16 years old (also attributed to Samuel van Hoogstraten, cat. 22.3). The young artist looks intently into the mirror. He has adopted the pronounced furrowed brow of his teacher – a typical Rembrandt motif (cf. cat. 22.1) – which conveys concentration. Maes uses strong washes to create a tonal, almost dramatic atmosphere of light and dark. This use of light, as well as the brightness of the paper, is modelled on Rembrandt's *Self-Portrait at a Window* of 1648 (cat. 20.7). The young Maes had clearly been taught by the master that a self-portrait is a matter not only of self-observation, but also of self-dramatisation.

The group of drawings showing Rembrandt in a working and studio environment includes the sheet now attributed to Willem Drost, which was long thought to be a self-portrait by Rembrandt (cat. 22.2). The draughtsman used Rembrandt's *Self-Portrait* in Vienna (Kunsthistorisches Museum), completed in 1652 and painted during Drost's time in the workshop, and the etched *Self-Portrait at a Window* as models.[7] An interesting detail is the corrected position of the right foot, which the artist had originally placed too high.[8] Drost was unable to copy this area from the Viennese painting, since the latter shows the master only to just below the belt. The facial expression with the inquiring look, the shoulders and the hat are based on the etching. The drawing may have been made in preparation for another, unrealised copy of the Viennese self-portrait.

In their self-portraits, most painters of the time favoured elegant costumes to suggest their noble social status, a strategy that Rembrandt also followed in other self-portraits. According to Raupp, Rembrandt presents himself here with an emphatically artisanal attitude in order to protest against academic norms.[9] Raupp refers to an artist's anecdote recounted by Lomazzo that Albrecht Dürer often went into town in his work clothes. Rembrandt may have been aware of this anecdote, as the corresponding book by Lomazzo was in the library of Jan Six.[10] JN

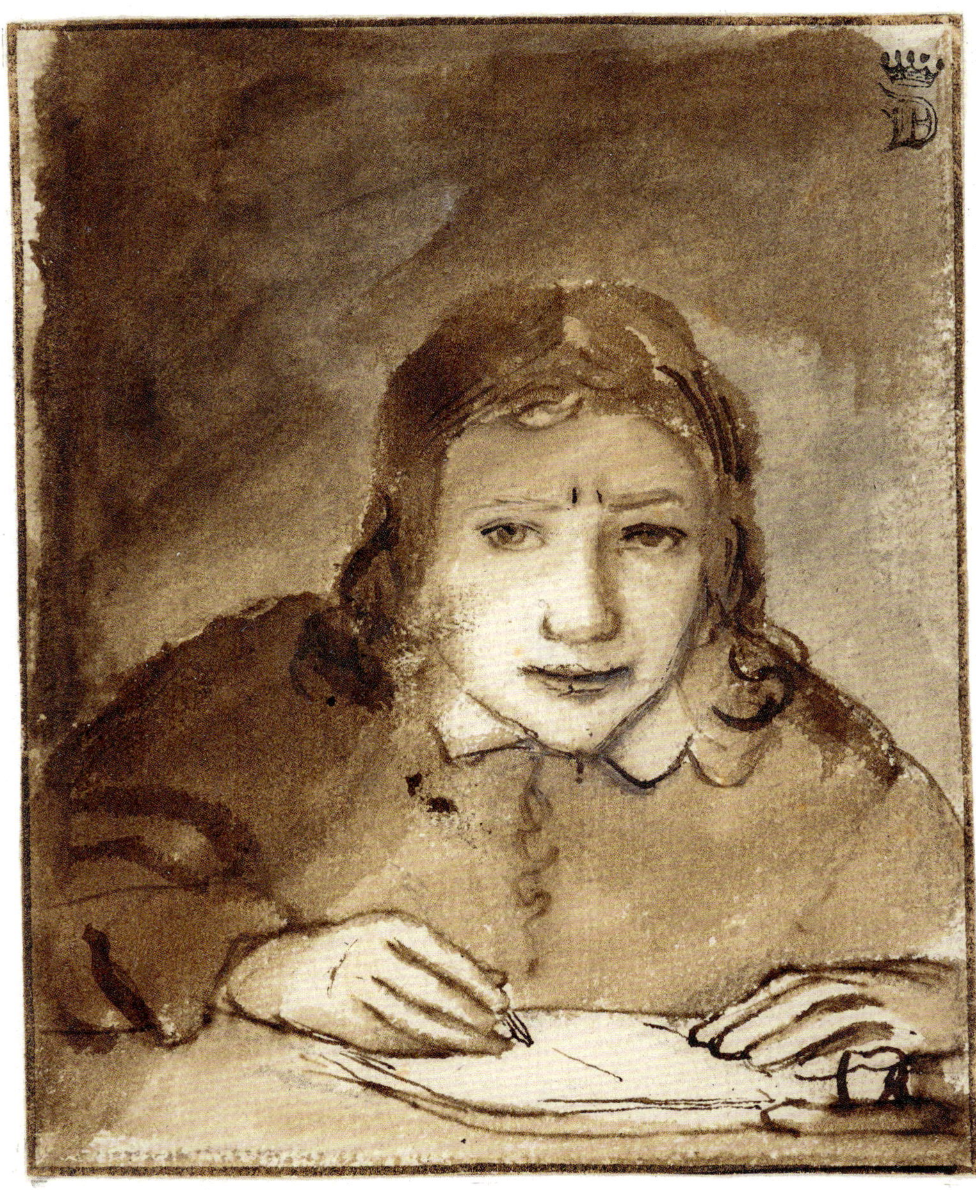

22.3

1 See Berlin/Amsterdam/London 1991, p. 34 (P. Schatborn).
2 Royalton-Kisch online, Benesch 432.
3 Corpus 1982–2015, vol. 4, pp. 155f.
4 Royalton-Kisch online, Benesch 432; Berlin 2006, pp. 78–80.
5 Ibid.
6 Amsterdam 2015, pp. 26–9.
7 Corpus 1982–2015, vol. 4, pp. 152f.; Amsterdam 2014, pp. 47f.
8 See Amsterdam 2014, pp. 47f. (P. Schatborn).
9 Raupp 1984, pp. 179f.
10 Corpus 1982–2015, vol. 4, p. 59 (M. de Winkel).

23.1 CAREL FABRITIUS

(Middenbeemster 1622–1654 Delft)

Self-Portrait

c. 1648–50
Panel, 65 × 49 cm
Signed (upper right): fabritius / f
Rotterdam, Museum Boijmans Van Beuningen, inv. 1205 (OK)
Lit.: Brown 1981, no. 4; Sumowski 1983–94, vol. 2, no. 603; London/The Hague 1999, no. 92; New York/London 2001, pp. 116f., 247–9, no. 17.

23.2 FERDINAND BOL

(Dordrecht 1616–1680 Amsterdam)

Self-Portrait

1646
Canvas, 102 × 85.5 cm
Signed and dated (left, next to the shoulder): Bol ... 1646
Dordrecht, Dordrechts Museum, inv. DM/887-372
Lit.: Blankert 1982, no. 60; Albert Blankert, 'Ferdinand Bol Zelfportret', in *Dordrechts Museum Bulletin* 1, 2006, pp. 14f.; Amsterdam 2017, p. 73.

A young man looks out from the painting with a questioning, confident gaze, his brightly lit face framed by dark curls (cat. 23.1). It has long been assumed that this signed work is a self-portrait by the artist, who took a number of liberties that run counter to the traditional conventions of portraiture. These include the low positioning of the sitter, the immediacy of the expression and the costume.[1] As Ariane van Suchtelen has pointed out, the visible dark hair on the chest is a breach of decorum and a novelty in portrait painting.[2] Fabritius could only have taken this liberty in an unofficial self-portrait or a tronie. What at first glance appears to be a smock is in fact part of a historicising costume: Fabritius is wearing a 'tabaard', a sixteenth-century housecoat still worn by painters in the seventeenth century.[3] Fabritius, who worked with Rembrandt from 1641 to 1643, seems to have followed the master's penchant for theatrical costumes and role-playing in his self-dramatisation. However, in contrast to the aristocratic gesture of Rembrandt's self-portraits of around 1640 (London, National Gallery, 1640, and the etched self-portrait of 1639, Bartsch 21), here naturalness and realism are evident as expressive aims.

The Rotterdam *Self-Portrait* is part of an iconographic tradition of artists' self-portraits that goes back to Albrecht Dürer's early *Self-Portrait* of 1498 (Madrid, Museo del Prado).[4] As in Dürer's work, the exposure of the artist's bare chest shows him with the sensuality and vitality of a young man. It is also a programmatic expression of the sober reproduction of reality as the aim of representation.[5]

The painting strikes a balance between astonishing realism and artificiality. On the one hand, the painter standing in front of a crumbling plaster wall, on which he casts a shadow, appears almost like a *trompe-l'œil*. On the other hand, the brushstrokes are recognisable as such and the painting style of the skin is not smooth, but patchy and almost raw, so that it is impossible to forget that one is looking at a painting.[6] As has often been pointed out in the literature, the painting is clearly influenced by Rembrandt's model in its impasto application of paint, emphasis on chiaroscuro and historicising costume.[7] The warm tones of the palette also belong in this context. Supplied with a false Rembrandt signature, the painting was thus attributed to the master until a cleaning in 1859 revealed the signature of Fabritius.[8] The open painting style of the Rotterdam picture, which bears a certain resemblance to the Leipzig *Self-Portrait* from Rembrandt's workshop (cat. 21.2), led Schmidt-Degener to attribute it to Carel Fabritius in 1916.[9]

The inventory of the estate of Fabritius's first wife in 1643 lists six tronies, including an 'antijckse troonij' (tronie in antique dress) and a 'schaduwe tronij' (tronie with shadow effects), which were presumably painted by him.[10] In these tronies, which were probably created during his time in Rembrandt's workshop, Fabritius may have experimented with the open painting style he masterfully employs in the Rotterdam painting. A few years later, now working in Delft, he turned away from this technique and smoothed out his style, as the 1654 *Self-Portrait* in London (National Gallery) shows.[11]

The *Self-Portrait* by Ferdinand Bol, a student of Rembrandt six years older than Fabritius, dates from around the same time, 1646. Like Fabritius's *Self-Portrait*, it was painted after Bol had already left his teacher's workshop, where he trained between 1636 and 1640.[12] Bol repeated the portrait type with the sitter leaning on his right arm in several self-portraits and in the *Portrait of a Man* in Munich (cat. 37.5).[13] The composition is derived from Rembrandt's above-mentioned self-portraits of 1639–40 (London, National Gallery, and Bartsch 21), where the artist presents himself as a *gentiluomo* in the manner of a Renaissance artist. For this work, Rembrandt had drawn on two famous paintings, Titian's *Portrait of a Man* (London, National Gallery) and Raphael's *Portrait of Baldassare Castiglione* (Paris, Musée du Louvre). The lighting of Bol's painting, with the left half of the face in shadow, also follows Rembrandt's example. Other students such as Gerbrand van den Eeckhout were also inspired by this type of portrait.[14]

The Dordrecht *Self-Portrait* is the earliest in a series of self-portraits by Bol. It shows a certain discrepancy between the self-confident pose in the historicising costume and the elegant gesture of the gloved hand

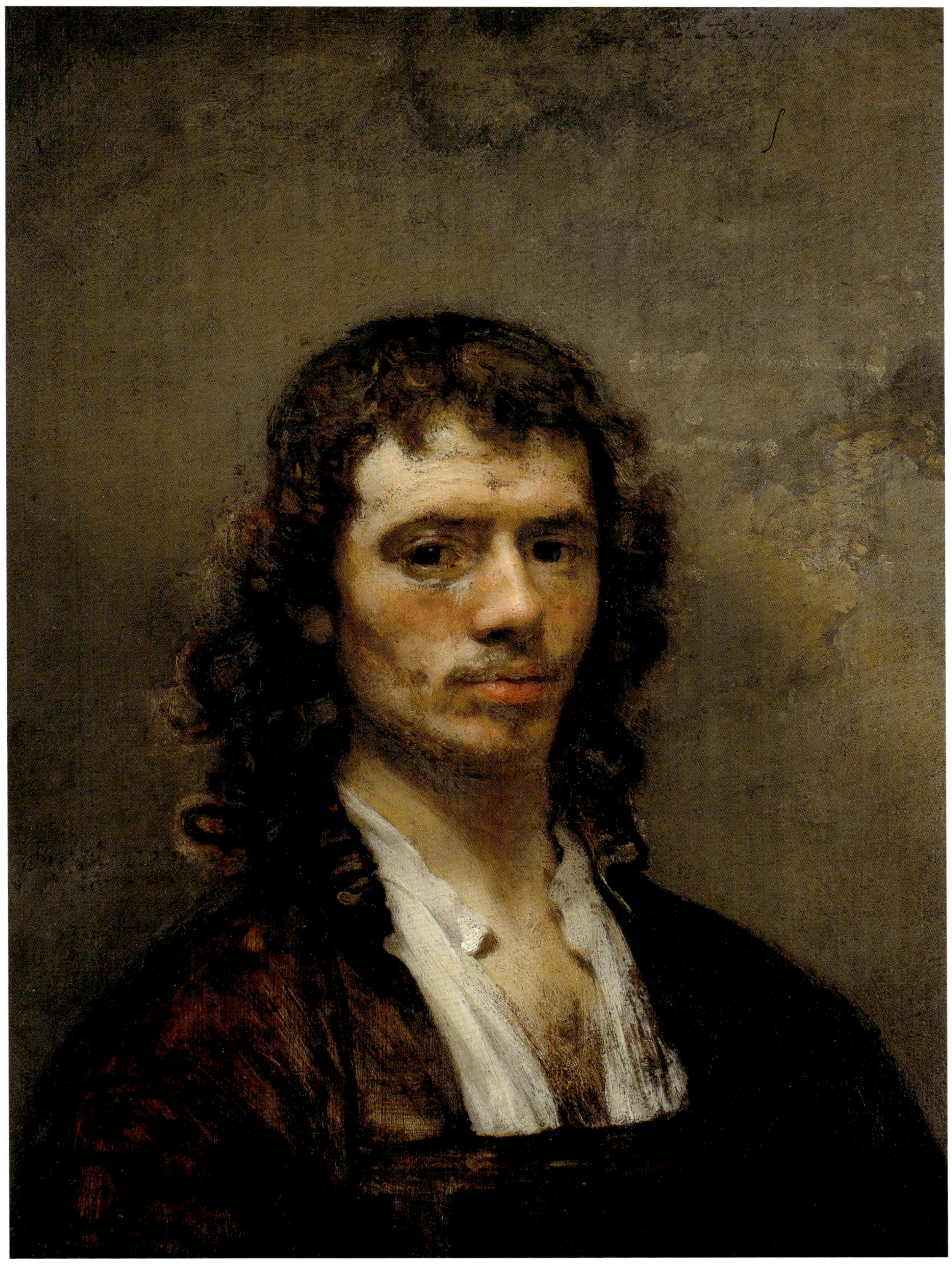

23.1

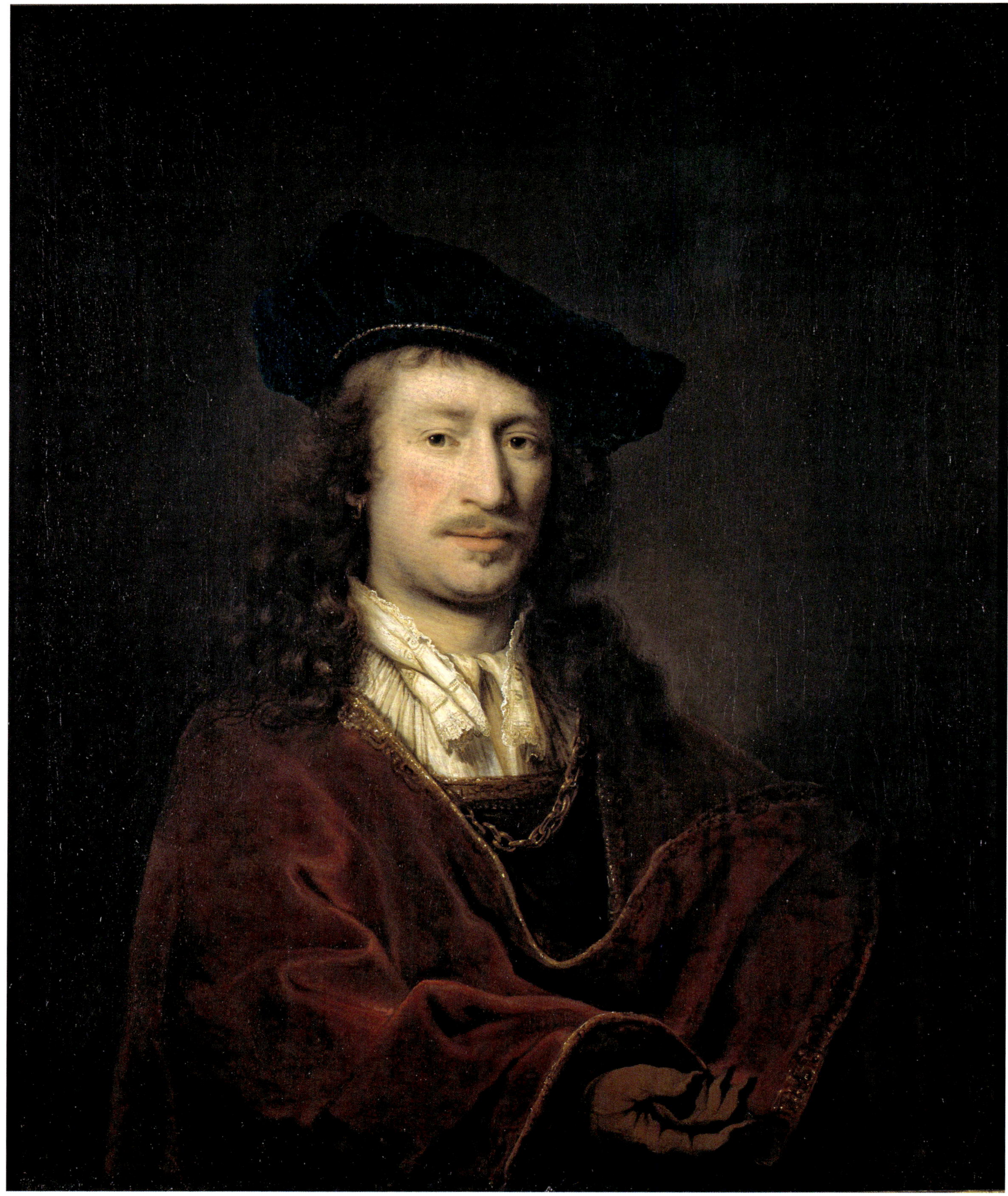

23.2

(which by no means had just been holding the brush) on the one hand and a somewhat stiff execution that still lacks lightness on the other. Bol took great care to render the red and green velvet of the cloak and beret, as well as the smoothness of the complexion. He prefers an objective elegance to the painterly expression of Fabritius. The artist wears an undergarment similar to that of Fabritius, but buttoned up in accord with the conventions of portraiture. With this self-portrait, Bol showed himself to be a technically skilled painter, capable of portraying his clients in a realistic and noble idiom. Even in this early work, Bol differs from Rembrandt in his smoother painting style and less dramatic lighting. The Dordrecht painting thus demonstrates his strategic sense of public taste, which would help him build a career as a portrait and history painter in Amsterdam. JN

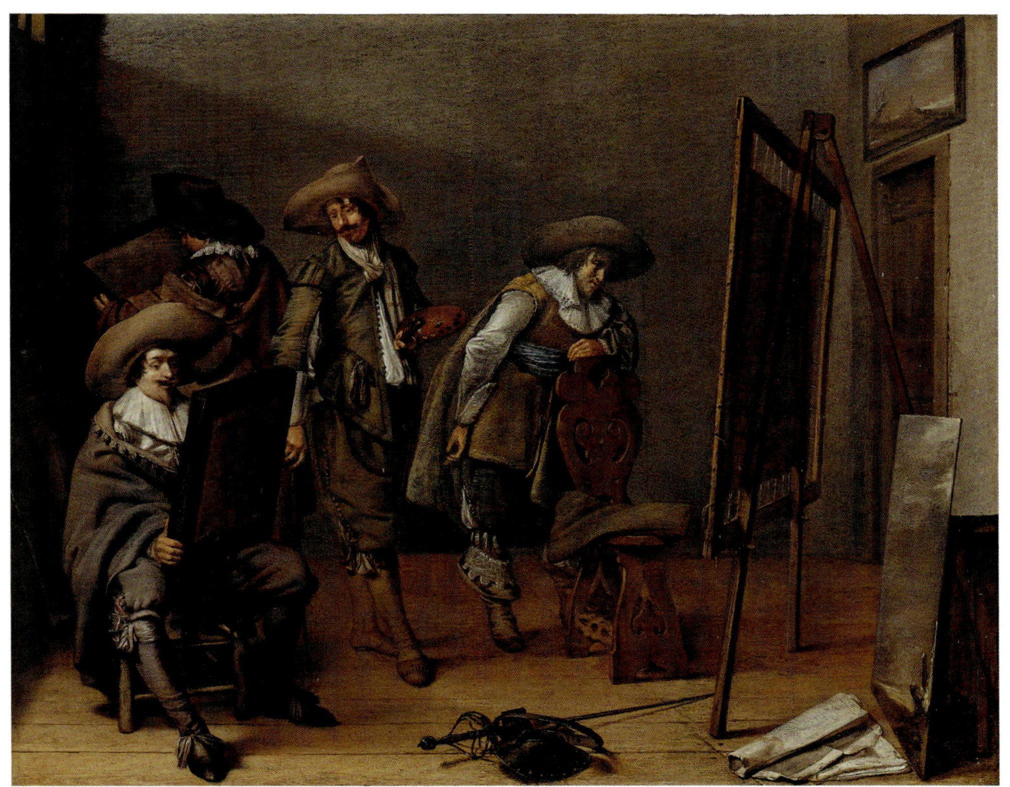

24.1

1 New York/London 2001, p. 247. Tragically, Fabritius died as a young man in the devastating explosion of the Dordrecht gunpowder magazine in October 1654. As a result, only a few of his paintings have survived.
2 London/The Hague 1999, p. 241.
3 Ibid.; cf. Brown 1981, p. 39; Corpus 1982–2015, vol. 4, p. 59.
4 For more on Rembrandt's relationship to Dürer in terms of the artist's self-representation, see Dickey 2004; Corpus 1982–2015, vol. 4, pp. 59f.
5 See Raupp 1984, pp. 311–14.
6 Sumowski 1983–94, vol. 2, p. 980.
7 London/The Hague 1999, p. 121.
8 Brown 1981, p. 123.
9 F. Schmidt-Degener, *Catalogus der schilderijen en tekeningen tentoongesteld in het Museum Boymans te Rotterdam*, Rotterdam 1916, p. 29; cf. Corpus 1982–2015, vol. 4, p. 255.
10 London/The Hague 1999, p. 121.
11 New York/London 2001, no. 19. According to Sumowski, in the second half of the 1640s the artist was still alternating between a Rembrandtesque and an individual style; see Sumowski 1983–94, vol. 2, p. 980.
12 Blankert 1982, pp. 17–19.
13 Amsterdam 2017, pp. 50–2, 72f.
14 Gerbrand van den Eeckhout, *Self-Portrait* (?), 1647, brush in black and grey ink, Paris, Fondation Custodia, Inv. 854a; cf. Schatborn 2010b, vol. 1, no. 61.

24.1 PIETER CODDE

(Amsterdam before 1599–1678 Amsterdam)

Art Lovers in a Painter's Studio

Early 1630s
Panel, 38.3 × 49.3 cm
Monogrammed (lower right): PC
Staatsgalerie Stuttgart, inv. 3249
Lit.: Kleinert 2006, no. 9; Winkel 2006, p. 152.

24.2 REMBRANDT

The Artist Drawing from the Model

c. 1639
Etching, drypoint and engraving, II (of IV); 23.2 × 18.2 cm (plate)
Kunstsammlungen der Veste Coburg, Kupferstichkabinett, inv. VII,380,194
Lit.: B. 192; NH 176; Berlin/Amsterdam/London 1991, vol. 2, no. 15; Sluiter 2006, pp. 281–5; Weimar 2011, no. 25; Coburg/Freiburg 2017, no. 14.

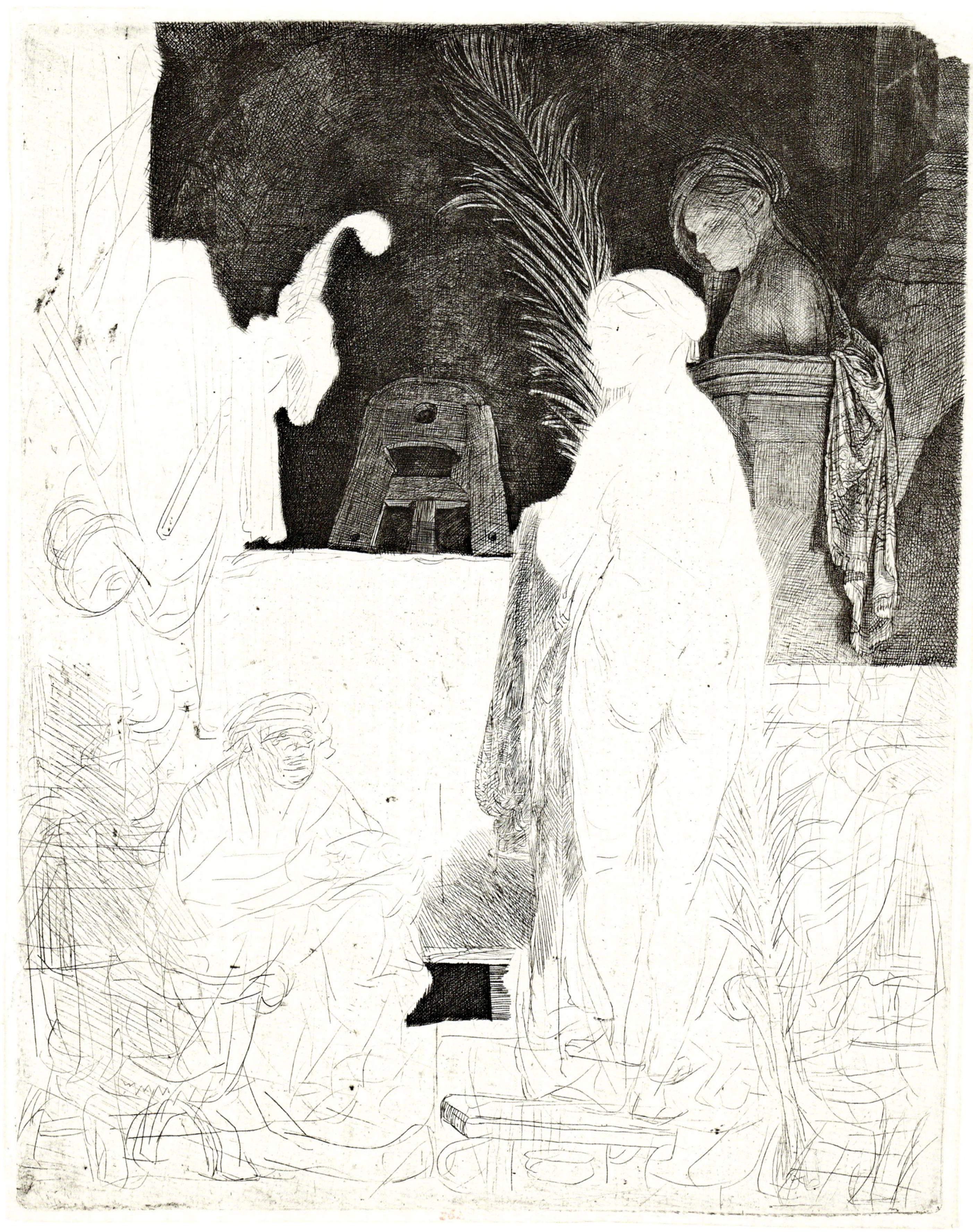

24.2

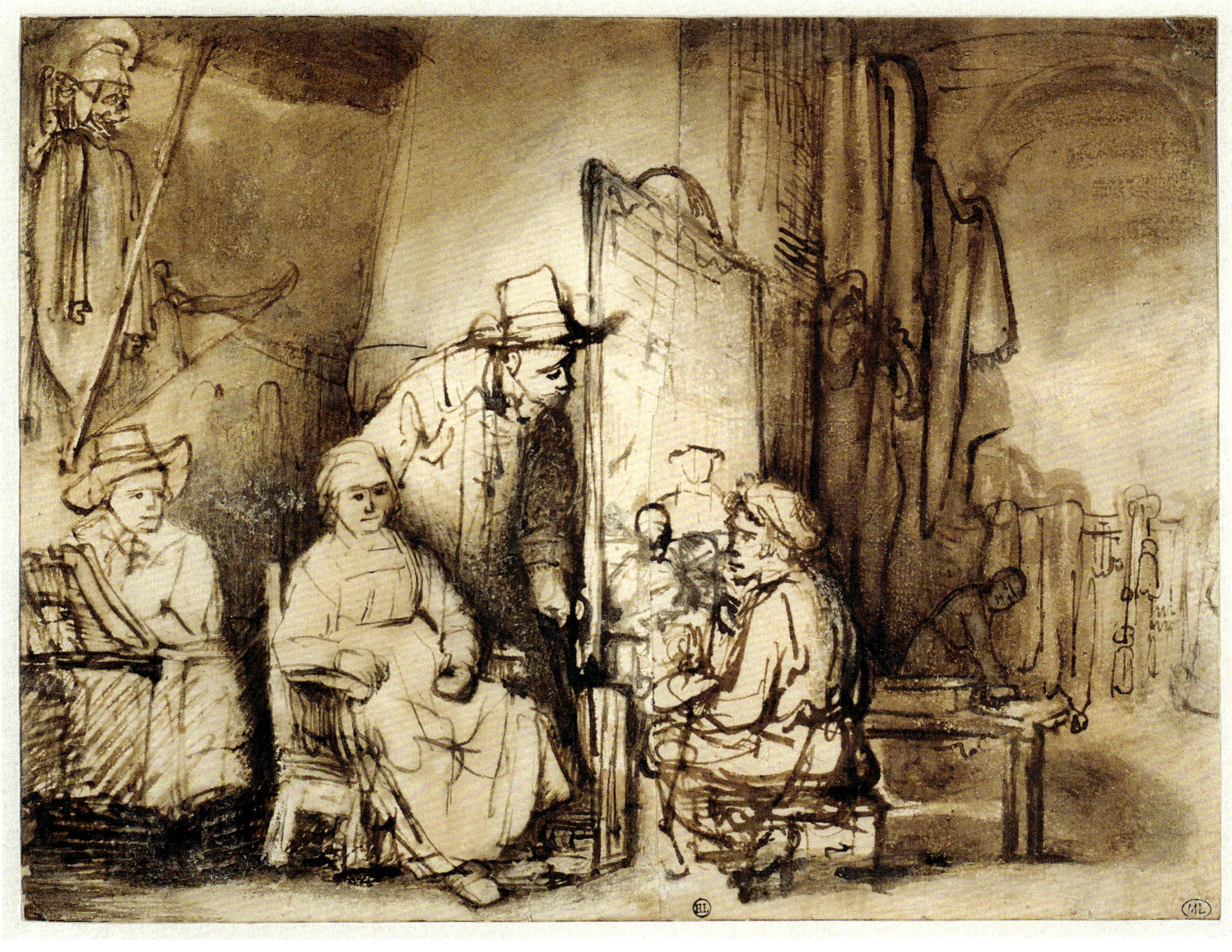

24.3

24.3 SAMUEL VAN HOOGSTRATEN

(Dordrecht 1627–1678 Dordrecht)

An Artist in His Studio Painting a Couple Portrait

c. 1640
Pen and brown ink, brush and brown wash, 17.5 × 23 cm
Paris, Musée du Louvre, Département des Arts graphiques, inv. RF 690
Lit.: Sumowski 1979–92, vol. 5, no. 1167a; Amsterdam 1984, no. 8; Munich/Amsterdam 2001, pp. 56–61; Los Angeles 2009, p. 4; Royalton-Kisch online, Drawings not in Benesch.

Rembrandt's unfinished etching *The Artist Drawing from the Model* (cat. 24.2) is both descriptive and allegorical in character. An artist sits drawing in front of a nude female model, who stands on a pedestal holding drapery and a large palm branch. In the background is the easel with a horizontal canvas. To the left are the props of the history painter, such as a shield, sword and cap with peacock feather. To the right is a female bust on a pedestal, draped in an oriental scarf that appears several times in Rembrandt's work.

Rembrandt had some difficulty reproducing the model's standing position, as can be seen from the corrected position of the feet (which shows that the artist etched directly onto the plate, that is, without a preliminary drawing). As early as the eighteenth century, the etching was interpreted as a depiction of the ancient sculptor Pygmalion, who fell in love with the ivory sculpture of a woman he had created. More recently, the figure of the artist has been interpreted as a depiction of the Greek painter Apelles, who painted Victoria, the goddess of victory.[1] Both interpretations are based on the art-theoretical topos of the transformation of *natura* into *ars*, nature into art, and vice versa.[2] The artist's precise study of nature is the basis for the convincing illusion of reality in painting. By alluding to ancient sources, Rembrandt sought to ennoble the role of the artist.

By the late 1630s when the etching was made, Rembrandt had enjoyed a successful decade in Amsterdam, where he was firmly established – the palm branch of the goddess of Victory was his own. However, it was not until the 1640s that he began to draw regularly from the live model, and his lack of experience may have contributed to the incorrect drawing on the plate and its unfinished state.[3] The composition and the female nude are closely modelled on prints, a fact that has long been recognised.[4] While working on the second state, Rembrandt made a drawing in which he corrected the position of the legs and completed the composition.[5] However, this drawing was never made into an etching.

In a painting by Pieter Codde from the early 1630s, three 'kunstliefhebbers', as they were called in Rembrandt's day – that is, art lovers and buyers – represent the audience that was important to the painter's fortune (cat. 24.1). Three elegantly dressed men are absorbed in the contemplation of various paintings, which they also hold in their hands to study them at close range. In the centre is the painter with his palette. An unframed landscape stands on the floor, while another hangs over the door. The stretched canvas on the easel, which can only be seen from the back, is being closely scrutinised. The picture reveals Codde's awareness of the importance of the reception of painting: in other words, the art market with potential buyers is presented here as a prerequisite for an artistic livelihood. The genre of the studio picture flourished in seventeenth-century Dutch painting, suggesting that artists increasingly reflected their status in the image of the artist's studio.[6]

Samuel van Hoogstraten was probably active in Rembrandt's workshop from 1642 to 1646. Sumowski has attributed to him the Paris drawing formerly thought to be by Rembrandt, which shows a studio in which a young painter is working on a couple portrait (cat. 24.3).[7] The picture on the stretched canvas is still at an early stage. The young painter focusses his inquiring gaze on the woman whose shoulders he is currently rendering, while the client leans forwards to look at the picture. This motif lends the drawing the charm of the momentary. On the left, another young artist is drawing, while an apprentice grinds pigments in the background on the right. On the walls hang draperies and weapons that were probably used as props for history paintings.

In Munich there is a smaller sketch of the same motif by Van Hoogstraten, which precedes the Paris sheet. Here, the man is shown standing statically next to his wife.[8] Thea Vignau-Wilberg has convincingly argued that Van Hoogstraten enlivened this composition after a correction by Rembrandt by inserting the man watching the painting in progress. To do so, the artist detached the left half of the sheet, redrew it and rejoined it to the right half, which follows the Munich sketch.[9] In front of the original, the vertical tear in the centre of the drawing clearly shows that it is composed of two halves. This method of correcting compositions by dividing and recombining drawings was common in Rembrandt's workshop (cf. cat. 47.1). The aim of this experimental process was to create compositions that were as natural and expressive as possible. JN

1 Sluijter 2006, pp. 281–5.
2 Royalton-Kisch online, Benesch 423.
3 Erich Hinterding convincingly refutes the older assumption that the artist deliberately published the plate with blank areas; cf. Emmens 1979, p. 224; Weimar 2011, p. 70.
4 Rembrandt must have been familiar with Pieter Feddes van Harlingen's 1615 etching of *Pygmalion* and Jacopo de' Barbari's 1498–1500 engraving of the *Allegory of Glory and Victory*; see Sluijter 2006, p. 283.
5 Pen and brown ink, wash, 18.8 × 16.4 cm, London, British Museum, inv. Gg.248 (see note 2).
6 Kleinert 2006.
7 More recently, Royalton-Kisch has again attributed the drawing to Rembrandt with a question mark (see Royalton Kisch online, Drawings not in Benesch).
8 Pen and brown ink, wash, 9.1 × 9.1 cm, Staatliche Graphische Sammlung Munich, inv. 1802/05; Munich/Amsterdam 2001, no. 2.
9 Ibid., p. 60.

25.1 REMBRANDT

A Man with a Penknife

1635–40
Pen and brown ink, brush and brown wash, red chalk, corrections in white, 12.5 × 12.3 cm
Klassik Stiftung Weimar, inv. KK 5492
Lit.: Benesch 263; Amsterdam/Weimar 1999, pp. 82f.; Dresden 2019, no. 55; Weimar 2022, p. 149.

25.2 REMBRANDT

Nude Man Seated and Another Standing, with a Woman and Baby in the Background ('Het Rolwagentje')

c. 1646
Etching, V (of VIII), 19.4 × 12.8 cm (sheet)
Museum der bildenden Künste Leipzig, Graphische Sammlung, inv. I. 5793
Lit.: B. 194; NH 233; Amsterdam/London 2000, no. 51; Weimar 2011, no. 44.

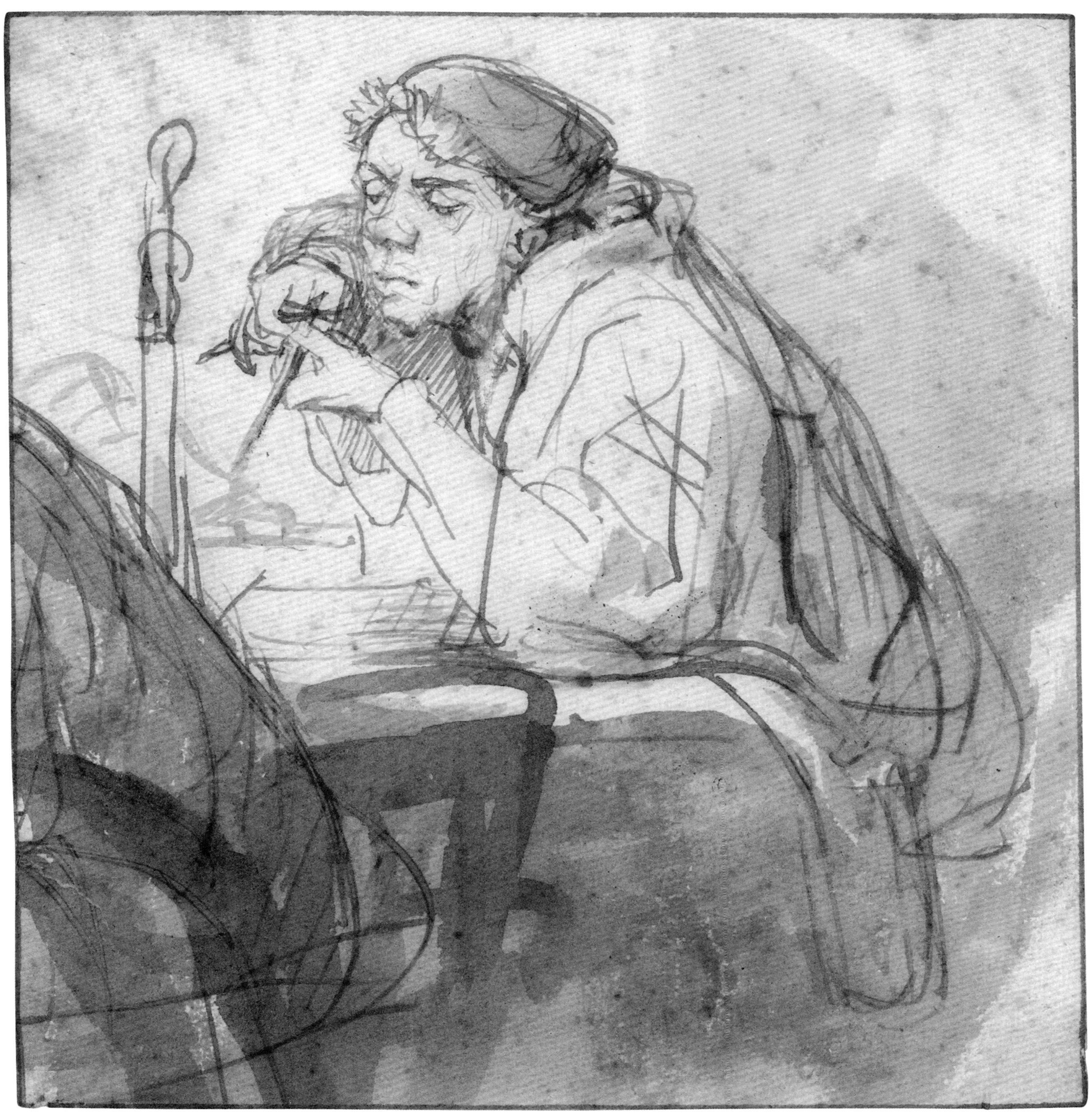

25.1

Practical exercises were essential for Rembrandt's students to develop their artistic skills. The importance of constant learning is illustrated both directly and indirectly in *A Man with a Penknife* and *Het Rolwagentje*, works that can be interpreted as allegories of teaching and practising.

With a concentrated look and knitted brows, a man sharpens his quill by the light of a burning candle (cat. 25.1). He leans forward at a table with a sheet of paper in front of him. In emblematics, the activity of sharpening a quill represented the intellectual work and diligent practice of scholars and artists as an allegory for the sharpening of the mind. The illustrated mottos read 'Senza taglio, non vaglio' (I am worthless if uncut) or 'Nil penna, sed usus' (It is not the pen that counts, but its use).[1] The motif was popular in seventeenth-century Dutch painting. Examples from Rembrandt's circle include Jan Lievens's *Quill Cutter* from 1627 and Gerrit Dou's *Scholar Sharpening His Quill* from c. 1632–5.[2] Rembrandt had already treated the subject in a painting in 1632.[3]

The attribution of the drawing, which is dated 1635–40, is the subject of debate. Peter Schatborn interpreted cat. 25.1 as a drawing by Rembrandt, while Martin Royalton-Kisch suggested his student Gerbrand van den Eeckhout as the possible author.[4] Royalton-Kisch surmises that the man cutting a quill is a draughtsman seen at work in Rembrandt's shop.

Rembrandt's etching (cat. 25.2) should be understood in the context of his workshop. In the foreground, two male nudes are developed in detail, one seated and the other standing. In the background, only sketchily indicated, a woman tries to teach a small child to walk in a trolley. Kneeling on the ground, she lovingly beckons the child towards her. In the emblem books and literature of the seventeenth century, the motif of a child in a playpen was seen as a symbol of 'exercitatio' (exercise).[5] Jan Emmens interpreted the child learning to walk as a symbol of artistic progress. In this interpretation, the nude studies symbolise the exercises by which the apprentices acquire the necessary artistic skills: just as a child painstakingly learns to walk, falling down and getting up again, so budding painters must pursue their studies conscientiously and persistently.

The two nudes show the same young man in different poses. Two other etchings by the master, dated 1646, show the same nude male model, once seated in front of a curtain and once with his leg outstretched (see cat. 26.4).[6] The slender youth has been identified as Christoph Paudiss, an 'excellent disciple of Rembrandt'.[7] Three student sketches have survived from the session in which *Het Rolwagentje* was made, which also show Rembrandt's pupil Paudiss from different angles.[8] From these working documents it can be concluded that Rembrandt sat with his pupils in a semicircle around the model and studied the nude together with them.[9]

A series of pentimenti on the etching and the reversed rendering of the figures suggest that Rembrandt incised the nudes directly into the etching plate during the joint session.[10] It is remarkable that the master, an advanced artist, drew together with his students and practised the discipline of drawing nudes with them.

In 1745, the French critic Dezallier d'Argenville reported that Rembrandt had compiled a small instruction or drawing book for art lessons consisting of ten or twelve sheets.[11] This booklet has not survived, but it is quite conceivable that it was part of Rembrandt's instruction and may have contained etchings by his hand as well as the aforementioned etchings of male nudes from 1646.[12] The material may have served as illustrative material for the students and may have been used for copying. LCS

1 Amsterdam/Weimar 1999, p. 83.
2 Jan Lievens, *The Quill Cutter*, 1627, canvas, 127 × 107.5 cm, Cologne, Wallraf-Richartz-Museum & Fondation Corboud, inv. WRM Dep. 943; Gerrit Dou, *Scholar Sharpening His Quill*, c. 1632–5, panel, 26.3 × 21.2 cm, New York, The Leiden Collection, inv. GD-104.
3 Rembrandt, *Portrait of a Man Trimming His Quill*, 1632, 103.5 × 84 cm, canvas, Kassel, Gemäldegalerie Alte Meister, inv. GK 234.
4 See Amsterdam/Weimar 1999, pp. 82f.; Royalton-Kisch online, Benesch 263. In Weimar 2022, p. 149, Royalton-Kisch's attribution is adopted without further discussion.
5 Emmens 1979, pp. 209–20.
6 Rembrandt, *Nude Man Seated before a Curtain*, etching, 1646 (B. 193).
7 Sandrart 1675, p. 78; Dresden 2019, nos. 40.1–40.3.
8 Carel Fabritius (attributed), Vienna, Albertina, inv. 8827; Samuel van Hoogstraten (attributed), Paris, Musée du Louvre, inv. RF 4713, recto; Rembrandt (Workshop), London, British Museum, inv. Oo,9.94.
9 Dresden 2019, nos. 40.1–40.3; Weimar 2011, no. 44.
10 Amsterdam/London 2000, no. 51.
11 Dezallier D'Argenville 1745, p. 27; Amsterdam 2016, p. 66 (S. Lobis).
12 Amsterdam 2016, p. 66 (S. Lobis).

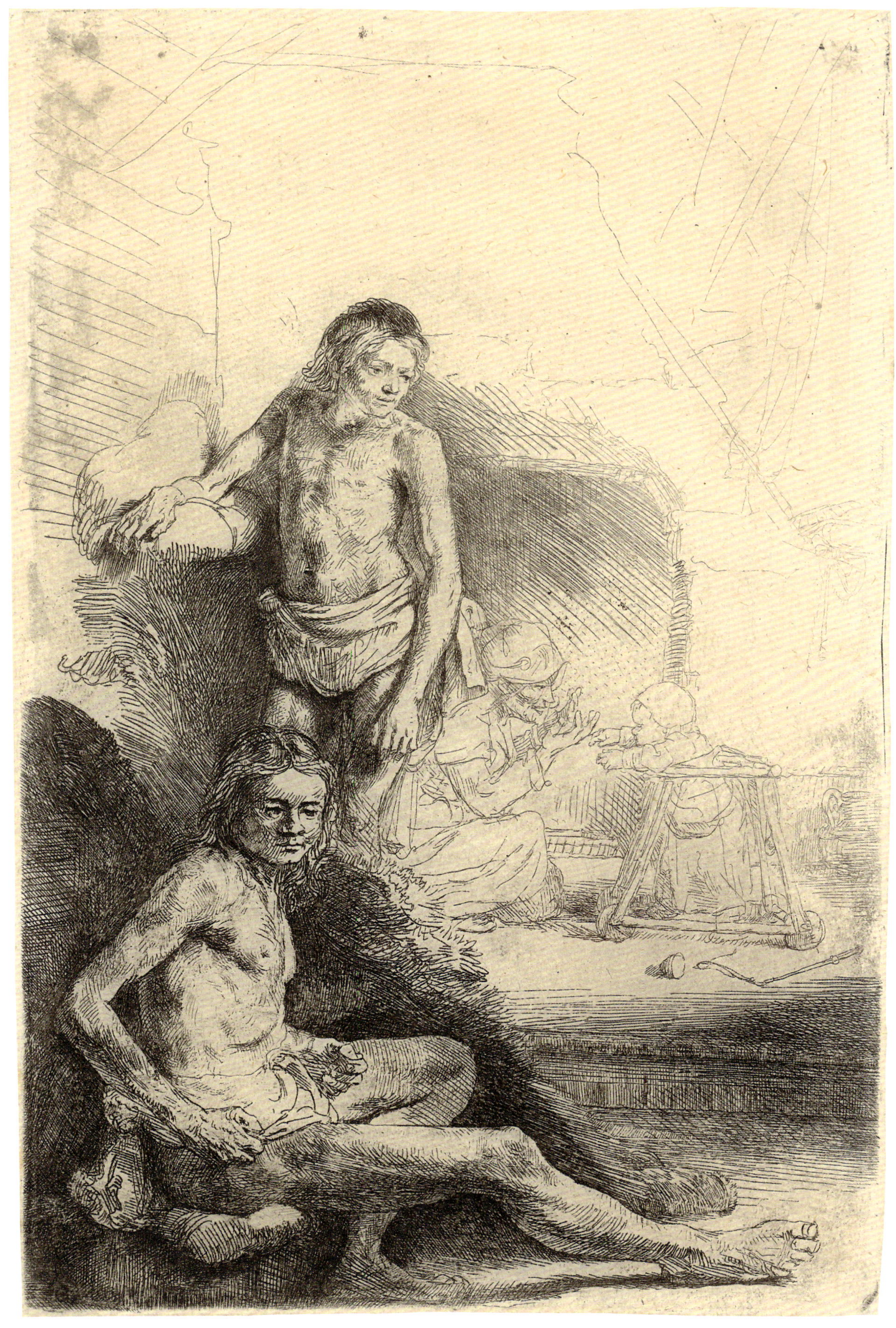

25.2

26.1 REMBRANDT

Naked Woman Seated on a Mound

c. 1631
Etching and engraving, II (of II), 17.8 × 16.2 cm (plate)
Signed (upper left): RHL
Kunstsammlungen der Veste Coburg, Kupferstichkabinett, inv. VII,380,201
Lit.: B. 201; NH 88; Berlin/Amsterdam/London 1991, no. 6; Edinburgh/London 2001, no. 12; Coburg/Freiburg 2017, no. 25; Dresden 2019, no. 37.1.

26.2 REMBRANDT

The Return of the Prodigal Son

1636
Etching, I (of I), 15.9 × 13.8 cm (sheet)
Signed and dated (on the step): Rembrandt f 1636
Museum der bildenden Künste Leipzig, Graphische Sammlung, inv. NI. 2072
Lit.: B. 91; NH 159; Schwerin 1995, no. 55.

26.3 REMBRANDT'S WORKSHOP

Boy, Seated on a Cushion

c. 1646
Pen and brown ink, brush and brown wash, corrections in white, 14.4 × 10.3 cm
Staatliche Graphische Sammlung Munich, inv. 01413 Z
Lit.: Munich/Amsterdam 2001, no. 8.

26.4 REMBRANDT

Man Seated on the Ground with One Leg Extended

1646
Etching and engraving, II (of III), 9.7 × 16.8 cm (plate)
Kunstsammlungen der Veste Coburg, Kupferstichkabinett, inv. VII,380,199
Lit.: B. 196; NH 234; Berlin/Amsterdam/London 1991, no. 21 (21b); Coburg/Freiburg 2017, no. 19.

26.5 GOVERT FLINCK

(Kleve 1615–1660 Amsterdam)

Reclining Female Nude

c. 1648
Black and yellowish-white chalk on blue paper, 24.9 × 41.2 cm
Inscribed in pencil (verso, lower centre): G. Flinck
Paris, Fondation Custodia, Collection Frits Lugt, inv. 2969
Lit.: Sumowski 1979–92, vol. 4, no. 939; Sluijter 2006, pp. 106f.; Schatborn 2010b, no. 82.

26.6 REMBRANDT FOLLOWER (?)

Rembrandt and His Students Drawing Nudes (?)

c. 1670–80
Pen and brown ink, brush and brown wash, black chalk, heightened in white, 18 × 26.6 cm
Hessisches Landesmuseum Darmstadt, inv. AE 665
Lit.: Edinburgh/London 2001, pp. 49f.; Sluijter 2006, pp. 324–6; Dresden 2019, pp. 151f.

26.7 REMBRANDT

Jupiter and Antiope (Larger Plate)

1659
Etching, II (of II), 14.2 × 20.4 cm (sheet)
Museum der bildenden Künste Leipzig, Graphische Sammlung, inv. I. 5493
Lit.: B. 203; NH 311; Berlin/Amsterdam/London 1991, no. 40; Amsterdam/London 2000, no. 90; Edinburgh/London 2001, cat. 134.

26.8 AERT DE GELDER

(Dordrecht 1645–1727 Dordrecht)

Back View of a Seated Female Nude

1660–62
Pen and brown ink, brush and brown wash, traces of red chalk, 22.3 × 18.6 cm
Staatliche Graphische Sammlung Munich, inv. 01487 Z
Lit.: Munich/Amsterdam 2001, no. 12.

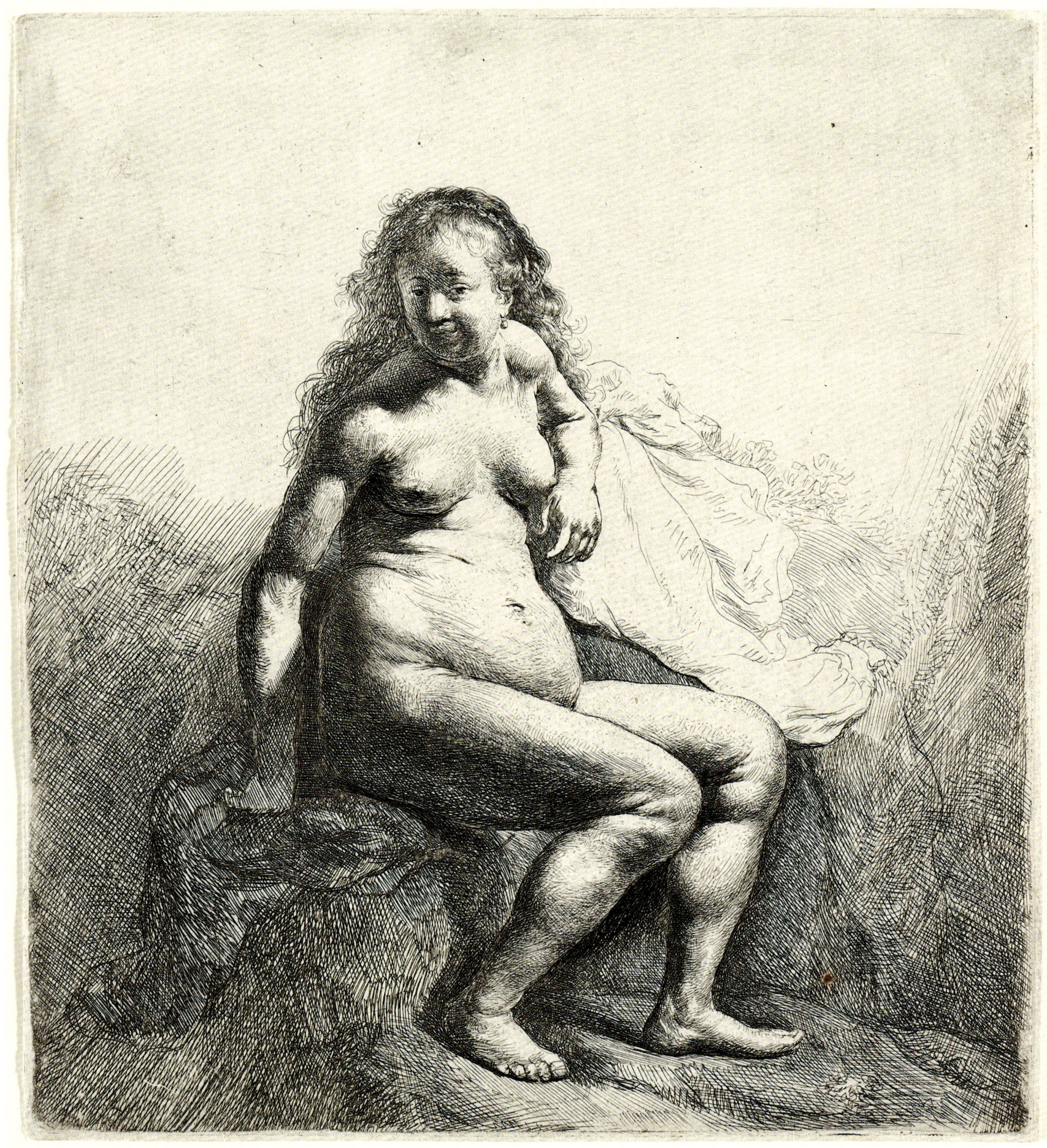

26.1

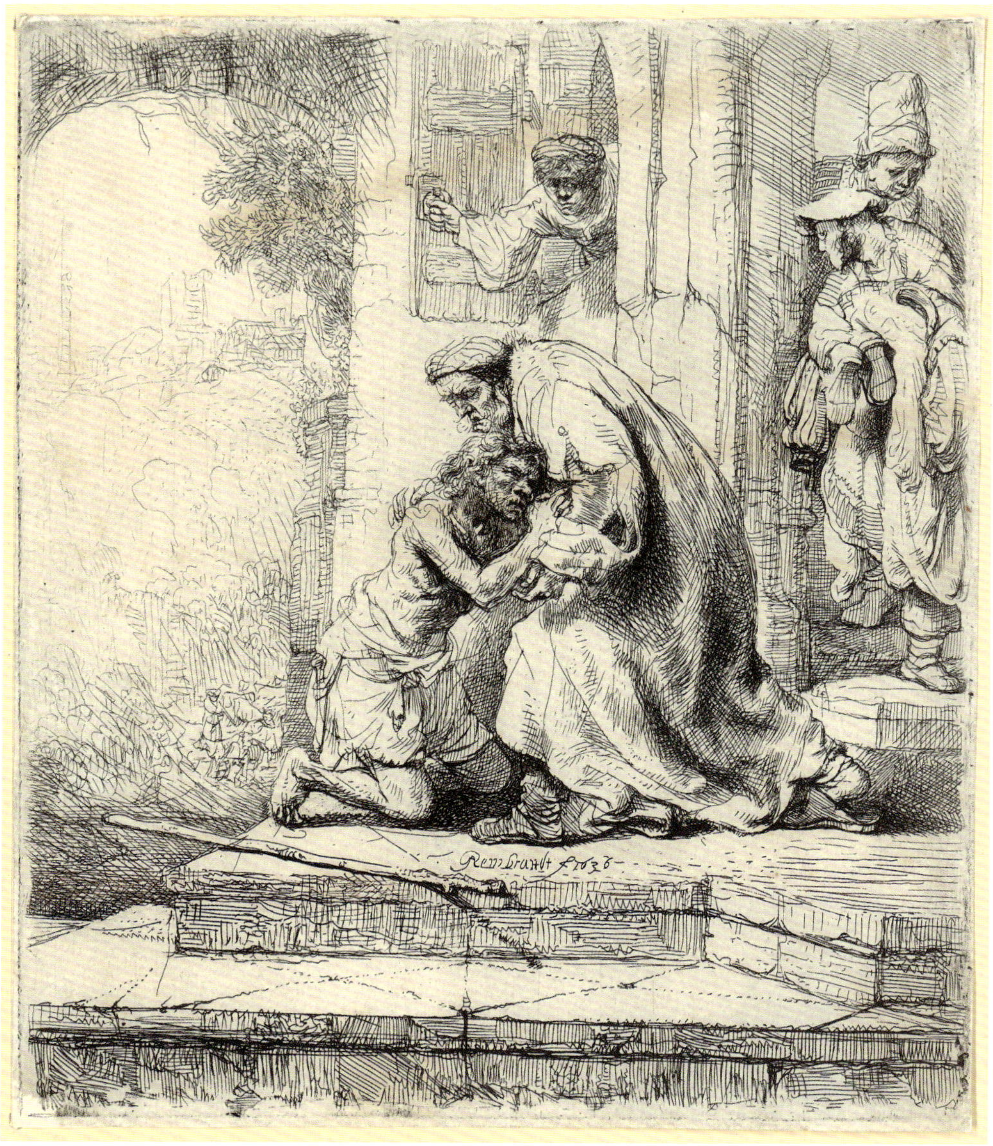

26.2

The study of the nude from a live model is part of a long artistic tradition and is considered one of the most important exercises in an artist's training. Rembrandt first devoted himself to the female nude in the early 1630s. From 1646, he and his students studied the male nude, and from around 1660 they worked from female models as well.[1]

In 1631, Rembrandt made the etchings *Jupiter and Antiope* and *Diana at the Bath*.[2] In the etching *Naked Woman Seated on a Mound* (cat. 26.1), which was produced at the same time, Rembrandt refrained from including specific details to identify the figure. The stylistic similarity to the Diana etching suggests that the sheets were designed as counterparts. The play with iconographic openness is striking, oscillating between a nude seemingly observed from life and the depiction of a mythological figure – presumably one of Diana's nymphs.[3] The vague localisation of the woman in a mythological context through the implied landscape probably served to legitimise such a revealing depiction.[4] With a cheeky smile on her lips, the voluptuous female figure turns directly towards the viewer; the accompanying erotic connotation seems overt.

The pose is probably a calculated one. In the early 1630s, the young artist was beginning to make a name for himself in Amsterdam, and such a sensational depiction probably increased his popularity. The deliberate provocation lay in the non-idealised depiction of the naked female body, which did not conform to the traditional rules for the representation of the female nude which prescribed classical proportions and a graceful pose. Samuel van Hoogstraten regretted that his teacher had chosen nude models that did not correspond to his idea of beauty.[5] And Govert Flinck, after leaving the Rembrandt workshop, rejected his teacher's realism and adopted a traditional view of the female nude. His *Reclining Female Nude* of 1648 (cat. 26.5) is a prime example. The model is of well-proportioned stature and reclines in a graceful pose on a decorative drapery – the stylistic contrast with his teacher's nudes could hardly be greater.

A written source from 1658 documents that a woman modelled 'poedelnaakt' for a group of artists, including Ferdinand Bol and Govert Flinck. [6] The model was accused of prostitution for posing 'stark naked'.[7] The situation of female nude models was precarious, as the moral code of the time made them liable to prosecution – and most of them were in fact prostitutes.

Although Rembrandt's naturalistic depictions of the female body give the impression of having been observed directly from life, it is unlikely that the artist studied fully nude models until the late 1650s.[8] Many of his earlier depictions of female nudes were modelled on prints – including his etching of a nude seated on a mound, whose somewhat inharmonious-seeming proportions were probably composed from individual observations of the human body.[9] Although Rembrandt

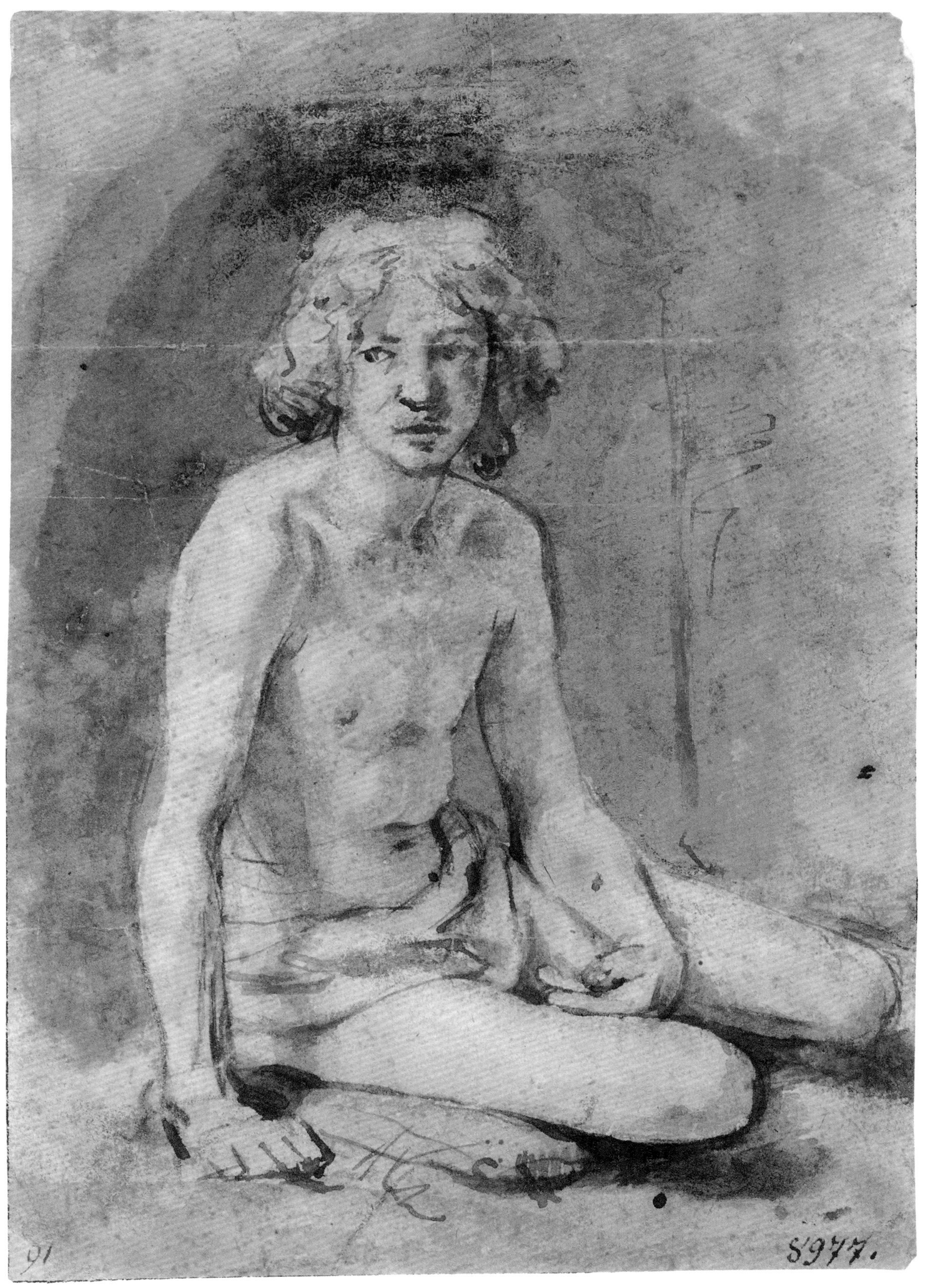

26.3

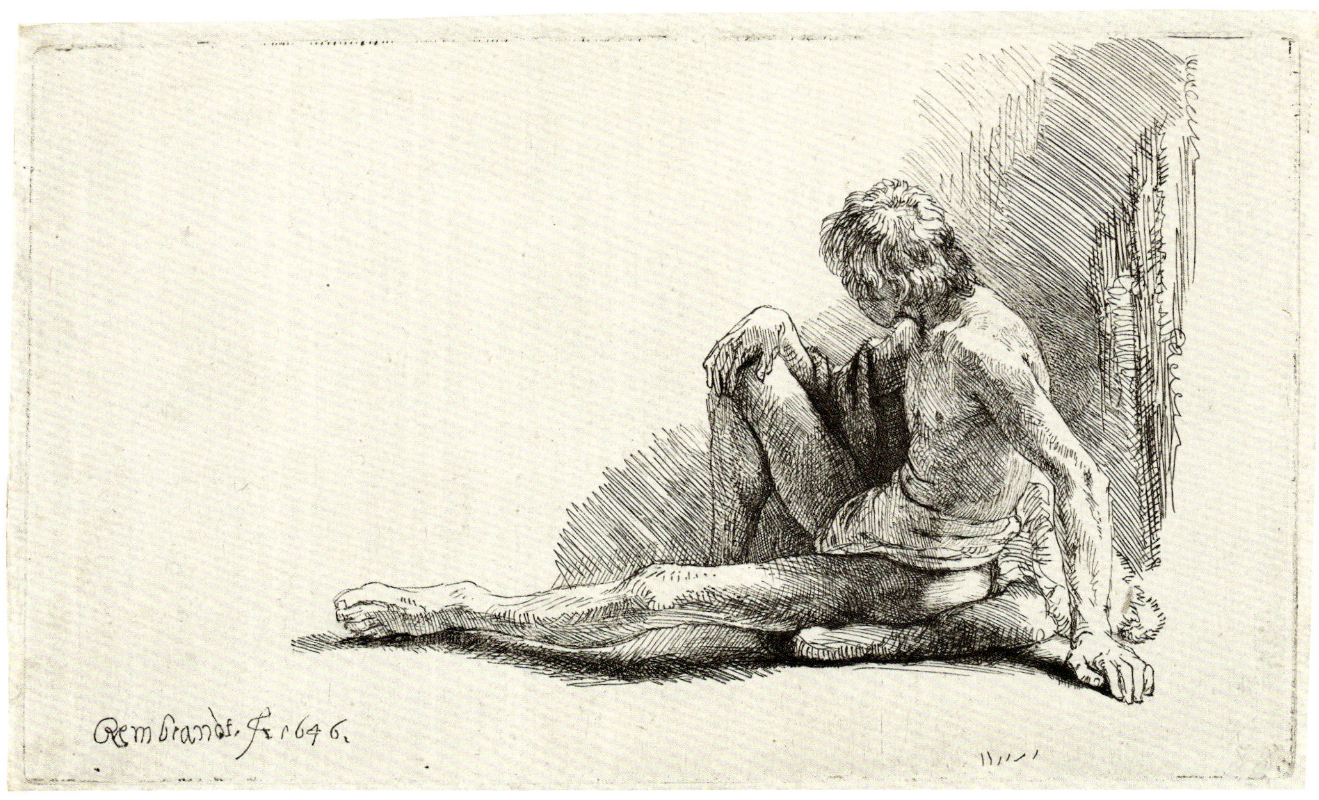

26.4

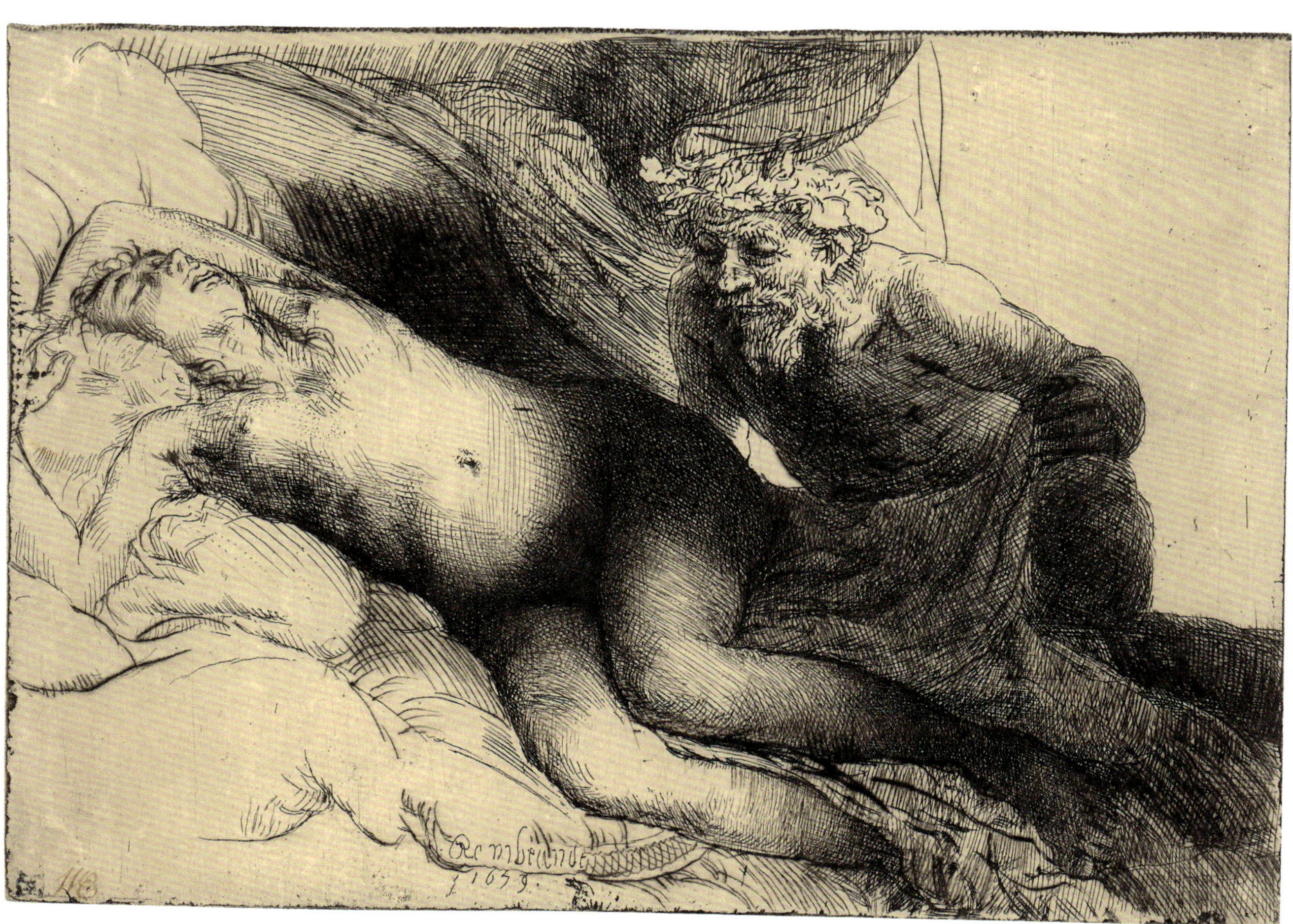

26.7

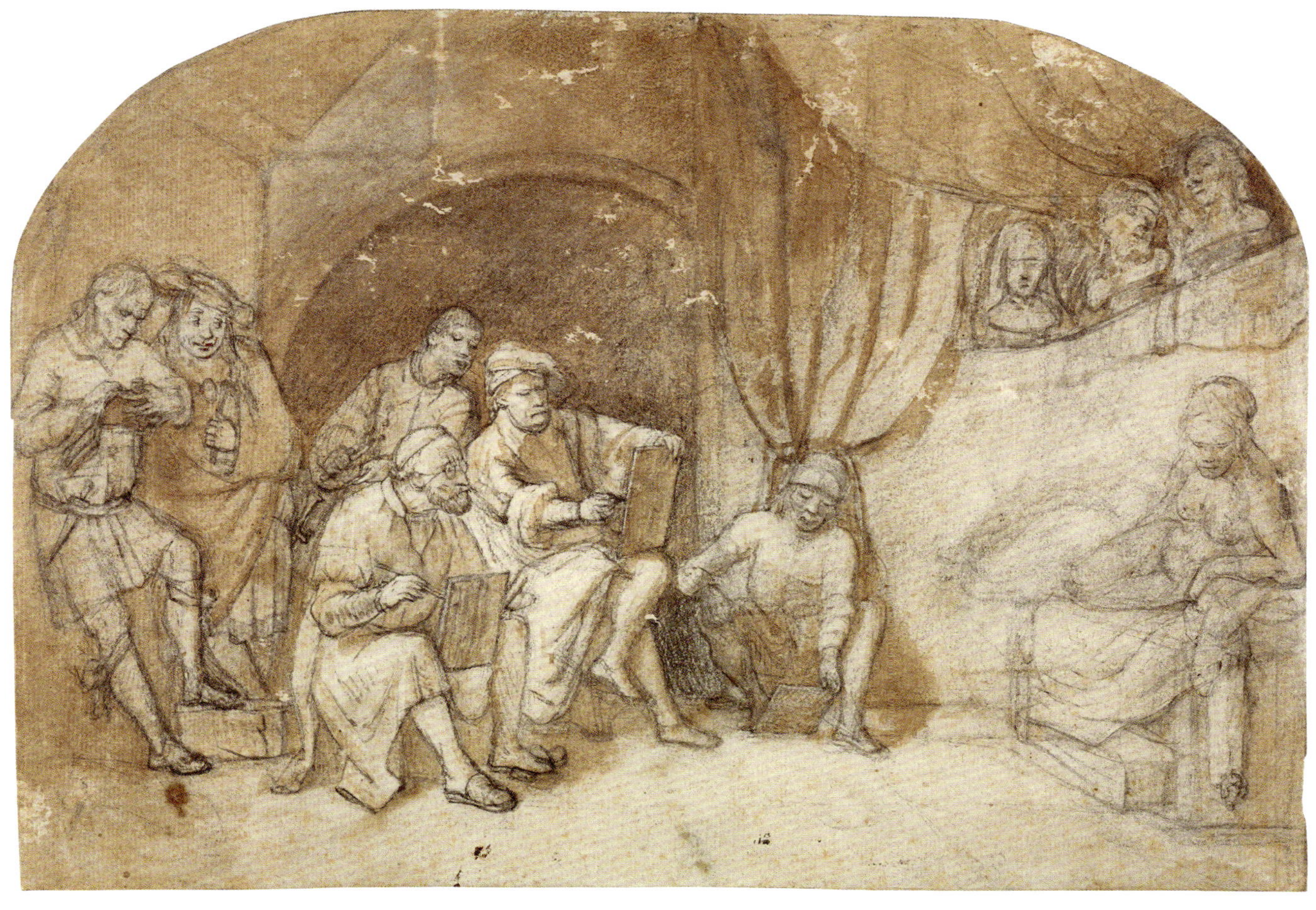

26.6

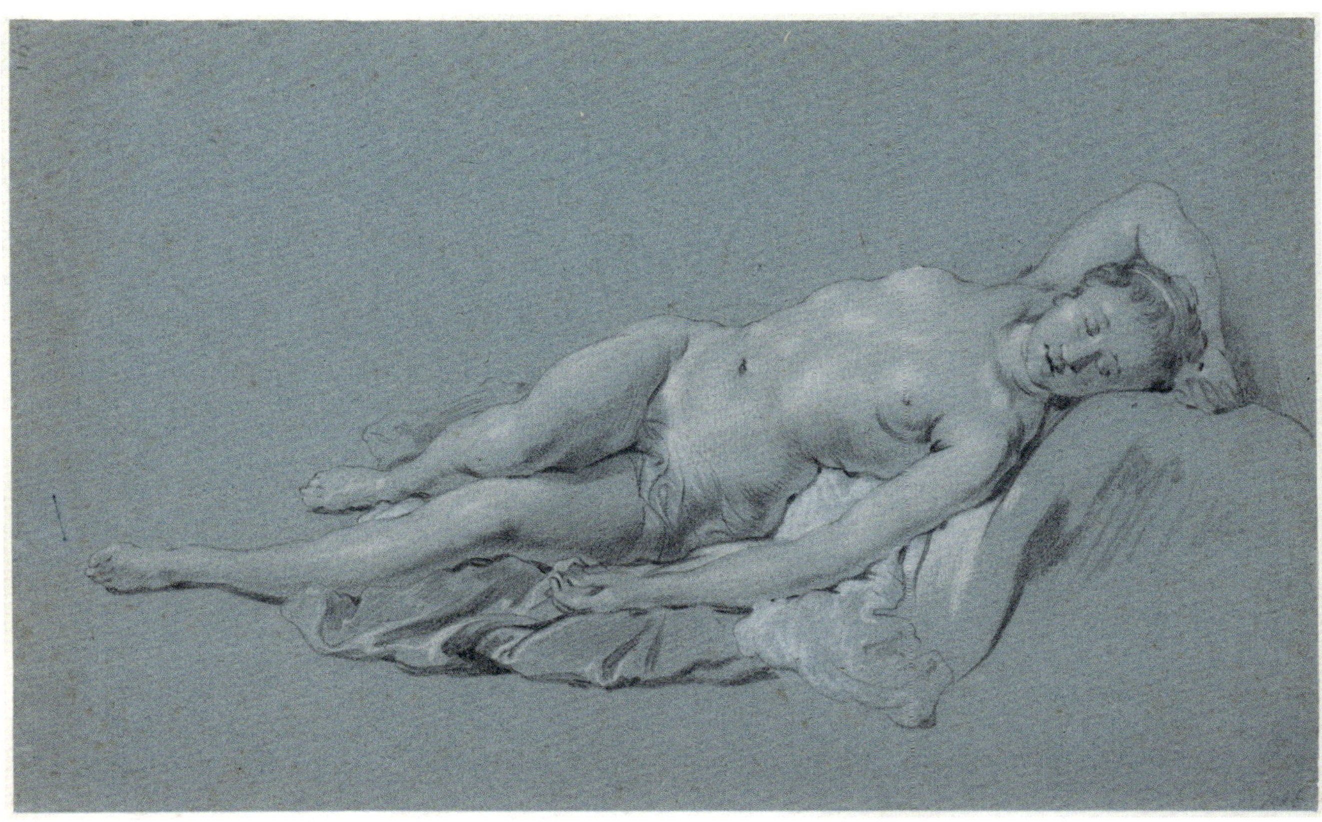

26.5

drew a female nude from the model in 1647, she is still partially clothed, with only her upper body bare.[10] The same is true of a drawing from 1654 and an etching from 1658.[11]

In 1646, Rembrandt and his students began to draw from a male model wearing only a loincloth. The joint drawing sessions resulted in several etchings by Rembrandt, as well as numerous drawings by his students, of young men who were the apprentices themselves, posing for each other.[12]

In his 1646 etching of a male nude with one leg extended (cat. 26.4), Rembrandt repeats the pose of the man sitting on the ground from *Het Rolwagentje* (cat. 25.2), probably using the same model. Rembrandt's attention to the texture of the soft skin and the delicate modelling of the body is remarkable. A similar focus on painterly qualities is evident in the student drawing of a nude youth with curly hair against a shaded background with brown washes, painted around 1646 (cat. 26.3). Rembrandt's 1636 etching *The Return of the Prodigal Son* shows how the nude is used in a biblical story (cat. 26.2).

A drawing presumably made after Rembrandt's death seems to reflect the practice of studying nudes in his workshop (cat. 26.6).[13] Several draughtsmen are seated in a semicircle in front of a reclining nude woman. Although the older man in the beret could be Rembrandt, next to him is an old man with spectacles who stares at the naked woman almost intrusively – more like a voyeuristic observer. It is striking that some of the figures wear historical costumes in the style of the fifteenth and sixteenth centuries. Sluijter has pointed out that the picture – long regarded as a faithful illustration of Rembrandt's workshop – should more likely be understood as a satire on the study of the nude and that it employs the usual clichés of such a drawing session.[14]

Rembrandt probably owned the 1592 etching of *Jupiter and Antiope* by the Italian Renaissance painter Annibale Carracci, which served as a direct model for his 1659 etching of the same subject (cat. 26.7).[15] Whereas in Carracci's work the woman's pose appears to be one of relaxed sleep, Rembrandt's view of Antiope gives the impression of lustful abandon: her arms are bent over her head, which is bowed low at the neck, and her lips are slightly parted.[16] This late etching illustrates how Rembrandt's artistic approach to the subject of the female nude had changed. In the early etching of *Jupiter and Antiope* from 1631, the sleeping woman is captured with delicate outlines, but is barely modelled. The late etching is very different, with dynamically placed lines and a keen sense of the sensuality of human flesh.

Even as a mature artist, Rembrandt continued the practice of studying the nude from a live model. Around 1660–2, he made two drawings of the same woman in different poses.[17] Two nude drawings from the same model by his student Aert de Gelder also survive from this period. This suggests that Rembrandt drew side by side with his student; this is supported above all by the fact that the model was captured from different angles.[18]

In De Gelder's Munich drawing, the generous use of washes evokes the impression of spatiality and plasticity (cat. 26.8). A comparison of Rembrandt's nudes with those of his student shows that the latter was trying to imitate his teacher's style, but without achieving the same degree of liveliness.[19] Nevertheless, the drawing of the model on a low stool upholstered with a cushion is a document of the importance of drawing 'naer het leven' (from life) in Rembrandt's workshop. The female figure is sensitively modelled with delicate outlines, shadows and light. LCS

1 Sluijter 2006, pp. 292–305.
2 Rembrandt, *Jupiter and Antiope* (Smaller Plate), 1631, etching (B. 204); Rembrandt, *Diana at the Bath*, c. 1631, etching (B. 201).
3 Amsterdam/London 2000, no. 11.
4 Dresden 2019, no. 37.1.
5 Hoogstraten 1678, p. 294.
6 Amsterdam 2016, p. 11 (J. Noorman).
7 Edinburgh/London 2001, p. 51 (V. Manuth).
8 Rembrandt, *Seated Naked Woman with a Hat Beside Her*, 1658, etching (B. 199); Amsterdam 2016, p. 19.
9 Dresden 2019, no. 37.1.
10 Rembrandt, *Seated Female Nude*, c. 1647, black chalk, 20.3 × 16.4 cm, Staatliche Museen zu Berlin, Kupferstichkabinett, inv. KdZ 5264.
11 Rembrandt, *The Artist's Studio*, 1654, pen and brush in brown ink, 20.6 × 19.1 cm, Oxford, Ashmolean Museum, inv. WA1855.8; Rembrandt, *Woman Sitting Half-Dressed beside a Stove*, 1658, etching (B. 197).
12 Amsterdam 2016, p. 13.
13 Sluijter 2006, pp. 325f.
14 Ibid.
15 Annibale Caracci, *Jupiter and Antiope*, 1592, etching, 15.4 × 22.5 cm, Philadelphia Museum of Art, inv. 1985-52-28057.
16 London/Amsterdam 2014, pp. 90f.
17 Rembrandt, *Seated Female Nude*, 1660–2, pen and brush in brown ink, brown wash, 21.1 × 17.7 cm, Art Institute of Chicago, Clarence Buckingham Collection, inv. 1953.38; Rembrandt, *Female Nude Seated in front of a Stove*, 1660–2, pen and brush in brown ink over black chalk, heightened in white, 29.2 × 17.5 cm, Amsterdam, Rijksmuseum, inv. RP-T-00-227; Aert de Gelder, *Seated Female Nude near a Stove*, 1660–2, pen and brush in brown ink, brown wash, corrections in white, 29.2 × 19.5 cm, Rotterdam, Museum Boijmans Van Beuningen, inv. R1 (PK).
18 Los Angeles 2009, nos. 41.1–2.
19 Munich/Amsterdam 2001, no. 11.

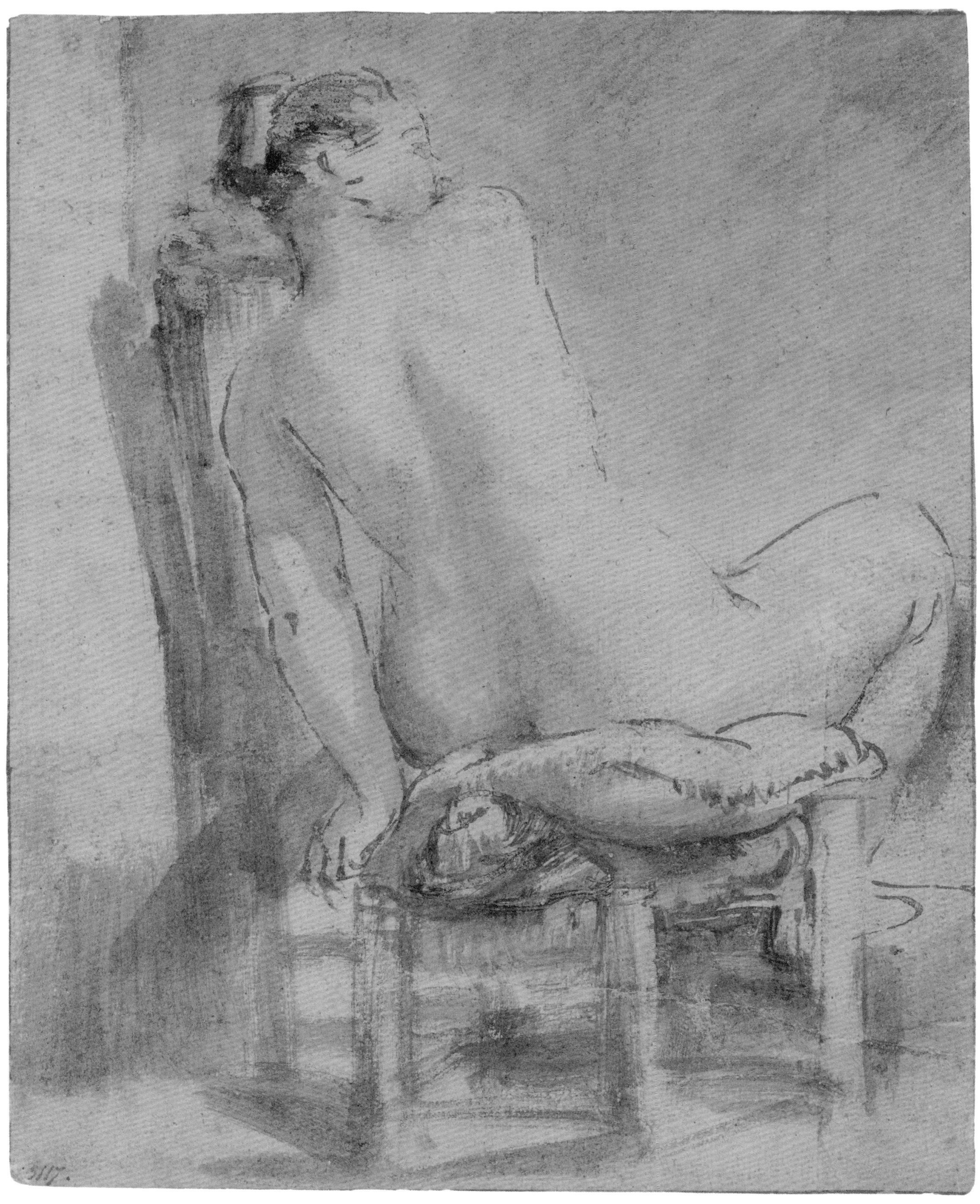

26.8

27.1 REMBRANDT (ATTRIBUTED)

Nude Study of a Young Man as Christ at the Column

c. 1646
Panel, 34.5 × 25.8 cm
Cologne, Wallraf-Richartz-Museum & Fondation Corboud, inv. WRM 2528
Lit.: Sumowski 1983–94, vol. 1, pp. 12, 22, note 32; Berlin/Amsterdam 2006, no. 51; Cologne/Prague 2019, no. 86.

27.2 BARENT FABRITIUS

(Middenbeemster 1624–1673 Amsterdam)

Standing Male Nude, Leaning against Beam

c. 1646
Pen and brown ink, brush and brown wash, black chalk, over preliminary drawing in black pencil, 20.4 × 15.8 cm
Rounded upper corners
Staatliche Kunstsammlungen Dresden, Kupferstich-Kabinett, inv. C 1363
Lit.: Sumowski 1979–92, vol. 4, no. 857xx; Dresden 2004, no. 15; Amsterdam 2016, pp. 121f.; Dresden 2019, no. 41.1.

27.3 REMBRANDT'S WORKSHOP

The Flagellation of Christ

1655–9
Pen and brown ink, brush and grey and brown wash
18.4 × 25.8 cm
Staatliche Kunstsammlungen Dresden, Kupferstich-Kabinett, inv. C 1323
Lit.: Dresden 2004, no. 52.

27.4 REMBRANDT'S WORKSHOP

Christ at the Column

c. 1650–5
Canvas, 93 × 72 cm
Inscribed later: Rembrandt.f.1658; beneath, overpainted signature: Rembra...
Hessisches Landesmuseum Darmstadt, inv. GK 251
Lit.: Sumowski 1983–94, vol. 4, no. 1922; Berlin 2006, no. 67; Cologne /Prague 2019, pp. 266, 268; Darmstadt 2022, no. 130.

The apprentices in Rembrandt's workshop modelled for each other. The same young men, drawn from different angles, thus reappear in various etchings by Rembrandt and drawings by his students (cf. cat. 25.2).[1] The model in the Cologne painting can be seen in a drawing in London attributed to Samuel van Hoogstraten.[2] Here, the master directed his students' attention more to the play of light and shadow on the naked skin than to the anatomy (cats. 26.3, 26.8). This painterly approach emphasises the sensuality of the skin and is suitable, for example, for expressing the vulnerability of the naked figure of Christ in scenes from the Passion and the sensuality of the human body in general.

The painting style of the study for *Christ at the Column* (cat. 27.1) appears technically routine: the thinly applied reddish imprimatura is used to suggest the curly hair, and the flesh tones are modelled with impasto paint. The bony left shoulder, the belly and the thighs are accentuated by white highlights, while the skin tones on the head are only sketched in. The slender body, stylised to the point of gauntness perhaps in view of Christ's suffering, shines in the light against a tonal background.[3] Sumowski has suggested that Rembrandt executed the study while his students drew the model.[4] It does not appear to have been translated into a painting. It cannot be ruled out that the study was made by a talented member of the workshop, such as Willem Drost, who was active there from around 1648 to 1653.[5]

To the right of the model, who poses on a pedestal like Christ at the column with his hands behind his back as if bound, the half-column is discernible in the shadow. The pose and the addition of this motif transform the nude study into a religious story. Rembrandt thus demonstrated to his students – for a painting of this kind was intended not for sale, but rather for use in the workshop – that the study of nature and religious narrative are linked.

A number of studies and compositional sketches suggest that Rembrandt's workshop was producing a multi-figure depiction of the Flagellation. For this purpose, individual aspects of the scene were likely reconstructed and drawn in the studio.[6] The Darmstadt painting, probably designed by Rembrandt but executed with the help of assistants, shows the moment before the flagellation, in which two henchmen bind the victim with iron shackles and a pulley (cat. 27.4).[7] The figure of a man pulling a rope appears in several drawings from Rembrandt's workshop.[8] In the Darmstadt painting (as in the Amsterdam drawing), he is dressed in a historicised sixteenth-century lansquenet costume.

One of the two Dresden drawings (cat. 27.3) shows Christ with similarly raised arms, but in profile on a pedestal; as in the Darmstadt painting, the pulley is anchored above the column. The sheet is probably to be understood as a combination of several approaches: working from the live model, 'uit de gheest' (from the imagination) and from other source images. With this combinatorial technique, the students attempted to find an independent composition. The

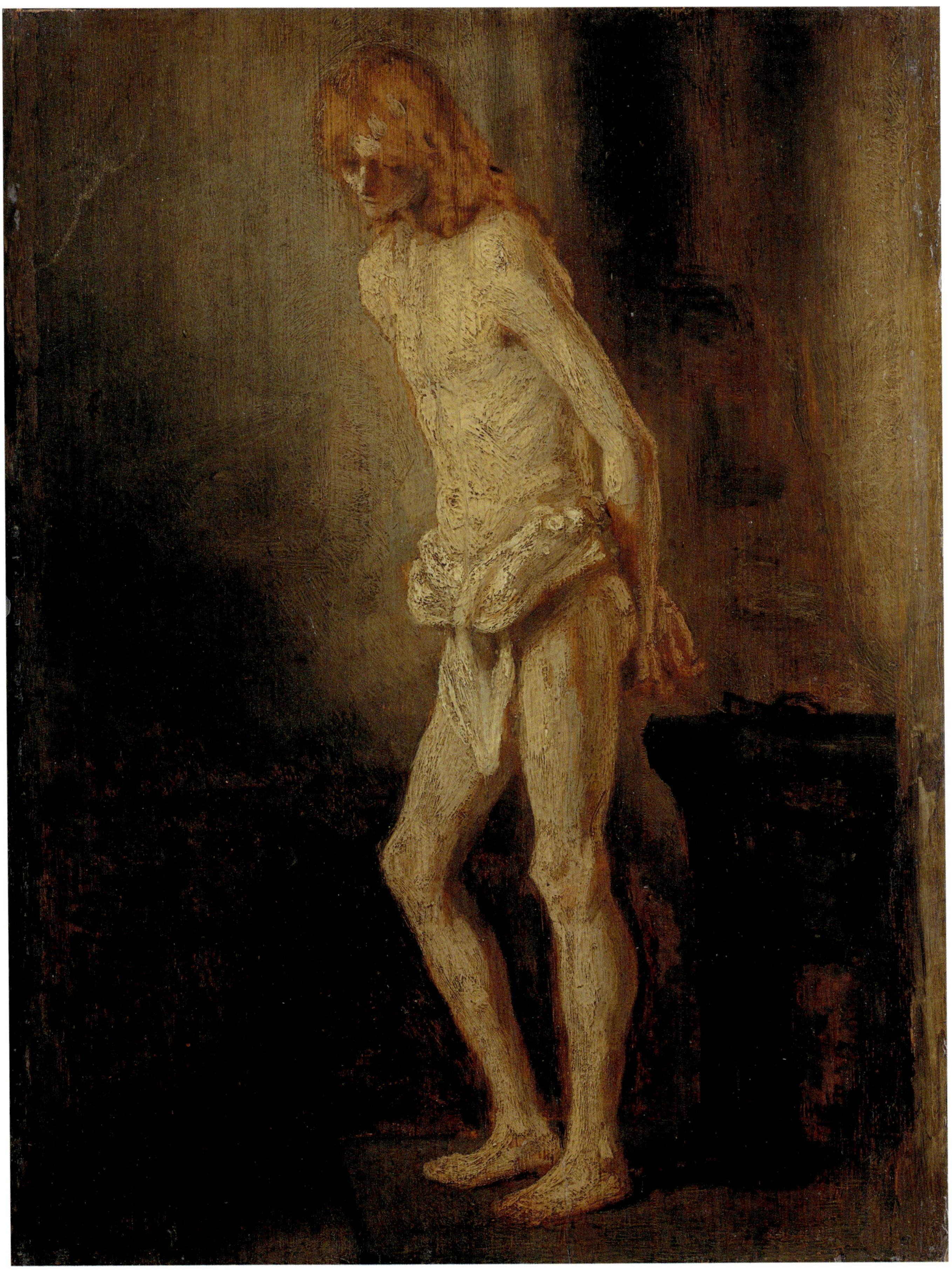
27.1

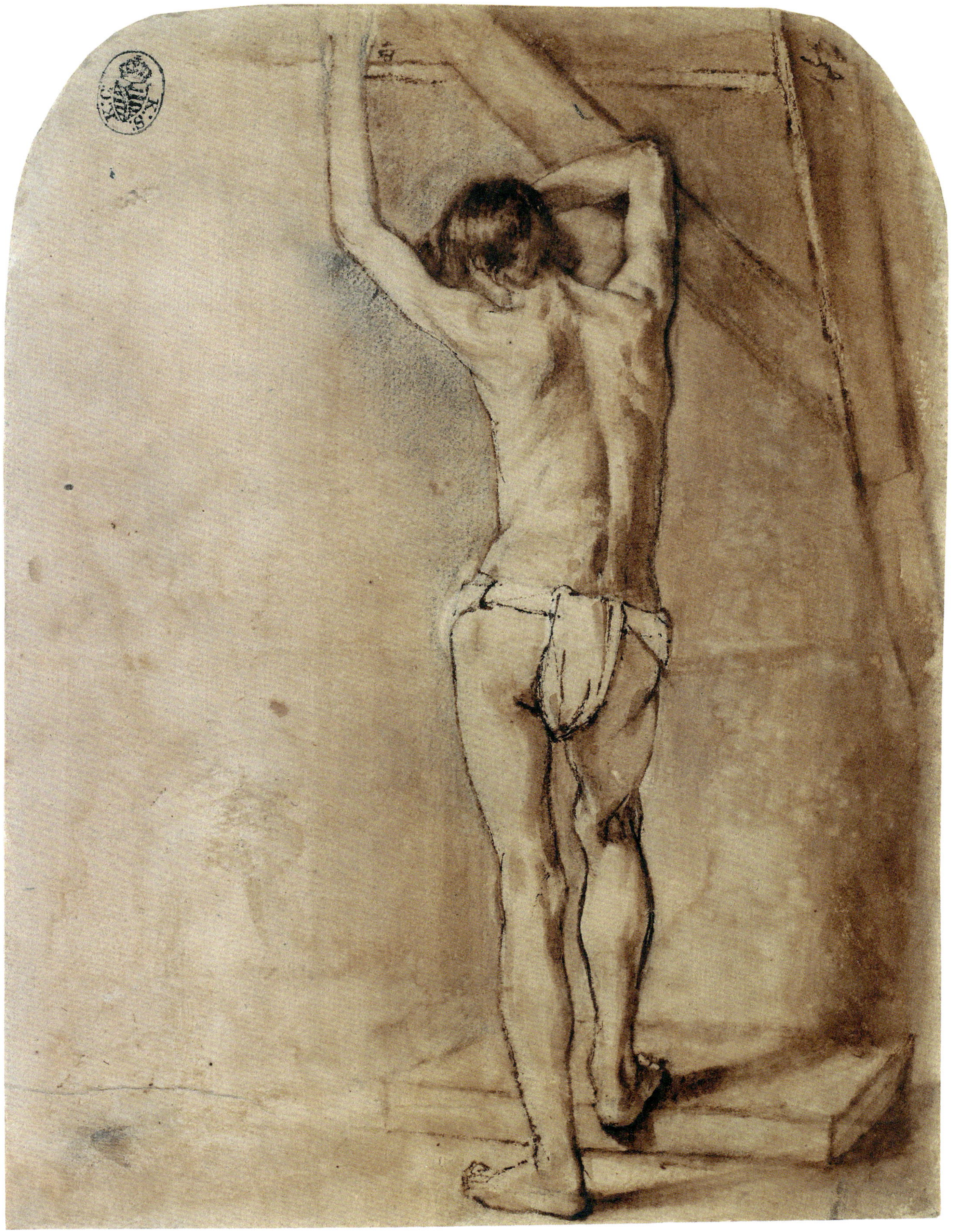

27.2

THE LANDSCAPE AS STUDIO

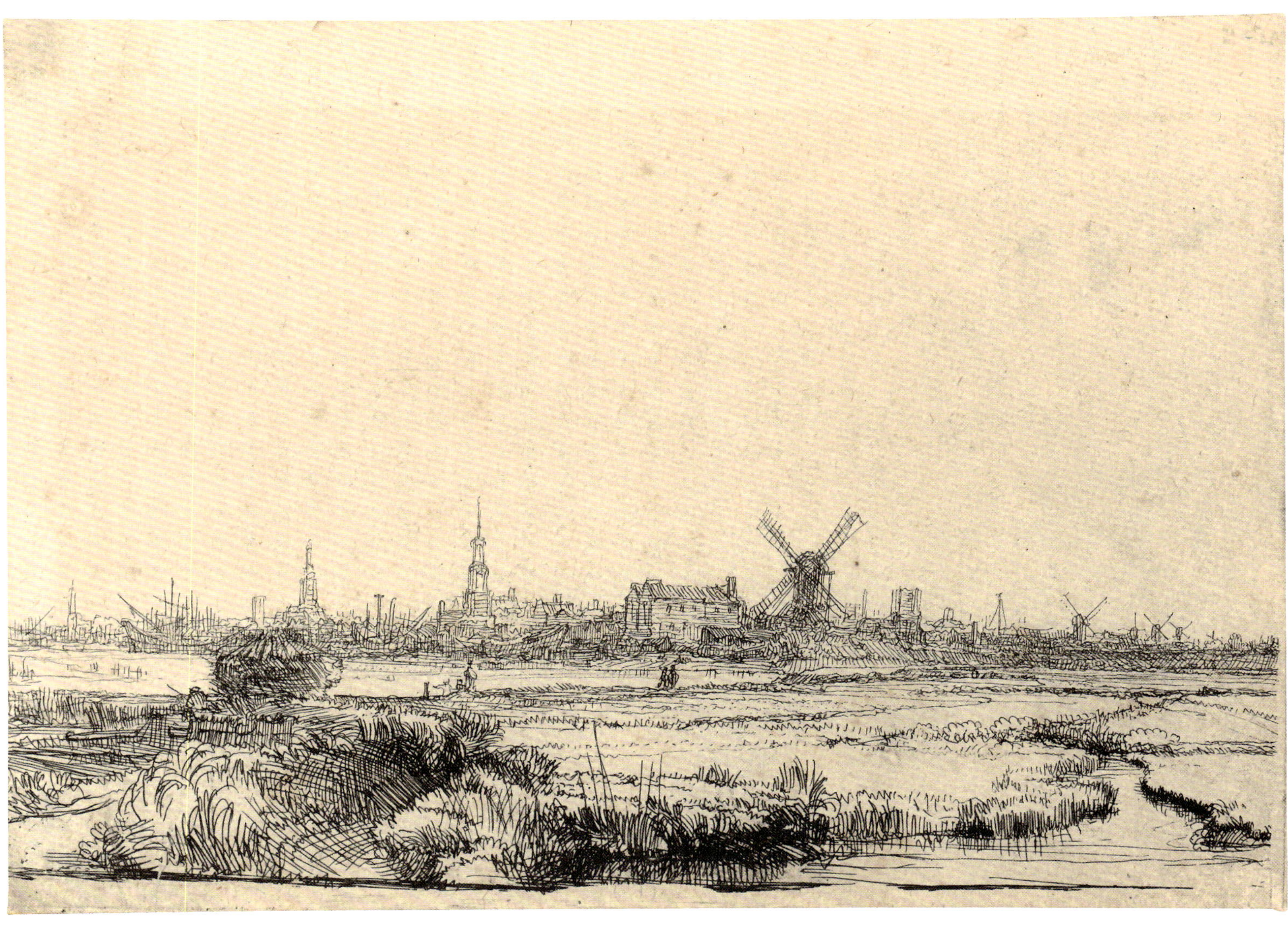

28.1

28.1 REMBRANDT

View of Amsterdam

c. 1641
Etching, I (of I), 10.7 × 15.5 cm (sheet)
Museum der bildenden Künste Leipzig, Graphische Sammlung, inv. NI. 2033
Lit.: B. 210; NH 203; Washington 1990, no. 74; Amsterdam 1993, no. 33; Amsterdam/Paris 1998, pp. 209–12; White 1999, pp. 215f.; Amsterdam/London 2000, no. 39; Hinterding 2006, no. 165; Coburg/Freiburg 2017, no. 84.

28.2 REMBRANDT

The Little Stink Mill on the De Passeerde Bulwark

1641
Etching with traces of drypoint, I (of I), 14.6 × 20.7 cm (sheet)
Signed and dated (lower right): Rembrandt f 1641
Museum der bildenden Künste Leipzig, Graphische Sammlung, inv. NI. 2074
Lit.: B. 233; NH 200; Washington 1990, no. 4; Amsterdam 1993, no. 34; Amsterdam/Paris 1998, pp. 191–5; Amsterdam/London 2000, no. 41; Hinterding 2006, no. 182; Coburg/Freiburg 2017, no. 85.

28.3 REMBRANDT

The Omval

1645
Etching and drypoint, II (of III), 18.4 × 22.4 cm (sheet)
Signed and dated (lower right): Rembrandt. 1645
Museum der bildenden Künste Leipzig, Graphische Sammlung, inv. NI. 2032
Lit.: B. 209; NH 221; Washington 1990, no. 54; Amsterdam/Paris 1998, pp. 265–71; Nevitt 1998, pp. 162–91; White 1999, pp. 226–8; Amsterdam/London 2000, no. 50; Schwartz 2019, pp. 251–5; Weimar 2011, no. 42; Coburg/Freiburg 2017, no. 87.

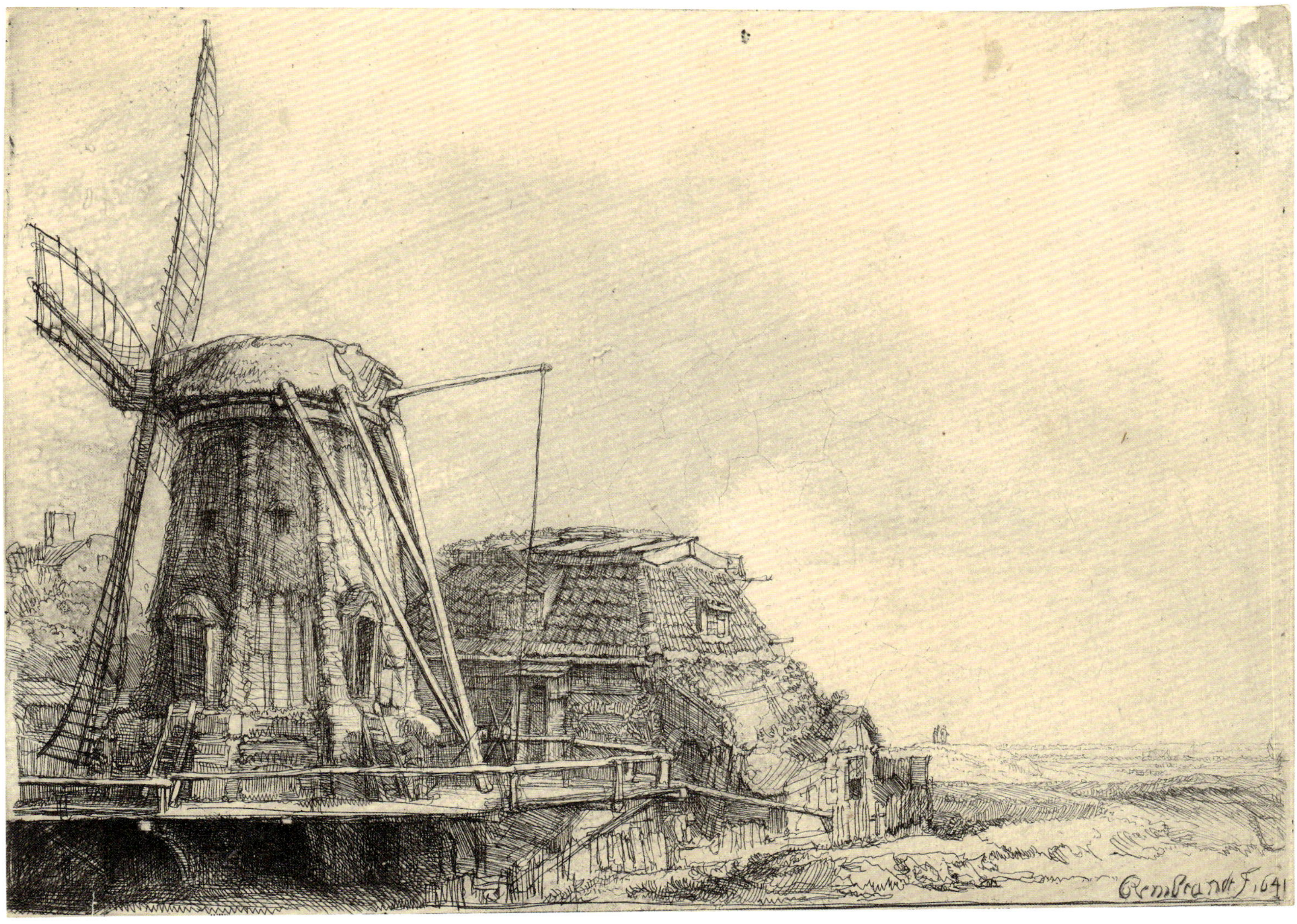

28.2

28.4 PHILIPS KONINCK

(Amsterdam 1619–1688 Amsterdam)

Landscape with Farmhouse and Windmill

1655–60
Pen and brown ink, brush and brown and grey wash, 26.1 × 38.4 cm
Later inscribed (upper right): Rembrandt
Maximilian Speck von Sternburg Foundation in the Museum der bildenden Künste Leipzig, Graphische Sammlung, inv. NI. 8303
Lit.: Leipzig 1837, no. 74; Sumowski 1979–92, vol. 6, no. 1494x; Leipzig/Munich 1998, no. II/51.

28.5 PHILIPS KONINCK

Dutch River Landscape

c. 1670
Pen and brown ink, brush and brown wash, 9.6 × 20.2 cm
Later signed: P. koning. P. D.
Museum der bildenden Künste Leipzig, Graphische Sammlung, inv. NI. 459
Lit.: Gerson 1980, p. 66, no. Z 46; Sumowski 1979–92, vol. 6, no. 1510x; Leipzig 1990, no. 49.

Rembrandt's etched and drawn landscapes are realistic impressions of often identifiable locations that he drew on walks outside the gates of Amsterdam. His landscape etchings date from relatively late in his graphic oeuvre, around 1640. In the 1640s, several Amsterdam artists, including Anthonie Waterloo, Jan Abrahamsz. Beerstraten, Simon de Vlieger, Reinier Nooms alias Zeeman and Roelant Roghman, began to draw from nature *en plein air*.[1] Rembrandt also worked outdoors with students, sometimes sitting a few metres apart and drawing the same motif.[2] The small *View of Amsterdam* and the

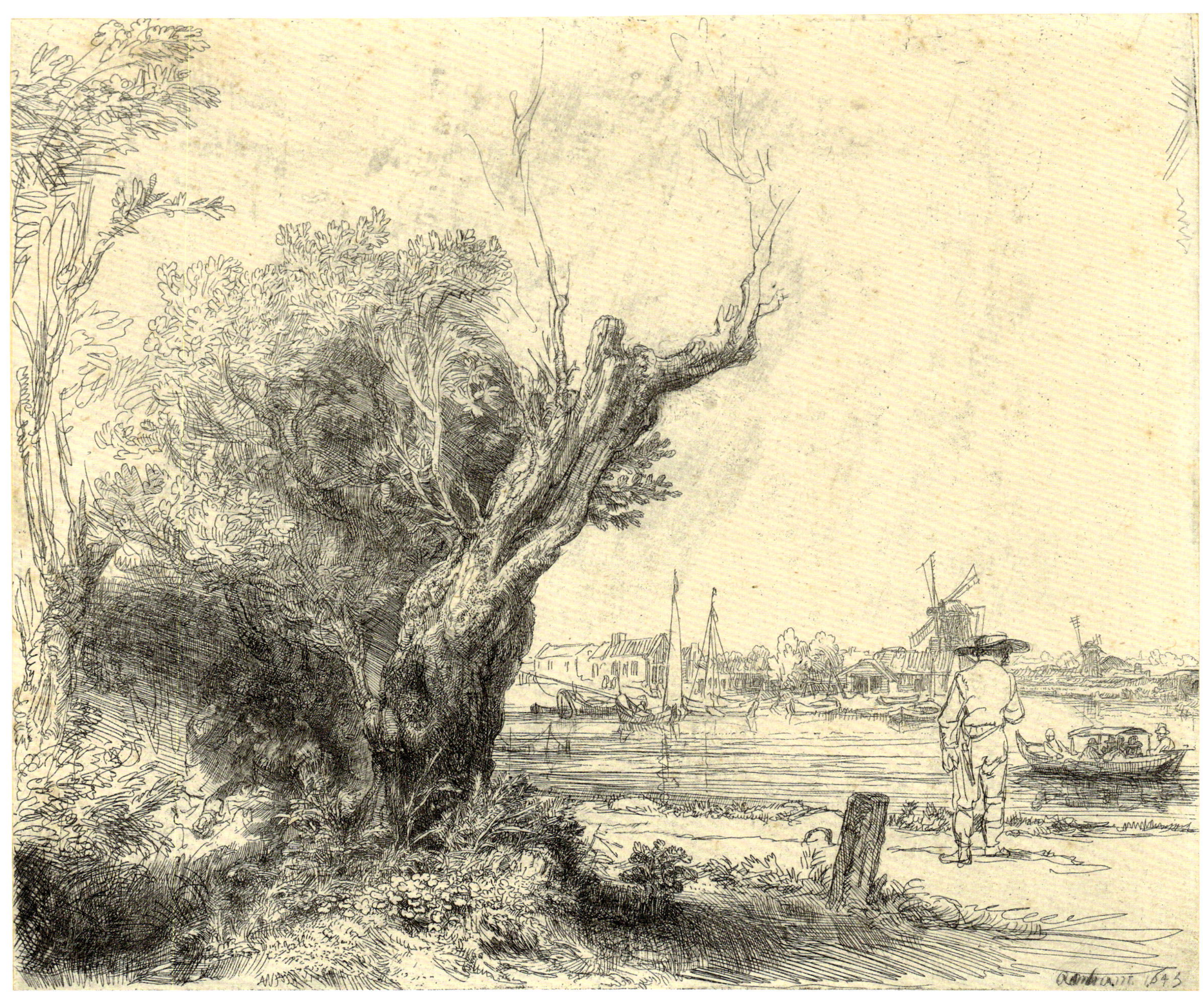

28.3

Little Stink Mill (cats. 28.1–2) are among Rembrandt's earliest landscape etchings. In the view of the city, he foregrounds the vast polder landscape, crisscrossed by the wide river IJ, wet meadows and ditches. The silhouette of the city with its prominent church steeples, windmills, ships' masts in the harbour and the warehouses and dockyard buildings of the United East India Company in the centre of the picture emerges above the individual blades of grass. Rembrandt captured the view from the Kadijk, north-east of the city.[3] Minor deviations from the topographical situation seem to indicate that it was created in the studio from drawings he had made on site. It was important to the artist that his picture have the same immediacy as a topographical study.

The same applies to the etching of the *Little Stink Mill*, so called because it was used by the leathermakers' guild to soften tanned leather with cod liver oil. The mill stood on the bulwark of the old Amsterdam fortifications known as 'De Passeerde'. It was a relatively modern tower windmill with a rotating roof and sails separate from the mill body, for which the beam construction served. Rembrandt rendered the construction with the precision of a technical draughtsman. On the protruding wooden gallery we see

While making the etching, he was looking at the drawing, which largely corresponds to it in size and composition.

With his wash brush, Rembrandt evokes the shimmer of silky fur and above all the play of light and shadow. In the late 1640s in particular, he studied the North African Barbary lions imported by the East India Company.[5] These studies helped him and his students lend authenticity to the setting of biblical stories through realism. Based on stylistic comparison with the Amsterdam work *Daniel in the Lion's Den* (Rijksprentenkabinet), the drawing can be dated to around 1649.[6] Wash is used to unify the lion and Jerome – tamed ferocity and the intellectual church father. The landscape background is rendered in delicate pen strokes, causing it to recede and enhancing the illusion of depth. In both etching and drawing, seclusion is emphasised as an expression of the scholarly life.[7] The architectural background, which is much more detailed in the etching than in the drawing, emphasises Rembrandt's efforts to create a historicising atmosphere. JN/JG

1 A total of 28 preliminary drawings for etchings have survived; see Amsterdam/London 2000, pp. 64–71 (M. Royalton-Kisch).
2 Schwartz 2019, p. 253.
3 Regarding cat. 29.1, see Hamburger Kunsthalle online (A. Stefes).
4 Berlin/Amsterdam/London 1991, no. 31; Amsterdam/London 2000, p. 293.
5 Cf. e.g. the drawing *A Lion Lying Down*, Paris, Musée du Louvre, Département des Arts graphiques; Berlin/Amsterdam/London 1991, no. 26.
6 Hamburger Kunsthalle online (A. Stefes).
7 See Weimar 2011, no. 38.

30.1 FERDINAND BOL

(Dordrecht 1616–1680 Amsterdam)

The Prophet of Bethel

c. 1645–50
Pen and brown ink, brush and brown wash on yellowish paper, 17.4 × 23.9 cm
Museum der bildenden Künste Leipzig, Graphische Sammlung, inv. NI. 3006 b/1
Lit.: Valentiner 1934, vol. 1, p. X; Sumowski, 1979–92, vol. 1, no. 254; Leipzig 1990, no. 46.

30.2 ERNST GOTTLOB

(Glogau 1744–1796 Leipzig)

The Prophet of Bethel (after Ferdinand Bol)

c. 1770
LE PROPHETE DE BETH EL.
Le Dessin original de Rembrand, imite et Dedié à Monsieur le Prince, Peintre et Membre de l'Academie Royàle de Peinture et de Sculpture de Paris. / Tiré de la Collection de Monsieur Winckler à Leipzig / Par son tres humble Serviteur E. C. Gottlob à Leipzig.
Aquatint, 24.2 × 29.5 cm
Kunstsammlungen der Veste Coburg, inv. IV, 428,1
Lit.: Coburg/Aachen 2007, pp. 247–54, fig. 176.

The drawing *The Prophet of Bethel* from the collection of the Leipzig art collector Gottfried Winckler (1731–1795) was considered by him to be a work by Rembrandt.[1] Comparison with the drawing of St Jerome (cat. 29.1), which is securely attributed to Rembrandt, shows that the draughtsman emulated Rembrandt's painterly washes to suggest a landscape with strong contrasts of light and dark. Valentiner attributed the drawing to Ferdinand Bol, who followed his teacher's style closely, but with less attention to detail and often with more summary strokes and large areas of ink. Nevertheless, the southern, light-flooded atmosphere is evocatively captured with nuanced washes. Rendered in fine lines as in Rembrandt's work, the outlines of the vegetation appear blurred, creating the illusion of distance. The stylistic similarity between Rembrandt's drawings and those of his students is a consequence of his teaching, in which students varied drawings by the master.[2] Valentiner noted that the composition of the Leipzig sheet was echoed with altered figures (for example, the standing prophet was replaced by Minerva) in a drawing in Rembrandt's workshop, which was presumably corrected by the teacher.[3]

The drawing, which Sumowski dates to the second half of the 1640s, could have been made from around 1645 on. Drawings by Bol from the mid-1640s are stylistically comparable. Examples include the drawings *Tobias Frightened by the Fish* (c. 1643–5, Staatliche Museen zu Berlin, Kupferstichkabinett, KdZ 4238), in which the architecture of the background is indicated by thin, loose lines, and *Tobias Healing His Father's Blindness* (c. 1645, Staatliche Museen zu Berlin, Kupferstichkabinett, KdZ 4236), with its dramatic, high-contrast lighting.[4] It is typical of Bol that he was still drawing in his teacher's style a number of years after leaving Rembrandt's workshop, where he was active from around 1636 to 1640.[5]

The sheet illustrates the story from 1 Kings 13:14–18 about the meeting of two prophets at Bethel near Jerusalem. While one of them follows the old ritual, the other – shown seated in the drawing – is a 'man of God'. The standing prophet invites him to return with him to Bethel for a meal. He refuses, saying that God has forbidden him to do so. But the old prophet lies to him, pretending to be authorised by God

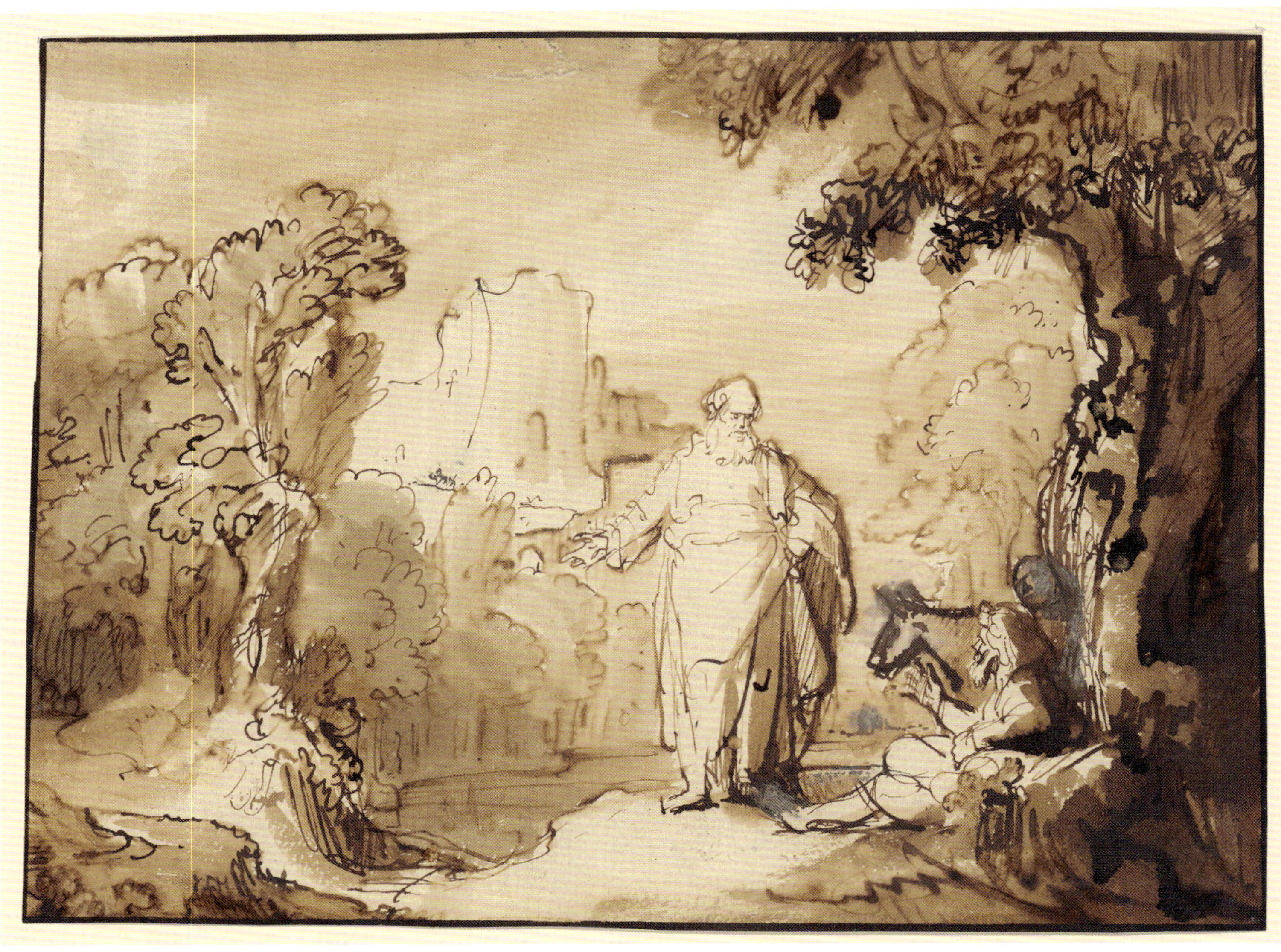

30.1

to make the invitation, so that the traveller goes back with him and eats the meal. As punishment for his disobedience to God and his gullibility, he is later killed by a lion. Bol stages the dialogue between the two men primarily through their spatial juxtaposition and the movement of their hands as an expression of their conversation, as he had learned from Rembrandt (cf. cat. 11). Ernst Gottlob reproduced the sheet in aquatint around 1770 (cat. 30.2). His teacher Oeser also made a copy after a drawing in the Winckler collection that was attributed to Rembrandt at the time (cat. 18.2). Around 1770, the aquatint technique, which was particularly suited to reproducing wash drawings, was still relatively new. One of its pioneers was the French painter and printmaker Jean-Baptiste Le Prince (1734–1781).[6] In Leipzig, the young artists Johann Carl Friedrich Dauthe (1749–1816) and Ernst Gottlob emulated the Frenchman under the guidance of Oeser. JN/JG

1 See the essay by Sven Pabstmann in this catalogue, p. 81.
2 See the essay by Jan Nicolaisen in this catalogue, p. 23.
3 Valentiner 1934, vol. 1, p. IX.
4 Berlin 2018, nos. 10, 11.
5 See Schatborn 2017, pp. 192–6.
6 See Rebel 1981, pp. 54–8.

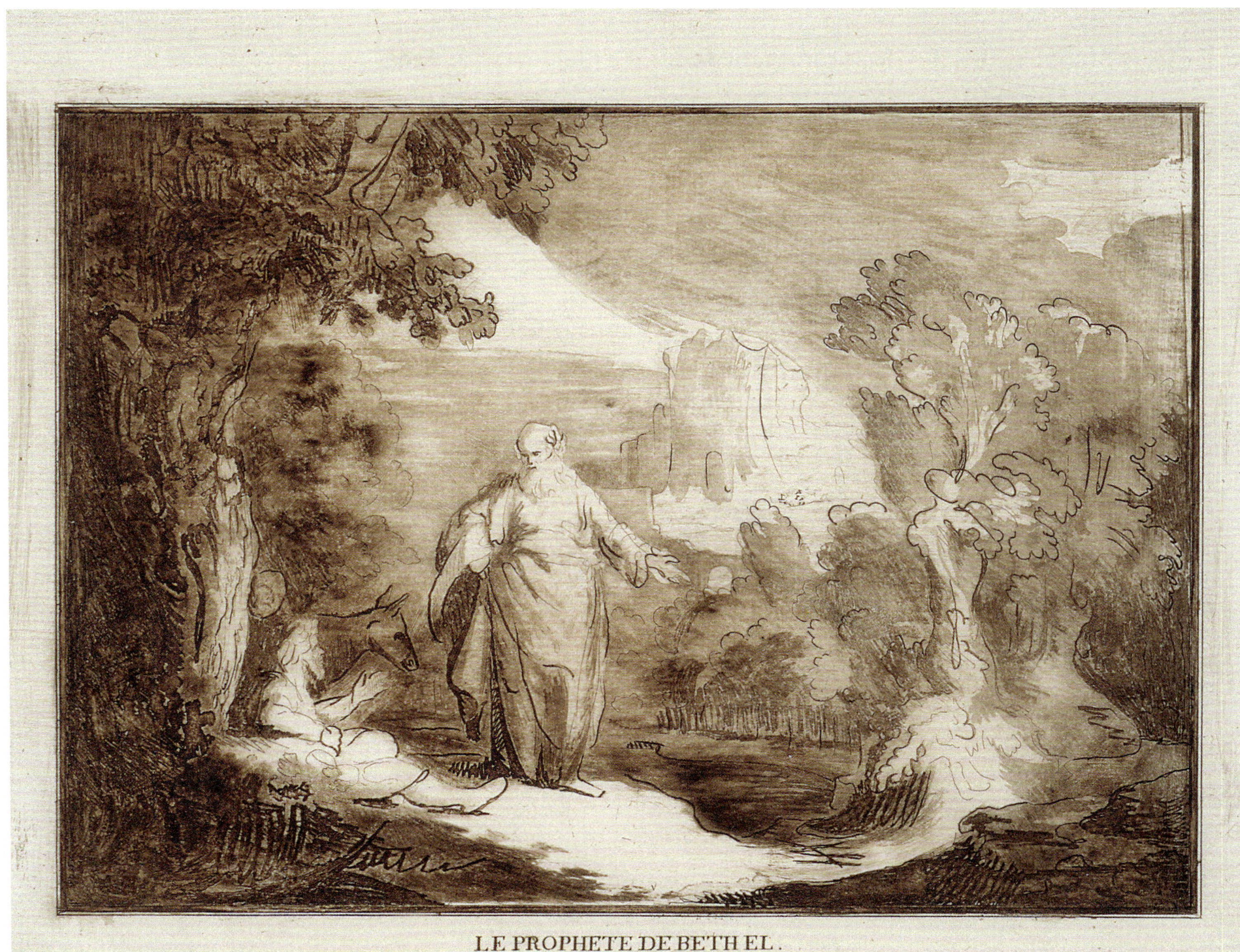
LE PROPHETE DE BETH EL.
Le Dessin original de Rembrand, imite et
Dedie à Monsieur le Prince, Peintre et Membre
de l'Academie Royale de Peinture et de Sculpture de Paris.
Tiré de la Collection de
Monsieur Winckler à Leipzig.
Par son tres humble Serviteur
E. C. Gottlob à Leipzig.

30.2

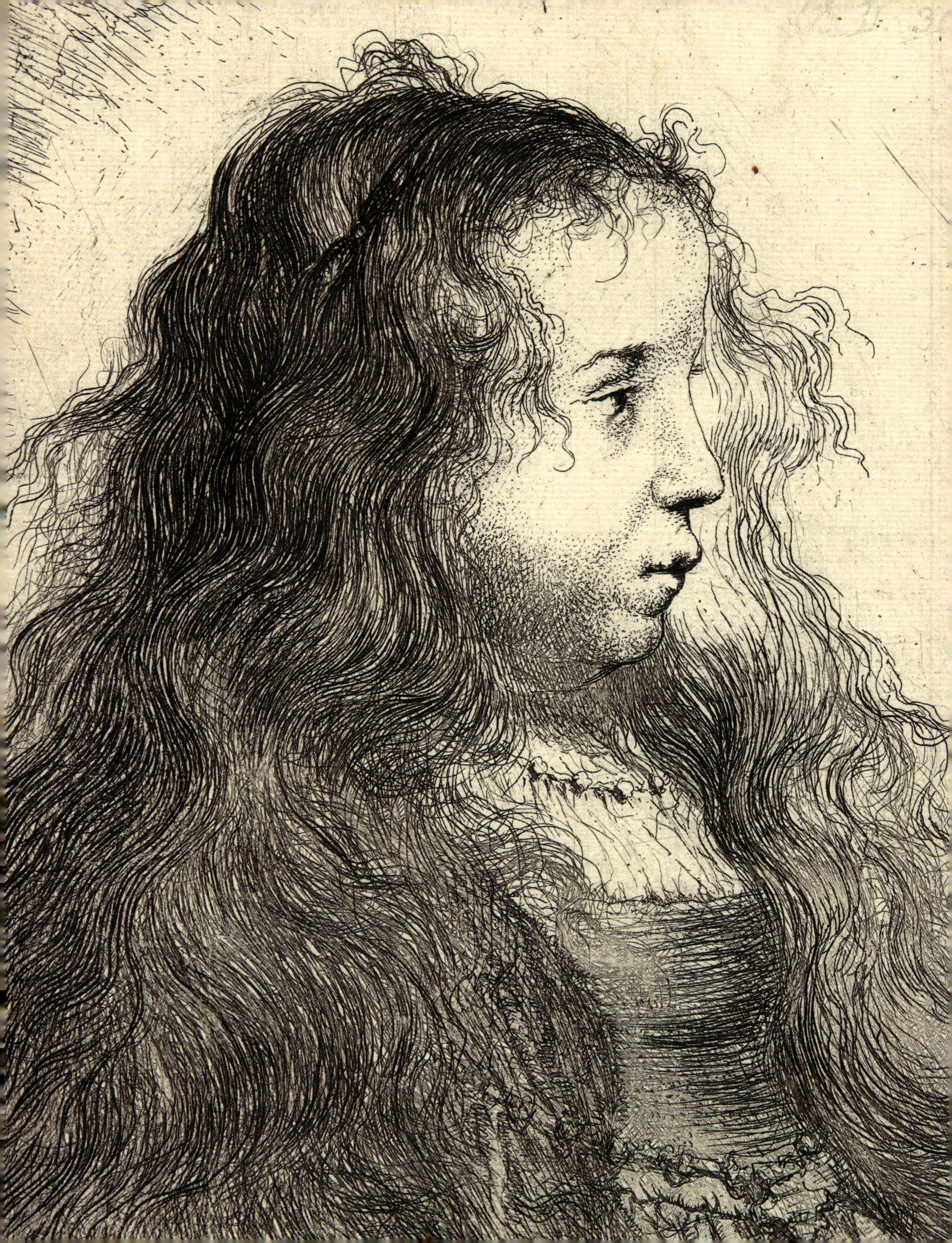

DISCOVERING THE FACE

BETWEEN TRONIE AND PORTRAIT

31.1 REMBRANDT

Study of an Old Man with an Open Book

c. 1627–8
Black and red chalk, lead white on reddish washed paper, 29.6 × 21.1 cm
Staatliche Museen zu Berlin, Kupferstichkabinett, inv. KdZ 5284
Lit.: Leiden 1991, p. 64; Berlin 2006, no. 1; Schnackenburg 2016, p. 108; Leiden/Oxford 2019, pp. 60f.

31.2 JAN LIEVENS

(Leiden 1607–1674 Amsterdam)

Old Man Reading

c. 1628–9
Pen and brown and black ink, brush and grey and black wash, over preliminary drawing in red chalk, white opaque paint, 33.6 × 27.4 cm
Paris, Musée du Louvre, Département des Arts graphiques, inv. 22729
Lit.: Sumowski 1979–92, vol. 7, no. 1631x; Washington/Milwaukee/Amsterdam 2008, no. 94; Schnackenburg 2016, no. 83; Abu Dhabi 2019, no. 39.

31.3 JAN LIEVENS

Head of a Bearded Old Man

c. 1629
Red chalk, 16.6 × 13.4 cm
Hessisches Landesmuseum Darmstadt, inv. AE 672
Lit.: Sumowski 1979–92, vol. 7, no. 1643x; Darmstadt 1998, no. 30; Schnackenburg 2016, no. 110; Leiden/Oxford 2019, p. 68.

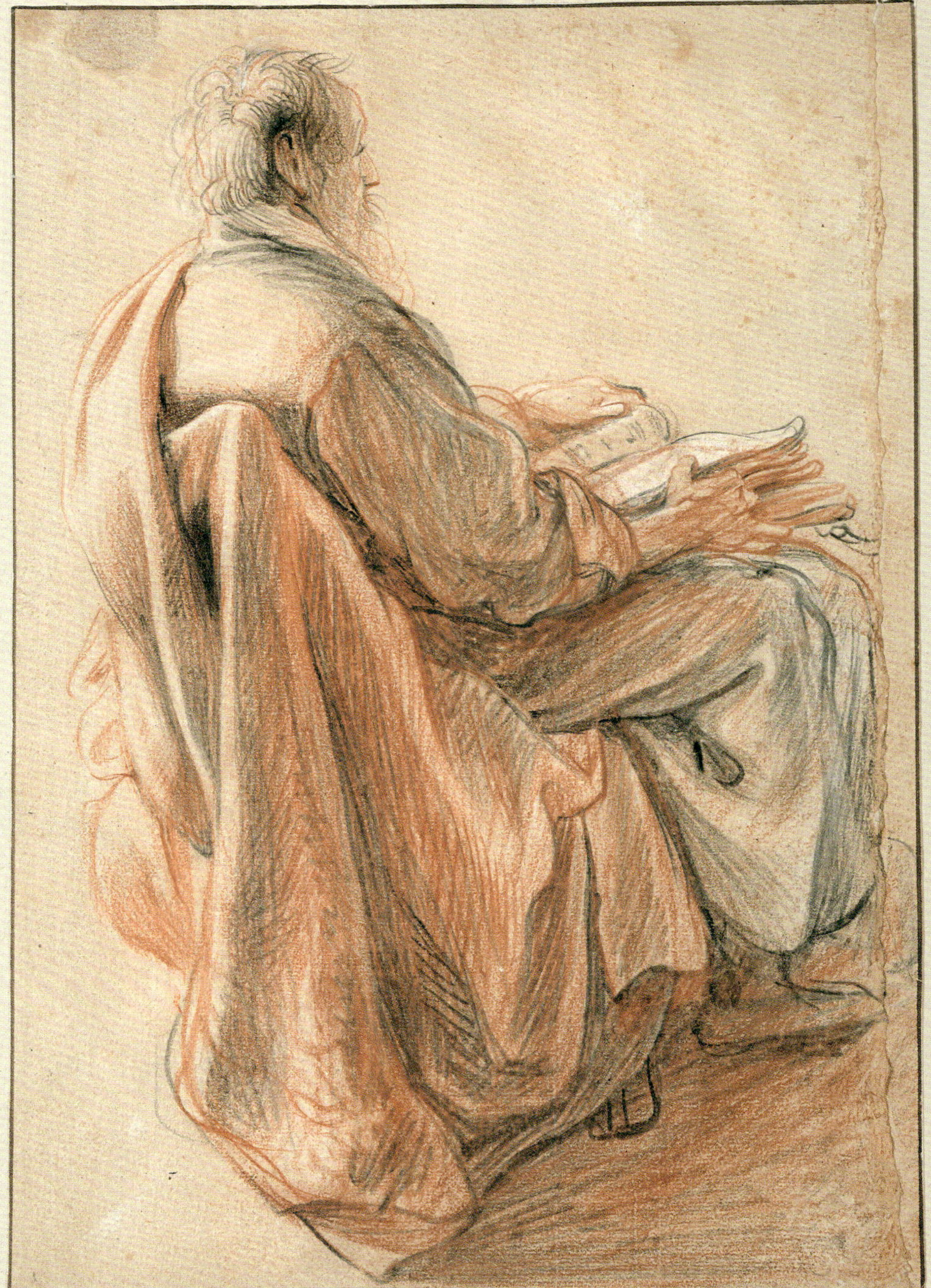

31.1

In the second half of the 1620s, Rembrandt and Lievens seem to have competed to see who could depict the most expressive heads of old men. They developed scenic narrative pictures from tronies by adding the special activity of reading, thinking or writing, evoking the expression of a spiritualised figure as a symbol of religious faith. The combination of male figures of proverbial biblical age with a book was suitable for depicting personages such as apostles.[1] The appeal of this motif in the university town of Leiden, where books were highly prized, corresponds to the still lifes with books that were popular there at the time.[2]

The three drawings illustrate the stylistic affinity between the artists during this period, both of whom combine red and black chalks with bold washes and white

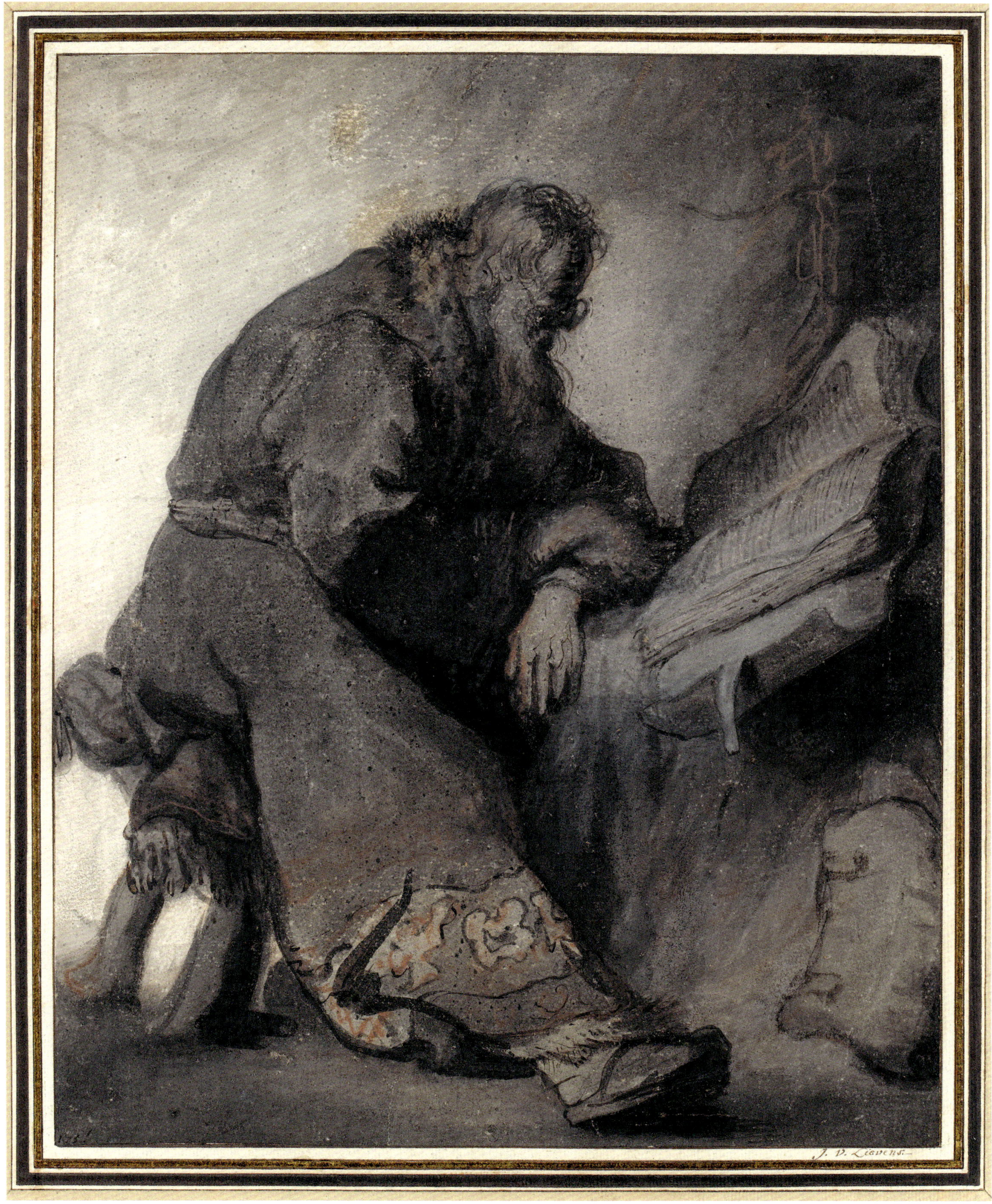

31.2

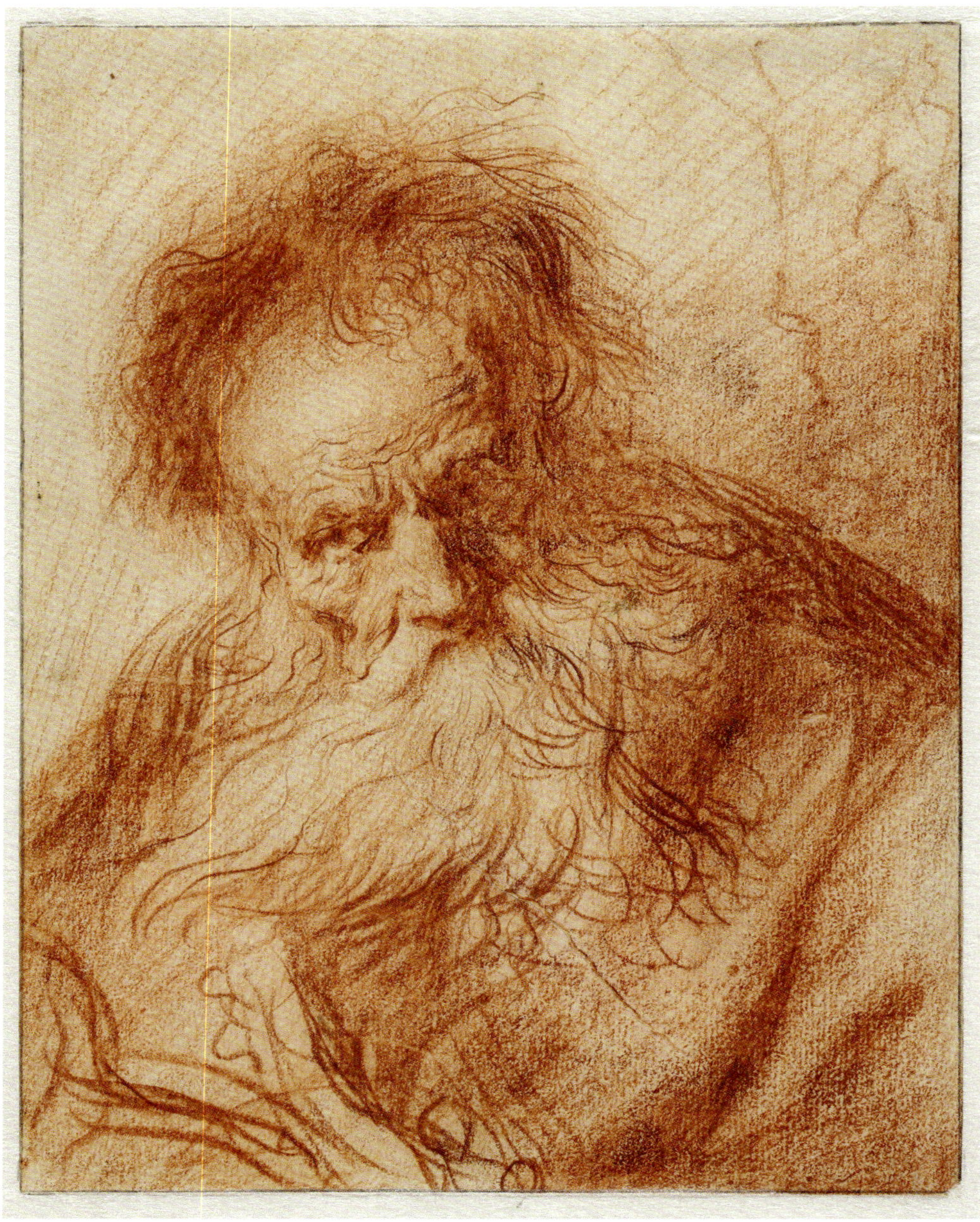

31.3

heightening to achieve decidedly painterly effects. On the one hand, these parallels suggest that they worked closely together in Leiden, even competitively, presumably in a shared studio, and were therefore familiar with each other's drawings. On the other hand, the similarities can also be traced back to the shared model of Pieter Lastman's drawings.[3]

The Berlin Rembrandt drawing (cat. 31.1) is a preliminary study for the figure of St Peter in the 1628 painting *Two Old Men Disputing*, also known as *Peter and Paul in Conversation* (Melbourne, National Gallery of Victoria). The apostle holds his fingers as a bookmark between the pages of the open book, the contents of which he is discussing with Paul. The situation of a dialogue, which interested the painter as a scenic interaction between the two learned men, is brought to life by the figure seen from behind turning towards his counterpart. The painting is executed in the chiaroscuro style typical of many of Rembrandt's works from this period, influenced by Utrecht Caravaggism. The drawing was made from a model, whom Rembrandt positioned in such a way as to be able to study the incidence of light on the garment in detail. This lighting was reproduced in the painting with only minor alterations.

The Darmstadt drawing (cat. 31.3) was made in preparation for the head in the painting *Old Scholar between Books* (New York, The Leiden Collection).[4] In contrast to the sculptural precision of Rembrandt's study, both of Lievens' drawings appear slightly more summarised and decorative, for example in the depiction of the drapery. Nevertheless, in the Darmstadt drawing the old man's furrowed face, as well as his head and beard, are rendered with great care, full of drama and temperament. It may have been based on the same model used by Lievens a few years later to paint the Leipzig *Bust of an Old Man* (cat. 34.4). The lively graphic suggestion of the beard with short and long strokes, the highlight on the tall forehead, the posture of the head and the indication of the cloak are similar.

The rather large sheet in the Louvre (cat. 31.2) belongs to a group of early drawings made by Lievens between 1625 and 1628–9 that are characterised by an experimental nature: as Olivia Savatier Sjöholm explains, Lievens tested bold, dark washes in different hues over a pencil or red chalk sketch.[5] His aim was to create an effect both painterly and dramatic. The brightly lit background is striking and similar to Rembrandt's Nuremberg painting (cat. 32.1), once again demonstrating the affinity between the two artists. Stylistically comparable is an early preparatory drawing for Rembrandt's etching of *Saint Paul*

(Bartsch 149).[6] The orientalising hem of the cloak is a recurring decorative motif in Lievens's work, evoking an historical era long past.[7] Lievens is primarily interested in suggesting the monumentality of the figure and the large tome, whereas in the Berlin drawing Rembrandt, in addition to studying the drapery, emphasises the scenic relationship to the opposite figure through the apostle's posture and body language. Rembrandt's students also used old men as models for tronies or religious paintings, as shown in a drawing attributed to Samuel van Hoogstraten.[8] In the early 1650s, Van Hoogstraten used a street beggar as a model for a painting in Vienna, *The Denial of Peter*.[9] JN

1 Bauch already pointed to the influence of Jacob de Gheyn III as a model, for example his 1616 etching *The Philosopher*; see Bauch 1960, p. 144, fig. 108.
2 Examples include Jan Davidsz. de Heem, *Vanitas Still Life*, 1628, Museum der bildenden Künste Leipzig; Jan Lievens, *Still Life with Books*, c. 1632, Amsterdam, Rijksmuseum; Jan Lievens, *Still Life with Books, Writing Utensils and Small Sculptures*, c. 1629, Munich, Bayerische Staatsgemäldesammlungen; cf. Schnackenburg 2016, nos. 112, 244.
3 Amsterdam 1991, p. 135; Berlin 2006, p. 26; Leiden/Oxford 2019, pp. 60f.
4 Schnackenburg 2016, no. 111.
5 Abu Dhabi 2019, p. 45.
6 Rembrandt, *Saint Paul*, c. 1627, Paris, Musée du Louvre, Département des Arts graphiques, inv. 22985; cf. Leiden 1991, p. 71; Abu Dhabi 2019, p. 45.
7 Schnackenburg 2016, p. 268.
8 Samuel van Hoogstraten (attributed), *A Pupil Painting an Old Man*, pen and brown ink, brush and brown wash, 9.1 × 13.9 cm, Paris, Fondation Custodia, inv. 5682; Schatborn 2010b, no. 100.
9 Hoogstraten 1678, pp. 113f.; Schatborn 2010b, vol. 1, p. 251.

32.1 REMBRANDT

St Paul at His Writing Desk

c. 1629–30
Panel, 47.2 × 38.6 cm
Nuremberg, Germanisches Nationalmuseum, inv. Gm 392
Lit.: Corpus 1982–2015, vol. 1, A 26; Nuremberg 1995, no. 92; Kassel/Amsterdam 2001, no. 32; Amsterdam 2006, pp. 49–51; Albers 2008, pp. 141–5; Nuremberg 2010, pp. 292f., no. 560, p. 448; Corpus 1982–2015, vol. 5, pp. 166f.; vol. 6, p. 494, no. 28; New York 2016, pp. 40f.

32.2 REMBRANDT WORKSHOP

Bearded Old Man

after 1633
Panel, 20 × 16.8 cm
Museum der bildenden Künste Leipzig, inv. G 804
Lit.: Corpus 1982–2015, vol. 1, C 25; Sumowski 1983–94, vol. 3, p. 1714; vol. 5, p. 3353; Nuremberg 1995, p. 192; Leipzig 2012, no. 270; Corpus 1982–2015, vol. 6, pp. 97, 498f.

32.3 REMBRANDT

Old Man in an Armchair

1652
Canvas, 111 × 88 cm
Signed and dated (upper right): f./1652
London, National Gallery, inv. 6274
Lit.: Bredius/Gerson 1969, no. 267; London 1991, vol. 1, pp. 376f., no. 6274; London 2006, no. 25; Wiesemann 2010, pp. 58f.; Wetering 2014, pp. 382–4.

32.4 REMBRANDT WORKSHOP (OR FOLLOWER)

Head of an Old Man

1650s (?)
Canvas, 60.2 × 49.2 cm
Later inscribed later (centre right): Rembrandt./f.1651
Maximilian Speck von Sternburg Foundation in the Museum der bildenden Künste Leipzig, inv. G1561
Lit.: Leipzig 1826, p. 36, no. 152; Sumowski 1983–94, vol. 4, pp. 2877, 2915; Leipzig 1996, pp. 24–6; Leipzig/Munich 1998, no. 1/70; Leipzig 2012, no. 272.

St Paul, once a fierce persecutor of the early Christian communities and later a convert and the most important missionary of Christianity, was depicted several times by Rembrandt. The Nuremberg painting shows the apostle deep in thought, sitting at a writing desk with an open tome; the oriental sword on the wall, a so-called yatagan, is a reminder of the bloody persecution of Christians.[1] In the Acts of the Apostles, Saul is said to have been 'breathing out murderous threats against the Lord's disciples' when he was surrounded by a heavenly light and blinded when he heard God's voice (Acts 9:1–15). Rembrandt's Caravaggesque lighting may recall this episode. The gleaming metal of the sword stands out against the plain, roughly plastered wall. Rembrandt was a passionate collector of historical weapons, which he used as props for history paintings. Prominently placed weapons appear a number of times in his early history paintings and those of his students (cats. 8, 9).[2]

Two sources of light – one coming from the top left, the other from a candle or lamp hidden behind the book – create a dramatic interplay of light and shadow. Areas almost completely in shadow contrast with

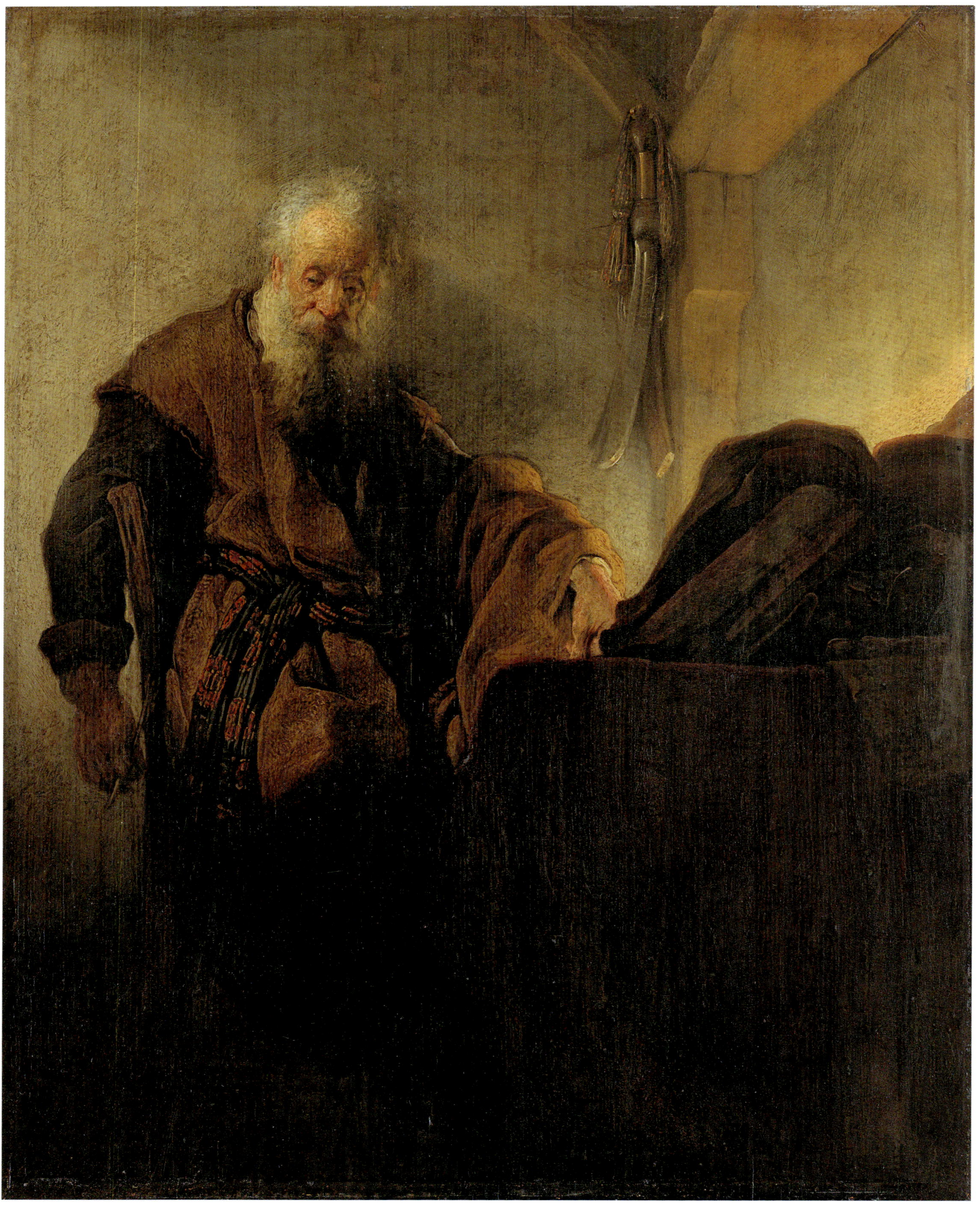

32.1

brightly illuminated motifs such as the apostle's forehead. The emphasis on the forehead expresses his spiritual importance as the author of the Epistles. In their early work, both Rembrandt and Jan Lievens repeatedly used the faces of old men to give biblical figures a special aura (cats. 31.1, 31.3). The artist depicted not only direct illumination but also reflected light on textiles and skin, with rich nuance and an impasto application of paint. Rembrandt's student, Samuel van Hoogstraten, described the compositional use of prominent areas of shadow ('schikschaduwen') as a characteristic of his teacher's art.[3]

Many years later, Rembrandt was still interested in the atmospheric staging of an old man's physiognomy and hands in alternating light and shadow. The London painting *Old Man in an Armchair* of 1652 (cat. 32.3) is not a portrait – no seventeenth-century patron would have allowed himself to be shown in such a pose – but a tronie. It is a representation of old age with the expression of a certain weariness and melancholy. The at times sketchy brushwork is all the more lively, building up the figure and the garment with loose, freely applied strokes. The open, rough style of painting is evident in the left hand and arm, which is only hinted at by the juxtaposition of brushstrokes. Rembrandt seems to be emulating 'sprezzatura', the loose painting style of the ItalianRenaissance. Scholars have also cited the model of Venetian painting, particularly that of Jacopo Tintoretto.[4] Other areas such as the face or the right hand are painted less sketchily. Because of these stylistic inconsistencies, the authenticity of the painting has been questioned since 1969.[5] Van de Wetering proposed a different interpretation in 2014, arguing that Rembrandt's first experiments with the rough painting style were at work here in the early 1650s. The medium of the tronie allowed the artist to take stylistic liberties that would have been unthinkable in a formal portrait. The strikingly loose painting style – similar to that of *Girl at a Window* (Stockholm, Nationalmuseum), painted the same year – seems to mark the beginning of Rembrandt's late style, which began in the 1650s. From this perspective, Rembrandt here appears as a searching, innovative artist, experimenting with different representational possibilities in *one* picture: the visualisation of a figure through a painting style that is both detailed and summary.

The physiognomies of the two old men in the paintings in Nuremberg and London occur multiple times in the work of Rembrandt and his circle – as shown, for example, by two tronies in Leipzig, which illustrate the copying and variation of characteristic head types in the workshop for purposes of teaching

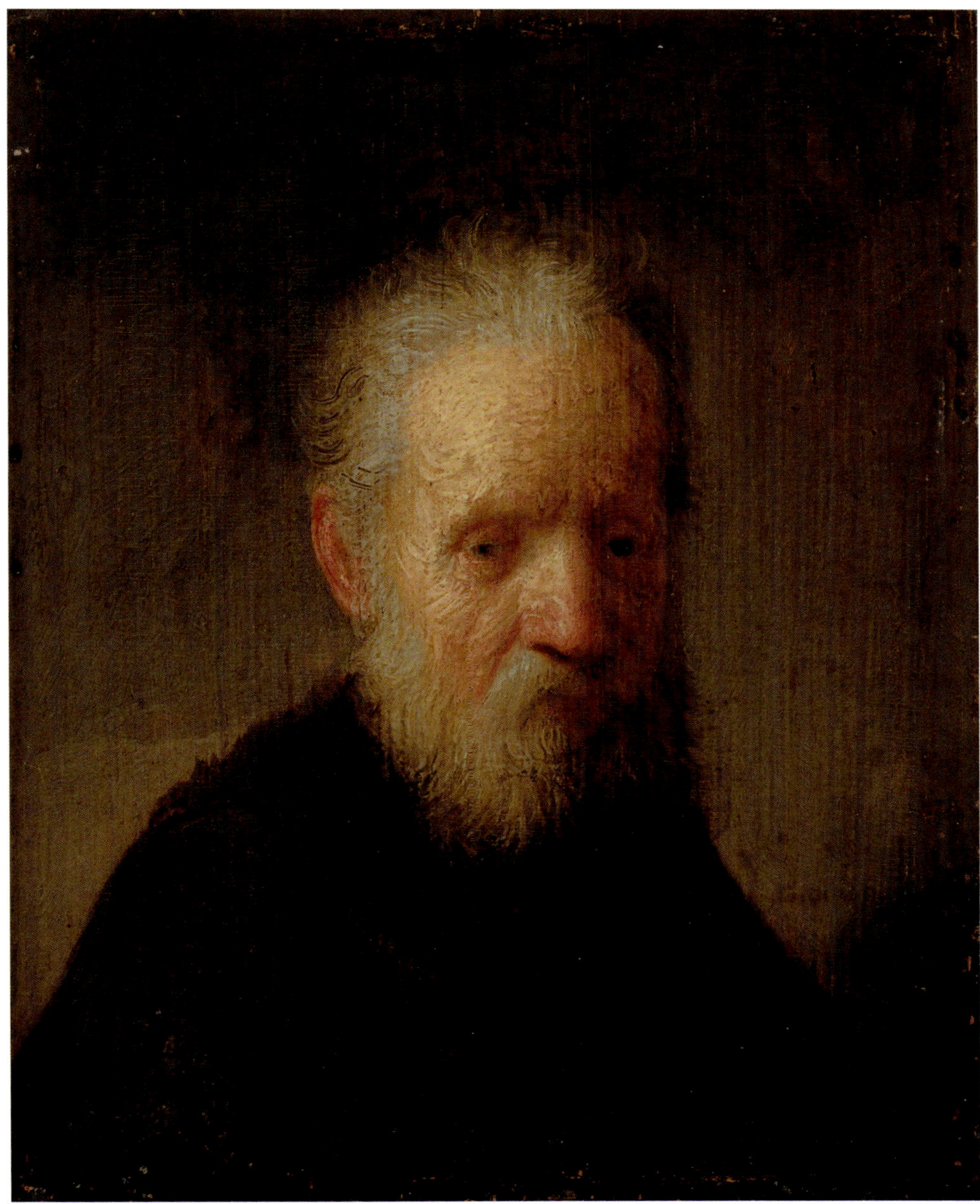

32.2

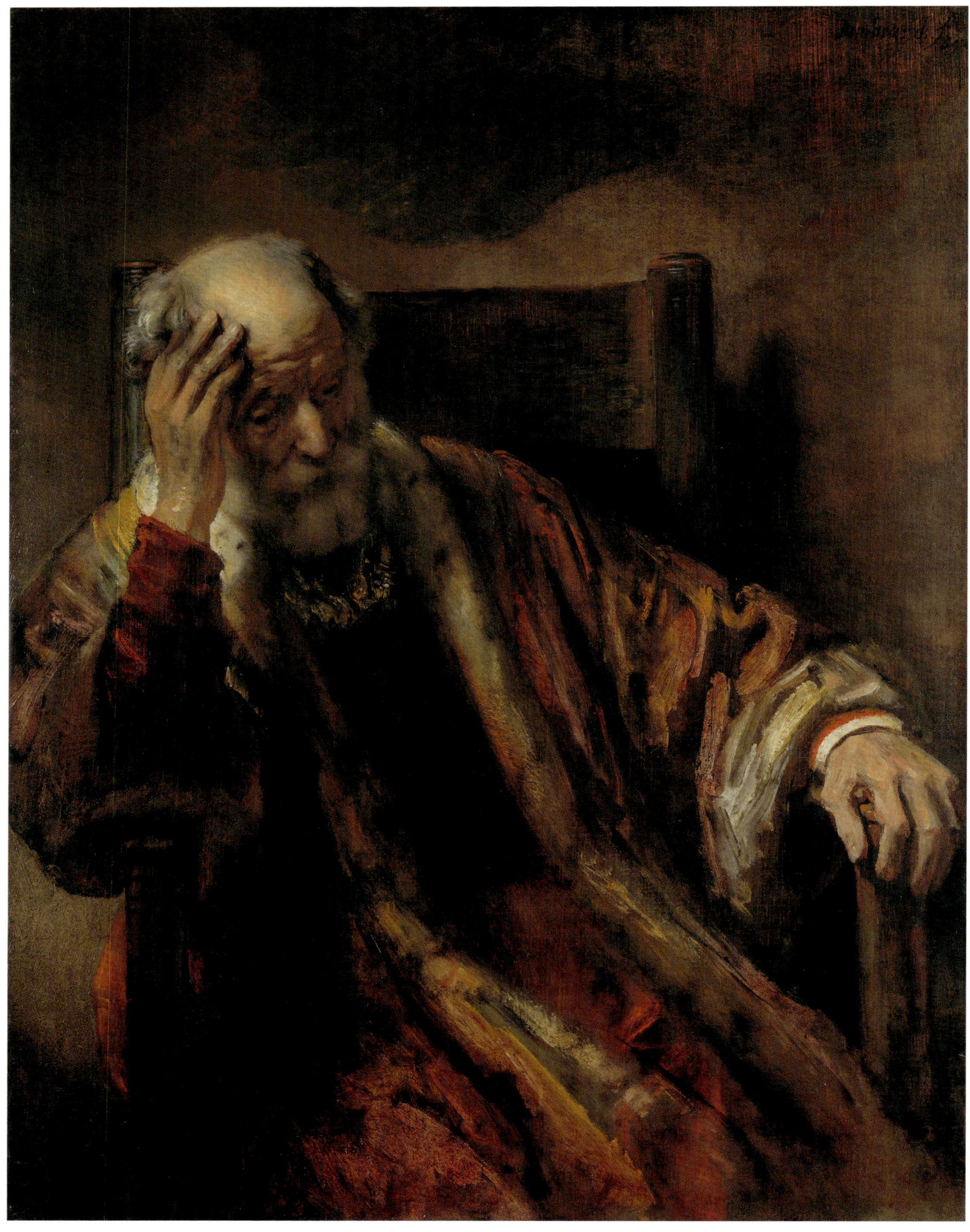

32.3

and probably also sale.[6] Students practised the convincing rendering of heads and faces, focusing on painting technique and lighting. The small-format Leipzig picture (cat. 32.2) is a detailed, true-to-scale copy of Rembrandt's *Tronie of an Old Man* (private collection), which shows the same model as the Nuremberg picture.[7] Following the teacher's example, the student scratched the hair into the fresh paint with the end of a brush. The painting also demonstrates how difficult it was to copy Rembrandt's impasto style, which he used to accentuate particularly light areas.

The Leipzig tronie *Head of an Old Man* (cat. 32.4) shows not only the same model as the London *Old Man in an Armchair*, but also a similarly impasto style of painting on the forehead to emphasise it in the light. The brown robe evokes a sense of softness and seems to merge with the dark background. It is uncertain whether the painting was created in Rembrandt's workshop or by a follower, but the painter certainly had access to studies from the workshop.[8] Tronies of old people enjoyed enduring popularity: the wrinkled faces of elderly people could symbolise a wide range of content, from exemplary wisdom to the transient *vanitas* of human life.[9] Max Speck acquired the painting with a later signature as a work by Rembrandt.[10] JN/JG

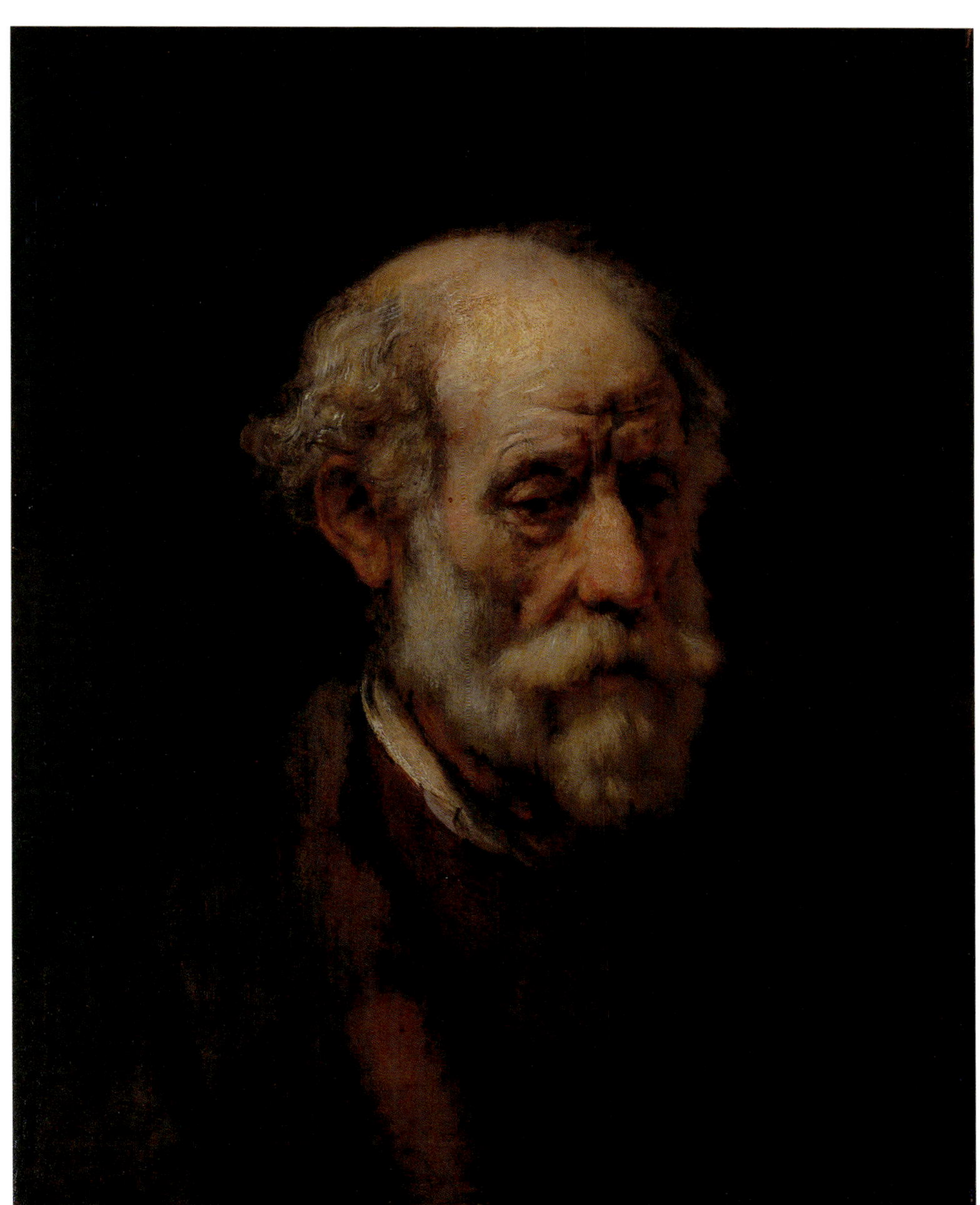

32.4

1 Nuremberg 1995, p. 192.
2 Kassel/Amsterdam 2001, p. 225.
3 Corpus 1982–2015, vol. 5, p. 167.
4 London 1991, p. 376; Wetering 2014, p. 384.
5 Bredius/Gerson 1969, no. 267; London 1991, p. 376.
6 See also the essay by Dagmar Hirschfelder in this catalogue.
7 Corpus 1982–2015, vol. 6, p. 97, no. 36.
8 Sumowski 1982–94, vol. 4, p. 2877; Leipzig 1996, p. 26; Leipzig 2012, p. 257.
9 Leipzig 2012, p. 257.
10 Leipzig 1826, no. 152, p. 36.

33.1 REMBRANDT

The Artist's Mother, Looking Down

1633
Etching, II (of III), 4.6 × 4.4 cm (sheet)
Signed and dated: Rembrandt. F. 1633
Museum der bildenden Künste Leipzig, Graphische Sammlung, inv. NI. 5802
Lit.: B. 351; NH 121; Leiden 2005, pp. 118–20.

33.2 GERRIT DOU

(Leiden 1613–1675 Leiden)

Old Woman with Spectacles, Reading a Newspaper

c. 1635
Panel (oval), 12.5 × 9 cm
Staatliche Kunstsammlungen Dresden, gal. no. 1719
Lit.: Dresden 2000, pp. 48f.; Leiden 2005, no. 21.

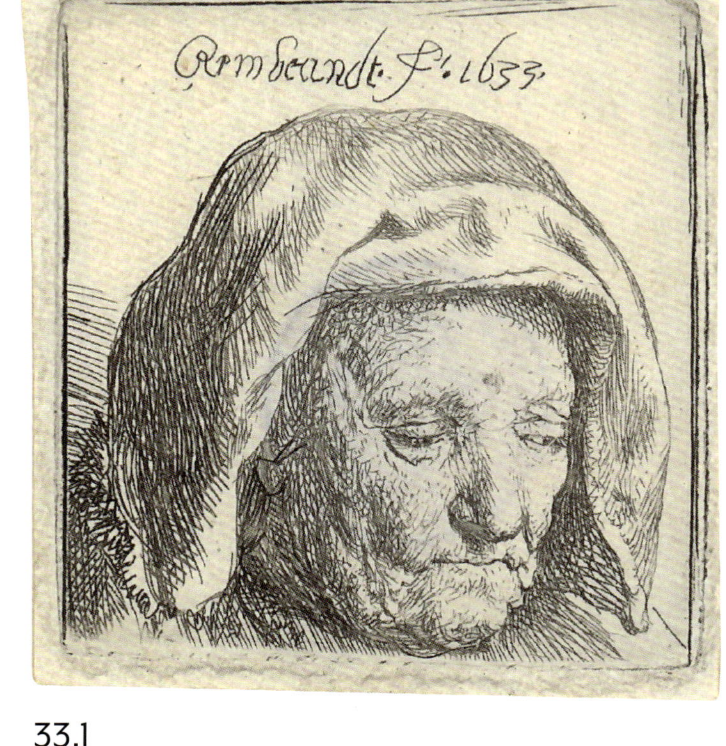

33.1

On 14 February 1628, at the age of 14, Gerrit Dou became the first student of Rembrandt, who was himself only 21 years old at the time.[1] Dou spent three years in Rembrandt's workshop. This period made a deep impression on his work, while at the same time early paintings such as *Old Woman with Spectacles* show how he emancipated himself from the influence of his teacher. An important aspect of his training was to copy and vary the character heads of old men and women created by Rembrandt at that time. Rembrandt's mother, Neeltgen Willemsdr. van Zuytbroek (c. 1568–1640), was probably the model for a number of his paintings and etchings between 1628 and 1633, including the small etching illustrated here (cat. 33.1).[2] Dou was probably not present at these sittings, but was certainly familiar with Rembrandt's paintings, from which he in turn developed his own pictorial ideas. These include the small Dresden painting (cat. 33.2), which shows the same model as Rembrandt's 1633 etching.

In Dou's work, the woman is engrossed in a printed pamphlet; the position of her head and her glasses emphasise her concentration as she reads. Dou adopted this motif from Rembrandt, who repeatedly depicted old women and men reading as an expression of piety and faith in early works such as the painting *Old Woman Reading (Prophetess Anna)* (cat. 7). The historicising costume of the old woman also varies the model of the teacher. Above all, however, it was Rembrandt's precise and delicate approach to painting during this period that influenced Dou. The representation of the velvety furred cloak and the light falling upon it follows the teacher's example. The young artist was particularly fond of the illusion of wrinkled, soft skin, which he brought to life with a very fine painting technique. This would become his trademark and transforms the small-scale picture into a precious miniature. With Rembrandt's etching, Dou had before him the formal experiment of a detailed representation on the smallest possible scale. In a personal touch, the old woman in the Dresden painting looks not at the Bible, but at a contemporary pamphlet, lending the scene a secular atmosphere. The juxtaposition of age and wealth represented by the gold chain has been interpreted as a remembrance of *vanitas*, the vanity and transience of all earthly life.[3] This seems unconvincing, however, as the woman's rapt attention imbues her with great vitality. Dou varied this head several times.[4]

From the 1679 inventory of the Amsterdam print dealer Clement de Jonghe, who owned many of Rembrandt's etching plates, we know that certain etchings were

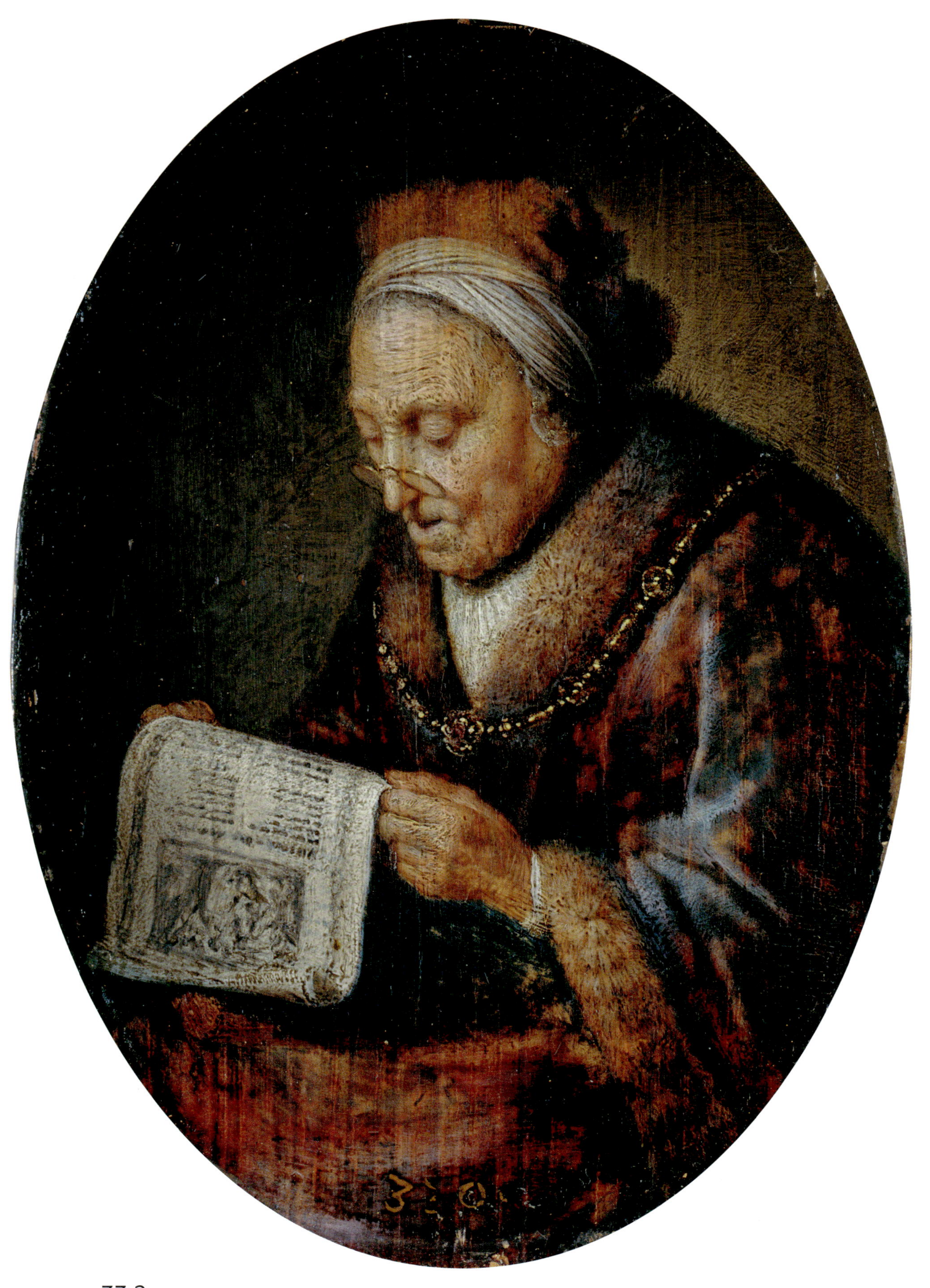

33.2

said to depict the artist's mother. These sheets were popular and were reprinted several times during the artist's lifetime.[5] Rembrandt also occasionally used this woman's features for the biblical figures in his images, such as the old prophetesses in the paintings from Hamburg and Amsterdam (cats. 4.1, 7). Rembrandt was thus part of a long tradition of artists since Albrecht Dürer who had depicted their parents.[6] He was certainly familiar with the head studies of old men and women that had been reproduced in drawings and engravings a generation earlier by Hendrick Goltzius (1558–1617) and Jacob de Gheyn II (1565–1629), which bear a striking resemblance in type and costume to his etchings of old women.[7] JN

1 Washington/London/The Hague 2000, p. 28.
2 Leiden 2005, p. 98.
3 Ibid., pp. 119f.
4 Cf. e.g. Gerrit Dou, *Old Woman with Fur Hat*, Staatliche Museen zu Berlin, Gemäldegalerie, inv. 847.
5 Leiden 2005, p. 21; Weimar 2011, p. 38.
6 Volker Manuth and Marieke de Winkel, 'De moeder van de kunstenaar: traditie, realiteit en verbeelding', in Leiden 2005, pp. 67–77.
7 I.Q. van Regteren Altena, *Jacques de Gheyn. Three Generations*, 3 vols., The Hague/Boston/London 1983, vol. 2, p. 124, no. 747; Hirschfelder 2008, pp. 69–71.

34.1 JAN LIEVENS

(Leiden 1607–1674 Amsterdam)

Boy with a Mask

Between 1626 and 1630
Panel, 57.4 × 43.8 cm
Cologne, LETTER Foundation
Lit.: E. Berckenhagen, *Antoine Pesne*, Berlin 1958, no. 504 (Pesne Workshop?); Bernd Ernsting, 'Realistik zwischen Leben und Tod – Die metamorphotische Maske. Zwei mysteriöse Gemälde von Jan Lievens', in *Wir sind Maske*, Kunsthistorisches Museum with the Museum für Völkerkunde and the Österreichisches Theatermuseum, Vienna 2009, no. VI.14; Schnackenburg 2016, no. 57.

34.2 JAN LIEVENS

Bust of a Girl with her Hair Down

c. 1632
Panel, 43.3 × 35 cm
Museum der bildenden Künste Leipzig, inv. G 1040
Lit.: Sumowski 1983–94, vol. 3, no. 1275; Melbourne/Canberra 1997, no. 34; Hirschfelder 2008, no. 285; Leipzig 2012, no. 193; Schnackenburg 2016, no. 237.

34.3 JAN LIEVENS

Bust of a Girl in Profile to Right

c. 1632
Etching, II (of II), 15.8 × 14.3 cm (sheet)
Monogrammed (lower right): IL [ligated]; (upper right, with publisher's address): Franc. van Wijngaerde excu
Braunschweig, Herzog Anton Ulrich-Museum, inv. J. Lievens AB 3.12
Lit.: B. 25; Hollstein 43; Washington/Milwaukee/Amsterdam 2008, no. 59; Nicolaisen 2014, pp. 90f.; Schnackenburg 2016, no. 239.

34.4 JAN LIEVENS

Bust of an Old Man

c. 1632
Panel, 53 × 40.5 cm
Monogrammed (lower left): IL.
Maximilian Speck von Sternburg Foundation in the Museum der bildenden Künste Leipzig, inv. G 1624
Lit.: Sumowski 1983–94, vol. 3, no. 1279; Leipzig/Munich 1998, no. I/71; Hirschfelder 2008, no. 310; Leipzig 2012, no. 194; Schnackenburg 2016, no. 235.

Praised by contemporaries for his talent even as a child, Jan Lievens led the way for Rembrandt in developing the tronie as an innovative pictorial genre in the 1620s. According to Hirschfelder, 'he gave the pioneering impetus for the production of tronies in Leiden'.[1] Rembrandt is known to have copied or varied four etchings of so-called Oriental heads after Lievens as late as 1635.[2] Lievens also produced tronies of children before Rembrandt.[3]

A stark example is the picture in the LETTER Foundation, which shows a boy holding the mask of a man in his hands, under whose peeling skin the complexion of old age can be seen (cat. 34.1). The smooth skin of the child contrasts with the face disfigured by death. It appears to be a grotesque mask of the kind used by actors on stage. The cheeks are theatrically made up, which in turn contrasts with the natural colouring of the boy's skin. Here, Lievens seems to be concerned with more than the idea of *vanitas*. He explores the contrast between appearance and reality in the sense of an artistic comparison, since the boy, rendered from the live model, presents a more truthful illusion than the artificial mask. In this respect, the tronie emphasises the virtuosity of realistic painting. The grotesque element may also have served as an opportunity to inspire

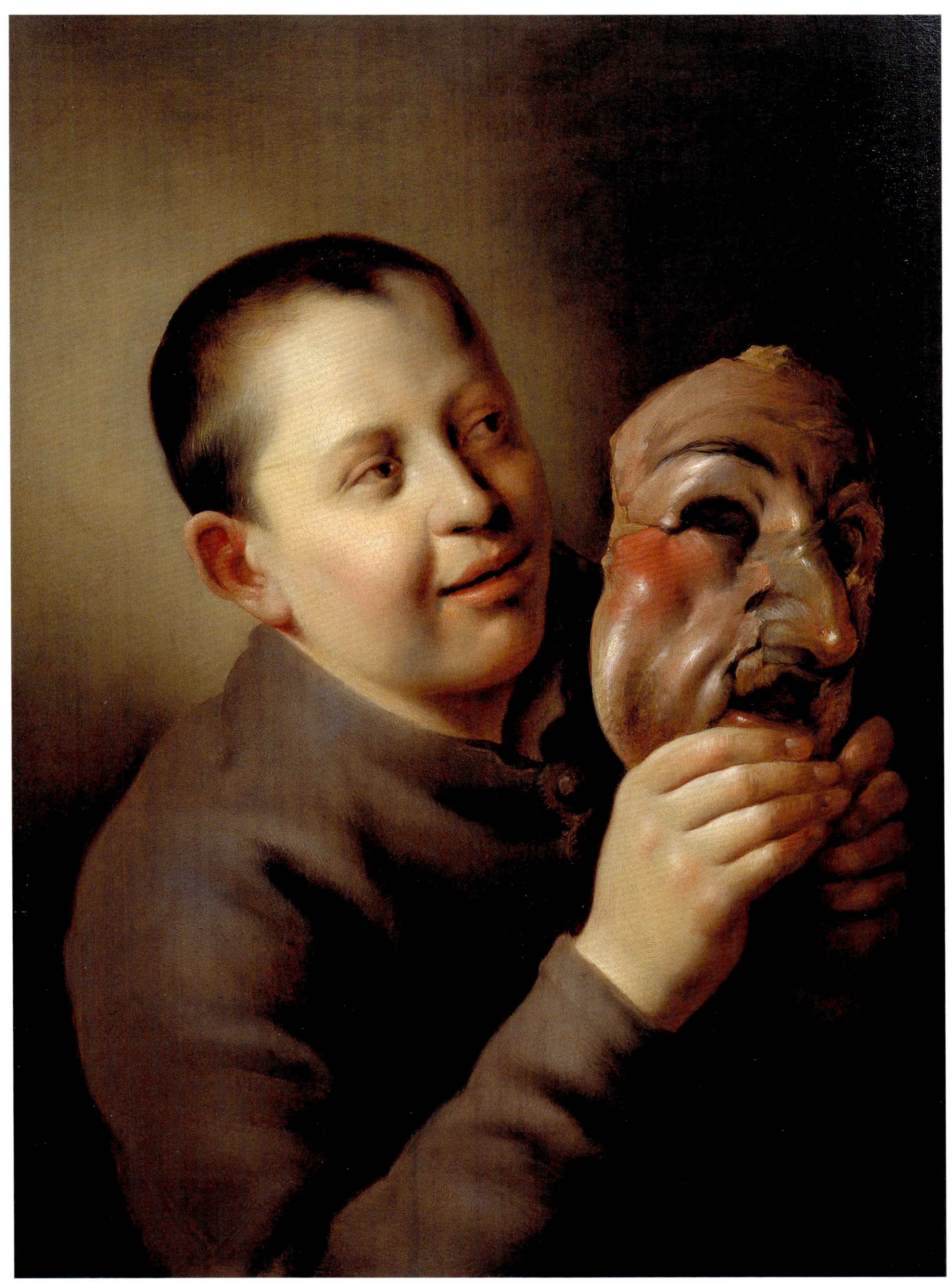

34.1

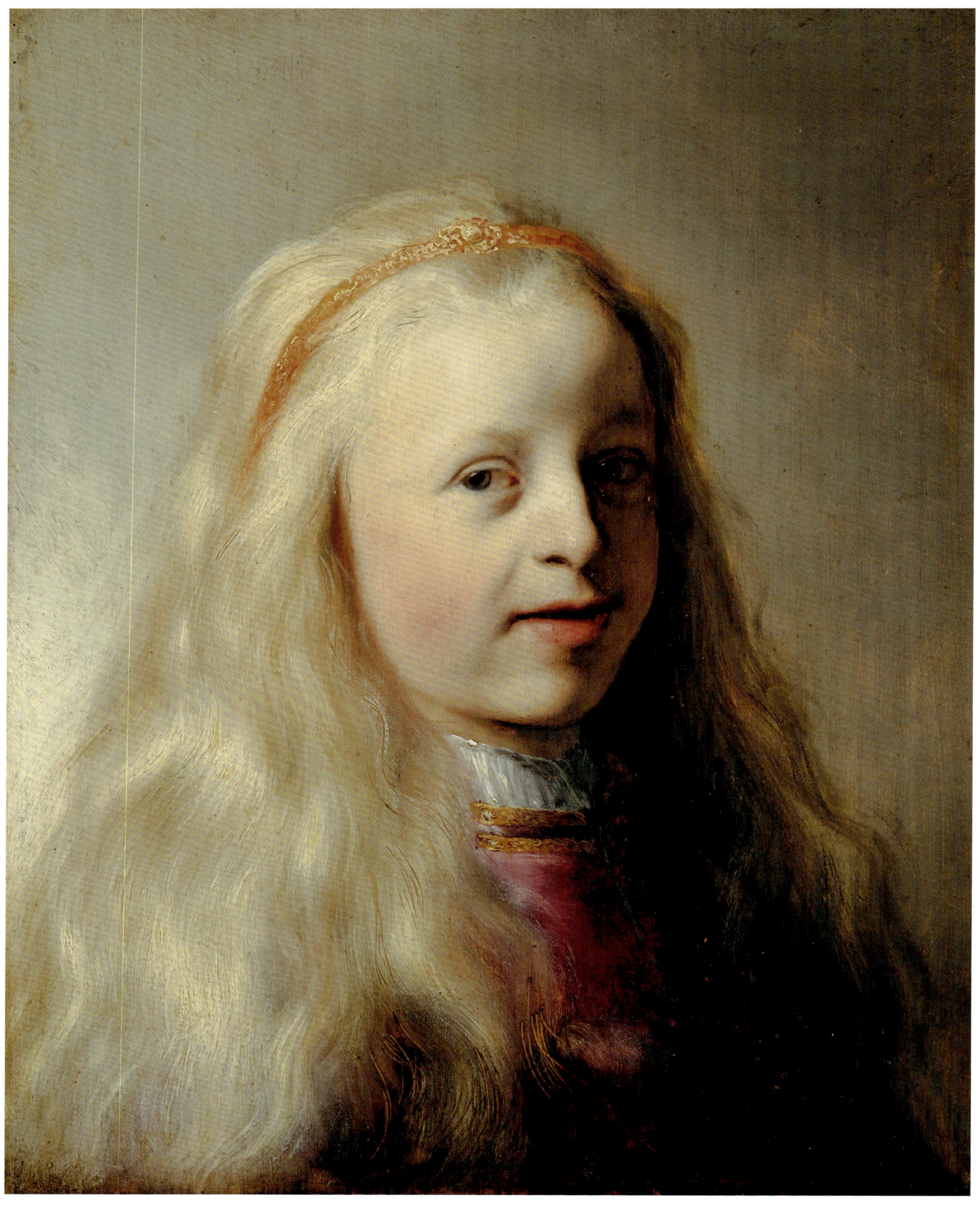

34.2

conversation among connoisseurs about these artistic issues. The boy's gaze, directed to the right, may hint at a pendant that has not survived. Stylistically, the painting probably dates from the second half of the 1620s.

The *Bust of a Girl with her Hair Down* (cat. 34.2) is a masterpiece by the artist, who was only 25 years old when he painted it. A young girl smiles at the viewer with an astonishingly self-confident, natural expression. She wears a historicising outer garment of red velvet with a gold-trimmed hem over a white shirt. The smoothness of her pale skin contrasts effectively with her more loosely painted hair, which cascades down her shoulders in magnificent abundance. The lively expression on her rosy-cheeked face is accentuated by her slightly open mouth, as if the girl were about to speak.

Lievens painted the unknown girl in profile a second time and seems to have been so taken with the head that he also made an etching of it (cat. 34.3).[4] Unlike the Leipzig painting, both of these images show the head in profile. In the three variations, Lievens presents the girl in different moods. In the second painting, the child wears a serious expression and appears more introverted. The etching shows an almost defiant expression with a closed mouth.

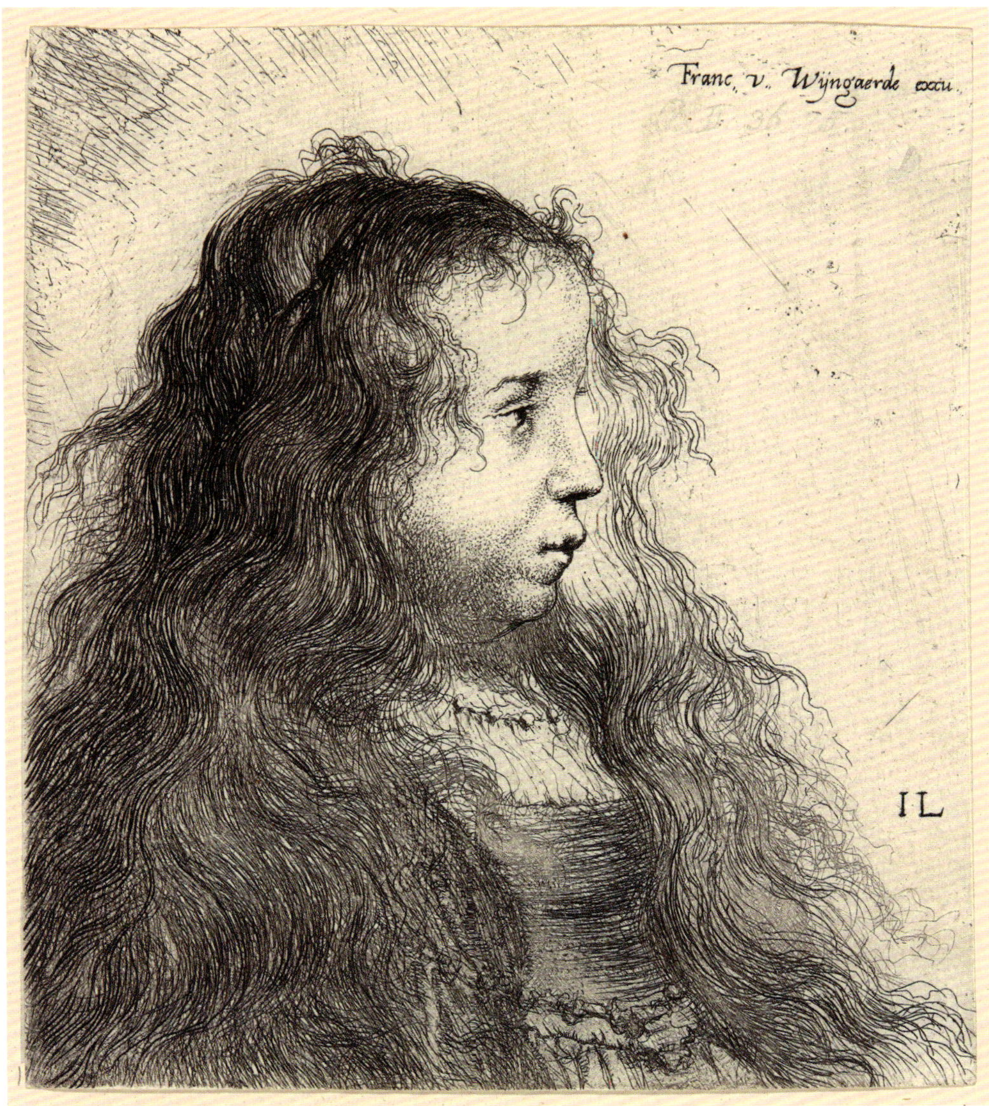

34.3

These psychological variations on a basic type speak to Lievens's interest in physiognomy as an expression of the 'gemoet'.[5] The head of a girl in Leipzig seems to reflect the joyful state of mind of a child who has not yet had the experience of old age. The latter is inscribed into the many heads of old men by Lievens and Rembrandt in the form of wrinkles, furrows, and a melancholy expression. Albert Blankert saw the tronie of an old woman as a possible counterpart to the girl's head in Leipzig.[6] In the seventeenth-century imagination, 'gemoet' meant the perceptions of the soul. It was an important category used by Dutch philosophers, physicians and art theorists to describe the inner and outer person. In contrast to sensory experiences, the impressions of the mind as mental sensations were also important for moral and religious feeling. In the early seventeenth century, Karel van Mander postulated the convincing reproduction of the emotions of laughing and crying as an artistic challenge.[7] The smooth forehead was considered a sign of light-heartedness.[8]

The artistic liberties Lievens takes with his tronies are remarkable. The hair is scratched into the still-wet oil paint with the end of a brush. This is particularly evident in the *Bust of an Old Man* (cat. 34.4). He also influenced the young Rembrandt with this technique during his Leiden period. On this artistic level, the differentiated and atmospheric characterisation of a state of mind in the tronie is on a par with a narrative history painting. Lievens's merit lies in having set this standard. The combination of a wealth of physiognomic and psychological observation, vivid execution, and an openness of meaning that stimulated the imagination made

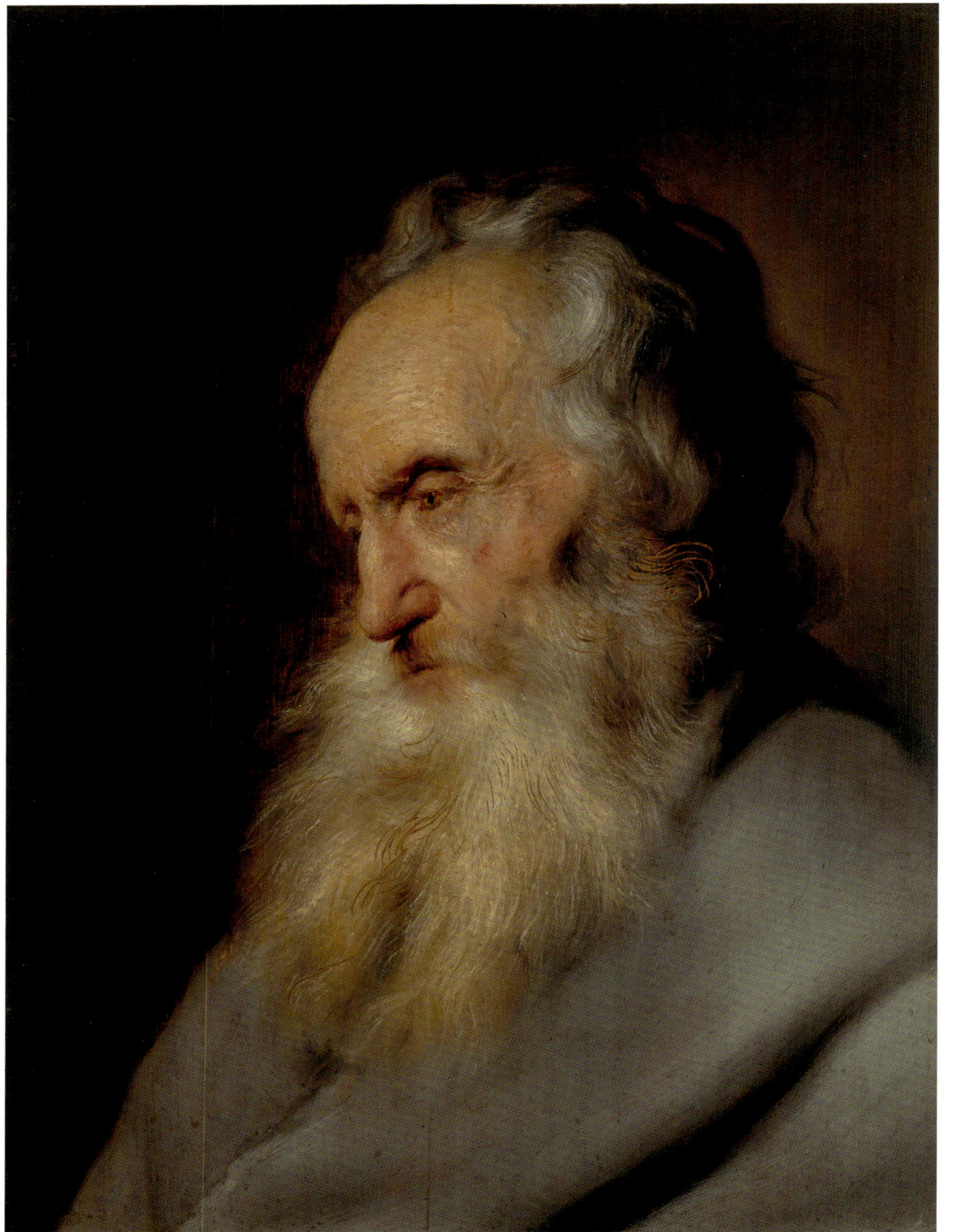

34.4

such tronies coveted collector's items. In all probability, the head of a girl in Leipzig is the same painting bequeathed by Jacob de Gheyn III to his cousin Jan Uytenbogaert in 1641 (cat. 38.3) and described as 'een jonck lachent meyskenstroinegen' (a tronie of young girl laughing).[9] JN

1 Hirschfelder 2008, p. 47.
2 Schnackenburg 2016, pp. 92–7.
3 Ibid., nos. 22–5, 34.
4 Jan Lievens, *Young Girl in Profile*, c. 1632, panel, 45 × 38.3 cm, Eijk and Rose-Marie van Otterloo Collection; Schnackenburg 2016, no. 238.
5 Cf. Nicolaisen 2013.
6 Melbourne/Canberra 1997, no. 35.
7 Cf. Mander/Miedema 1973, p. 169; Nicolaisen 2013, p. 92.
8 Mander/Miedema 1973, p. 166.
9 Hirschfelder 2008, p. 51.

35 REMBRANDT

Man in Oriental Costume

1632
Canvas, 152.7 × 111.1 cm
Signed and dated (lower right): RHL [monogrammed] van Rijn / 1632
New York, The Metropolitan Museum of Art, inv. 20.155.2
Lit.: Corpus 1982–2015, vol. 2, pp. 8, 26, 38, 144, 151–7, no. A48; New York 1995, no. 2; London/Amsterdam 2006, pp. 129f.; New York 2007, vol. 2, no. 142; Hirschfelder 2008, no. 405, p. 119; Corpus 1982–2015, vol. 6, no. 84; Paris 2016, no. 20; Leiden/Oxford 2019, no. 144.

Orientalising motifs were widespread in Dutch painting in the first half of the seventeenth century. The trade of the Dutch provinces with the Near and Far East forms the historical background for this interest. However, most artistic representations of the Orient, including Rembrandt's works, are characterised more by pictorial tradition, fantasy and cliché than by personal observation. So-called Orientals play a special role in the young Rembrandt's tronie paintings.[1] Based on paintings by Lastman and Rubens, who depicted Oriental rulers in strikingly foreign garments and turbans in biblical stories such as the *Adoration of the Magi*, Rembrandt created monumental standing figures in drawings and paintings.[2] As early as 1628, Jan Lievens painted the large-scale *Old*

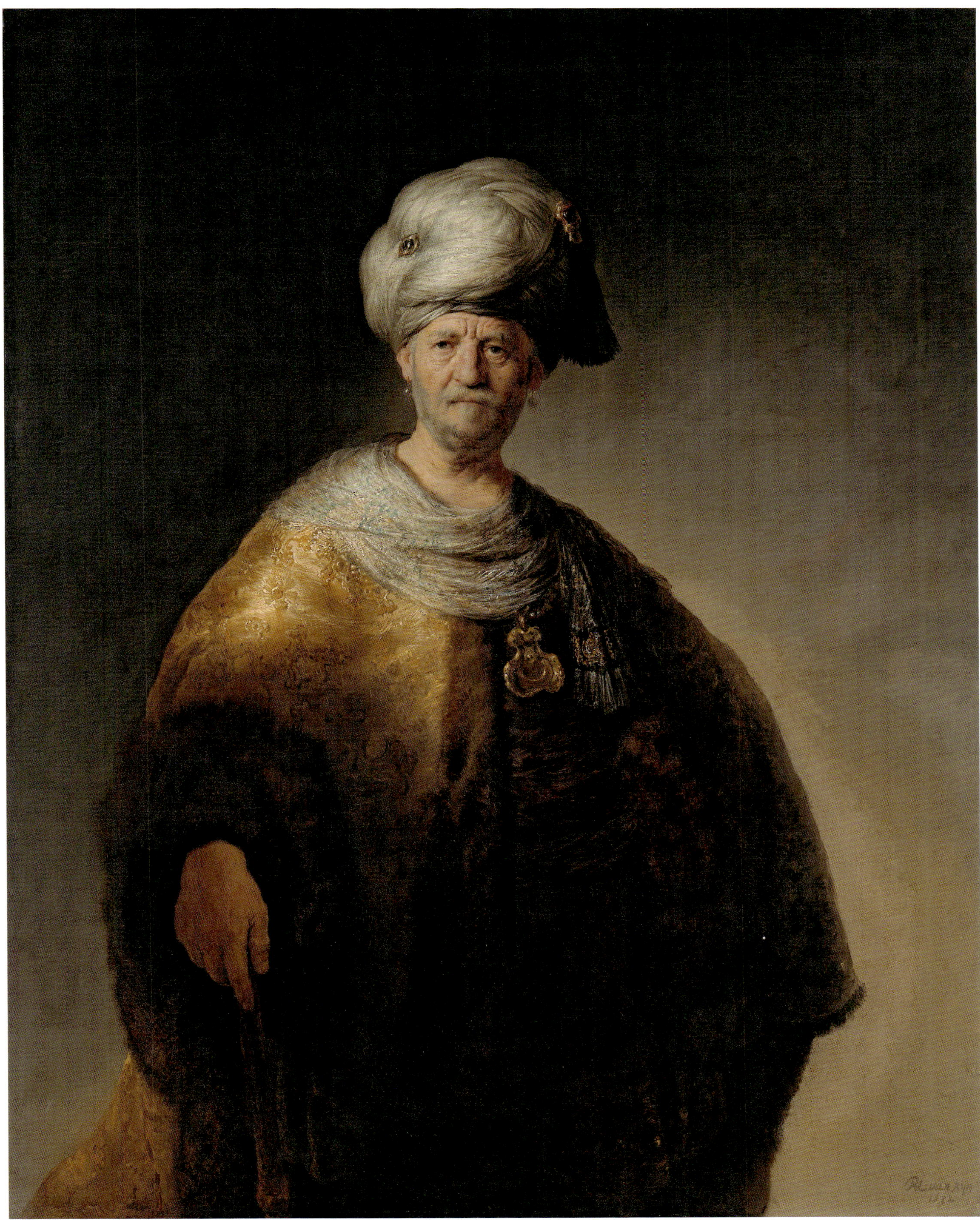

35

Man in Oriental Costume (Potsdam, Stiftung Preußische Schlösser und Gärten, canvas, 135 × 100.5 cm), which is recognisably similar to the New York painting in terms of composition and lighting and which probably inspired Rembrandt's version.[3]

Rembrandt depicts a dignitary, marked by age but imposing in his overall appearance. The costume, which includes a white damask turban with gold-set pearls, earrings, a shawl and a fur-trimmed robe with a golden sheen as well as a golden crescent pendant, suggests a Turkish origin. In the 1729 auction catalogue of Govert Looten's collection, the painting was described as 'Een Turkse Vorst of Primo Vezier' (A Turkish Prince or Primo Vizier).[4] The sumptuous costume provided Rembrandt with an opportunity for the virtuosic rendering of various fabrics in predominantly warm tones with nuanced transitions and dramatic lighting effects. Cooler colours, such as the white of the turban, glow against the darkness of the background.

The varying degrees of painterly execution are striking, ranging from delicate precision to summary suggestion in both shaded and illuminated areas. Here, the 26-year-old artist demonstrates his technical skill. The garment's dazzling colour was the antithesis of the clothing worn by Amsterdam's urban elite, who dressed and had themselves portrayed in elegant black. Scholars have noted the similarity to the early portraits of the Amsterdam period (*Portrait of Nicolaes Ruts*, 1631, New York, The Frick Collection; *Portrait of Joris de Caullery*, 1632, San Francisco, M. H. de Young Memorial Museum). Walter Liedtke has pointed out that not only the monumental scale, but also the lighting is similar to that of the portraits.[5] The painting of the *Man in Oriental Costume* may have originally belonged to Marten Looten – an ancestor of Govert Looten (1668–1772) – whose portrait Rembrandt also painted in 1632 (Los Angeles County Museum of Art).[6] The works were produced during Rembrandt's collaboration with the art dealer Uylenburgh, who arranged lucrative commissions for the young painter from wealthy collectors.

With the large-scale, three-quarter-length figure, Rembrandt gave the young genre of the tronie a monumental format in contrast to previous, mostly small-scale tronies that focussed on the head. It is reasonable to assume that the large dimensions were also linked to the young painter's artistic ambition to ennoble the genre by assimilating it to the formal portrait and blurring the boundaries between the two types of works. Rembrandt was also able to charge a correspondingly high price for the large format. The portrait-like expression of the face and the elaborate lighting may also have served this strategy.

The appeal of such paintings to contemporary viewers may have consisted in their multiple layers of meaning. On the one hand, they stand for 'qualities such as authority, dignity, and power that characterised the personality of a ruler'.[7] This could tempt us to view them as portraits of particular personalities, as with the 'Oriental' by Jan Lievens in Potsdam, which around 1700 was interpreted as a Turkish sultan and thought to be a work by Rembrandt.[8] On the other hand, they are ingenious role-plays that live from the charm of combining different levels of reality.[9] The observant Constantijn Huygens noted this peculiarity of the tronie and wrote of the Potsdam painting in his diary: 'In the collection of our prince there is a painting of a man, the so-called Turkish potentate after the head of a Dutchman.'[10] Contemporaries thus realised that such paintings were not an entirely realistic depiction of a person, but a fantastical combination of foreign costume and native model. JN

1 See Basel/Potsdam 2020, pp. 56–73 (G. Schwartz).
2 See Rembrandt, *An Oriental Standing, Full-Length*, c. 1638, pen and brown ink, 22.2 × 17.3 cm, London, British Museum, inv. PD 1895.1214.100; Paris 2016, no. 38.
3 See Leiden/Oxford 2019, p. 278 (Ch. Brown).
4 Ibid.
5 New York 1995, vol. 2, p. 44.
6 Corpus 1982–2015, vol. 6, no. 72.
7 Quoted in Hirschfelder 2008, p. 314 [translated].
8 Schneider/Ekkart 1973, p. 45, no. 153.
9 See Nicolaisen 2014.
10 Schnackenburg 2016, p. 270 [translated]. The model recurs in various paintings by Rembrandt and other artists. For example, the physiognomy appears in Rembrandt's *Apostle Peter* of 1632 (Stockholm, Nationalmuseum) and the *Bust of a Man in Oriental Costume* of 1633 (Munich, Alte Pinakothek); see Corpus 1982–2015, vol. 6, nos. 83, 104. The same man is also said to have modelled several times for the Amsterdam painter Jacob Backer; New York 1995, p. 45.

36 REMBRANDT

Tronie of a Man with a Feathered Beret

c. 1635–40
Panel, 62.5 × 47 cm
Signed (right edge): Rembrandt. f:
The Hague, Mauritshuis, inv. 149
Lit.: The Hague 2004, no. 48; The Hague 2006, no. 48; Corpus 1982–2015, vol. 6, no. 157.

Turning his head to the right over his shoulder, the young man in elegant costume looks out at the viewer. He wears a black coat with elaborate gold embroidery and a gorget with a greyish-white scarf. His magnificent curls are adorned with a dark purple feathered beret, which sits at an angle.

The reserved gaze of the man in three-quarter view fixes the viewer from the corners of his eyes. His softly modelled facial features with slightly open mouth and flushed cheek give him a gentle, almost vulnerable expression. Rembrandt practised rendering facial expressions with great vividness. There is a sense of immediacy in this painting, as if

37.6 FERDINAND BOL

Portrait of a Lady

c. 1648
Canvas, 87 × 72.5 cm
Munich, Bayerische Staatsgemäldesammlungen, Alte Pinakothek, inv. 610
Lit.: Hirschfelder 2008, no. 51, p. 280; Ottawa/Frankfurt 2021, pp. 153, 173.

37.7 FERDINAND BOL

Portrait of a Man

1652
Canvas, 111 × 89.9 cm
Inscribed (upper right): FB[ligated]ol. 1652
Maximilian Speck von Sternburg Foundation in the Museum der bildenden Künste Leipzig, inv. G 1620
Lit.: Leipzig/Munich 1998, pp. 143f., no. I/72; Leipzig 2012, no. 32.

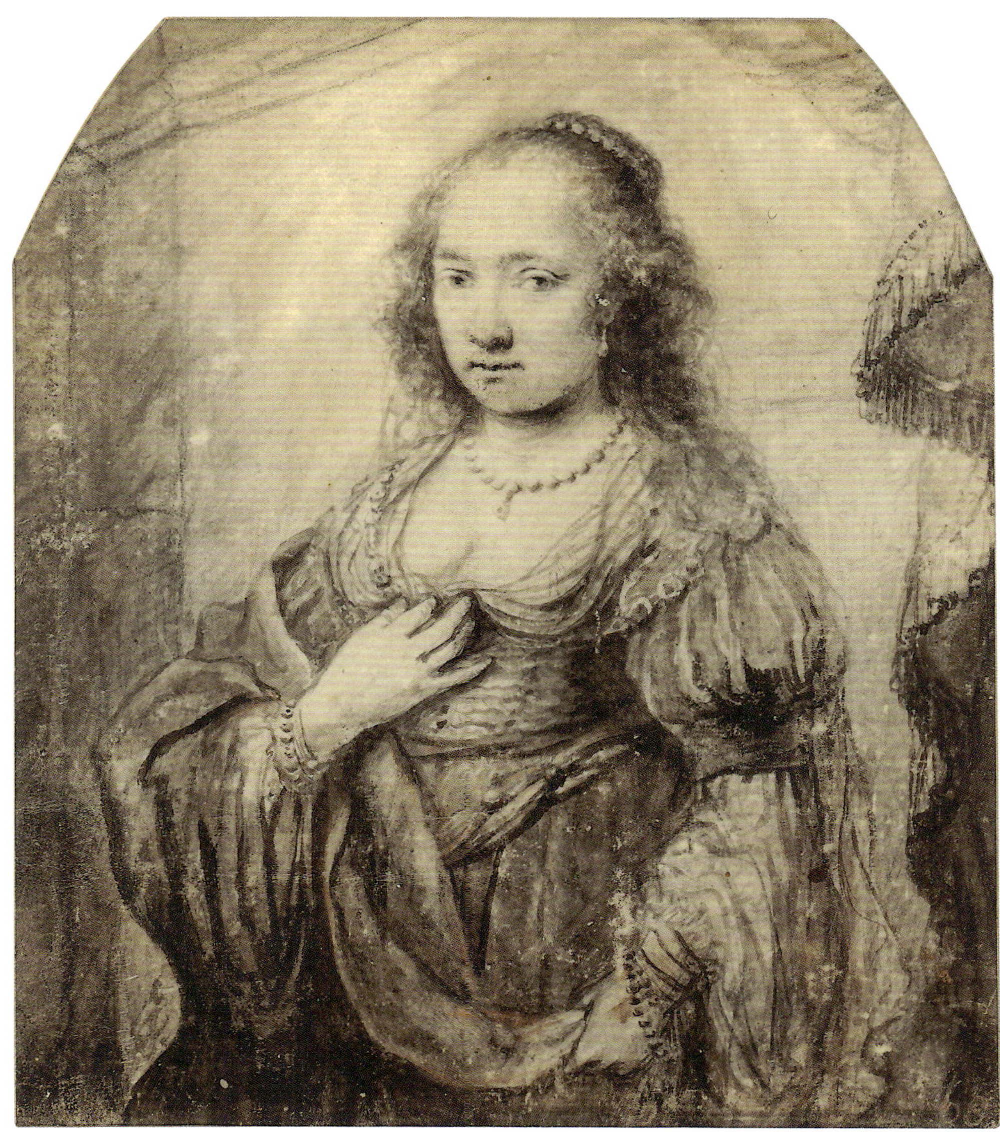

37.3

With the economic boom in the seventeenth-century Netherlands, portrait painting reached a zenith between 1630 and 1670. The prestige of affluent townspeople grew, and with it the desire to have their wealth correspondingly represented in art. As a result, portraiture developed a wide variety of forms and expressive possibilities.[1] Rembrandt was able to capture the human presence in his portraits with a high degree of realism and astonishing vividness. In the 1630s, he became one of the most sought-after portrait painters in Amsterdam.

The early etchings of Rembrandt's wife Saskia, however – the couple had married in 1634 – are not formal portraits.[2] Rembrandt often depicted his wife in role-portraits and period costumes, as in the etching *Saskia van Uylenburgh in Rich Costume* from their wedding year 1634 (cat. 37.1). A year earlier, shortly after the young couple had pledged their troth, Rembrandt made a drawing of his wife as a bride.[3] The same pose appears in similar form in a 1637 etching with three female heads (cat. 37.4). Saskia is at the centre of the composition, fixing the viewer with an open and penetrating gaze. The fluid lines suggest that the heads were drawn directly onto the plate.

In addition to formal portraits in contemporary dress, Rembrandt also made portraits in historical costume, *portraits historiés*. Imaginative costumes could evoke biblical, mythological, or historical allusions. One example is Rembrandt's Kassel portrait of Saskia in pompous fantasy dress.[4] The above-mentioned etching of Saskia from 1634, in rich traditional costume and with precious pearls in her hair, belongs to the genre of such 'historicising portraits'.

The portrait of *Saskia as a Shepherdess* by Rembrandt's student Govert Flinck also appears to be a *portrait historié* (cat. 37.2). It has been interpreted as a counterpart to a portrait of Rembrandt as a shepherd by Flinck.[5] Saskia wears a hat decorated with flowers and a dress with wide, slit sleeves,

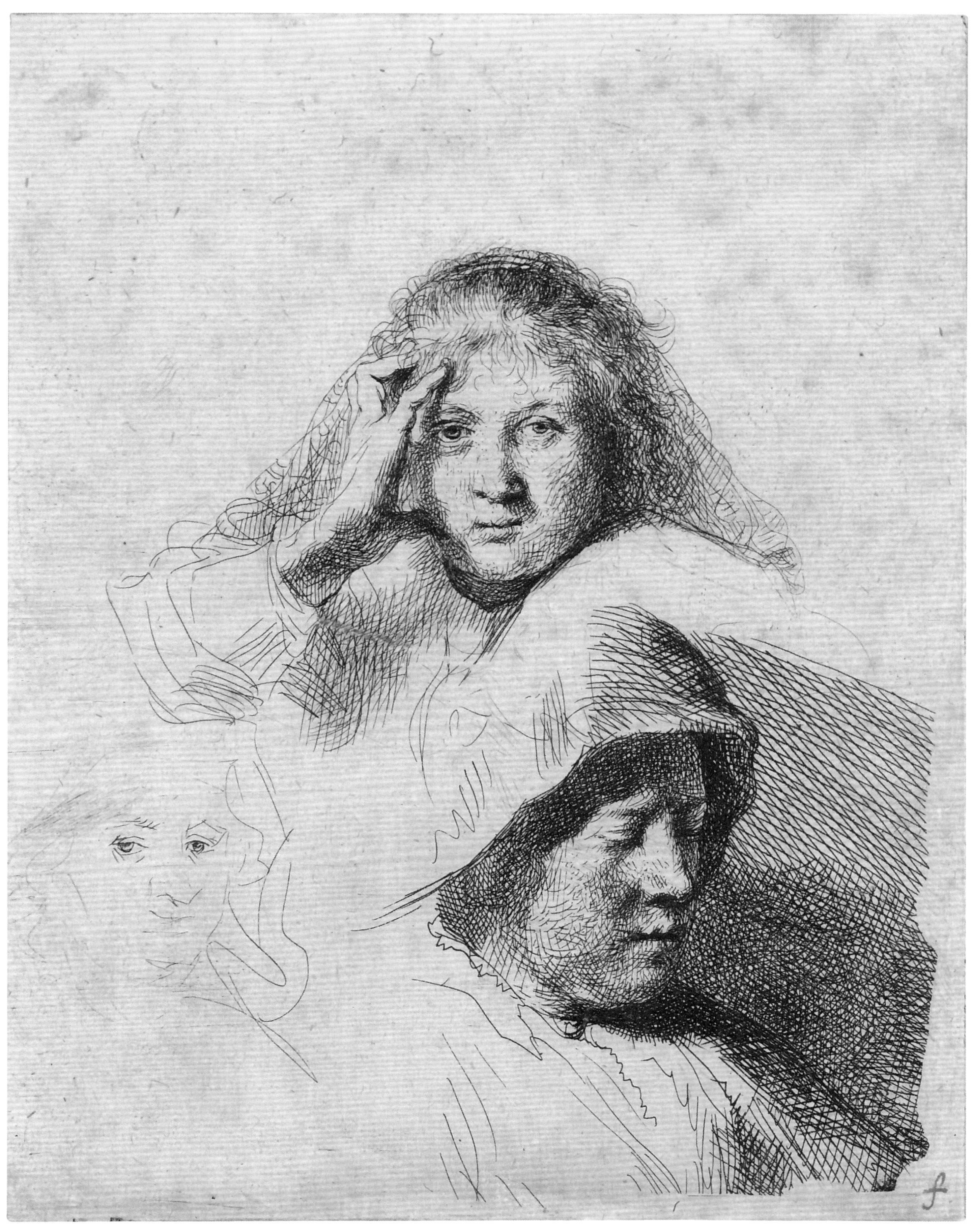

37.4

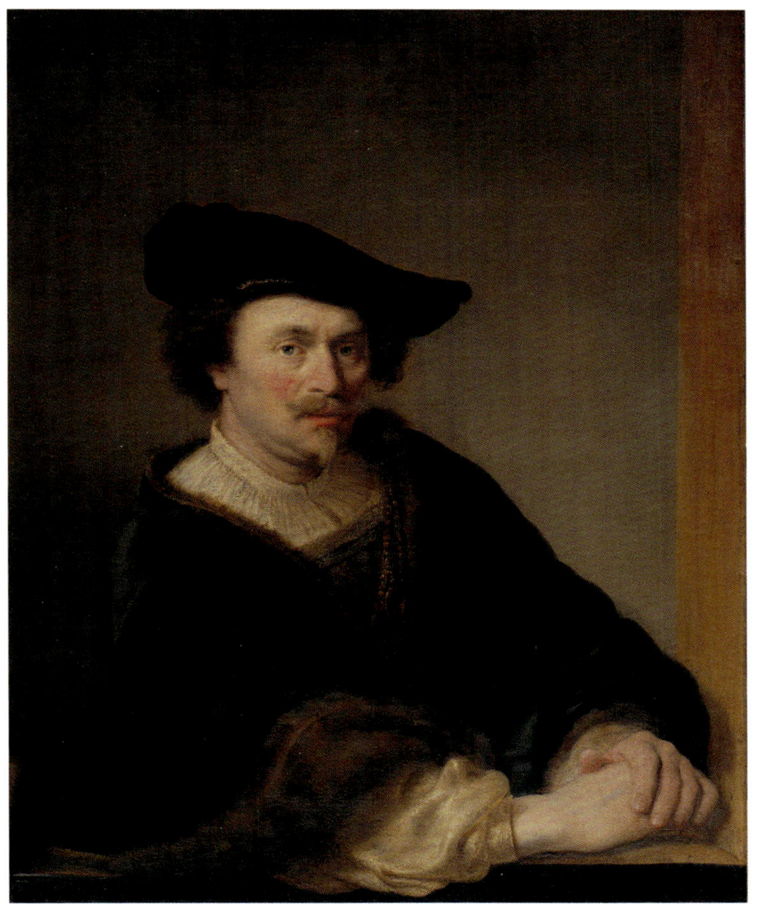

37.5

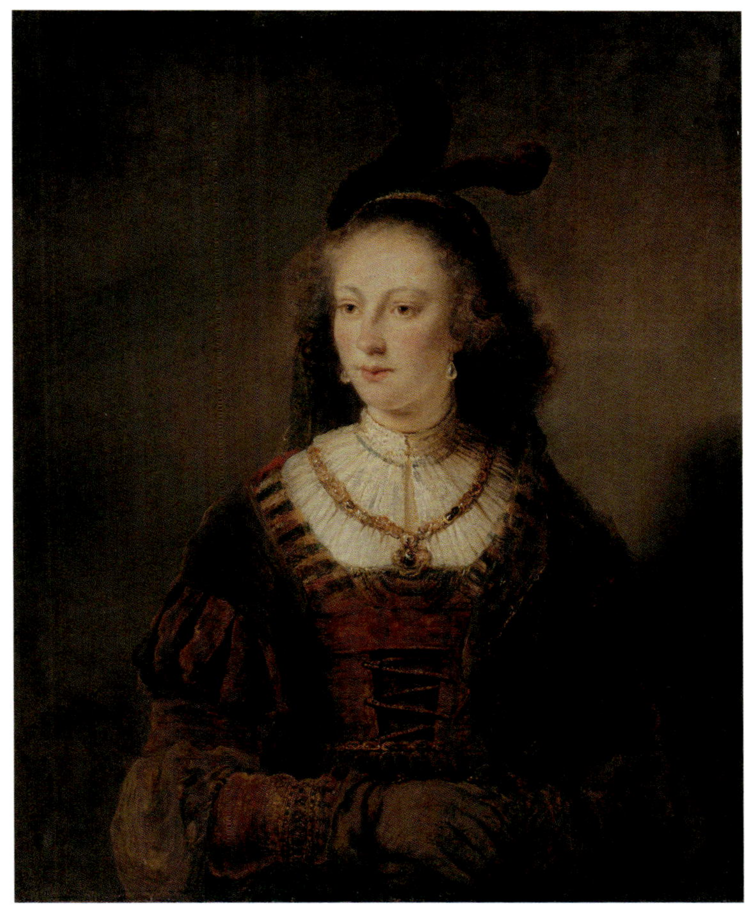

37.6

long since out of fashion. Flinck's painting of the shepherdess is based on Rembrandt's *Flora* of 1634, whose features are modelled on those of Saskia.[6]

Scholars have repeatedly questioned whether the paintings are actually portraits of Rembrandt and Saskia. In particular, the identity of the female model has been questioned, as she bears little resemblance to Rembrandt's wife.[7] It is possible that these are not historicising portraits, but rather tronies.[8] Flinck had established his own business in 1636 after training under Rembrandt. Inger Krog suggests that he gave his pastorals a certain portrait-like quality, especially in the case of Rembrandt as a shepherd, in order to increase the market value of the paintings, since Rembrandt's face already had a high recognition value.[9]

Ferdinand Bol learned the craft of portrait painting in Rembrandt's workshop in the 1630s. The Leipzig drawing of a woman in historicising costume, dated 1635–6 (cat. 37.3), was made in this context. It follows his teacher's depictions of women from the mid-1630s.[10] The portrait, drawn on vellum, is of particular delicacy, making doubts about Bol's authorship untenable.[11] Stylistically, it is akin to works that can clearly be attributed to Bol, such as his drawings *Flora* in London, *Woman with a Pear* in Cambridge, and *Woman as Granida* in Copenhagen,[12] which are very similar in their treatment of the hands, décolleté and facial features. They bear witness to Bol's artistic beginnings in the Rembrandt workshop, and the smile of the young woman looking out of the picture already reveals his ability to create sensitive portraits.

After his time in Rembrandt's workshop, Bol established himself as a successful portrait artist beginning in the early 1640s. Around 1645–6 and around 1648, he painted portraits of an unknown gentleman and an unknown lady in historicising costumes (cats. 37.5–6). The warm, brownish colouring of the works, the precisely rendered faces, and the three-dimensional effect of the figures show the formative influence of his teacher. Indeed, the portraits were previously thought to be works by Rembrandt and bore his forged signature.[13] The costumes are executed with great finesse. The female figure's antique garments are rich in detail,

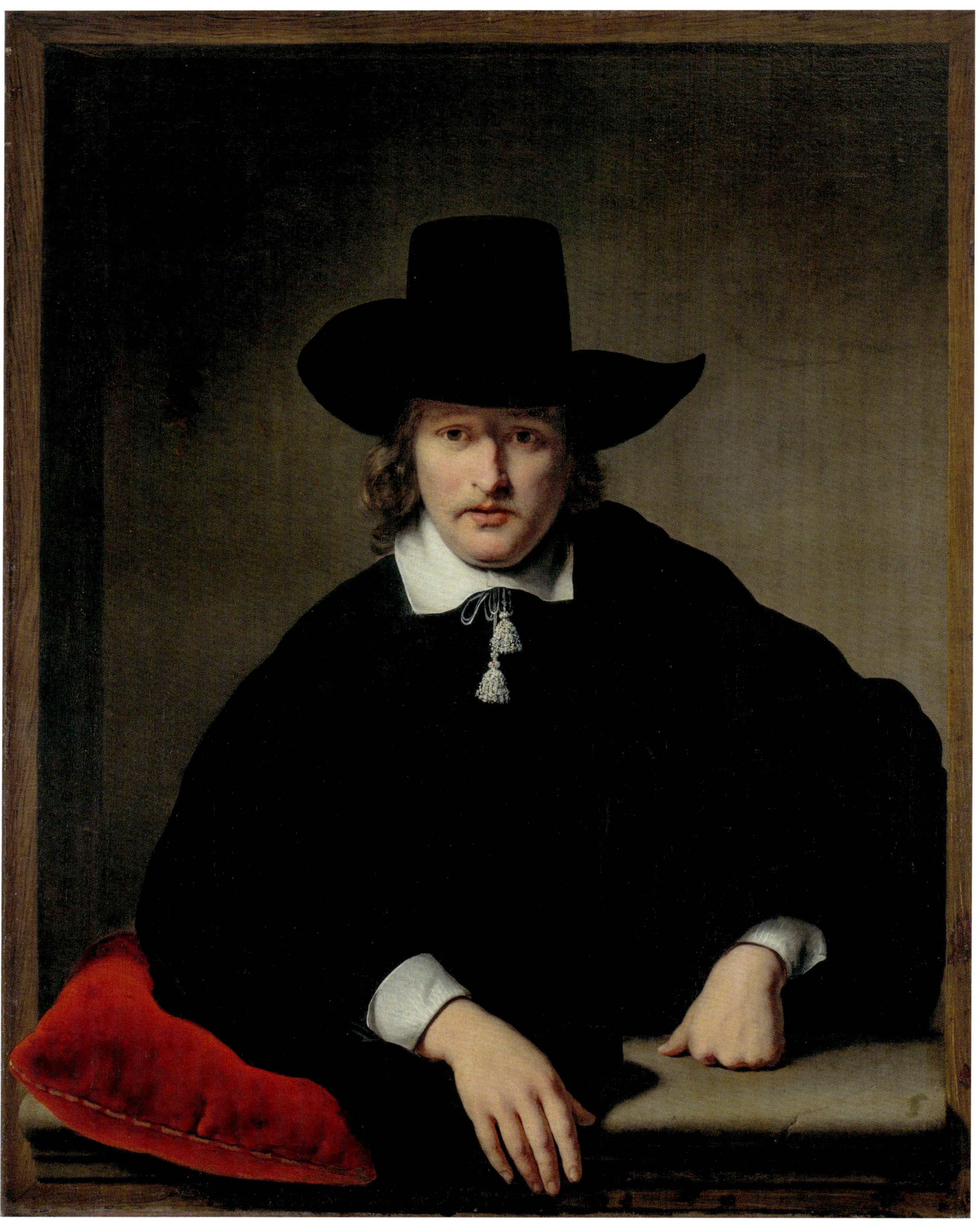

37.7

such as the fine embroidery on the trims of her sleeves, the translucent, delicate fabric of the veil falling over her shoulder and the multi-linked, heavy gold chain with reflections of light. Rembrandt's 1640 *Self-Portrait* in the National Gallery in London was an important source of inspiration for Bol's portrait of a man.[14] It served Bol as a model for many portraits of a half-length male figure in side view, usually standing behind a balustrade.[15]

The *Portrait of a Man* from 1652 shows that Ferdinand Bol gradually developed his own style while still emulating his former teacher (cat. 37.7). The young man casually drapes his hand over the stone in front of him and turns towards the viewer. His posture and elegant clothing convey an expression of self-confidence. The bright white of his collar, cuffs and detailed tassels, as well as the strong red of the velvet cushion on which the sitter's right arm rests, provide striking colour accents. A pendant to this is a *Portrait of a Lady* showing a young woman in contemporary dress, also dated 1652.[16]

Bol's smooth and precise painting style is modelled on his master's portraits from around 1640. The appearance of the fashionably dressed man, however, is influenced by the Flemish style of portraiture, particularly that of the painter Anthony van Dyck.[17] Also inspired by Rembrandt is the recourse to the type of illusionist window portraits, with which the master experimented from the late 1630s on (cf. cat. 39). Bol's two portraits are also characterised by a strong *trompe-l'œil* effect: The elements projecting over the painted wooden frame, such as the balustrade and the cushions, seem to break through the boundaries of the image and enter the viewer's space.[18] The painter masterfully plays with the fascinating tension between closeness and distance – a staging device he had learned during his apprenticeship in Rembrandt's workshop. LCS

1 Hirschfelder 2008, p. 82.
2 See Leeuwarden/Kassel 2019.
3 Rembrandt, *Portrait of Saskia as a Bride*, 1633, silverpoint, 18.5 × 10.6 cm (upper corners rounded), Staatliche Museen zu Berlin, Kupferstichkabinett, inv. CC BY-NC-SA.
4 Rembrandt, *Saskia van Uylenburgh in Profile, in Pompous Dress*, c. 1633/34–1641, panel, 99.5 × 78.8 cm, Kassel, Gemäldegalerie Alte Meister, inv. GK 236.
5 Govert Flinck, *Shepherd*, c. 1636, canvas, 75.1 × 64.4 cm, Amsterdam, Rijksmuseum, inv. SK-A-3451.
6 Rembrandt, *Flora*, 1634, canvas, 124.7 × 100.4 cm, St Petersburg, Hermitage, inv. ГЭ-732.
7 See Sumowski 1983–94, vol. 1, p. 305; Utrecht/Frankfurt/Luxembourg 1993, p. 155.
8 'Govert Flinck, Shepherd, c. 1636', Bikker (2023), https://www.rijksmuseum.nl/en/collection/SK-A-3451.
9 Copenhagen 2006, no. 33f.; see also Leeuwarden/Kassel 2019, pp. 59–63.
10 Leipzig 1990, no. 45; e.g., Rembrandt, *Artemisia (Sophonisba?)*, 1634, canvas, 142 × 153 cm, Madrid, Museo Nacional del Prado, inv. P002132.
11 Leipzig 1990, no. 45.
12 Sumowski 1979–92, vol. 1, no. 129; see ibid., nos. 105, 127, 148.
13 Ferdinand Bol, *Portrait of a Man*, c. 1645–6, Munich, Bayerische Staatsgemälde-sammlungen, Alte Pinakothek, https://www.sammlung.pinakothek.de/en/artwork/OrLb50yx1V.
14 Rembrandt, *Self-Portrait at the Age of 34*, 1640, canvas, London, National Gallery, inv. NG672.
15 Sumowski 1983–94, vol. 1, p. 305; see ibid., nos. 136, 138, 143, 145.
16 Ferdinand Bol, *Portrait of a Lady*, 1652, canvas, 110 × 89 cm, private collection; Leipzig/Munich 1998, no. I/72. On 8 July 2021, the painting was sold at Christie's, London (as Lot 25).
17 Blankert 1982, p. 60.
18 Leipzig 2012, no. 32.

38.1 REMBRANDT

The Preacher Jan Cornelisz. Sylvius

1633
Etching, II (of III), 16.7 × 14.3 cm (sheet)
Museum der bildenden Künste Leipzig, Graphische Sammlung, inv. NI. 5801
Lit.: B. 266; NH 124; Dickey 2004, pp. 28, 33–5.

38.2 REMBRANDT

The Preacher Johannes Uytenbogaert

1635
Etching and engraving with drypoint, IX (of IX), 23.5 × 19.5 cm (sheet)
Museum der bildenden Künste Leipzig, Graphische Sammlung, inv. NI. 5805
Lit.: B. 279; NH 153; Dickey 2004, pp. 35–42.

38.3 REMBRANDT

Jan Uytenbogaert ('The Gold Weigher')

1639
Inscribed (lower left): Rembrandt f / 1639 [in the plate]
Etching and drypoint, III (of III), 25 × 21.3 cm (sheet)
Museum der bildenden Künste Leipzig, Graphische Sammlung, inv. NI. 2031
Lit.: B. 281; NH 172; Dickey 2004, pp. 66–88; Schwartz 2019, pp. 260–3.

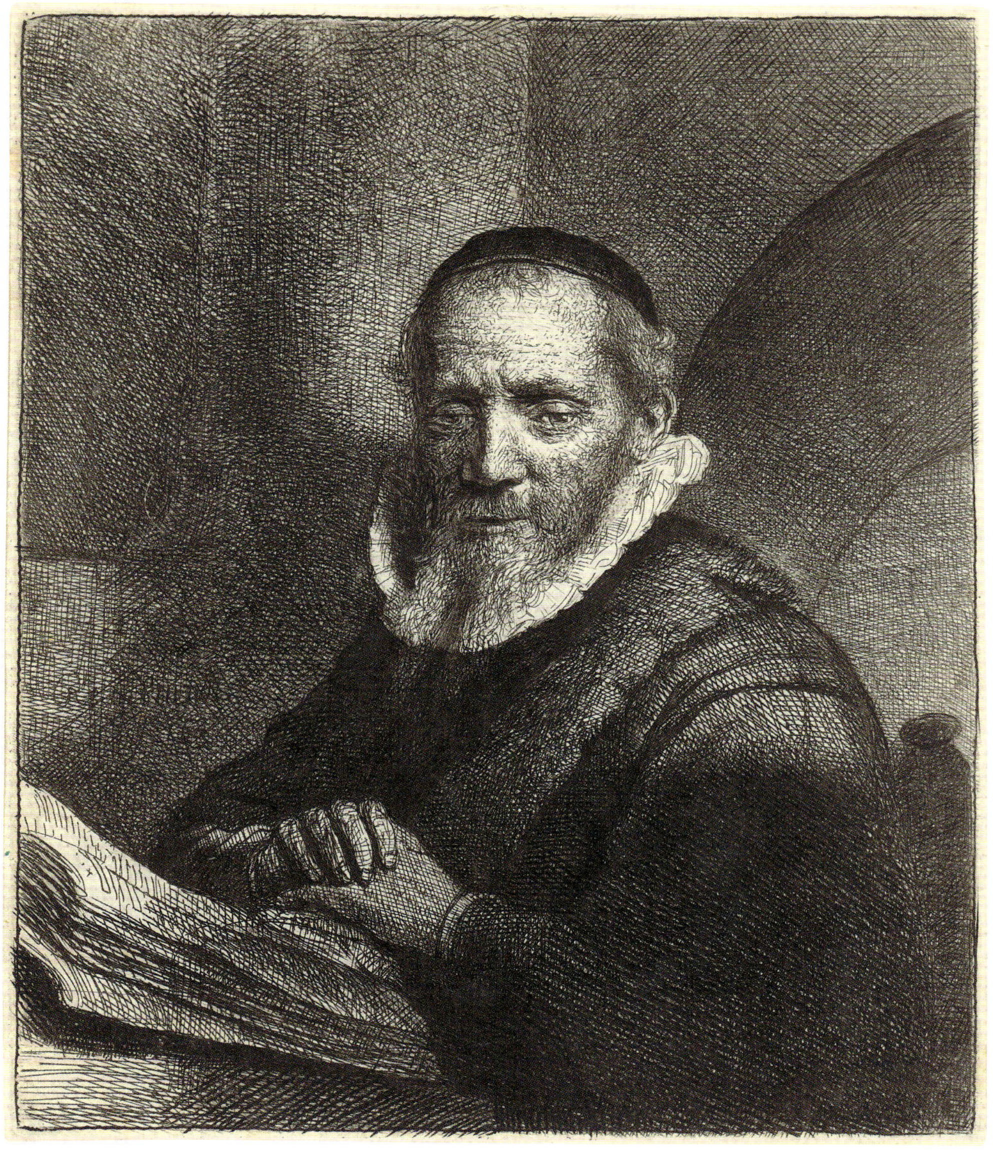

38.1

38.4 REMBRANDT

Jan Six

1647
Etching, drypoint, and engraving, V (of V), 24.7 × 19.7 cm (sheet)
Museum der bildenden Künste Leipzig, Graphische Sammlung, inv. NI. 2052
Lit.: B. 285; NH 238; Dickey 2004, pp. 112–19.

38.5 REMBRANDT

The Painter Jan Asselijn ('Krabbetje')

c. 1647 (?)
Etching and drypoint, V (of VII), 18.8 × 17.2 cm (sheet)
Museum der bildenden Künste Leipzig, Graphische Sammlung, inv. NI. 2057
Lit.: B. 277; NH 236; Dickey 2004, pp. 120–5.

38.6 REMBRANDT

The Apothecary Abraham Francken

c. 1657
Etching, drypoint, and engraving, XII (of XII), 16.1 × 20.8 cm (sheet)
Museum der bildenden Künste Leipzig, Graphische Sammlung, inv. NI. 2029
Lit.: B 273; NH 301; Dickey 2004, pp. 142–9.

Rembrandt's etched portraits comprise a relatively small and thematically specific group within his extensive oeuvre of etchings. As Rudi Ekkart has pointed out, their fragile combination of etching, engraving, and drypoint made them unsuitable for large editions and therefore generally unusable for commercial purposes.[1] The portraits span four decades, from the 1630s to the 1660s. In most cases, there seems to have been a personal connection between the sitter and the artist.

The portrait of the preacher Jan Cornelisz. Sylvius (1564–1638), who, as Saskia's guardian and relative, was present at her engagement and the baptisms of her first two children, dates from 1633 (cat. 38.1).[2] Two years later, the artist made a portrait of the preacher Johannes Uytenbogaert (1557–1644) that shows remarkable technical progress (cat. 38.2). The fur trim of the cloak, the ruff and the skin and beard as well as the pages of the book are rendered in a materially differentiated manner. The learned preacher looks up as if his reading had just been interrupted, using the thumb of his left hand as a bookmark on the page, a recurring motif in the work of Rembrandt and his students (cats. 31.1, 41.2). Uytenbogaert, one of the most prominent Remonstrants, became court preacher in The Hague and

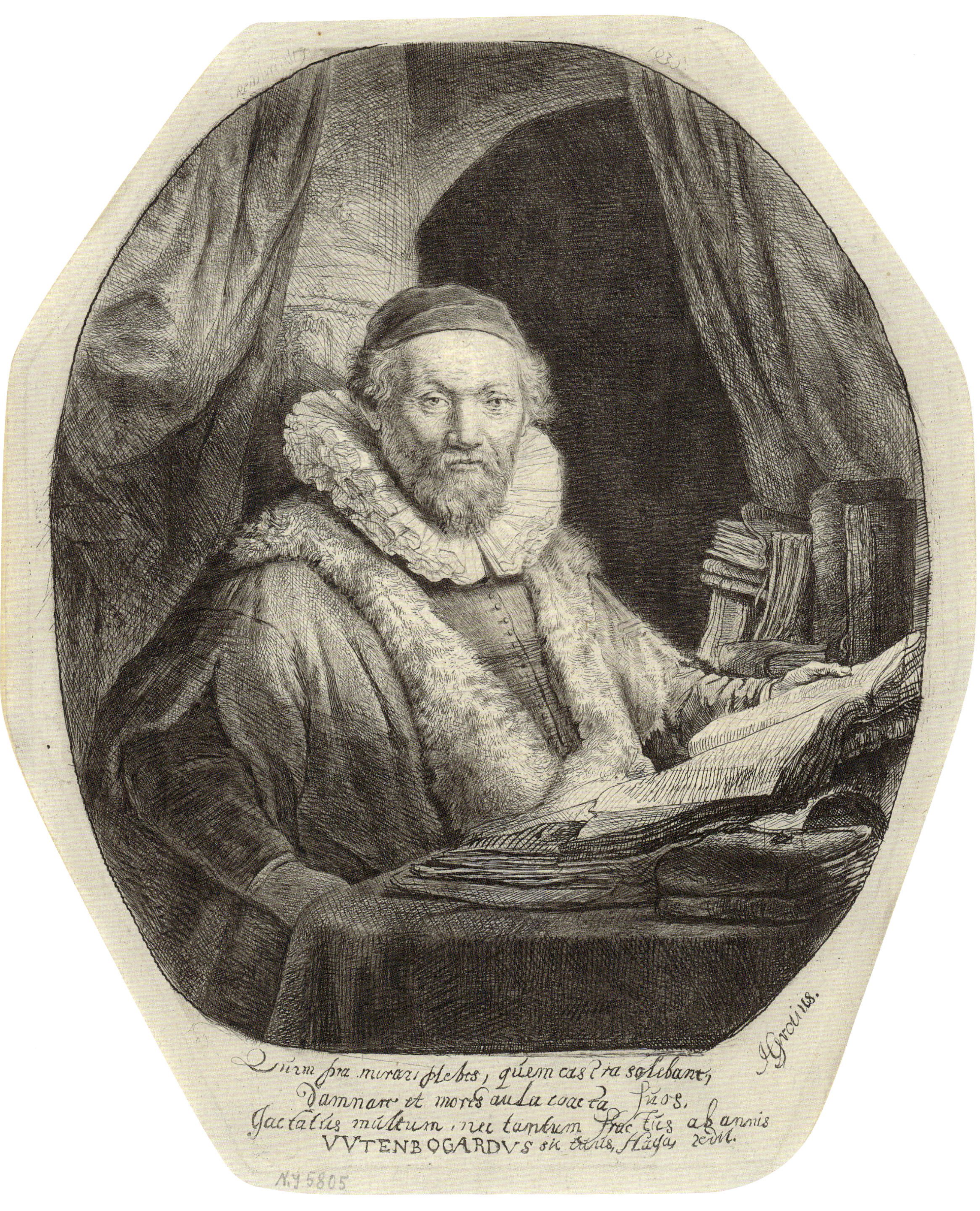
Quem pia mirari plebes, quem castra solebant,
Damnare et mores aula coacta suos.
Iactatus multum, nec tantum fractus ab annis
VVTENBOGARDVS sic tuus, Haga, redit.
H. Grotius.

38.2

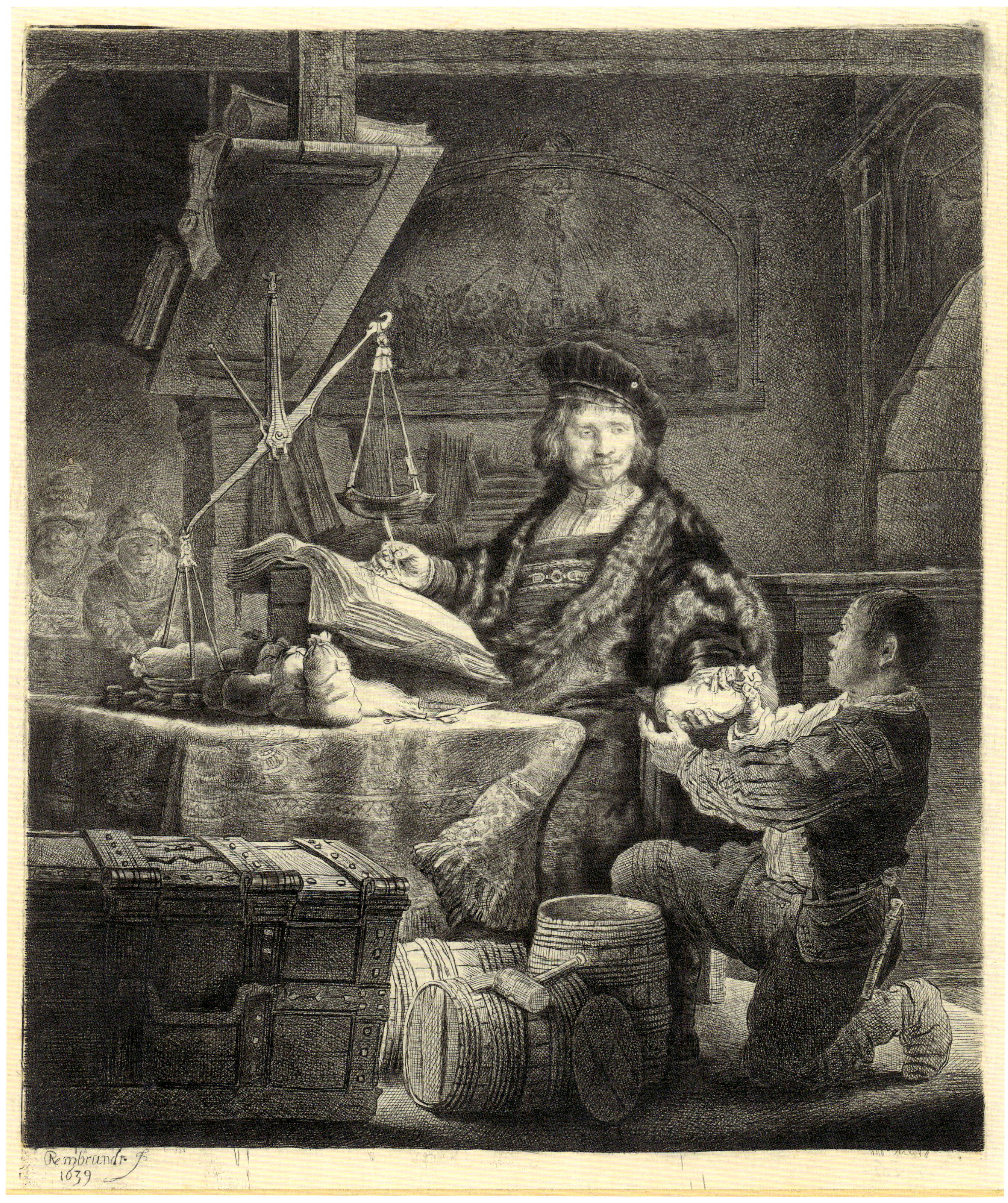

38.3

was later dismissed in the course of the conflict with the Counter-Remonstrants. Rembrandt was also commissioned to create a painted portrait of Uytenbogaert, for which the latter sat for the artist in his studio on 13 April 1633.[3]

The narrative portrait of Jan Uytenbogaert, a wealthy general tax collector and a relative of the famous preacher, was made in 1639 (cat. 38.3). Uytenbogaert was also responsible for paying the fees for Rembrandt's paintings for the stadtholder in The Hague and probably already knew the artist from the latter's student days in Leiden. Uytenbogaert is known to have visited him in his Amsterdam studio in January 1639 and was a passionate collector of paintings, prints and naturalia. In 1641, he inherited the art collection of his cousin, Jacob de Gheyn III, which included paintings by Rembrandt and Jan Lievens such as the latter's *Bust of a Girl with her Hair Down*, now in Leipzig (cat. 34.2). The painting in the background alludes to his activity as an art collector. His collection was so famous that it was visited by Cosimo de' Medici in 1667. His passion for older art is indicated by the historicising clothes, which transform the etching into a *portrait historié*. Rembrandt depicts Uytenbogaert as a gold weigher – a popular motif in Dutch art in the first half of the sixteenth century, which he himself used for a painting in 1628. This painterly image, Rembrandt's hitherto most ambitious etched portrait, was probably intended to offer his services to this wealthy art collector and important man at the court of The Hague.

In 1647, Rembrandt etched a portrait of another art collector, Jan Six (1618–1700), who promoted him and also supported him financially (cat. 38.4). The young man leans against the window in a casual pose, absorbed in reading. On the wall in the background is a painting, partially obscured by a curtain. Six came from a wealthy aristocratic family, worked in the family business of trading in cloth and dyeing silk until around 1652, served as a judge of matrimonial disputes in 1656 and became one of the mayors of Amsterdam in 1691. His real passion, however, seems to have been the fine arts: he was also a poet and wrote the tragedy *Medea*, for which Rembrandt designed the title page (cat. 10.4). The collector also owned paintings by Rembrandt such as *St John the Baptist Preaching* (c. 1634–5, Staatliche Museen zu Berlin, Gemäldegalerie) and *Saskia in a Red Hat* (c. 1633–42, Kassel, Gemäldegalerie Alte Meister). As Rembrandt's financial difficulties increased in the 1650s, Six lent him the large sum of 1,000 guilders in 1653.[4] The artist portrayed Six again

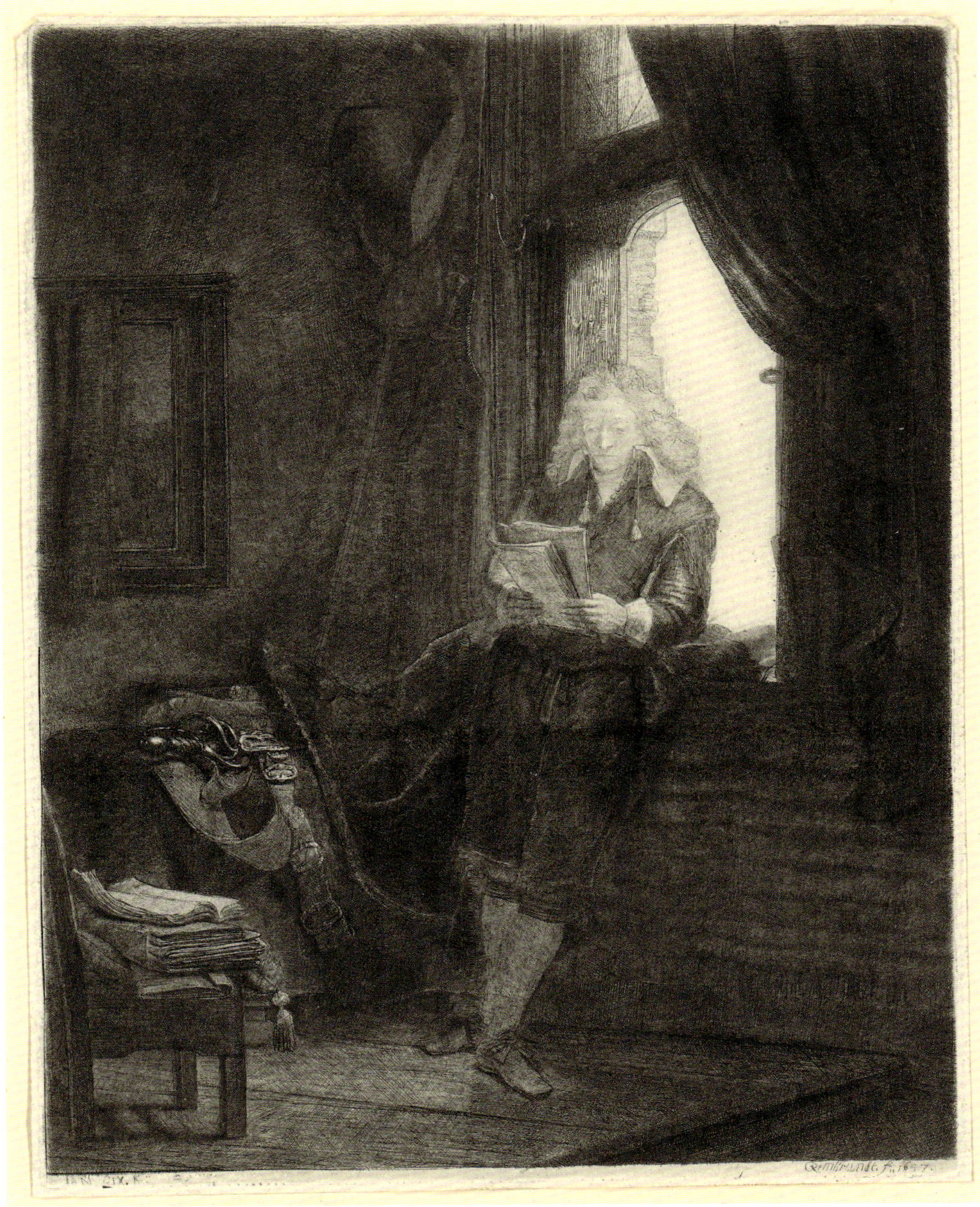

38.4

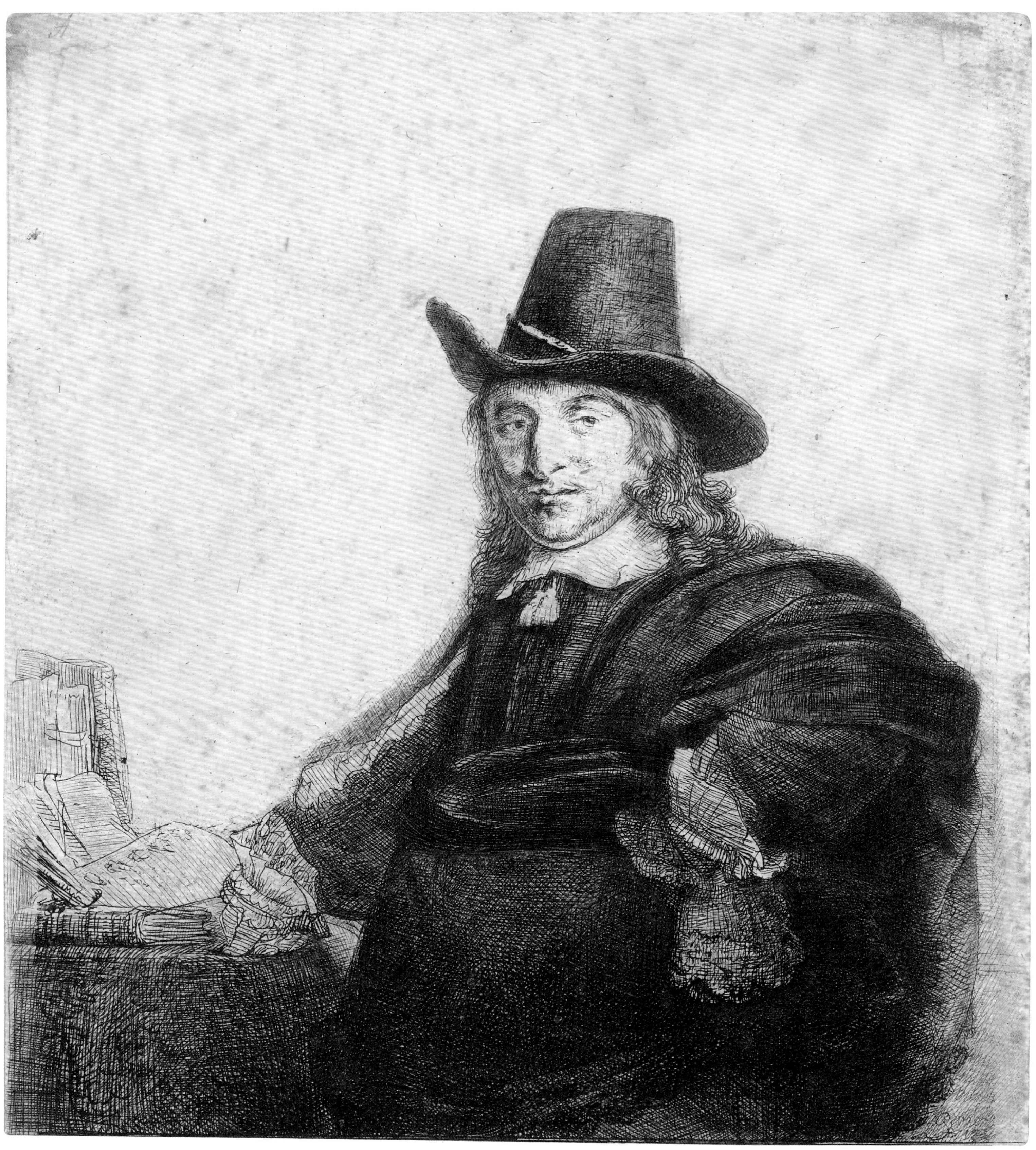

38.5

in 1654 in a painting that is still in the family's possession.

The portrait of Jan Asselijn (1610–1652), an Italianate painter (cat. 38.5), is much simpler. The exact nature of Rembrandt's relationship with the sitter is unclear, although we do know of his connection with Thomas Asselijn, Jan's younger brother, who was a poet and merchant. In the 1650s, Asselijn appeared several times as a witness for Rembrandt in business and legal matters.[5] It is possible that this portrait was commissioned by him. Jan Asselijn is dressed in the elegant black silk fashionable at the time. In the first state of the etching, an easel with a painting can be seen in the background, which Rembrandt later removed for unknown reasons.

Rembrandt was a friend of the apothecary Abraham Francken (1613–after 1678) and depicted him around 1657 as an art collector in an atmospheric interior (cat. 38.6). He shows the collector holding a work of art in his hands, examining it closely. Dickey assumes that it is a print or a drawing, but the position of the hands suggests that Francken is holding a painting on wood.[6] On the table in front of him is an album used to hold drawings and prints, while a number of paintings are visible on the wall in the background. In 1656, Rembrandt reached a low point in his career, both financially and socially, and had to declare bankruptcy and sell his art collection. The interior, a poetic expression of spiritual freedom and leisure, seems to be a counter-image to his own existence at the time. Throughout the 1650s, Abraham Francken acted as a supportive witness for Rembrandt in both business and personal matters.[7] After his death, he became the guardian of Cornelia, Rembrandt's daughter from his relationship with Hendrickje Stoffels. However, two other identifications of the sitter have also been discussed, one of which seems particularly plausible. Dickey suggests that the man is Daniel Francken, Abraham's brother, a successful surgeon who likewise collected art. Furthermore, he lent Rembrandt more than 3,000 guilders in 1656. The etching could have been made as a token of gratitude or in return for the loan.[8] However, Abraham Francken, who is said to have been a collector of modest means but of great passion and a friend of Rembrandt, remains a likely candidate.[9] JN

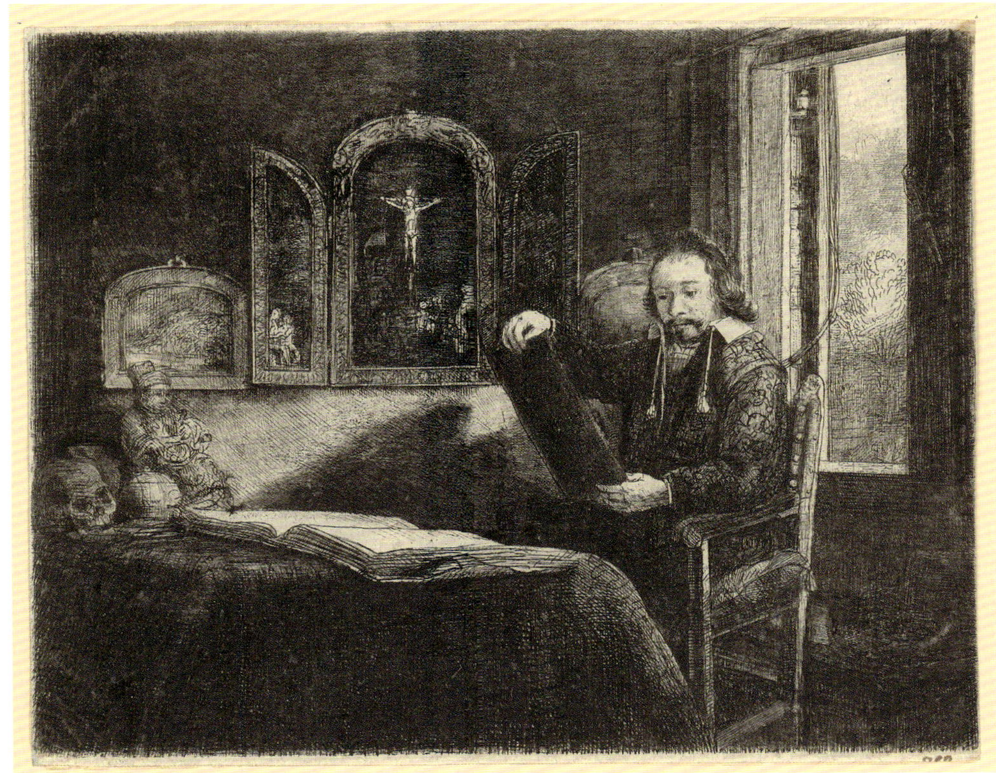

38.6

1 R.E.O. Ekkart and E. Ornstein-van Slooten, *Oog in oog met de modellen van Rembrandts portret-etsen / Face to Face with the Sitters for Rembrandt's Etched Portraits*, exh. cat. Amsterdam, Museum Het Rembrandthuis, 1986, pp. 13f.
2 Dickey 2004, p. 33.
3 Rembrandt, *Portrait of the Preacher Johannes Uytenbogaert*, 1635, Amsterdam, Rijksmuseum; cf. ibid., p. 36.
4 Ibid., p. 112.
5 Ibid., p. 123.
6 Ibid., p. 142.
7 Ibid., p. 143.
8 Otto van Cattenburch, a wealthy civil servant, is also discussed as a candidate. According to an agreement from 1655, he was supposed to receive an etched portrait by Rembrandt in return for a loan of 400 guilders; ibid., pp. 144, 148.
9 Amsterdam 2019, p. 55.

39.1 JAN VICTORS

(Amsterdam 1619–c. 1676 Dutch East Indies)

Young Woman at a Window

1640
Canvas, 93 x 78 cm
Signed and dated: S.D.b.d. : Jan Fictoor fe. 1640.
Paris, Musée du Louvre, Département des Peintures, inv. 1286; MR 711
Lit.: Paris 2009, p. 288; Ottawa/Frankfurt 2021, no. 88, p. 193; Veldman 2021.

39.2 NICOLAES MAES

(Dordrecht 1634–1693 Amsterdam)

Girl at a Window (The Daydreamer)

1650–60
Canvas, 12.3 × 96 cm
Signed (on the lower ledge of the window frame): N. Mae
Dordrecht, Dordrechts Museum, loan Amsterdam, Rijksmuseum, inv. SK-A-245
Lit.: Sumowski 1983–94, vol. 3, no. 1330; Robinson 1996, no. A 25; Copenhagen 2006, no. 42.

39.3 GERRIT DOU

(Leiden 1613–1675 Leiden)

The Lacemaker

1667
Panel, 30.5 × 25.5 cm
Signed and dated: GDOV 166[3]
Staatliche Kunsthalle Karlsruhe, inv. 267
Lit.: Kleinmann 1996, p. 120; Sonntag 2006, pp. 28, 42, 44, 88, 92, 112f., 130 note 271; Karlsruhe 2015, no. 110.

Trompe-l'œil images (optical illusions) involving windows and illusionistic picture frames were popular in seventeenth-century Dutch painting, including that of Rembrandt and his students. Samuel van Hoogstraten, Ferdinand Bol, Gerrit Dou and Philips Koninck were particularly devoted to this theme. The sensitive depiction of young women and girls was influenced not only by Rembrandt, but also by Jan Lievens, who made a study of a girl's head around 1630 (cat. 34.2).

An early window painting from 1640 is by Jan Victors (cat. 39.1). A written source from 1722 identifies him as one of 'Rembrandt's best students'.[1] His *Young Woman at a Window* was probably inspired by a drawing by Rembrandt from 1633–6, which shows Saskia van Uylenburgh at an open window.[2] Victors's sumptuously dressed female figure impressively demonstrates his ability to capture materiality. The fabric woven with delicate gold threads, the soft leather of the gloves and the shimmering pearls and gems evoke a tactile allure.

Ilja M. Veldman has convincingly demonstrated that this could be the Old Testament figure of Michal[3], who is described in 2 Samuel 6:16 as looking out a window, watching her husband, King David, behaving indecently in public. The realistic and illusionistic pictorial elements produced by the shadows on the window frame and shutter and the extension of the woman's hands beyond the frame are remarkable.

Jan Victors's early realisation of the motif of a girl at a window anticipates his teacher, for it was not until 1641 that Rembrandt devoted himself to the subject in the medium of painting.[4] Nicolaes Maes's *Girl at a Window* (cat. 39.2) is influenced by this. Maes had probably seen Rembrandt's *Kitchen Maid* of 1651 during his apprenticeship in the workshop. The genre painting shows a young woman leaning forward at a window, deep in thought. The open shutter projects outward in a highly illusionistic way. Like Rembrandt, the painter chose a colour scheme dominated by reds and browns, giving the picture a warm, soft glow.[5] Macro-XRF images of the painting indicate that the girl was originally shown looking out from the picture.[6] With her gaze turned slightly to the side and downwards, Maes's *Daydreamer* appears introverted.

Few seventeenth-century Dutch painters explored the window motif as intensively as Gerrit Dou, who enjoyed great popularity for his meticulous painting and is regarded as the founder of the Leiden Fijnschilders. He learned this style of painting from Rembrandt, with whom he apprenticed from 1628 to 1631. Dou perfected the technique over decades, while Rembrandt later developed a rough, impasto style. Around 40 of Dou's window paintings have survived, all showing a stone parapet with figures in the foreground.[7]

Gerrit Dou's *Lacemaker* of 1667 looks up from her needlework and seems to spontaneously make eye contact with the viewer (cat. 39.3). An open book and a rose lie on the ledge in the foreground, suggesting that the young woman's virtue may be in jeopardy.[8] The open book has been identified as the *Groot Liedboeck*, which among other things condemns arrogance and dalliance.[9] Most of Dou's window paintings contain such elements alluding to modesty, indicating that he took a different direction from his teacher, whose images did not primarily aim to convey moral meaning.

Rembrandt taught his students how to create evocative compositions of figures, objects and motifs. They were able to apply this knowledge to great effect in the subject of a girl at a window, creating a harmonious consonance of figure and architecture. Their play with the illusionist devices of painting offers astonishing optical illusions that blur the line between painting and reality. LCS

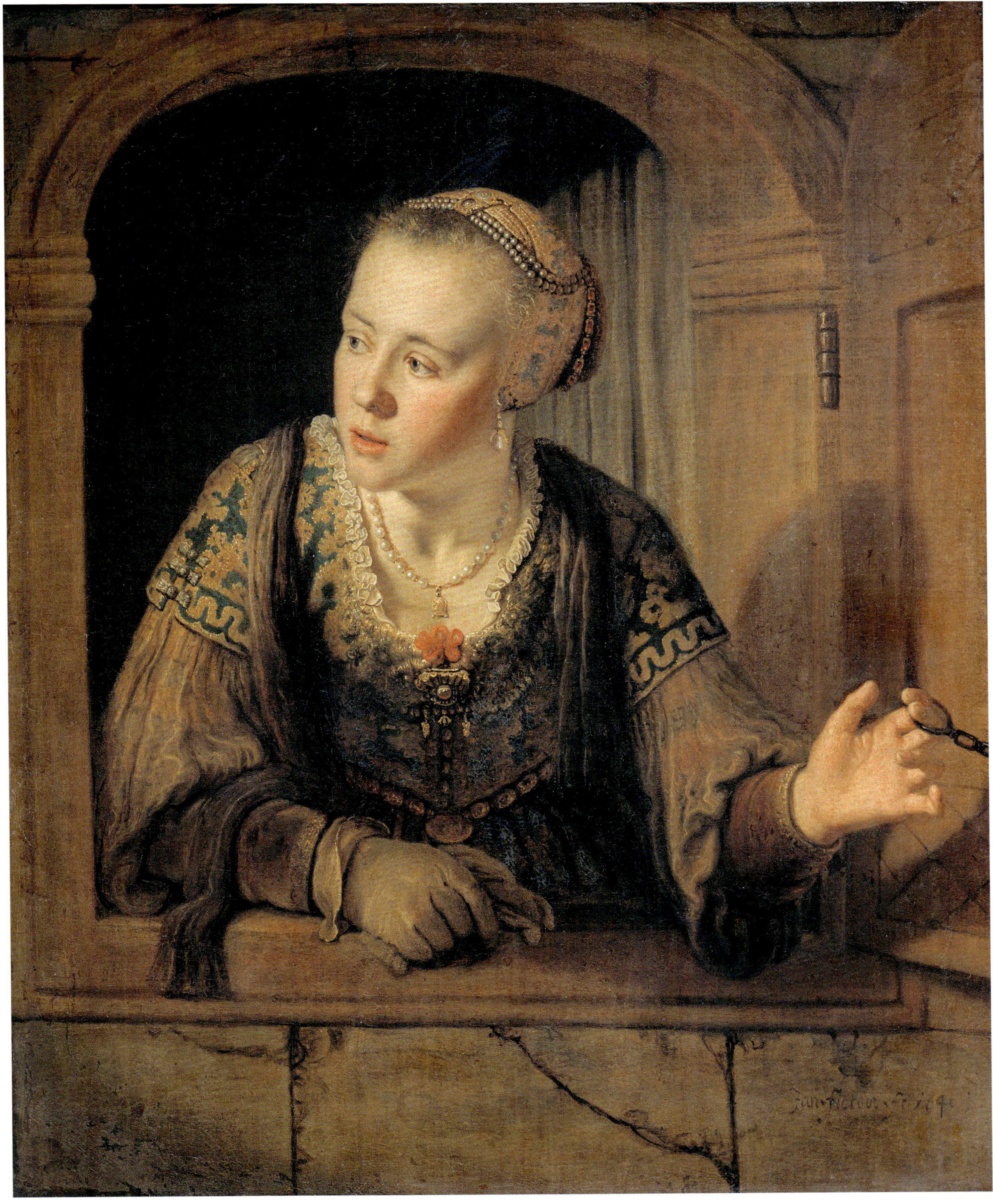

39.1

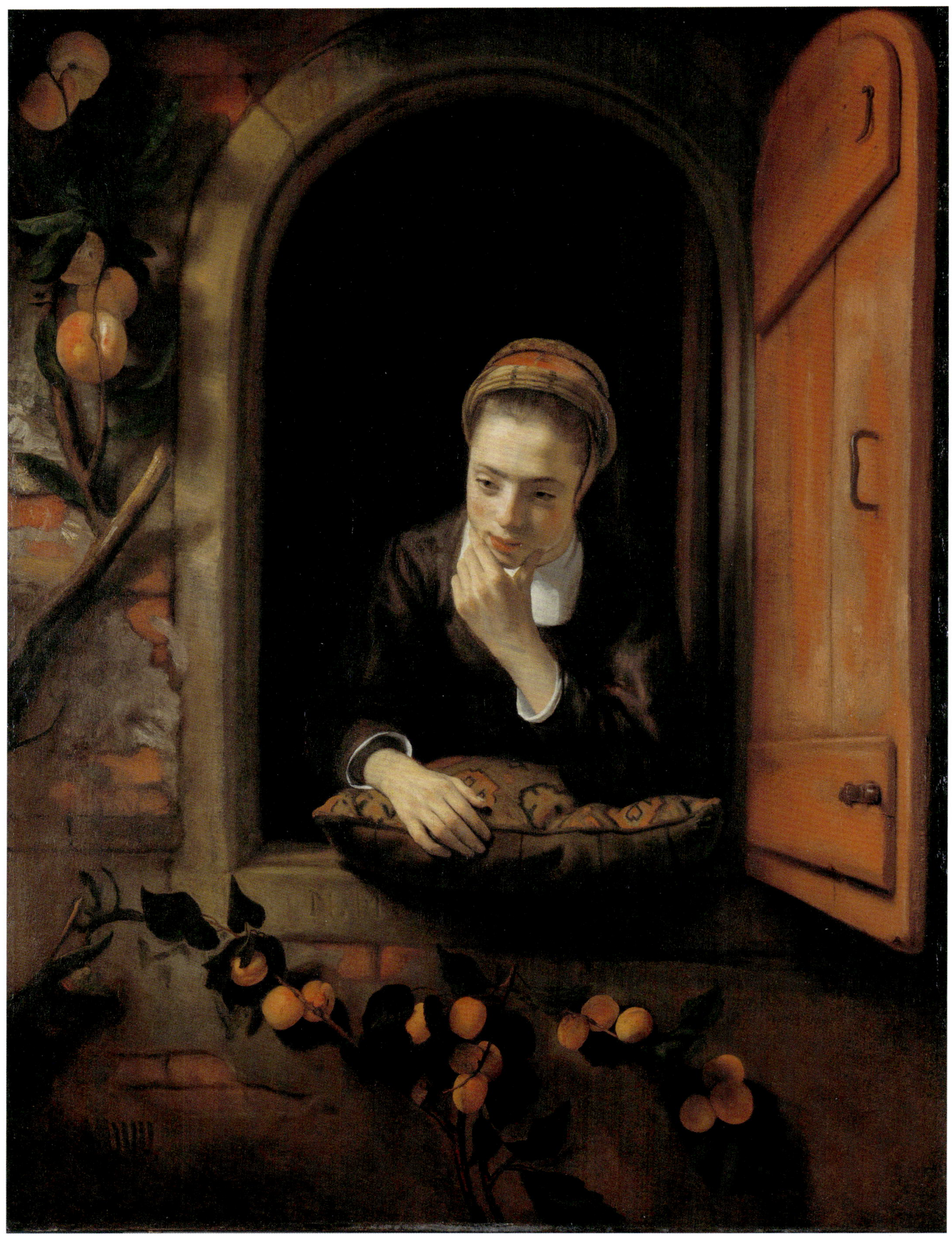

39.2

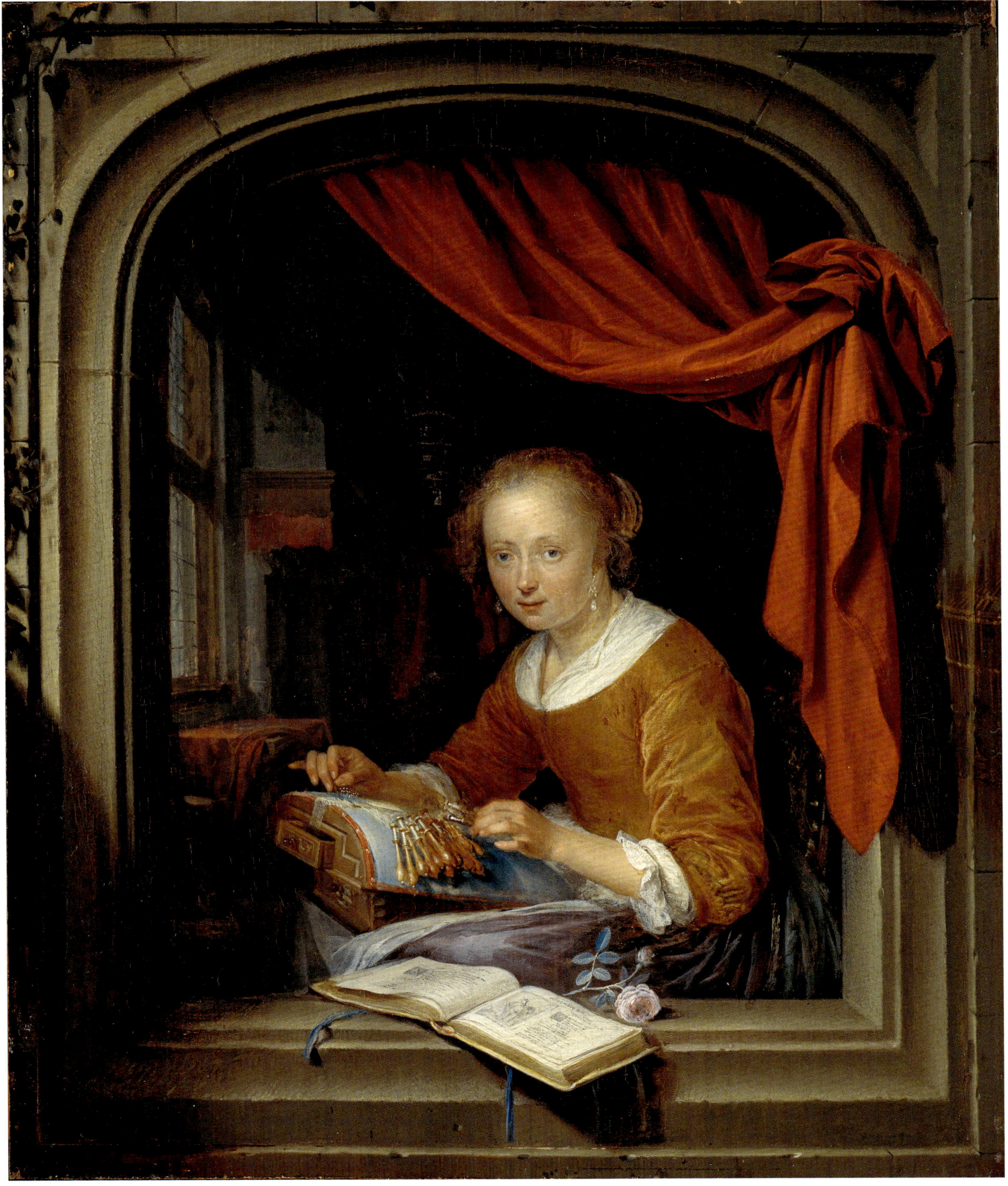

39.3

1 A Haarlem inventory from 1722 lists 'a male portrait of Bol or Victors, Rembrandt's best students'; see Biesboer 2001, p. 345, no. 79 [translated]; E. Haverkamp Begemann, in Chicago 1969, p. 26; Veldman 2021, p. 71. See also cat. 48.
2 Rembrandt, *Saskia van Uylenburgh at the Open Window*, c. 1633–6, pen and brush in brown ink, brown wash, 23.6 × 17.8 cm, Rotterdam, Museum Boijmans Van Beuningen, inv. R 131 (PK).
3 Veldman 2021.
4 Rembrandt, *Girl in a Picture Frame*, 1641, panel, 10.4 × 76 cm, Warsaw, Royal Castle, inv. ZKW / 3906; Rembrandt, *Girl at a Window*, 1645, canvas, 81.8 × 66.2 cm, London, Dulwich Picture Gallery, inv. DPG163; Rembrandt, *The Kitchen Maid*, 1651, canvas, 78 × 63 cm, Stockholm, Nationalmuseum, inv. NM 584, Copenhagen 2006, no. 13.
5 According to Sumowski, the peaches as a symbol of love could be a reference to the girl's thoughts; Sumowski 1983–94, vol. 3, no. 1330.
6 The Hague/London 2019, no. 6, pp. 72–5.
7 See Sonntag 2006.
8 Karlsruhe 2015, no. 110, p. 264 (H. Jacob-Friesen).
9 Ibid.

40 REMBRANDT PUPIL

Costume Tronie of an Old Man in Armour (so-called *Man with the Golden Helmet*)

c. 1650–5
Canvas, 67.5 × 50.7 cm
Staatliche Museen zu Berlin, Gemäldegalerie, cat. 811 A
Property of the Kaiser Friedrich Museumsverein
Lit.: Rifkin 1969; Stockholm 1992, no. 68, pp. 224f.; Hirschfelder 2008, no. 492, pp. 129, 141, 205, 249, 269, pl. 103; Warnke 2013.

The work known as *The Man with the Golden Helmet* is one of the most famous paintings in the Berlin Gemäldegalerie. It owes its extraordinary and still fascinating effect to the interplay between the darkness that envelops the ageing soldier and the light that dramatises the figure, casting metallic reflections on his helmet and gorget. The figure thus oscillates between visibility and invisibility, between physical presence and dissolution – characteristics typical of Rembrandt's late work. The focus is on the cabasset, a precious helmet not used in battle, decorated with feathers and repoussé work. In contrast to the other parts of the composition, the paint here is applied impasto, making the helmet stand out sculpturally. It is therefore unlikely that the work was intended as a portrait, but rather as a study of this magnificent helmet.

The contrast between the helmet and the subordinate figure, together with details of the painting technique, was the reason for the attribution of the work to 'Rembrandt's circle'. The lead white, characteristic of Rembrandt's flesh tones, is almost entirely absent, as is vermillion, a pigment typically used by Rembrandt. The intricately hatched brushwork of the face is also difficult to reconcile with Rembrandt's painting style.[1]

The artist and restorer Joseph de Landerset (1753–1824), into whose hands the work came while in a Swiss private collection, probably made significant changes to the composition. In any case, early interventions include a change in format by trimming on all sides, replacement of the original stretcher and lining as well as damage to the finely applied, transparent layers of paint, followed by extensive over-painting.[2] In 1897, the Berlin restorer Alois Hauser further obscured the work's appearance by relining it, concealing the ruinous condition with further overpainting and applying a thick layer of pigmented varnish. The latter was removed in 1985–6.[3] What the work actually looked like in the seventeenth century, therefore, remains partially unknown. Its fragile condition has thus far prevented a clear attribution to a student or follower of Rembrandt. Carel van der Pluym, Heyman Dullaert, Carel Fabritius, Wilhelm Drost and Ulrich Mayer have all been suggested.[4]

The painting is a prime example of a common practice in seventeenth-century Dutch painting: for the purpose of inventing new pictorial ideas and for practice, but also in order to produce objects for the art market quickly, props such as pieces of armour were combined with fictitious pictorial characters, often using so-called tronies.[5] The results were in great demand. Rembrandt is known to have used many such head studies, although sometimes they were based on a real portrait.[6] In the *Old Man in Armour* we encounter a tronie that also appears in a group of works associated with Rembrandt's workshop.[7] His studio also contained many objects that could be used to depict historical or ritual scenes. Rembrandt's inventory of 1656 even includes a 'carabetse helmet'.[8] The artistic task was therefore to depict the materiality of the helmet, which was completed with a tronie. The painter may well have been a student or assistant of Rembrandt, although the painting would not necessarily have to have been made in the workshop, since its members could appropriate the tronie repertoire for themselves. SW

1 See Kelch 1986; Pieh 1986, pp. 9–34; Fischer 1986, esp. p.47.
2 Busche 2015, p. 102.
3 See the extremely critical assessment of the 1985 restoration in Moroz 1993, pp. 38–48.
4 Rifkin 1969 and Adams 1984 (Van der Pluym); Grimm 1983 (Dullaert); Moffitt 1984 (Fabritius); Binstock 1999 (Drost); Nystad 1999 (Mayer).
5 On tronies, see the essay by Dagmar Hirschfelder in this catalogue, pp. 39–49; Hirschfelder 2008; Gottwald 2011; and the conference proceedings Munich 2014.
6 For such cases, Dagmar Hirschfelder has coined the term 'porträthaft wirkende Tronie' (portrait-like tronie); Hirschfelder 2009, p. 50.
7 The best-known are the 1650 portrait in The Hague (Mauritshuis), a work in Moscow (Pushkin Museum) and a canvas in Paris (Musée du Louvre); see Bauch 1966, no. 199, p. 11; Hirschfelder 2008, pl. 103, nos. 491–4, p. 129, note 86; Giltaij 2022, pp. 109f., nos. 145–8.
8 See Amsterdam 1999; Nystad 1999, p. 247.

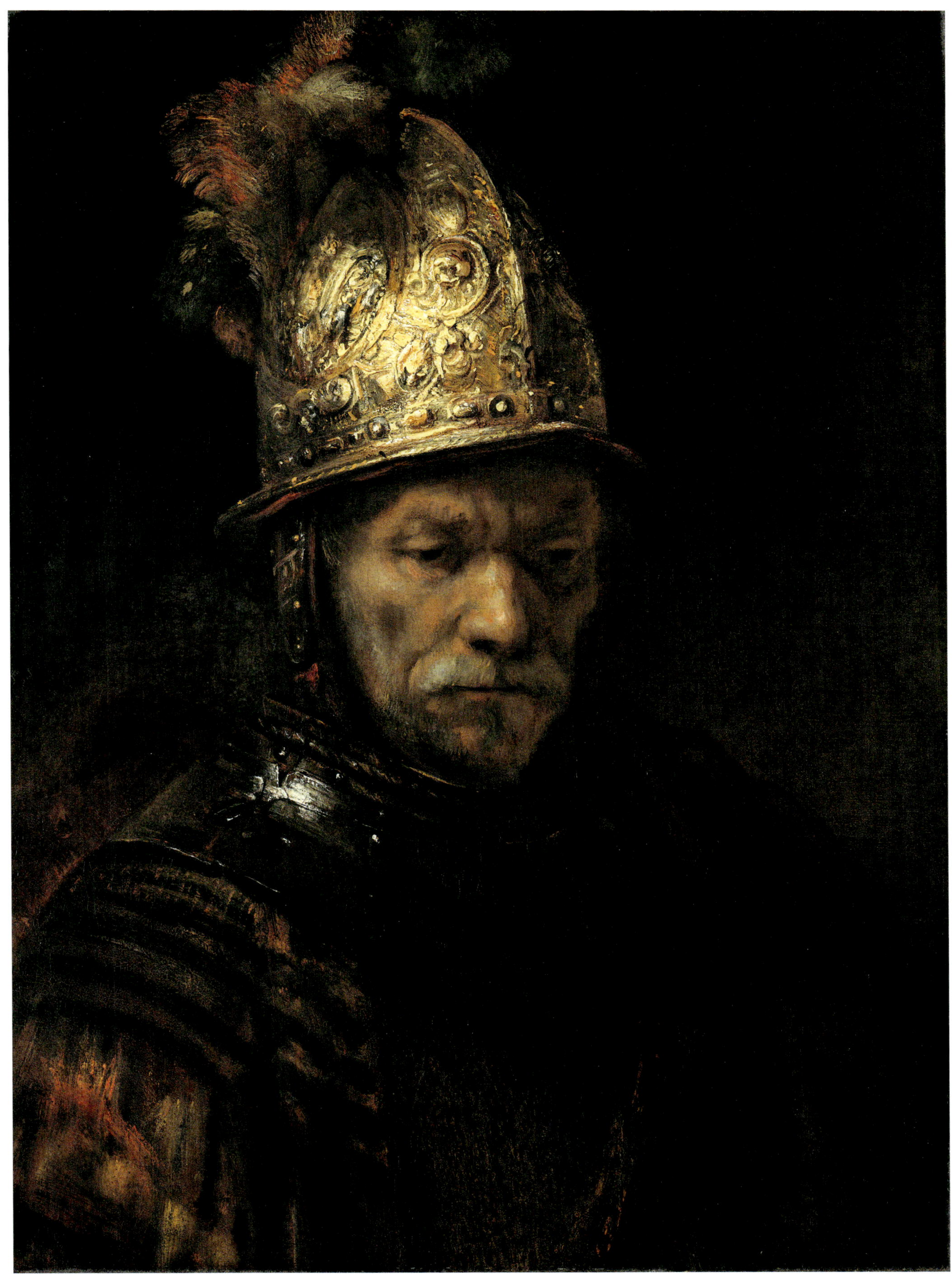

41.1 ABRAHAM VAN DIJCK

(Amsterdam [?] c. 1635–1680 Dordrecht)

Old Woman Reading (The Prophetess Anna?)

c. 1655
Canvas, 37.7 × 36.9 cm
Maximilian Speck von Sternburg Foundation in the Museum der bildenden Künste Leipzig, inv. G 1593
Lit.: Leipzig 1826, no. 12; Sumowski 1983–94, vol. 1, no. 372; Leipzig 2012, no. 68; Witt 2020, P 18.

41.2 ABRAHAM VAN DIJCK

An Old Woman Interrupts Her Reading ('Old Prophetess')

c. 1660
Canvas, 109.2 × 89 cm
Gotha, Friedenstein Stiftung, Herzogliches Museum, inv. SG 701
Lit.: Leipzig 1768, no. 494; Sumowski 1983–94, vol. 1, no. 375; Witt 2020, P 45.

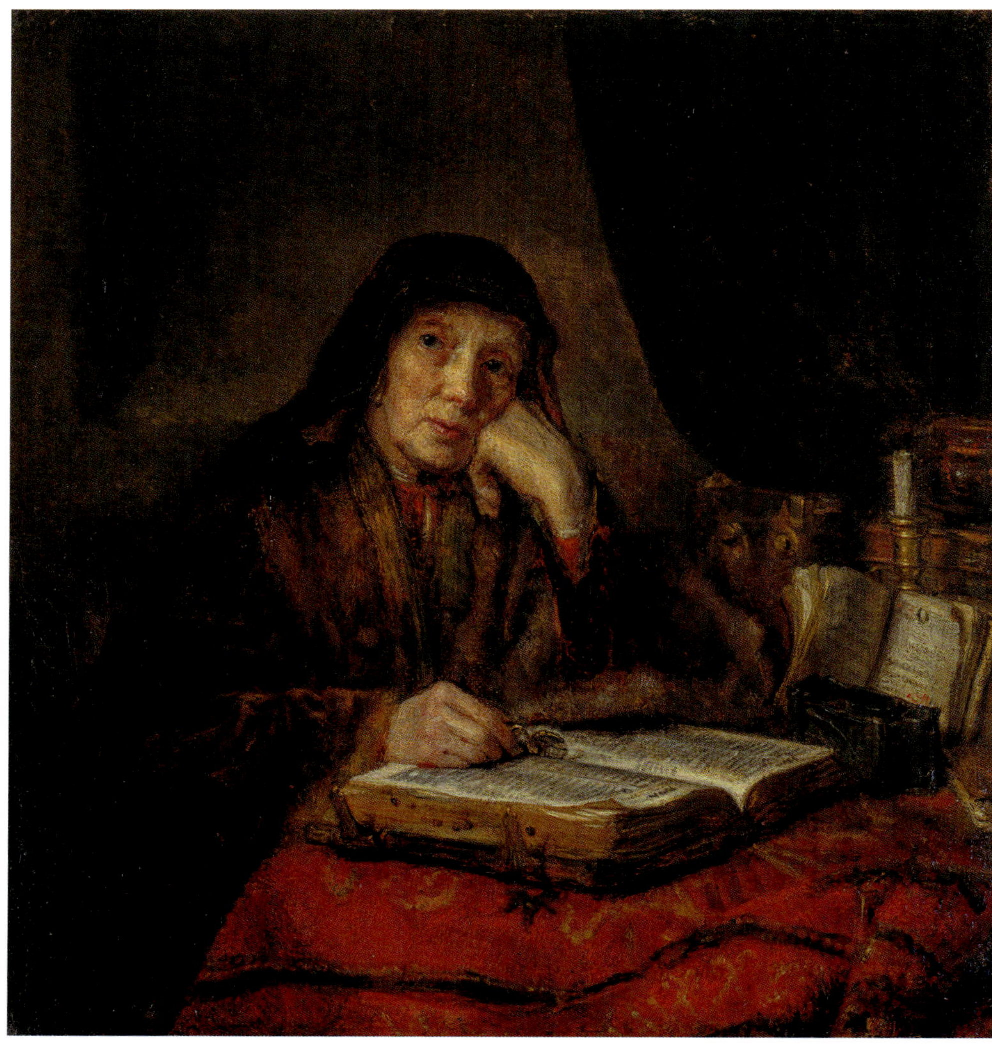

41.1

Abraham van Dijck was just 15 years old when he entered Rembrandt's workshop as an apprentice in 1651. He came from a merchant family in Dordrecht, like Nicolaes Maes, who was active in Rembrandt's workshop at around the same time (cat. 22.3). Van Dijck had previously studied in Dordrecht with Rembrandt's student Samuel van Hoogstraten in the second half of the 1640s.[1] Van Hoogstraten, a native of Dordrecht, who had himself begun an apprenticeship in Rembrandt's workshop ten years earlier, probably encouraged some of his students to learn from the master. Van Dijck specialised in the depiction of quiet moments and introspective feelings, a common feature of Rembrandt's late work.[2] An example of this is the *Old Woman Reading (The Prophetess Anna?)* (cat. 41.1), which was probably painted in Dordrecht shortly after Van Dijck had completed his training with Rembrandt.

As if interrupted at her reading – a pictorial idea that originated with Rembrandt – the woman looks up, lost in thought. In her right hand she holds her spectacles between the open pages, while her left hand supports her weary head. In the 1650s, van Dijck produced a series of images of pious old women, varying the same physiognomic type in different ways.[3] The motif also appears in the work of his fellow student Nicolaes Maes.[4] Van Dijck was probably familiar with Rembrandt's 1655 painting *Old Woman Reading*, which shows the same model.[5] Rembrandt had already explored the theme of the reading prophetess Anna in his early work (cat. 7).

Van Dijck reproduces the various materials such as fur, brass or paper with subtle shades of colour. The wrinkled skin around the mouth is also aptly characterised. The suggestion of an old woman studied from life is the result of Rembrandt's training and also shows the influence of Gerrit Dou. However, the lighting is harmonious and balanced, far removed from the dramatic chiaroscuro of the teacher. The picture strikes a balance between

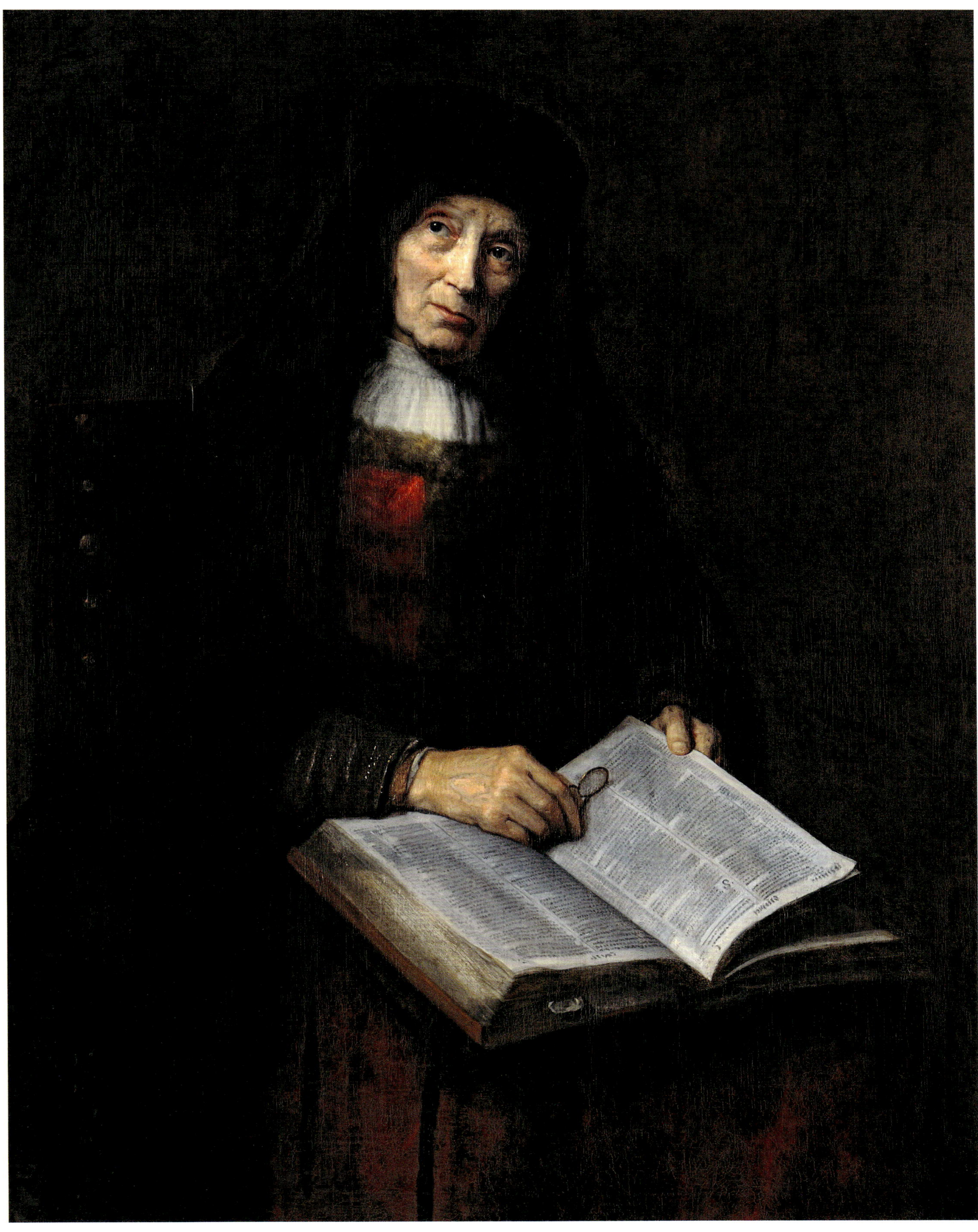

41.2

naturalistic everyday life and atmospheric devotional painting. It is only on closer inspection that one notices the historicising clothes, with the fur coat and headscarf falling over the shoulders, and the precious earring. On the table next to the book are an inkwell, a candle and several leather-bound folios, indicating the figure's erudition.[6] These motifs suggest that she is the pious prophetess Anna, whose old age did not prevent her from worshipping day and night in the temple (Luke 2:36–38). From Rembrandt, Van Dijck adopts the pictorial form of a scene that is more suggestive than it is clear. The multiple possible interpretations of the picture probably contributed to the popularity of this type of small-scale, inexpensive painting among dealers and contemporary collectors.

The painting was probably acquired by Max Speck in 1809 for the princely sum of 1,840 thalers (given its small format) as a work by Rembrandt and published as such in his collection catalogues.

In the eighteenth century, Van Dijck's painting *An Old Woman Interrupts Her Reading* from the important collection of Gottfried Winckler (1731–1795) in Leipzig was also regarded as a Rembrandt painting (cat. 41.2). Here, the upward gaze returns, illustrating the inner dialogue with God and at the same time exemplifying the economical reuse of models in Van Dijck's workshop. Once again, the subject is the contemplation of a devout reader, absorbed in her study of the Book of Ezekiel, an Old Testament scripture dealing with visions and prophecies. In contrast to the historically dressed prophetess in the Leipzig painting, the woman in the Gotha painting wears contemporary clothing. In the 1768 catalogue of the Winckler collection, we read:

'A respectable matron, perhaps the master's mother, sits in domestic devotion in an armchair, turned to the right. A black crape covers her trembling head and part of her red, fur-trimmed undergarment. Her expression is one of edifying contemplation as she reads the Bible, open in her lap. She turns the pages with her left hand, while her other hand, holding her spectacles, rests calmly on the sacred book.'[7]

The interpretation of the old woman as Rembrandt's mother was already widespread at the time and gave the painting additional meaning. When Winckler's house on Katharinenstraße in Leipzig was hit by a cannonball during the Battle of the Nations on 18 October 1813, the painting, which hung close to the windows, narrowly escaped destruction.[8] JN

1 Witt 2020, pp. 11f.
2 London/Amsterdam 2014, pp. 268f.
3 See Sumowski 1983–94, vol. 1, nos. 367, 370, 371, 375, 377; Witt 2020, D 11.
4 Nicolaes Maes, *Old Woman Dozing*, c. 1656, Brussels, Koninklijke Musea voor Schone Kunsten van België, inv. 2983; The Hague/London 2019, no. 13.
5 Canvas, 78.7 × 66 cm, Duke of Buccleuch and Queensberry, KBE; Edinburgh/London 2001, no. 121.
6 Further examples of the motif of reading in the work of Abraham van Dijck include his drawings *Young Man Reading at a Table* (Witt 2020, no. 54) and *Old Woman with Glasses, Reading*, c. 1650 (Berlin 2018, no. 55).
7 Quoted in Leipzig 1768, p. 495, no. 494 [translated].
8 Friedrich Rochlitz (1769–1842), husband of Henriette Winckler (1770–1834), who had previously been married to Friedrich Daniel Winckler (1760–1809), one of the art collector's three sons, reports: 'A six-pound cannonball hit the oriel … and damaged it badly. My share of the Winckler painting collection is located directly above it; right next to the windows is the large, splendid Rembrand …'; quoted in 'Der Verkauf von Teilen der Wincklerschen Kunstsammlung durch Friedrich Rochlitz', in Carl-Maria-von-Weber-Gesamtausgabe.de [translated].

42 BARTHOLOMEUS VAN DER HELST

(Haarlem 1613–1670 Amsterdam)

Old Woman at the Window

c. 1665
Canvas, 99.1 × 84.8 cm
Inscribed (lower centre, beneath book): B. van H… [illegible]
Maximilian Speck von Sternburg Foundation in the Museum der bildenden Künste Leipzig, inv. G 1619
Lit.: Leipzig/Munich 1998, no. I/74; Edinburgh/London 2001, pp. 60f.; Winkel 2006, pp. 82–5; Gent 2011, no. 144; Leipzig 2012, no. 130.

A woman leans over a window frame, surprisingly from the outside in. This departure from tradition might suggest that something is amiss here, and upon closer inspection we notice that the matron, characterised as an old woman with a wealth of meticulously rendered wrinkles, is dressed in a bright red, tight-fitting gown, appropriate only for young women. This is a blatant breach of propriety that was no doubt noticed by contemporaries. Her black veil is to be understood not as a garment of mourning, but as a sunscreen to protect her skin from tanning and wrinkling. Marieke de Winkel explains the veil using a verse by Jacob Cats in which a woman laments the loss of her youth: 'Although I always wear a veil or a mask and rarely go out, my youthful nature is turning into wrinkled skin.'[1]

Bartholomeus van der Helst depicts the woman as an allegory of *vanitas*, visualising the inexorable passage of time. The work is painted in virtuosic detail, evoking the materiality of the jacket, the leather binding and the pages of the book in the woman's hand as well as the linen of the handkerchief. The painting belongs to the category of 'bedriegertje', images that deceive the eye and play with the senses. Through the painted frame, the

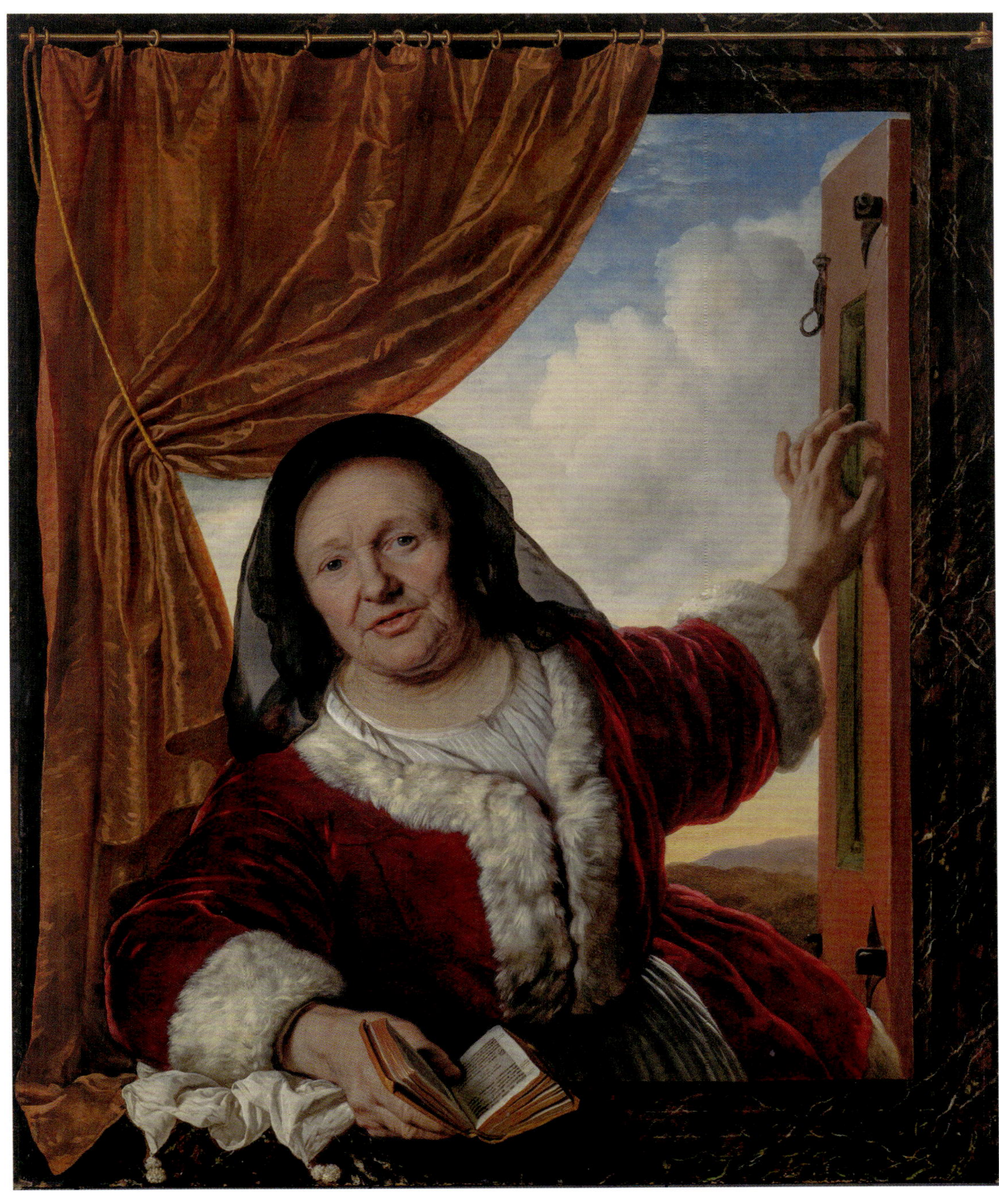

42

woman almost seems to enter the viewer's world.

The head type of the Leipzig work appears with younger facial features in the 1652 painting by Van der Helst in Dresden *Young Woman Behind a Green Curtain* (Staatliche Kunstsammlungen Dresden, Gemäldegalerie Alte Meister). Stylistically related is his 1665 painting *Woman with a Book* (Dijon, Musée Magnin). Bartholomeus van der Helst was a leading portrait painter in Amsterdam and as such a rival of Rembrandt. As portraitist of the Amsterdam upper classes, he was well acquainted with the vanities of his clients, about which he makes a witty joke here. Acquired by Max Speck in Brussels in 1822 for 1,500 francs, this painting belongs to the tradition of tronies of old women established by Rembrandt, Lievens and Dou. The lively staging in the window follows the tradition of window paintings, which was further developed in Rembrandt's workshop (cf. cats. 39.1–3). JN

1 Quoted in Leipzig 2012, p. 142 [translated]; cf. Edinburgh/London 2001, pp. 61, 250, note 66.

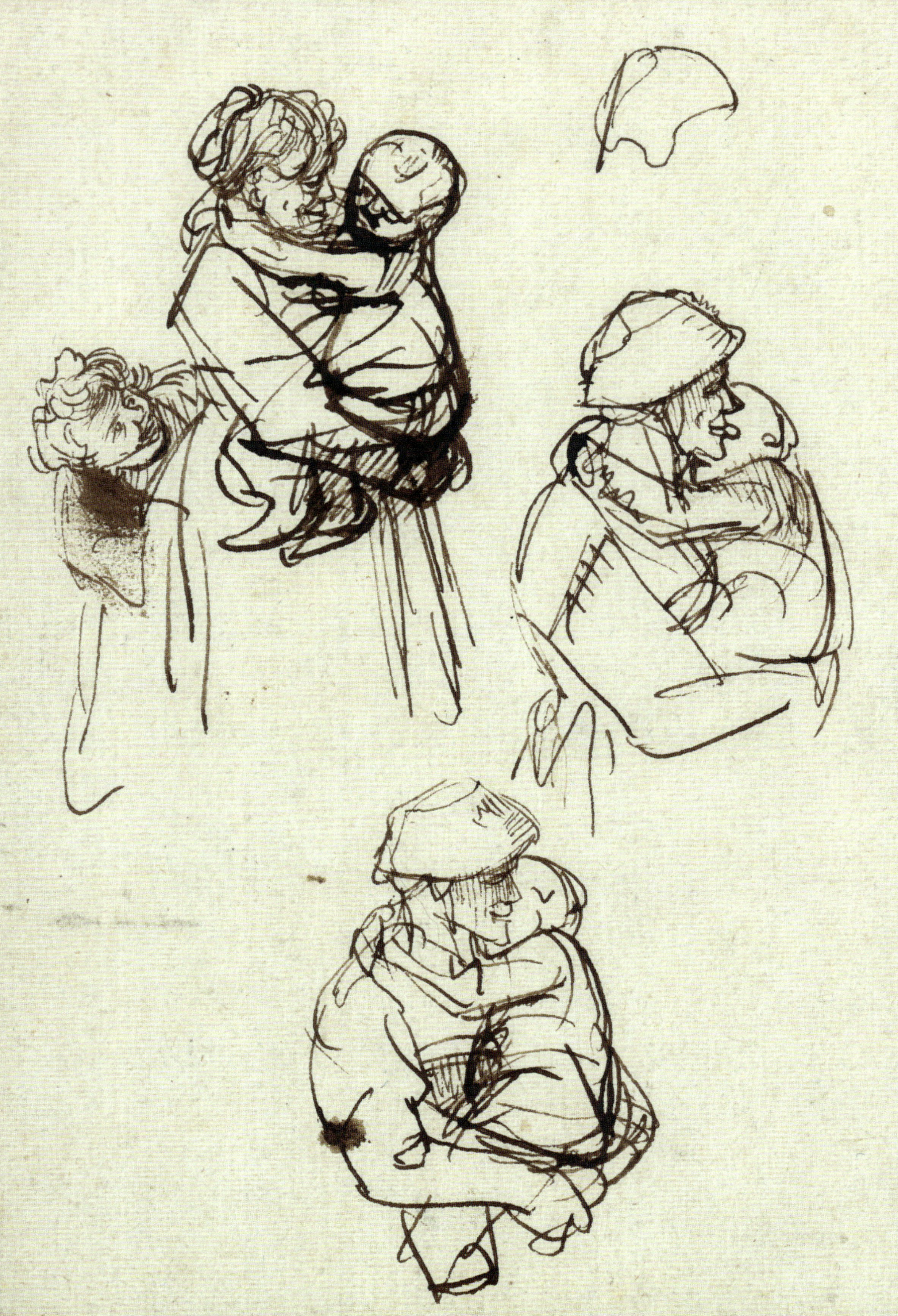

EMOTION AND HUMANITY IN EVERYDAY LIFE

43.1 WILLEM BUYTEWECH

(Rotterdam 1591/92–1624 Rotterdam)

The Pancake Baker

c. 1620
Brush and black-brown and grey ink and wash, 9.7 × 14.2 cm
Museum der bildenden Künste Leipzig, Graphische Sammlung, inv. I. 336
Lit.: M. Monkiewicz, 'Willem Buytewech's "Market Quarrel" in the National Museum, Warsaw', in *Master Drawings*, 35, 1997, pp. 397–400.

43.2 REMBRANDT

The Pancake Woman

c. 1635
Pen and brown ink, 10.8 × 14.4 cm
Amsterdam, Rijksprentenkabinet, inv. RP-T-1891-A-2424
Lit.: Benesch 409; Peter Schatborn (2017), 'Rembrandt van Rijn, The Pancake Woman, Amsterdam, c. 1635', in Turner online; Schatborn/Hinterding 2019, no. Z 235.

43.3 REMBRANDT

The Pancake Woman

1635
Etching, III (of III), 11.1 × 8.1 cm (sheet)
Signed and dated: Rembrandt ft 1635
Museum der bildenden Künste Leipzig, Graphische Sammlung, inv. NI. 2060
Lit.: B. 123; NH 144; Berlin/Amsterdam/London 1991, no. 10; Amsterdam/London 2000, no. 28.

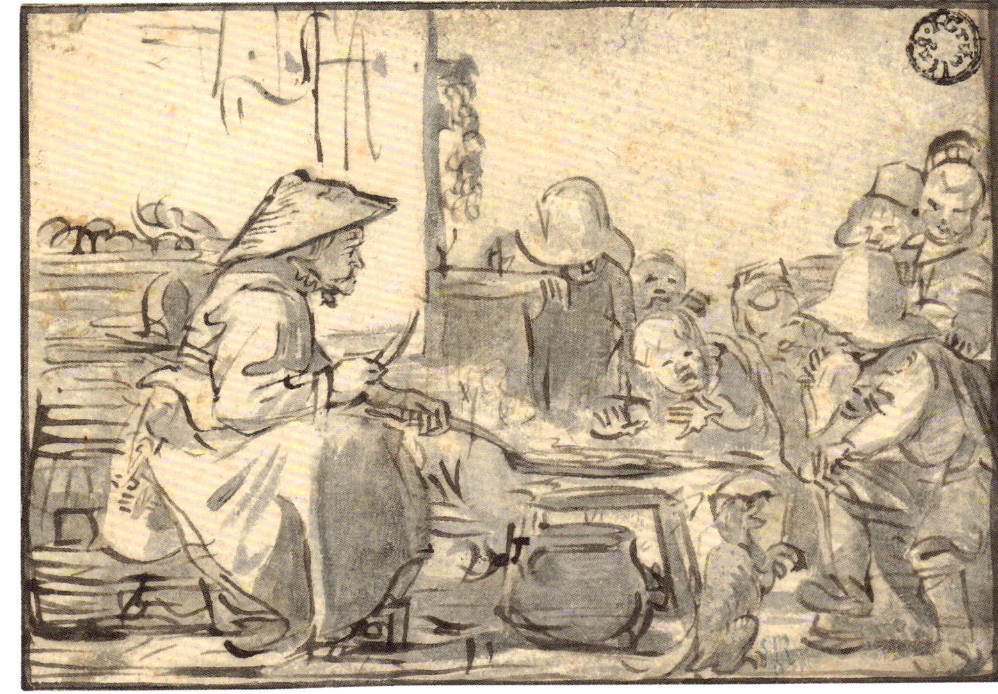

43.1

43.4 REMBRANDT

Christ Preaching

c. 1652
Etching and drypoint, I (of II), 15.6 × 20.8 cm (sheet)
Museum der bildenden Künste Leipzig, Graphische Sammlung, inv. NI. 2041
Lit.: B. 67; NH 298, I (of II); Amsterdam/London 2000, no. 68; Weimar 2011, no. 64.

43.5 REMBRANDT

A Woman with a Child Frightened by a Dog

c. 1635–6
Pen and brown ink, heightened with opaque white, 10.3 × 10.2 cm
Paris, Fondation Custodia, Collection Frits Lugt, inv. 5155
Lit.: Benesch 403; Schatborn 2010b, no. 3; Wetering 2016, p. 114f.; Leeuwarden/Kassel 2019, pp. 65–71; Schatborn/Hinterding 2019, no. Z 236.

43.6 REMBRANDT

Three Studies of a Woman with a Child in Her Arms

c. 1637–8
Pen and brown ink, 18.7 × 15.3 cm
Paris, Fondation Custodia, inv. 4904
Lit.: Benesch 343; Schatborn 2010b, no. 4; Holm Bevers, 'Review: Peter Schatborn, Rembrandt and His Pupils: Drawings in the Frits Lugt Collection', in Master Drawings, 50, 2012, pp. 397–408, no. 1; Schatborn/Hinterding 2019, no. Z 230.

Rembrandt's drawings of children are fascinating for their combination of spontaneous sketching and subsequent elaboration, which are difficult to separate. Many of the drawings of children were probably sketched by the artist directly in front of the model and later embellished and refined.[1] In the Paris drawing, a small child clings anxiously to its mother's arm as a dog approaches,

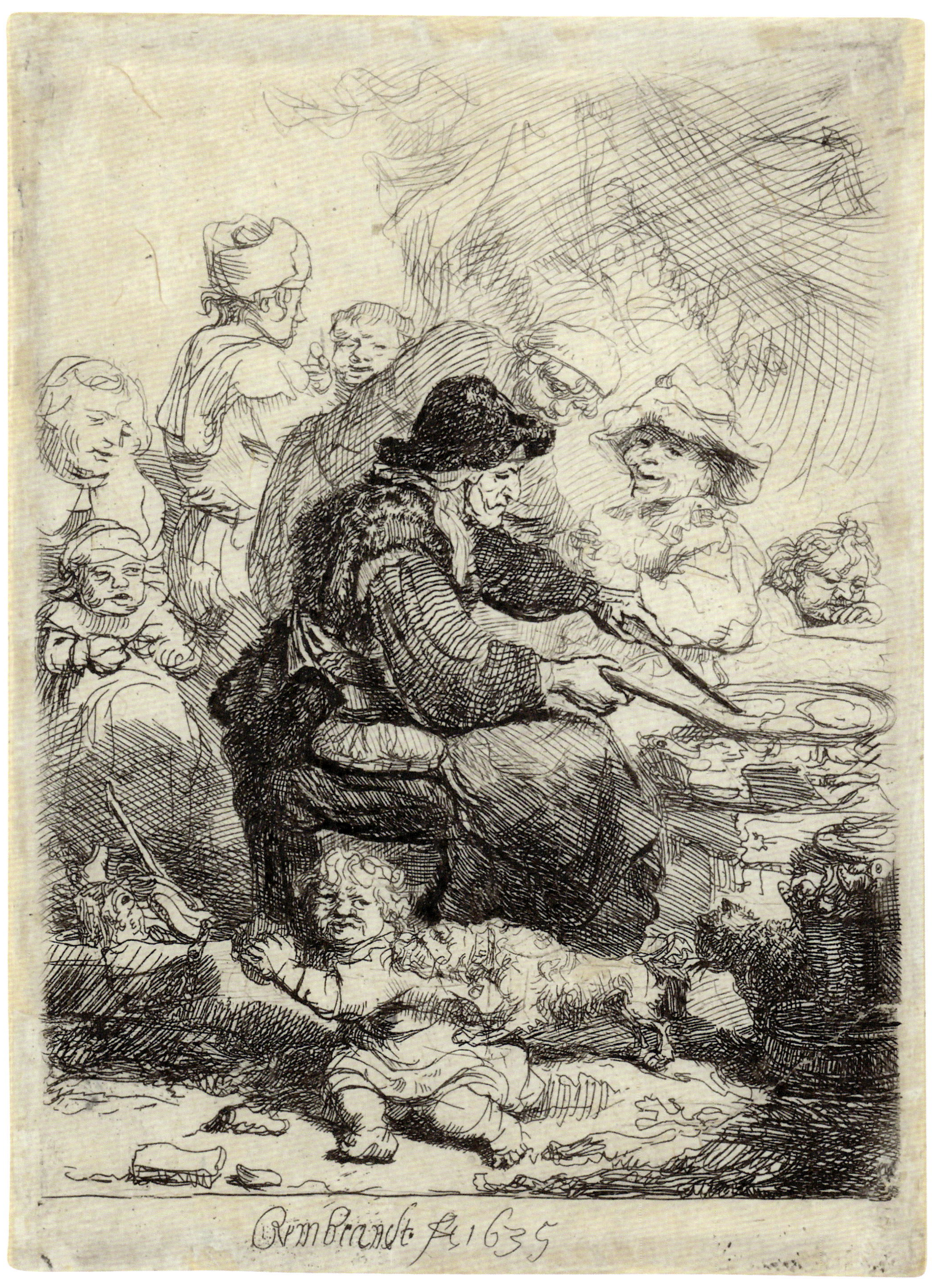

43.3

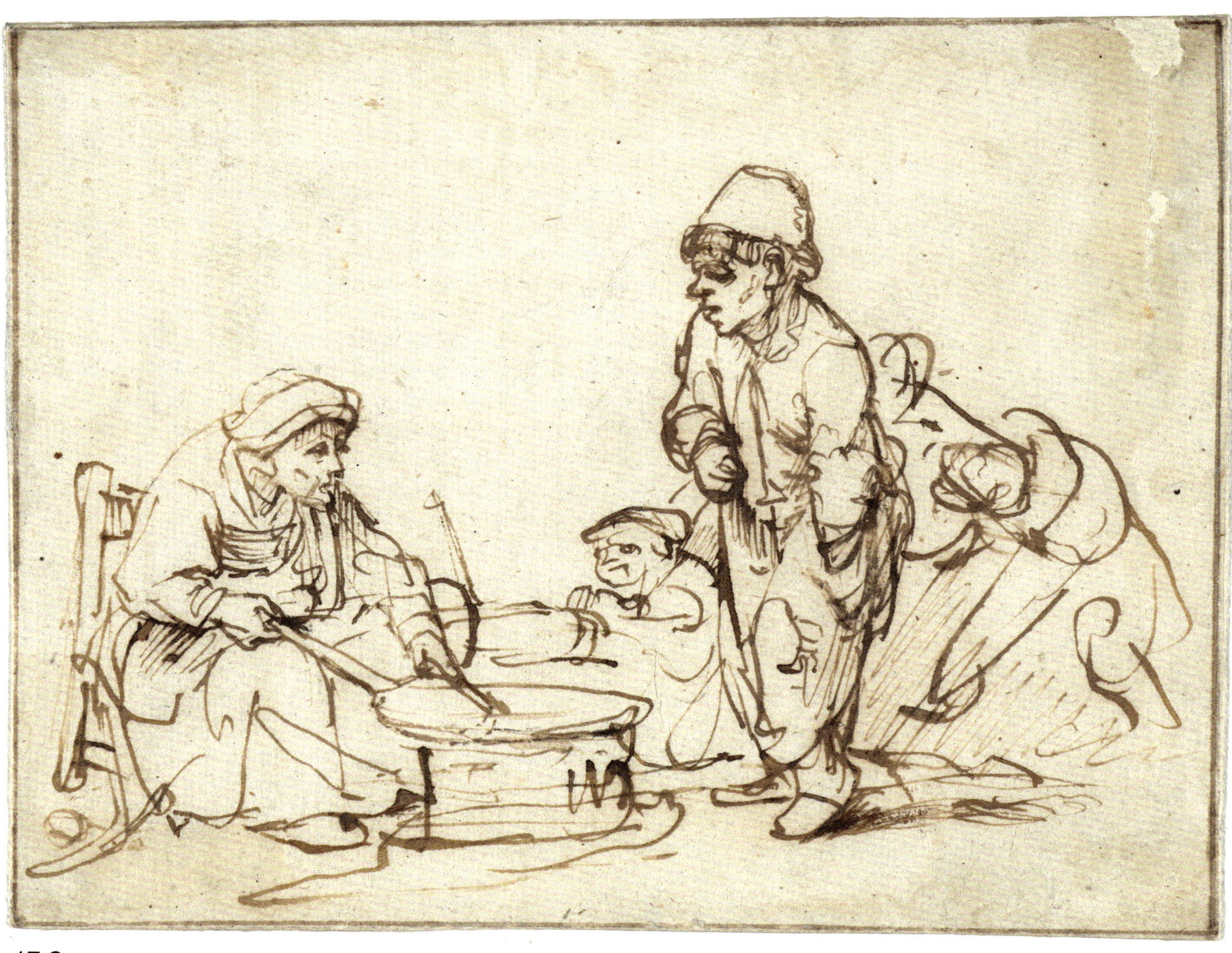

43.2

curiously sniffing a basket holding a dead duck (cat. 43.5). In this everyday scene, Rembrandt presents a small drama of emotions. No artist before him had paid such attention to the feelings of children. Rembrandt developed the composition further in a drawing in Budapest.[2]

Also from the second half of the 1630s is a sheet with three studies of a woman with a child in her arms (cat. 43.6). In one of the studies, another child, perhaps an older sibling, plays with the baby. The latter looks down from above in anticipation of the child's appearance; in the other studies, it hides its head on its mother's shoulder. The mother, in turn, responds to the infant's intense emotional life with an affectionate smile. Rembrandt captures the child's seated posture in the woman's arms in a spatially objective manner, while at the same time visualising the inner movement of the figures. Schatborn cites several variations of the motif in other drawings by Rembrandt.[3]

In the Amsterdam drawing (cat. 43.2), the artist uses his great observational skill to capture a boy reaching deep into his pocket to take out money for a pancake, at which he gazes with appetite.[4] Rembrandt also revisited the motif of the pancake baker, popular since the Reformation, in an etching dated 1635 (cat. 43.3). Here in the foreground, a small child protects his pancake from a dog. The Amsterdam drawing did not serve as a direct preliminary study for the etching, but may have been made

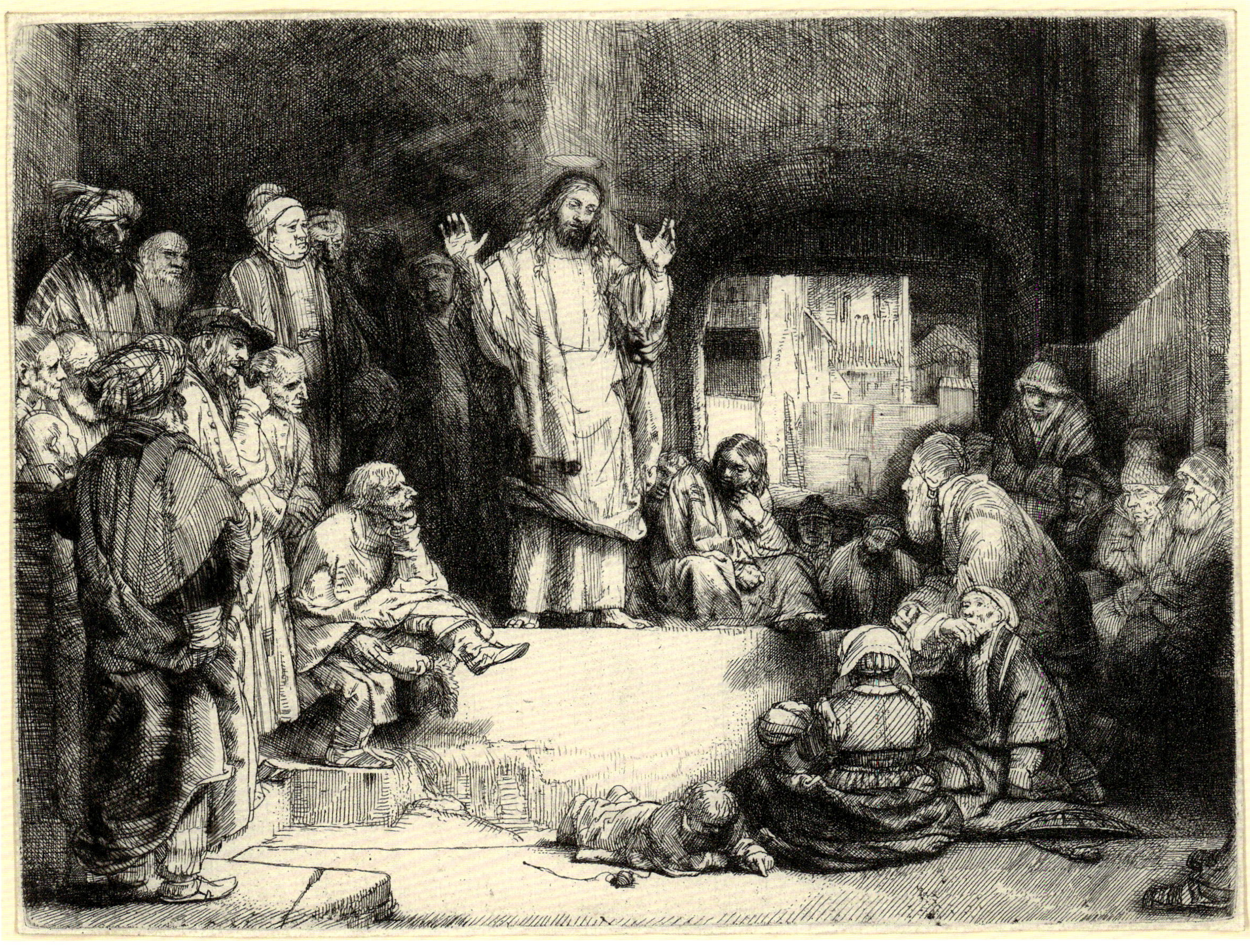

43.4

in the course of its preparation. The artist owned a painting of the same subject by Adriaen Brouwer, whom he particularly admired for his depiction of emotions.[5] What interested Rembrandt in his own drawing and etching was the most natural expression possible of the sensual desire aroused in the boy by the fragrant pancakes.[6] In the parallel actions of the boy looking and reaching into his pocket, he shows how his appetite is translated into physical movement. A drawing by Willem Buytewech demonstrates that here, Rembrandt is relying on an iconographic tradition that prefigures motifs such as the old woman in profile, the children and the dog (cat. 43.1).

More than almost any other artist, Rembrandt was interested in depicting the emotions of children and infants, which he observed closely. Small children could be studied among the offspring of his relatives. This curiosity stemmed from his general interest in subjects of everyday life, as well as his desire to portray the 'meeste ende die naetuereelste beweechgelickheijt' (the highest degree of natural movement), as he wrote in a letter to Constantijn Huygens in 1639.[7] The depiction of human emotion had preoccupied him from the beginning of his career, as Huygens noted during a visit to his studio in the 1620s, surprised by the 'accuracy and vividness of emotion' in his paintings. Rembrandt claimed to show the inner life of a person, whether in biblical stories, portraits or genre paintings. In this sense, children, who are often unable to

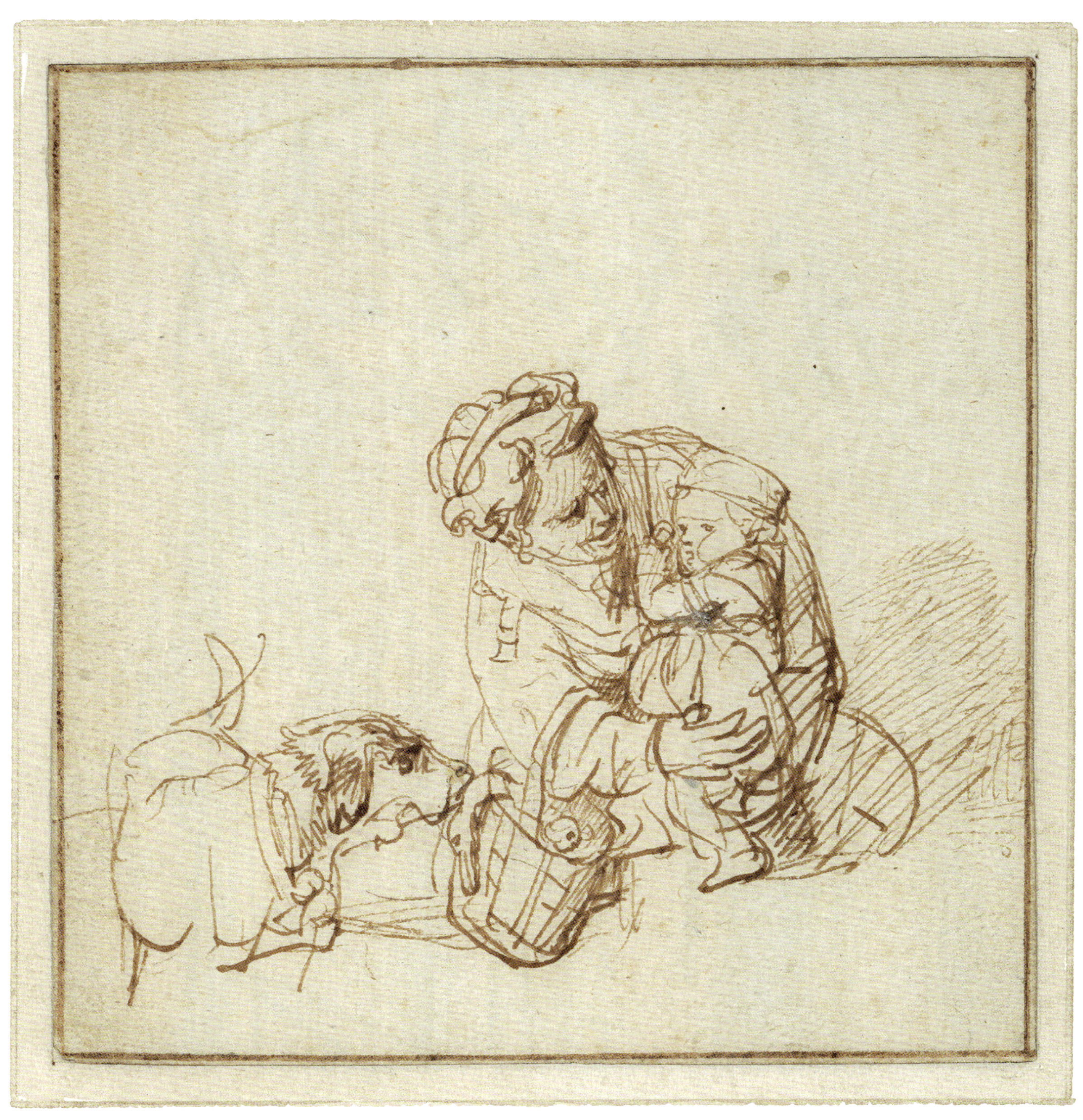

43.5

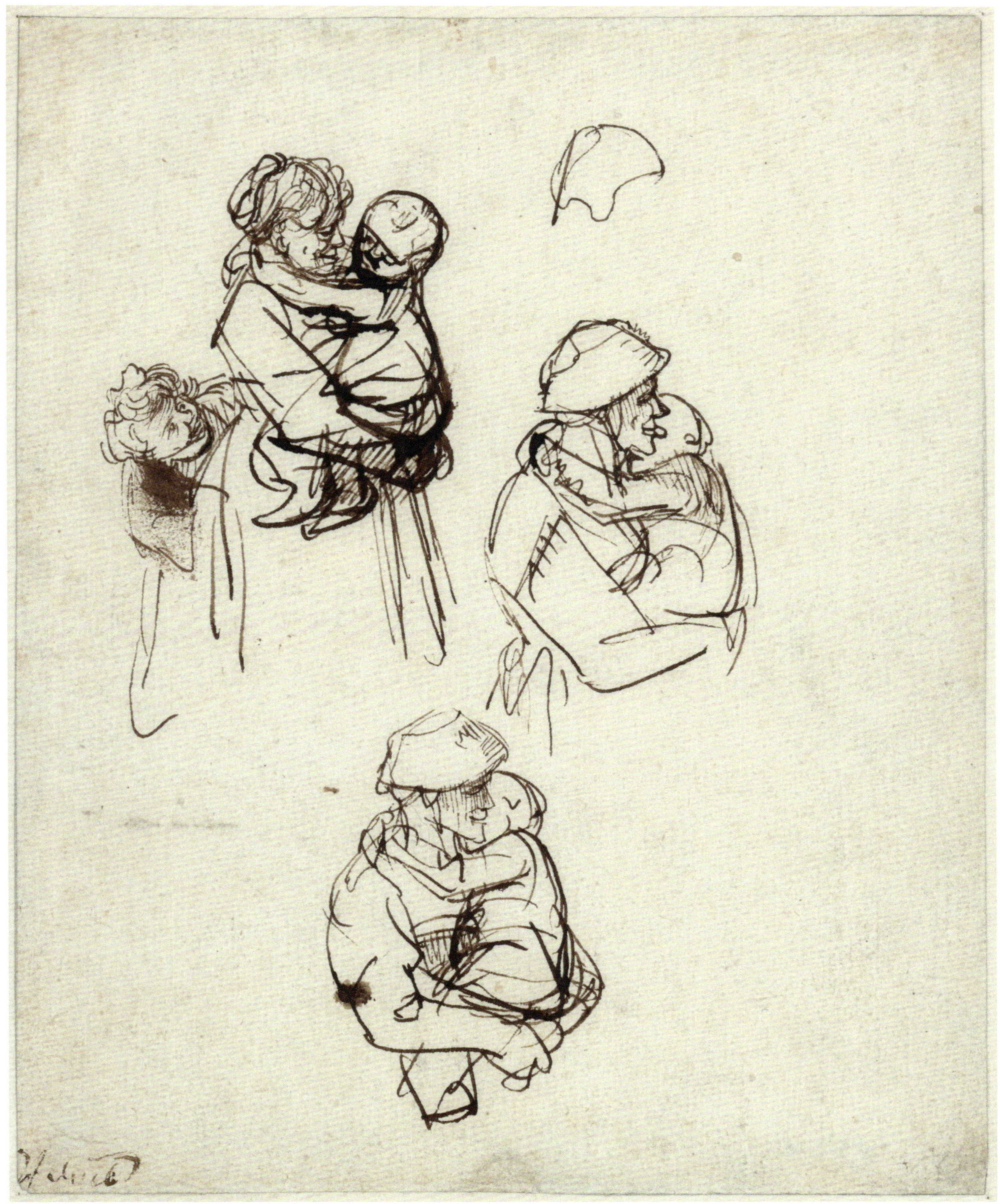

43.6

hide their strong emotions, provided him with suitable subjects. Just as he went to the theatre to experience and study the portrayal of strong emotions and passions on stage in tragedies and comedies (cf. cat. 10.1), he perceived the power of emotions such as love or anger in family life at home. In the etching *Christ Preaching* (cat. 43.4), the child placed prominently beneath the Saviour, immersed in his play despite the sermon, emphasises the realism of the depiction.

Rembrandt collected his drawings of children in a separate book. The painter Jan van de Capelle (1626–1679) owned an album with 135 drawings 'sijnde het vrouwenleven mit kinderen van Rembrandt' (the life of women with children by Rembrandt), according to his estate inventory of 1680. Van de Capelle had acquired the album, along with other drawings by Rembrandt, at the bankruptcy auction of 1656. Many of the drawings of children known today probably came from this album. They served not only as study material used by Rembrandt to develop later compositions, but also as a vivid and multifaceted visualisation of the sensuality and emotionality of human existence, which preoccupied him as an artist throughout his life. JN

1 Vogel-Köhn 1981, pp. 7–11.
2 Schatborn 2010b, vol. 1, p. 29.
3 Ibid., pp. 32f.
4 See Peter Schatborn (2017), in Turner online.
5 Ibid.
6 For a moralising interpretation of the motif, see Coburg/Freiburg 2017, no. 74.
7 See the essay by Jan Nicolaisen in this catalogue, pp. 22f.

44.1 REMBRANDT (?)

A Woman Standing in Profile to Left

c. 1638–9
Pen and brown ink, opaque white, 21.1 × 13.5 cm
Kunsthalle Bremen, inv. 744
Lit.: Benesch 217; London 1983, no. 4; Bremen 2000, no. 62.

44.2 REMBRANDT

Woman in Bed (Saskia?) with a Visitor

c. 1638
Pen and brown ink, brush and brown wash, 22.7 × 16.4 cm
Staatliche Graphische Sammlung Munich, inv. 01402 Z
Lit.: Benesch 405; Edinburgh/London 2001, no. 43; Munich/Amsterdam 2001, no. 17; Dresden 2019, no. 26.4.

44.3 WILLEM DROST

(Amsterdam 1633–1659 Venice)

Sleeping Woman

c. 1656
Pen and brown ink, brush and brown wash , 13.9 × 9.9 cm
Amsterdam, Museum Het Rembrandthuis, inv. 247
Lit.: Amsterdam 1972, no. 2 (as Rembrandt); Amsterdam 1991, no. 6; Amsterdam 2014, no. 7.

Hardly another artist of his time was able to perceive the world around him and capture it in drawings like Rembrandt. His genre pictures seem free of idealisation and reflect subtle, natural observations of everyday life. However, Rembrandt also stylised what he saw in order to create a particular mood.

The study of a *Woman Standing*, dated 1638–9 and attributed to Rembrandt, depicts a domestic scene (cat. 44.1). It is not clear what the figure is doing; Benesch has suggested that the drawing shows Rembrandt's wife, Saskia van Uylenburgh (1612–1642), choosing a piece of jewellery in front of a mirror.[1] However, there is no evidence to support this interpretation, since there is no such mirror in the depiction. It is more likely that she is leaning slightly forward in front of a tall table or a door. Rembrandt captured the woman's body and dress with bold, swift strokes of the pen. Shading in fine parallel and zigzag strokes creates shadows and volume. Martin Royalton-Kisch suggests that this drawing may have served as a drapery study for the portrait of Saskia in the Gemäldegalerie Alte Meister in Kassel.[2]

Such studies drawn from nature were described in contemporary parlance with the term 'naer het leven' (from life). Rembrandt's drawings of genre scenes and everyday life provided him with a wealth of material he could use when working on etchings and paintings. This is also true of a group of sheets depicting Saskia in bed, made between the second half of the 1630s and the early 1640s.[3] Saskia's four pregnancies (only one of her children survived to adulthood) and a serious illness to which she succumbed in 1642 often confined her to bed.

In the Munich drawing from around 1638, the artist's wife is shown lying in a massive alcove bed, her upper body propped up on pillows (cat. 44.2). She gazes at the viewer with a serious, weary expression and rests her head in her right hand, possibly alluding to Dürer's 1528 engraving *Melancolia*. Rembrandt drew the reclining woman with delicate, precise strokes of the pen. The visitor at her side, on the other hand, is rendered in broad, sweeping lines. In contrast to the detailed figure of Saskia, she is evoked with rapid brushstrokes and may have been added later by the artist. Rembrandt seems to have deliberately used varying degrees of figural development to keep the focus on the image of his wife. The view of the bedroom is captivating for its familiarity and intimacy. It is likely that Rembrandt sat and sketched by his wife's bed. The studies of Saskia in bed served him as a model for the 1639 etching of the *Death of the Virgin* and helped him to depict Mary's death in a powerful and convincing way.[4]

As a teacher, Rembrandt also sharpened his students' eye for the pictorial in everyday life. Willem Drost had studied drawing 'naer het leven' during his apprenticeship in the late 1640s and early 1650s. His *Sleeping Woman* of around 1656 (cat. 44.3) seems to have been strongly inspired by a drawing by Rembrandt from two years earlier, which shows an intimate view of the sleeping Hendrickje Stoffels (1626–1663), Rembrandt's partner probably from the late 1640s onwards.[5] The head of Drost's sleeping woman rests on a pillow lying on a bed (cat. 44.3). The young woman's relaxed facial features bear witness to her deep sleep. Strongly varying hatching lines and finely placed shadows give the figure great vividness. Her bonnet is depicted a second time to the right above the figure – an indication that Drost drew the headdress from a model and repeated the motif to ensure its accuracy.[6]

The depiction of sleeping figures, especially young women, was a popular subject in the Netherlands in the seventeenth century. The motif was particularly common in genre painting, where it often suggested hidden moral meanings – either in

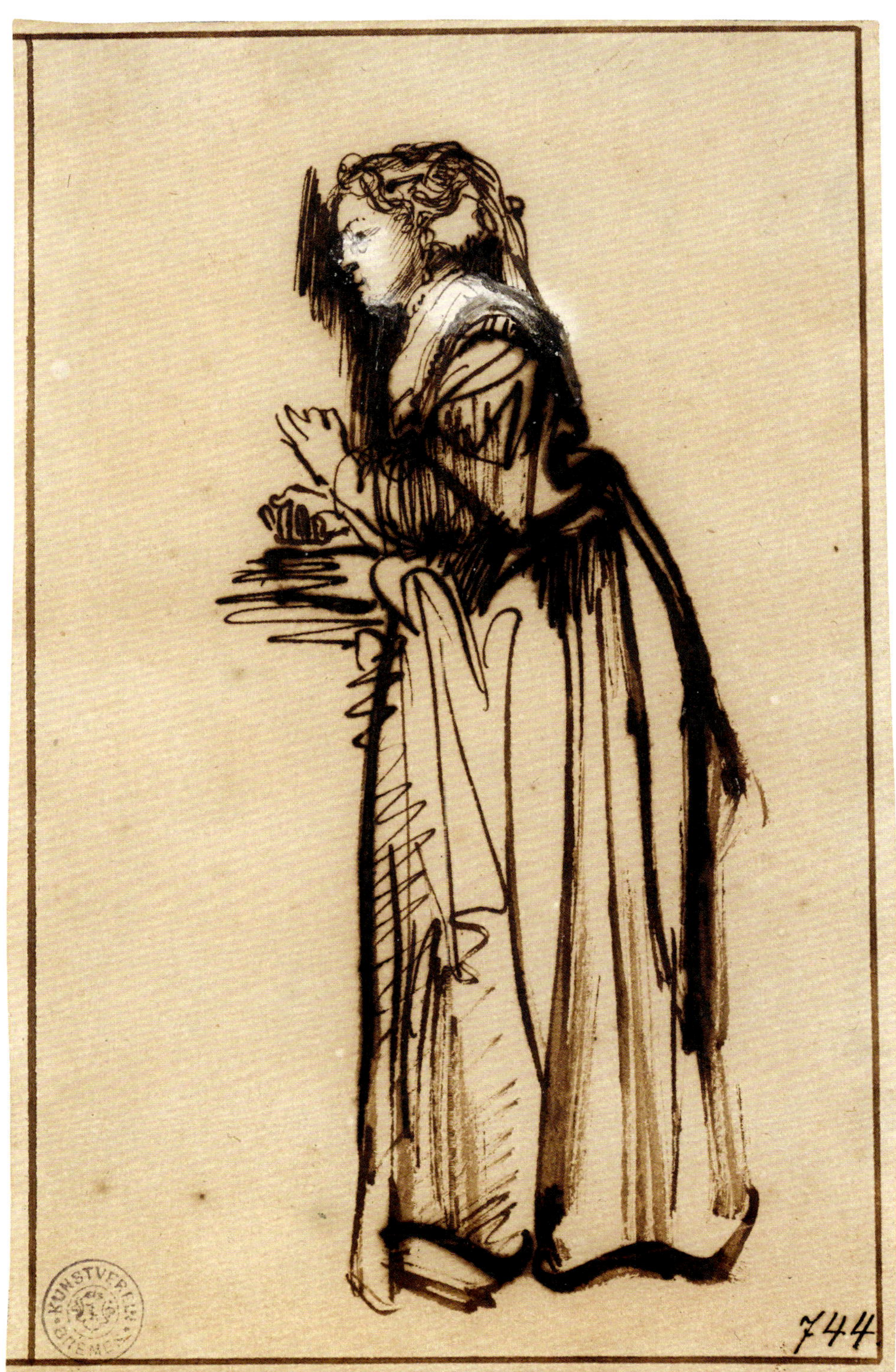

44.1

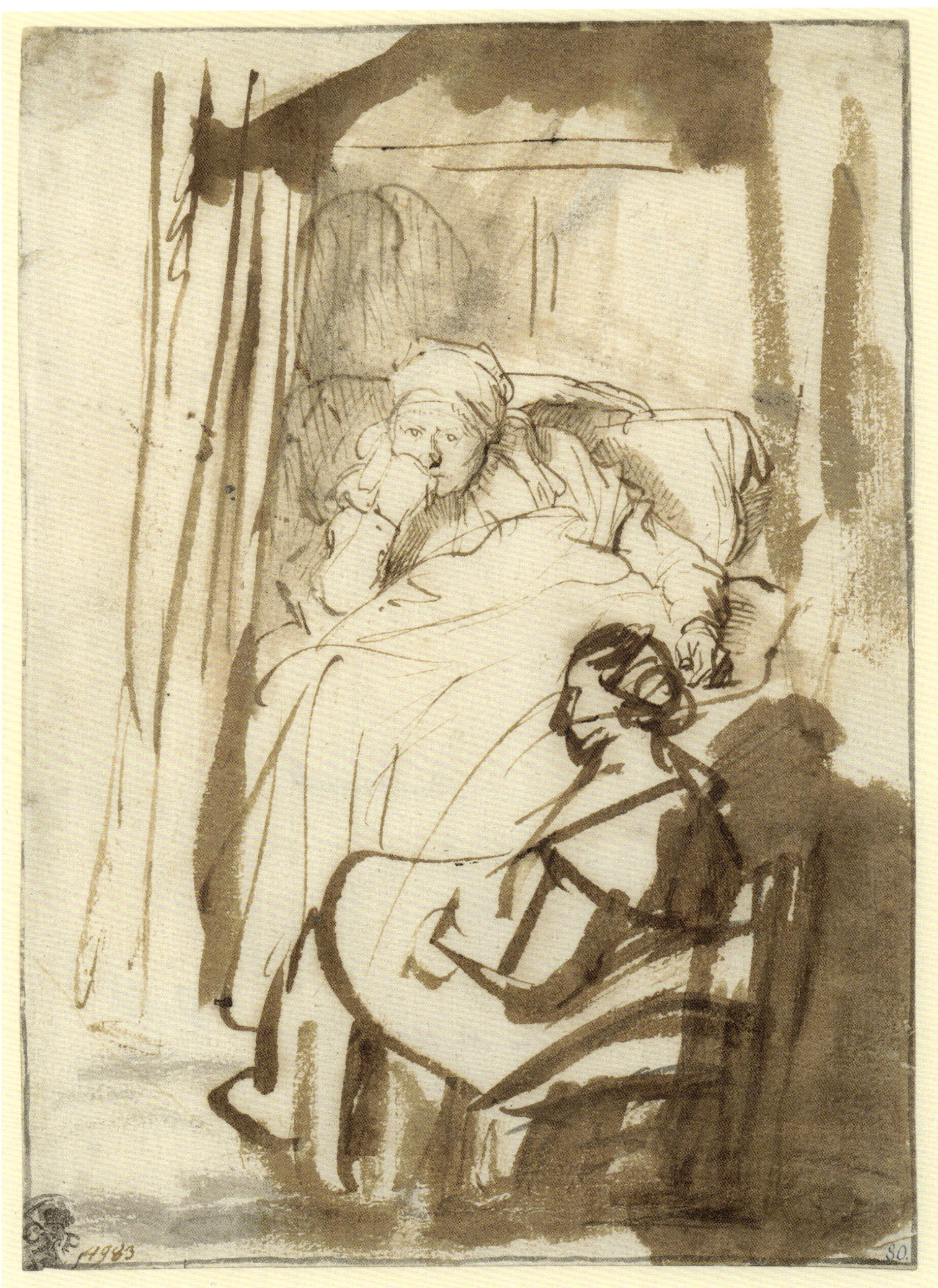

44.2

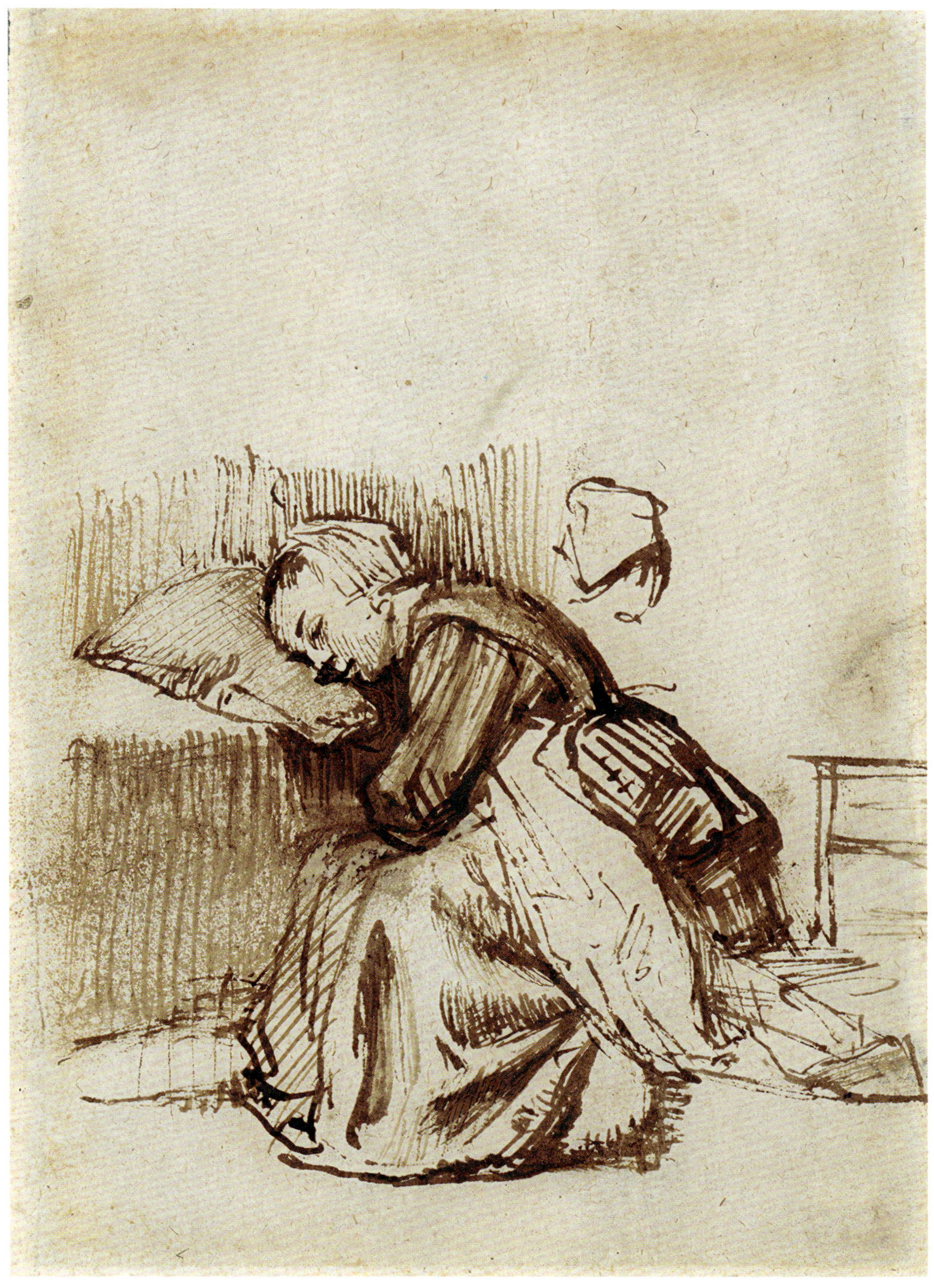

44.3

the form of erotic allusions or as a reference to the sin of idleness. The two drawings by Rembrandt and Drost are far removed from any such moralising intent. LCS

1 Benesch 217.
2 Rembrandt, *Saskia van Uylenburgh in Profile, in Pompous Dress*, c. 1633/34–41, panel, 99.5 × 78.8 cm, Kassel, Gemäldegalerie Alte Meister, inv. GK 236; Royalton-Kisch online, Benesch 217.
3 See Edinburgh/London 2001, nos. 41f.
4 Rembrandt, *The Death of the Virgin*, 1639, etching (B. 99); Dresden 2019, p. 138.
5 Rembrandt, *A Young Woman Sleeping (Hendrickje Stoffels)*, c. 1654, brush in brown ink, brown wash, 24.6 × 20.3 cm, London, British Museum, inv. 1895,0915.1279. Hendrickje Stoffels remained with Rembrandt until her death in 1663; Dresden 2019, no. 118.
6 Amsterdam 2014, no. 7.

45 REMBRANDT

Christ Healing the Sick ('Hundred Guilder Print')

1648
Etching with drypoint and engraving, II (of IV), 30.4 × 41.4 cm (sheet)
Staatliche Graphische Sammlung Munich, inv. 1964:0460 D
Lit.: B. 74; NH 239; Amsterdam/London 2000, no. 61; Dresden 2019, no. 49 (H. Bevers); Golahny 2021; Amsterdam 2024, pp. 100f.

Convinced of the quality of his work, Rembrandt always aimed to make as much money as possible from his art. It is only logical that one of his most ambitious etchings should be named after the exorbitant price that one of the impressions allegedly fetched on the art market during the artist's lifetime: the 'Hundred Guilder Print'.[1] In the midst of a crowd of over thirty figures, including a Black man in a fur hat (at the right edge of the composition), Jesus stands upright under a high vault with his hand raised, blessing the sick and needy who flock to him. Due to reversal caused by the printing process, it is his left hand that is elevated, a fact that does not seem to have bothered Rembrandt. A young woman with a baby in her arms approaches Jesus and is rejected by Peter (to his left); Jesus, however, welcomes her with outstretched arm. In the foreground, a sick woman lies on a stretcher covered with straw. Other old and infirm people stream in through a gateway on the right, including a blind man with a stick and a man with a bandaged head lying on a pushcart. Orientalising costumes place the events at a distance in time and space.

The scene simultaneously illustrates several episodes from Matthew 19, notably the healing of the sick and the blessing of the children. The sceptical Pharisees are depicted as old men at the left

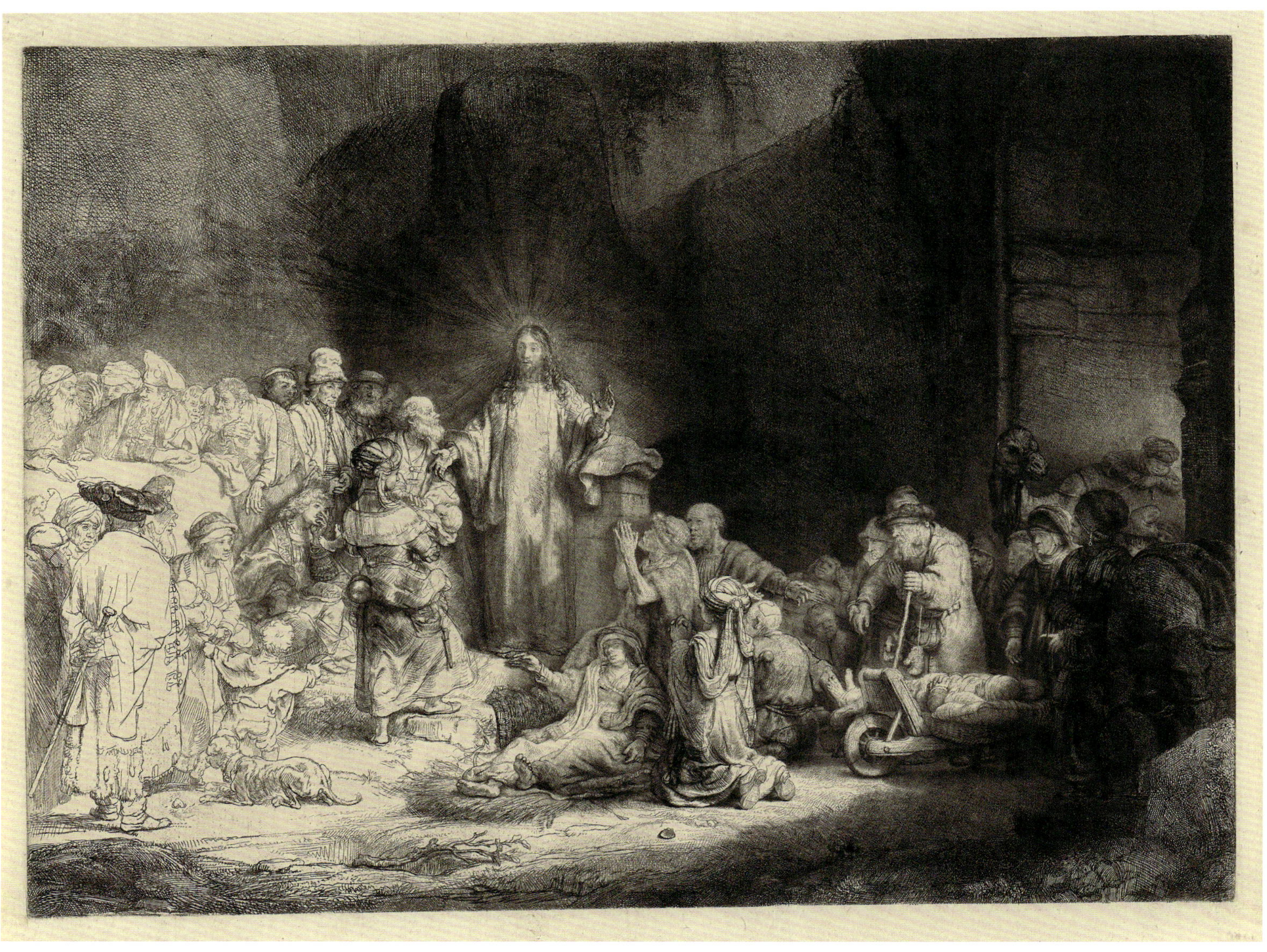

45

edge of the picture, while some of the disciples likewise appear to the left of Jesus. Rembrandt also alludes to the story of the rich young man who is advised by Jesus to give up his worldly possessions in order to enter heaven. The curly-haired young man sits on the steps with a pensive expression. In the gateway to the right, a camel can be seen in the semi-darkness, symbolising Jesus's words: 'It is easier for a camel to go through the eye of a needle than for a rich man to enter the kingdom of God' (Matthew 19:24).

Rembrandt dramatises the human desire for salvation through the movement of the many figures from the darkness towards the luminous figure of Jesus Christ. The shadow of the praying hands and profile of a woman kneeling beneath him stand out against his light-coloured robe. The individual figures are rendered in drypoint with a wealth of velvety nuances. Some are precisely formulated in the materiality of their clothing and show differentiated facial expressions, while others are sketchily indicated with only a few lines. The artist experimented with the technique of etching to create different levels of reality. The result is a vivid picture composed of many individual scenes – according to Van Hoogstraten, 'troeping' and 'verscheydenheyt' are the key terms in this compositional method – which does not appear illustrative, but rather virtuosic and at the same time imaginary. One never loses sight of the fact that this is a technically sophisticated work of art. Six preparatory drawings (undoubtedly there were more) have survived, in which individual figures and groups of figures are developed. As compositional studies, they aim to emphasise the narrative cohesion of the groups and their orientation towards the figure of Jesus, aspects that Rembrandt also sought to convey to his students.[2]

Rembrandt juxtaposes the profane and the sacred, emphasising the connection between them. His pictorial narratives are touching precisely because of the proximity of realistically depicted everyday life and apparitional miracles. As an accomplished master, he combined the radiant light of the Saviour with the figures of the wretched in semi-darkness in order to arouse the viewer's compassion. By inserting numerous studies 'naer het leven' – such as the motifs of mothers with children – he increased the impact of the pictorial narrative (cf. cats. 43.5–6).[3] JN

1 London/Amsterdam 2014, p. 153.
2 See Martin Royalton-Kisch, 'The role of drawings in Rembrandt's printmaking', in Amsterdam/London 2000, pp. 77–80; Holm Bevers in Dresden 2019, pp. 207–13.
3 Vogel-Köhn 1981, pp. 11, 223, nos. 57, 58.

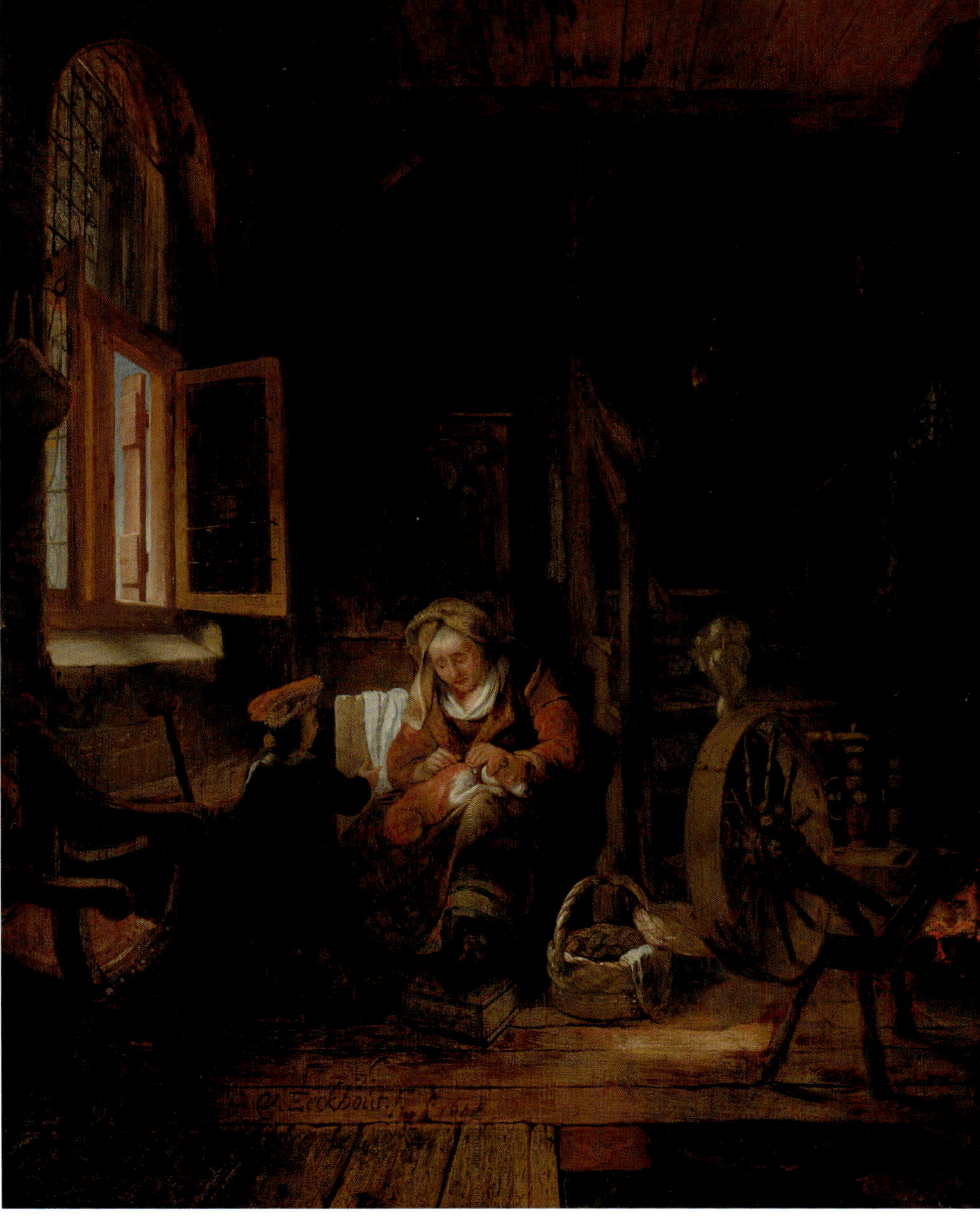

46.1

46.1 GERBRAND VAN DEN EECKHOUT

(Amsterdam 1621–1674 Amsterdam)

Anna and the Young Tobias

1648
Panel, 39.7 × 31.6 cm
Museum der bildenden Künste Leipzig, inv. G 328
Lit.: Sumowski 1983–94, vol. 2, p. 728, no. 405; Leipzig 2012, no. 80.

46.2 GERBRAND VAN DEN EECKHOUT

Study of a Dog Lying Down

1650–60
Point of the brush and brown ink, brown wash, 29.4 × 19.9 cm
Paris, Fondation Custodia, Collection Frits Lugt, inv. 5822
Lit.: Sumowski 1979–92, vol. 3, no. 797* and with no. 782*; Schatborn 2010b, vol. 1, no. 70.

The son of a goldsmith, Gerbrand van den Eeckhout probably trained in Rembrandt's workshop in the second half of the 1630s. His earliest dated painting is from 1641, and according to Houbraken he remained on friendly terms with Rembrandt after his apprenticeship. He was an accomplished painter and draughtsman who did not specialise in one subject, but painted biblical stories as well as portraits, genre scenes and landscapes. He also designed book illustrations and ornamental engravings and was active as a writer.

The small 1648 painting *Anna and the Young Tobias* shows the influence of Rembrandt and Gerrit Dou on the young artist (cat. 46.1). In a dusky interior, an old woman sits with a dog on her lap, checking it for fleas, while a young boy watches her. Next to her are a sewing basket

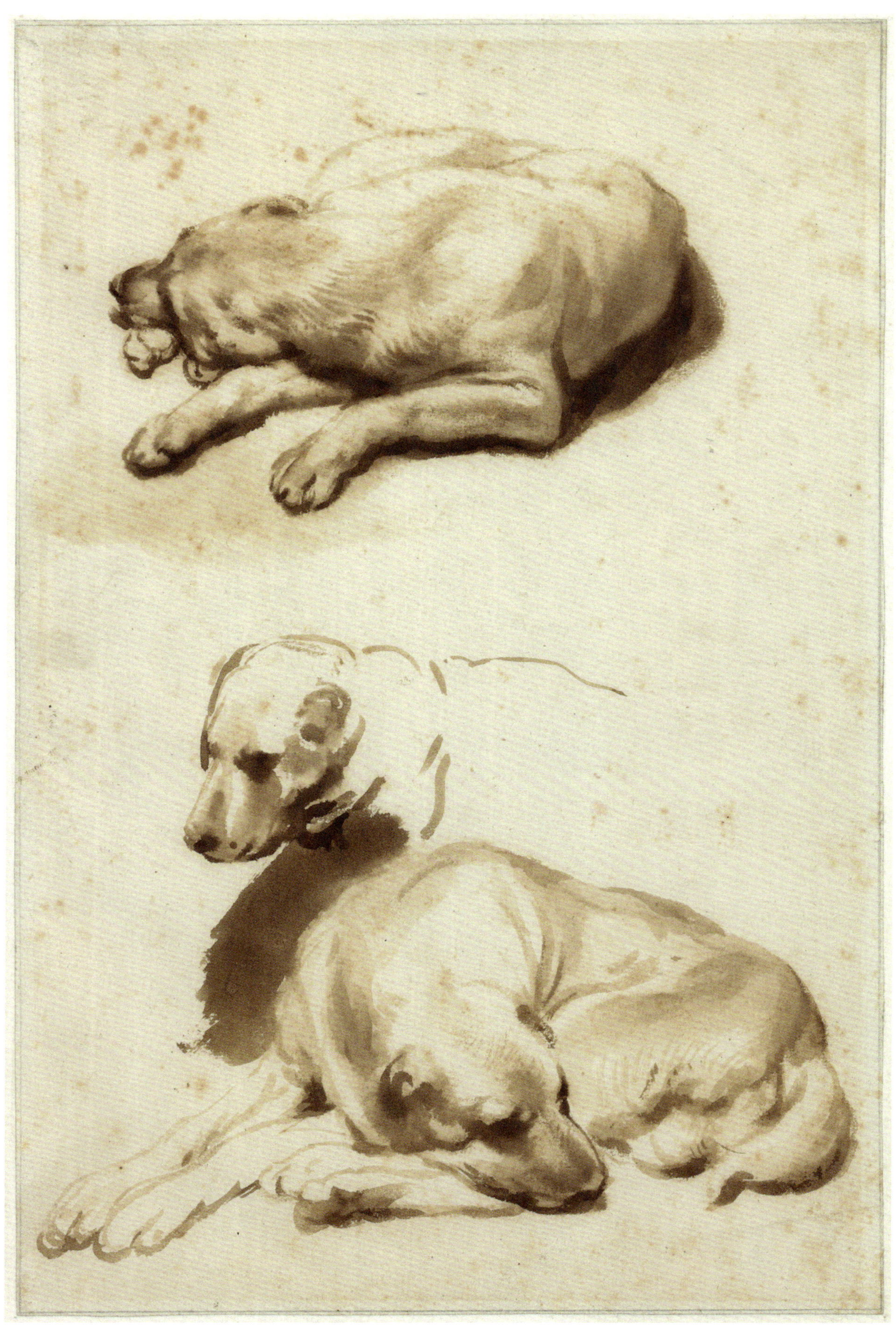

46.2

and a spinning wheel with wool attached to it to be spun into yarn. A small fire burns on the right, while faint sunlight enters the room through the open window, illuminating the woman and the dog. The lighting is far less dramatic than is usual in Rembrandt's work. The relatively matter-of-fact depiction of domestic utensils and the addition of still life elements such as the basket of sewing implements and the wool on the spinning wheel are inspired by paintings by Gerrit Dou from the 1630s and 1640s.[1] At the same time, these motifs and the historicising clothing of Anna and her son Tobias – the velvet cap, the boy's girdled robe and the old woman's headdress – hint at the scene's biblical origins. The apocryphal Book of Tobit was the inspiration for many works by Rembrandt and his circle. Anna 'brought home what she could get for their living by the labour of her hands' (Tobit 2:19). The young Tobias is later accompanied by his little dog on his journey to find a cure for his blind father. The walking stick can be seen to his left.

Anna's head and the impasto painting on her wrinkled forehead recall the heads of old women by Rembrandt and Dou from the 1620s and 1630s (cf. cats. 33.1–2). The genre-like details of the painting are an indication of the taste of the art market and the interest in mixing Old Testament motifs with everyday observations. This is precisely what Rembrandt taught his students, and it is what gives the biblical stories their historicising, yet true-to-life charm. Around the same time, the engraver Geertruydt Roghman (1625–1651/57) – the sister of the landscape painter Roelant Roghman, a friend of Rembrandt and Van den Eeckhout – published a series of engravings showing women doing domestic chores, one of them at the spinning wheel. As Eddy de Jongh notes in his commentary on Roghman's engravings, spinning was seen as an exemplary sign of housewifely virtue.[2] Ridding the dog of fleas was also seen as a symbol of care and cleanliness. This scene is accentuated by the lighting.

The artist showed great sensitivity for the rendering of material details in light, as is vividly illustrated in an ink drawing with three studies of a dog lying down, its fur shimmering in the light (cat. 46.2). The varying degrees of brightness are captured in fine brushstrokes. With its reliance on precise observation, this view is comparable to the snapshots of everyday life captured in drawings of people sleeping by Rembrandt and his workshop (cf. cat. 44.3). The draughtsman is concerned with expressing tranquillity and introspection. Schatborn rightly compares Van den Eeckhout's Paris study with Rembrandt's drawing of *Hendrickje Sleeping* from around 1654 in the British Museum.[3] Rembrandt also drew and etched the motif of a sleeping dog, which probably influenced Van den Eeckhout.[4] JN

1 Leipzig 2012, p. 99.
2 Amsterdam 1997, p. 268, no. 54.
3 Benesch 1103; cf. Schatborn 2010b, vol. 1, p. 188.
4 Rembrandt, *Sleeping Dog*, c. 1637–40, Pen and brush in brown ink, 14.3 × 16.8 cm, Boston, Museum of Fine Arts (Benesch 455); Rembrandt, *Sleeping Puppy*, 1639–40, etching and drypoint, 3.8 × 8.1 cm (B. 158); cf. Boston/Chicago 2003, nos. 54, 55.

47.1 REMBRANDT

Men Slaughtering an Ox

c. 1635–40
Pen and brown ink, partially rubbed with a finger, opaque white (oxidised), 11.7 × 15 cm
Staatliche Graphische Sammlung Munich, inv. 4979
Lit.: Benesch A 18; Munich/Amsterdam 2001, no. 31; Schatborn/Hinterding 2019, no. 246; Royalton-Kisch online, Drawings not in Benesch.

47.2 ISACK VAN OSTADE (?)

(Haarlem 1621–1649 Haarlem)

Slaughtered Pig

c. 1640
Panel, 33.7 × 46.5 cm
Inscribed (lower right).: Is … [illegible]
Museum der bildenden Künste Leipzig, inv. G 1050
Lit.: Leipzig 2012, no. 257.

With an axe in his hands, a man raises his arms high to slaughter an ox that another man is holding by its horns. A woman with a wooden bucket stands by, ready to catch the blood about to spurt out. The sheet is an interesting example of how Rembrandt developed a highly dramatic composition in a gradual process. Closer inspection reveals that the drawing is composed of two parts, with a dividing line running down the middle.[1] The artist cut apart a drawing that no longer survives, leaving only the man holding the ox head by the horns. On a new sheet of paper, he added the left half with the butcher and the female figure. Here the main figure is the butcher, whose sweeping gesture recalls the biblical scene of the beheading of John the Baptist.[2] The movements of the body, especially the wide-legged stance on the

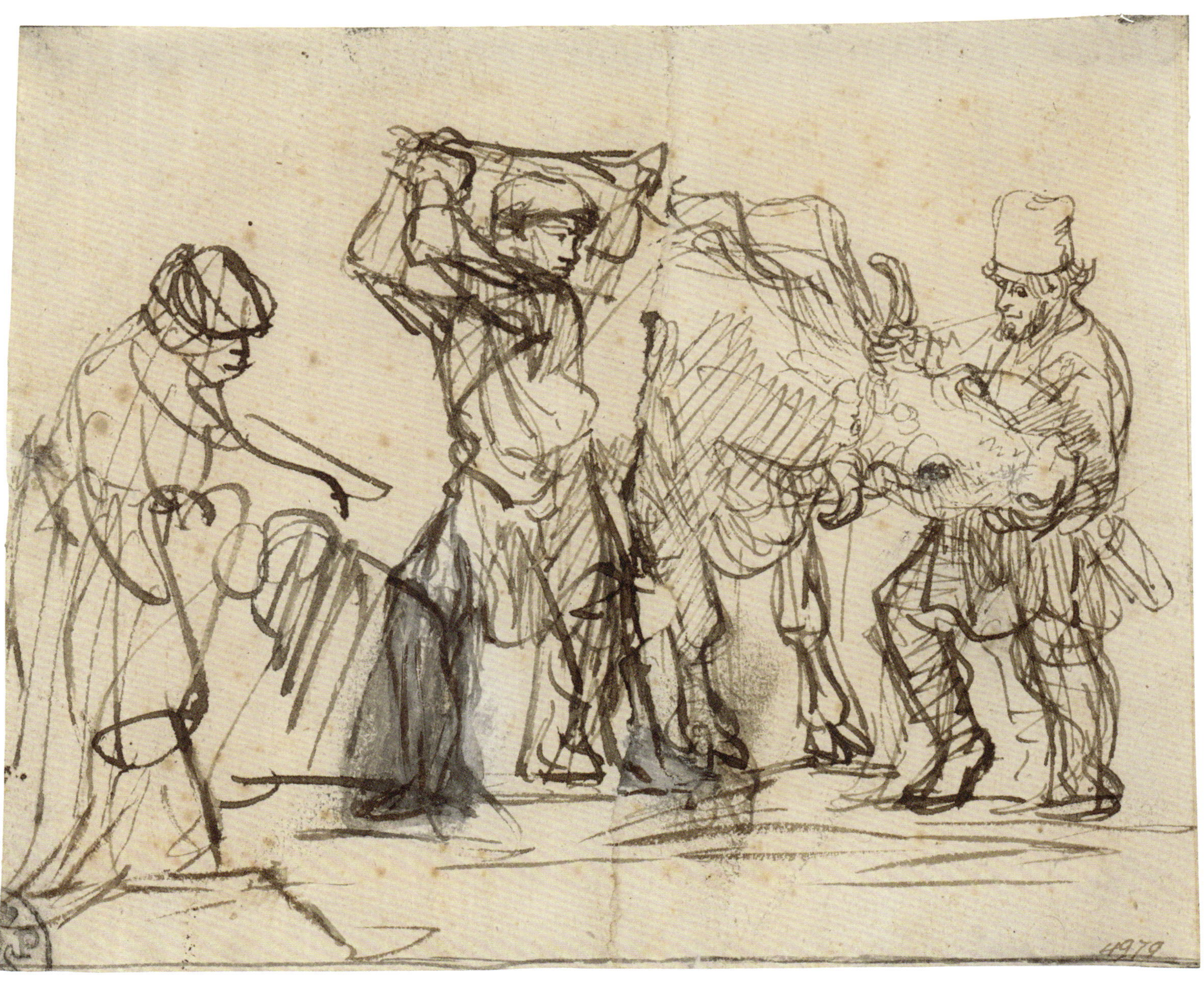

47.1

ground and the outstretched arms, were later drawn with bold contours in broad strokes over finer lines. Rembrandt thus suggests strong physical tension in order to depict the moment before the axe strikes the ox's neck. The body language serves to dramatise the scene. The borrowings from religious imagery are not accidental, but deliberate: Rembrandt imbues a subject taken from everyday peasant life with an emotionally moving note befitting a history painting. Here we can see the strong influence of Peter Paul Rubens, who played an important role in Rembrandt's work in the 1630s.[3] The genre painting becomes, as it were, a history painting.

At first glance, it is easy to overlook the absence of the ox's rump and hindquarters, as the focus is entirely on the relationship between the raised arms and the animal's head. Rembrandt not only physically divides the scene into two sheets of paper, but also draws our attention to individual motifs, like film clips that only become plausible when combined. What at first appears to be a realistic depiction of a brief moment is in fact a carefully composed scene. This selective realism was a central component of Rembrandt's drawing practice and instruction. It has been suggested that the right half of the picture with its finer lines could be by Gerbrand van den Eeckhout.[4] However, it

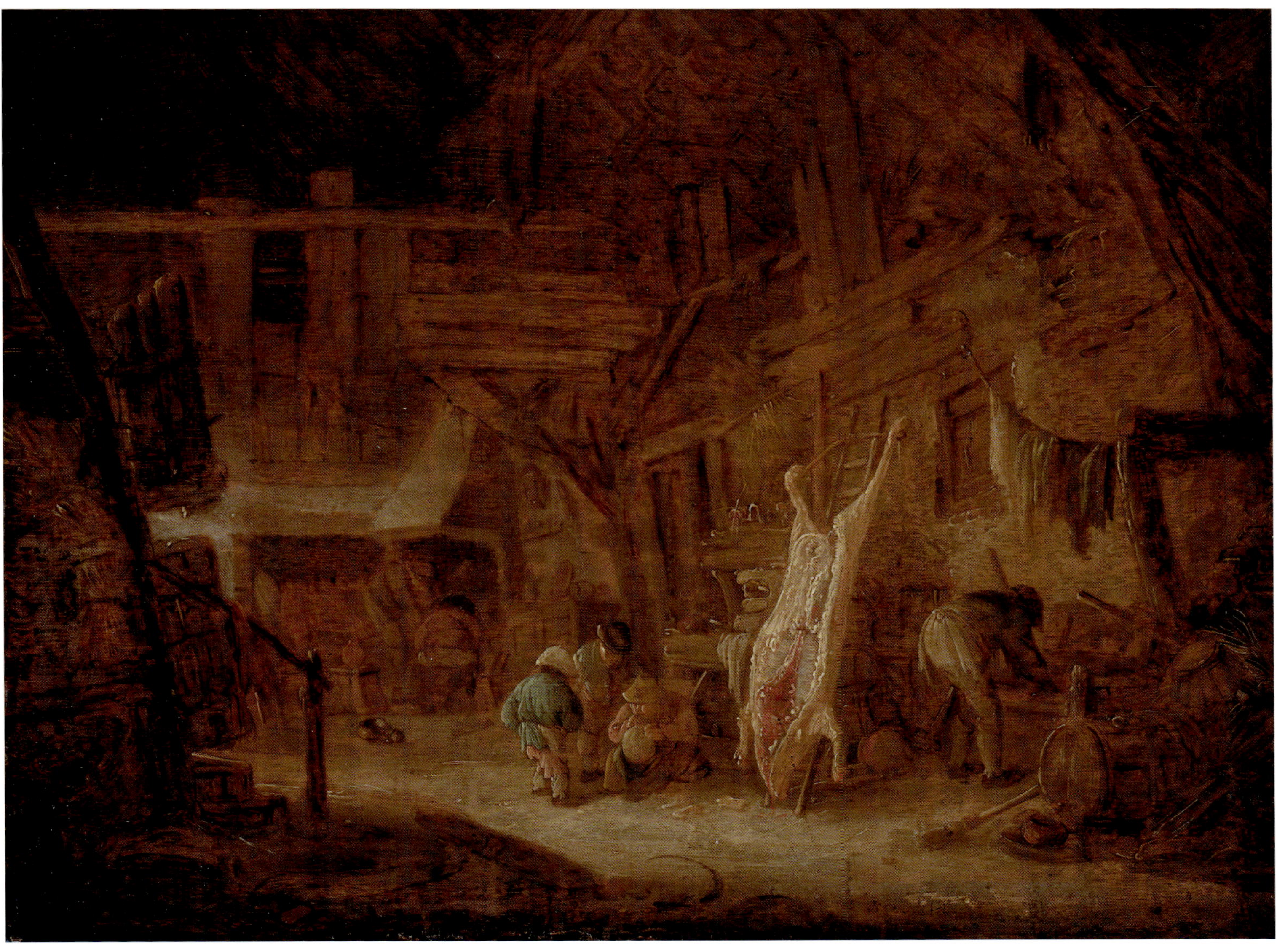

47.2

could just as well be a correction made by Rembrandt to his own drawing.

The method of recombining individual motifs underlines the functional purpose of drawing in Rembrandt's workshop (cf. cat. 24.3). The aim was not to produce a beautiful drawing, let alone one that could be sold. Rather, the intent was to generate the image through trial and error in order to create a harmonious, that is, coherent, dramatic composition that would appeal to the viewer's emotions. The convincing quality of the scene arises from the naturalness of the movements of multiple figures, making it appear as if it had been studied from life, when in fact it had not.

The slaughter of pigs is a common motif in Dutch genre painting and printmaking. In Isack van Ostade's painting from around 1640, a freshly slaughtered pig is tied to a ladder in a barn (cat. 47.2). A child blows up the pig's bladder – a popular motif that, like the soap bubble, was seen as a moralising symbol of the brevity of human life. The slaughter could also be interpreted as a reminder of one's own death, but also as foresightful householding.[5] Rembrandt explored the theme of slaughter on several occasions, for example in a painting from 1655 (Paris, Musée du Louvre) and a drawing in Berlin (Staatliche Museen zu Berlin, Kupferstichkabinett, KdZ 8516).[6] In a 1643 etching (B. 157), he shows an unsuspecting pig being prepared for slaughter with its legs tied.[7] Pig slaughter was also a popular subject among Rembrandt's students.[8] JN

1 Munich/Amsterdam 2001, pp. 136f.
2 Comparable works include the drawings by Rembrandt, *The Beheading of Prisoners*, New York, The Metropolitan Museum of Art, (Benesch 478), and Rembrandt's Workshop, *Beheading*, Staatliche Graphische Sammlung Munich (Munich/Amsterdam 2001, no. 32).
3 See Sumowski 1983–94, vol. 1, p. 16.
4 See Royalton-Kisch online, Drawings not in Benesch for A 18.
5 Leipzig 2012, no. 257.
6 Berlin 2006, p. 165, no. 48.
7 See Dresden 2019, no. 39.
8 See the paintings by Gerbrand van den Eeckhout, 1646, in Bonn (Rheinisches Landesmuseum) and by von Barent Fabritius, 1656, in Berlin (Gemäldegalerie) and Rotterdam (Museum Boijmans Van Beuningen); Sumowski 1983–94, vol. 2, nos. 500, 595, 596.

48.1 ADRIAEN VAN OSTADE

(Haarlem 1610–1685 Haarlem)

The Dentist

1637
Panel, 19.1 × 24.9 cm
Museum der bildenden Künste Leipzig, inv. G 655
Lit.: Leipzig 2012, Nr. 248.

48.2 ADRIAEN VAN OSTADE

The Balladeer (The Reader)

1644
Panel, 45.1 × 35.5 cm
Maximilian Speck von Sternburg Foundation in the Museum der bildenden Künste Leipzig, inv. G 1604
Lit.: Leipzig 1826, no. 39; Leipzig/Munich 1998, no. I/96; Leipzig 2012, no. 251.

48.3 JAN VICTORS

(Amsterdam 1619–c. 1676 Dutch East Indies)

The Tooth Breaker

1650s
Canvas, 74.5 × 87.7 cm
Maximilian Speck von Sternburg Foundation in the Museum der bildenden Künste Leipzig, inv. G 1637
Lit.: Leipzig 1826, no. 14; Miller 1985, no. 110, pp. 233f.; Sumowski 1983–94, vol. 4, no. 1799; Leipzig/Munich 1998, no. I/97; Leipzig 2012, no. 347.

Jan Victors was probably a student in Rembrandt's workshop from 1637 to 1639, possibly as early as 1635.[1] After his apprenticeship, he specialised in history paintings, commissioned by wealthy Amsterdam collectors. From the 1650s, however, he responded to the increasing demand for genre paintings on the Amsterdam art market.[2] The Leipzig painting *The Tooth Breaker* (cat. 48.3) reveals stylistic and thematic differences between teacher and student. These include the smooth painting style and the bright, cool colouring, but above all the bold and moralising view of the subject. As an orthodox Calvinist, the artist aims for didactic caricature rather than observation of nature and humanity or painterly finesse.[3] The genre paintings of artists such as Jan Miense Molenaer (c. 1610–1668) were more of a model here than the works of Rembrandt. The figures are largely arranged parallel to the picture plane, as if on a stage. The main figures such as the tooth puller, his 'patient' – a young girl whose clenched fists express pain – and the quack's assistant, wearing a red velvet dress and holding up a tincture of dubious efficacy, are highlighted in bright colours against a brownish background. A man in a jester's costume fiddles on a violin to underline the questionable medical expertise of the tooth puller and the gullibility of the people who entrust themselves to him. The gleeful expressions on the faces of the onlookers evoke not so much sympathy as a sense of distance from what is happening.

Rembrandt's influence might be seen in the young woman in the left half of the picture, bending down to her child and explaining what is happening. In the second half of the 1630s, during what is thought to have been Victors's period of collaboration in his workshop, Rembrandt produced many drawings of women and children (cf. cats. 43.5–6). Rembrandtesque is the preference for exotic props: the parasol – an Indonesian pajong – also appears in Rembrandt's work, for example in the 1641 etching *The Baptism of the Chamberlain* (B. 98). Victors apparently used such a parasol as a studio prop, as it appears in several paintings from the 1650s.[4] The historicising clothing of the tooth puller may also have been inspired by Rembrandt's fondness for sixteenth-century theatrical costumes.

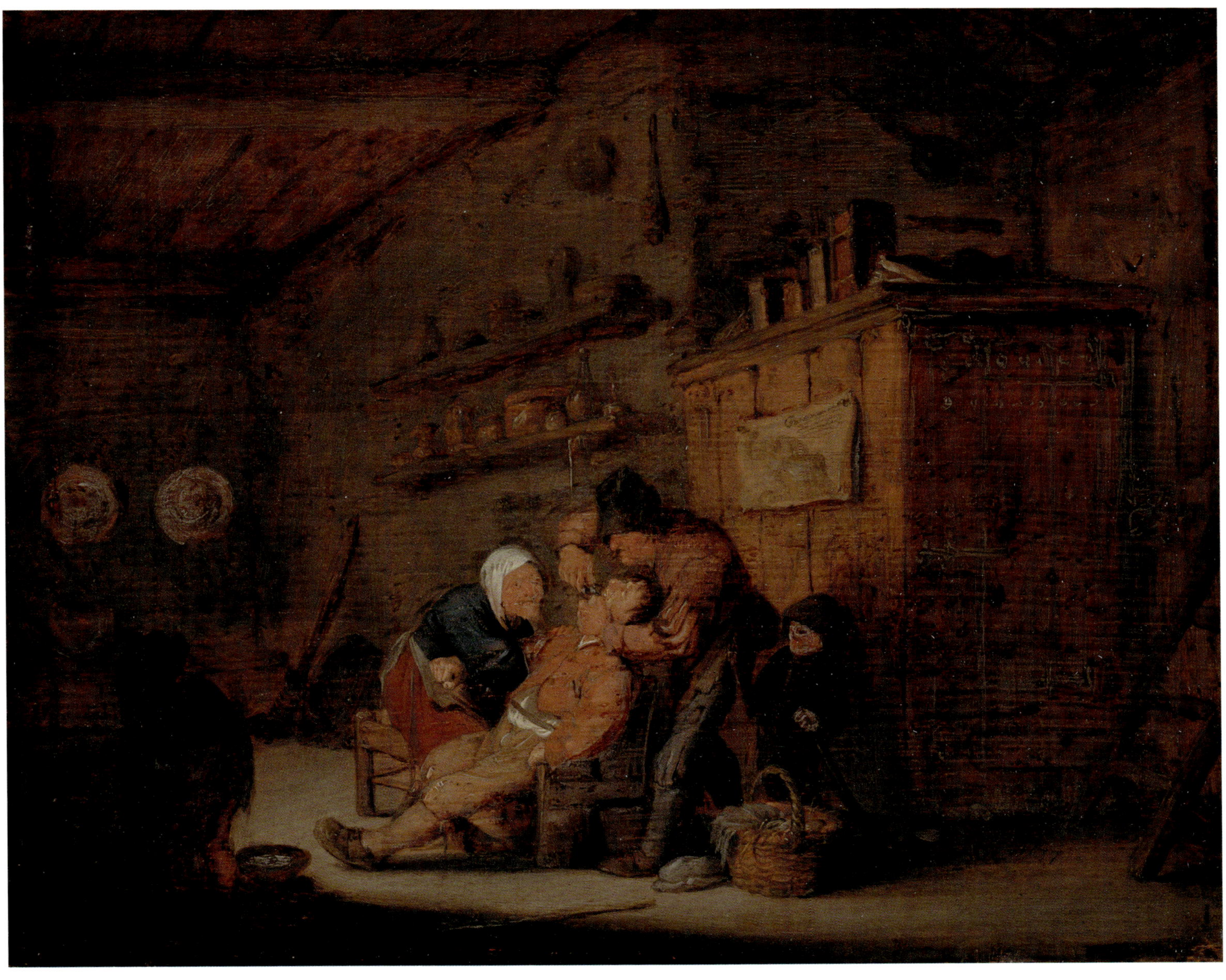

48.1

Adriaen van Ostade's painting *The Dentist* by (cat. 48.1) also combines a depiction of the senses – touch and sensitivity to pain – with a warning not to be deceived by appearances and thereby come to harm.[5]
Here, too, the tooth puller wears a historicising sixteenth-century costume with a slit jacket. Books are lined up on a large wooden cupboard to simulate literacy. An old woman holds the arm of the 'patient', whose wide-open eyes communicate his pain. The dim interior and the selective lighting recall Rembrandt's paintings of the 1630s (cf. cats. 6.1, 8). The latter's influence on Adriaen van Ostade was recognised early on by scholars.[6] The incidence of light that overlays the figure in the left foreground, reducing it essentially to a dark outline, is a compositional element that can also be found in Rembrandt's work.[7] In Van Ostade's painting, small reflections of light on the tongs visualise the hard metal in the man's mouth. This immediacy of observation, aimed at capturing the viewer's senses, is similar to Rembrandt's narrative strategy.

Adriaen van Ostade, who was himself a talented etcher, was also influenced by Rembrandt's etched genre scenes. For example, the Leipzig *Balladeer* of 1644 (cat. 48.2) seems to have been inspired by Rembrandt's *Rat Poison Seller* of 1632 (Bartsch 121). The composition, lighting, and detailed rendering of the figures in picturesque costume, as well as the village setting, are similar. Whereas Rembrandt's early genre scenes

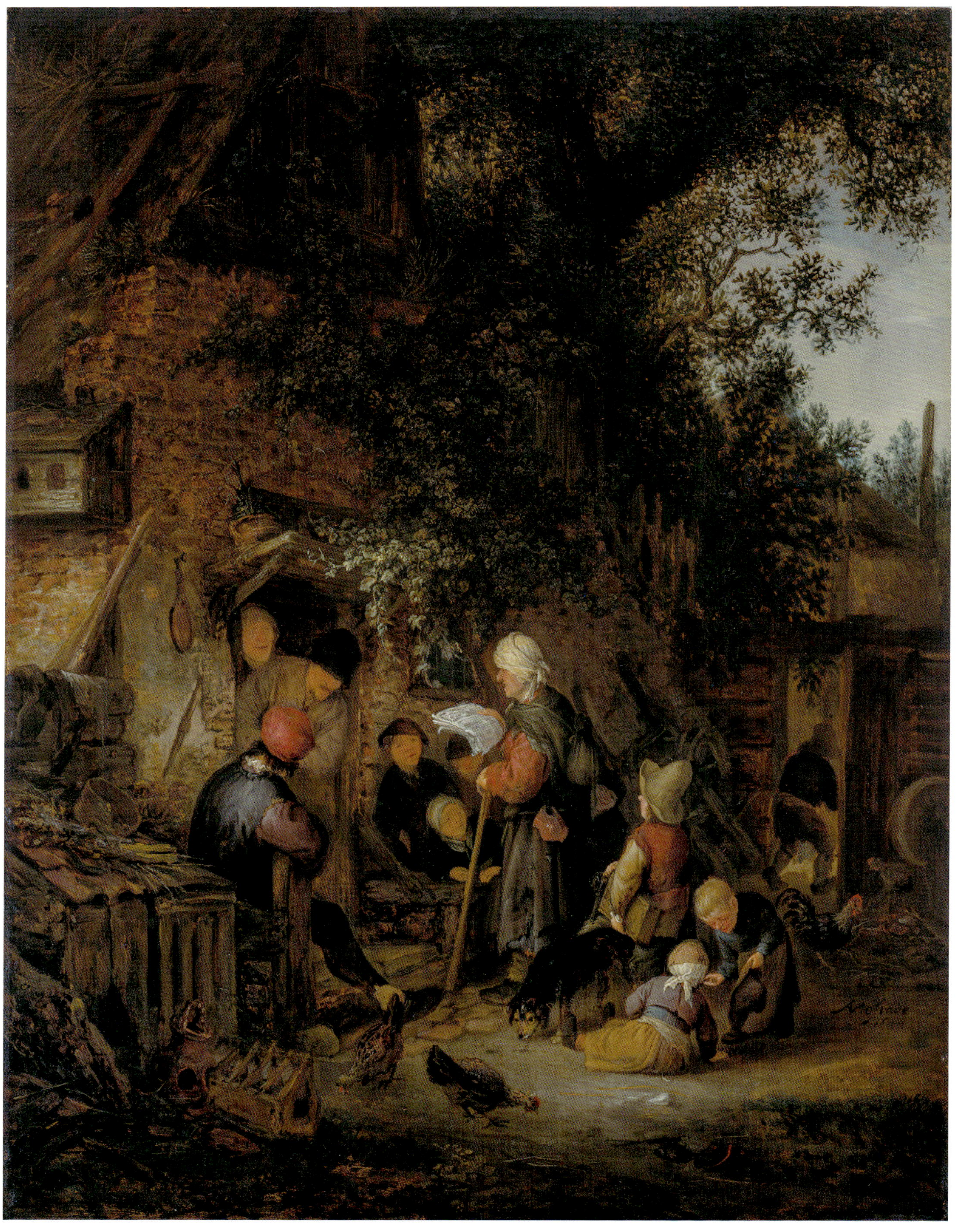

48.2

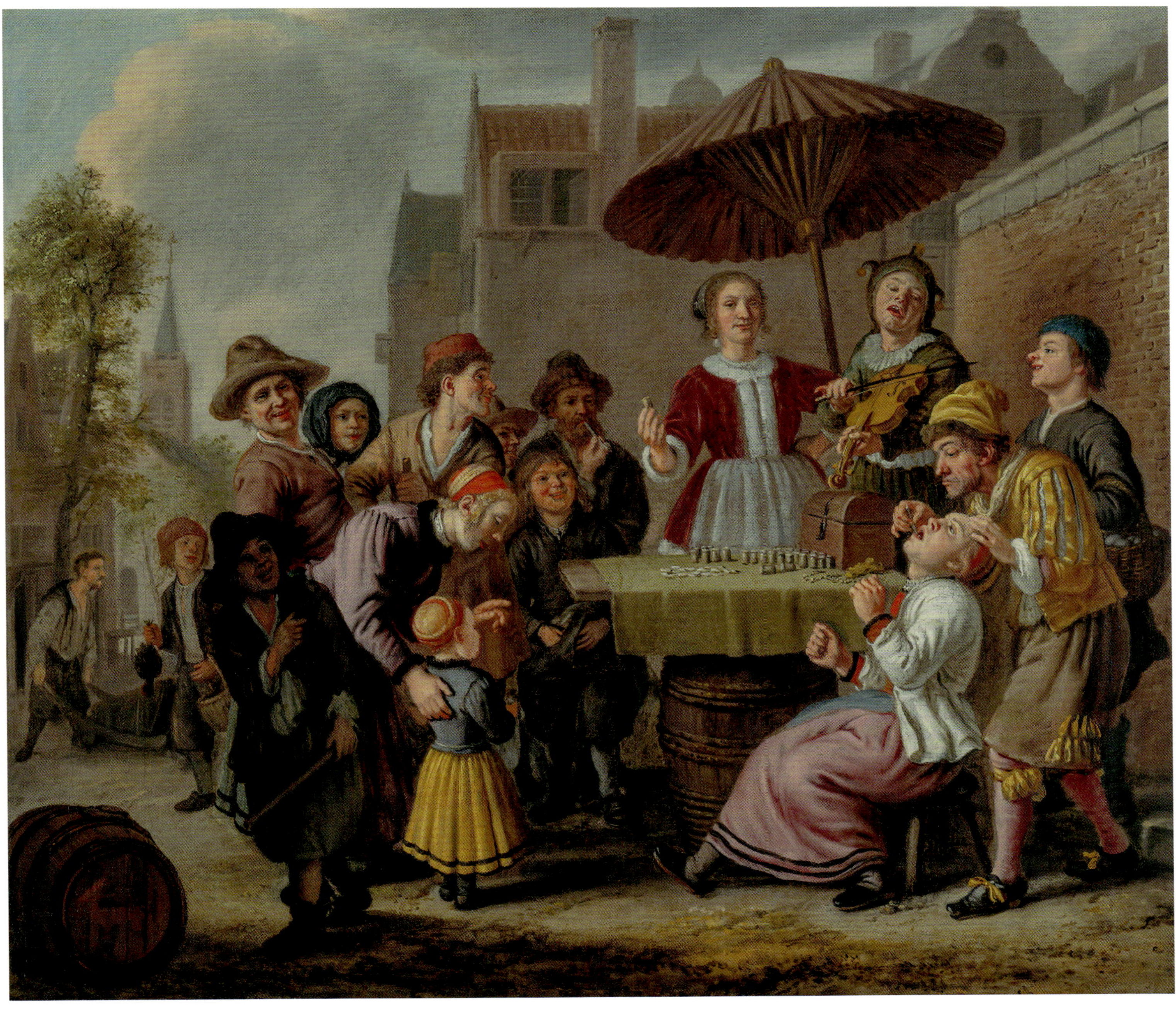

48.3

are intended to elicit pity from the viewer, Van Ostade's painting mixes caricatural humour – for example the beer mug on the old woman's belt as an indication that she likes to be paid in beer – with a certain idealisation of rural life through elements such as the cosy, warm lighting.[8] Like Rembrandt, Adriaen van Ostade paid great attention to the depiction of small children, who populate and enliven the picture. JN/JG

1 See Sumowski 1983–94, vol. 4, pp. 2589–93; Melbourne/Canberra 1997, p. 256; Los Angeles 2009, p. 2. Deviating from this: Broos 1983, pp. 35–58; Sluijter 2015, p. 363.
2 See Sluijter 2015, pp. 372f.; Ottawa/Frankfurt 2021, p. 289 (S. Dickey).
3 For more on the religious attitude of Victors, see Sluijter 2015, p. 362; Veldman 2021.
4 Leipzig 2012, p. 320.
5 Ibid., p. 238.
6 See Sumowski 1983–94, vol. 1, p. 84.
7 See Rembrandt's painting *Supper at Emmaus*, c. 1629, Paris, Musée Jacquemart-André.
8 Leipzig 2012, p. 241.

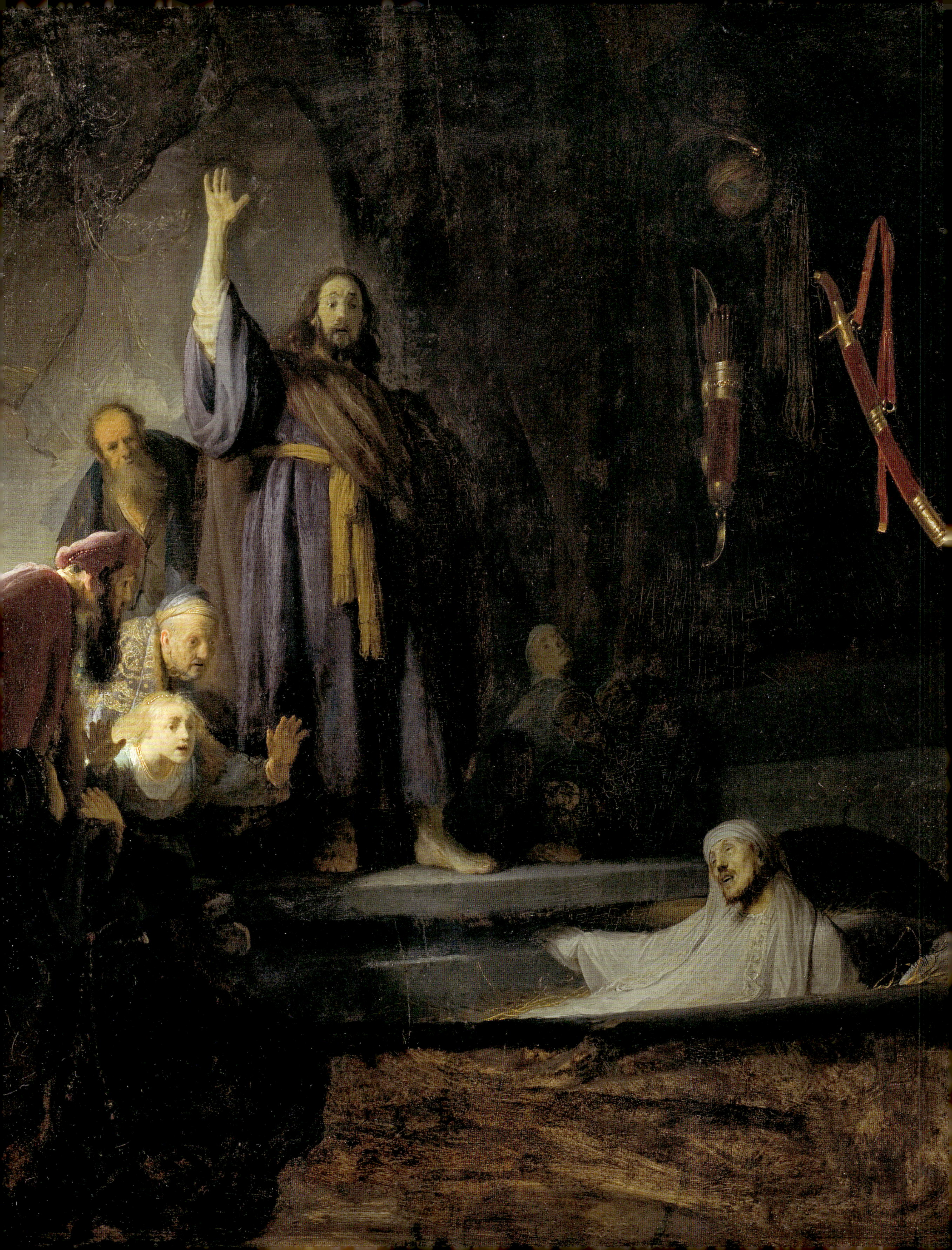

THE GOTTFRIED WINCKLER COLLECTION IN LEIPZIG

CHRISTIAN FRIEDRICH WIEGAND

(Leipzig 1752–1832 Leipzig)

The Hanging of the Gottfried Winckler Collection in the Garden Palace in Front of the Grimma Gate, Leipzig

c. 1800 (?)

49.1 CHRISTIAN FRIEDRICH WIEGAND

18 miniature copies of paintings
Watercolour, 34 × 32.5 cm
Stadtgeschichtliches Museum Leipzig, inv. IV/76/1

49.2 CHRISTIAN FRIEDRICH WIEGAND

38 miniature copies of paintings
Watercolour, 49 × 76 cm
Stadtgeschichtliches Museum Leipzig, inv. IV/75/1

49.3 CHRISTIAN FRIEDRICH WIEGAND

28 miniature copies of paintings
Watercolour, 49 × 76.5 cm
Stadtgeschichtliches Museum Leipzig, inv. IV/65/1

49.4 CHRISTIAN FRIEDRICH WIEGAND

34 miniature copies of paintings
Watercolour, 39 × 68 cm
Stadtgeschichtliches Museum Leipzig, inv. K/431/2002

49.5 CHRISTIAN FRIEDRICH WIEGAND

12 miniature copies of paintings
Watercolour, 48 × 35 cm
Stadtgeschichtliches Museum Leipzig, inv. IV/66/1

Lit.: Schulz 1937; Gleisberg 2011–12; Hommel 2018.

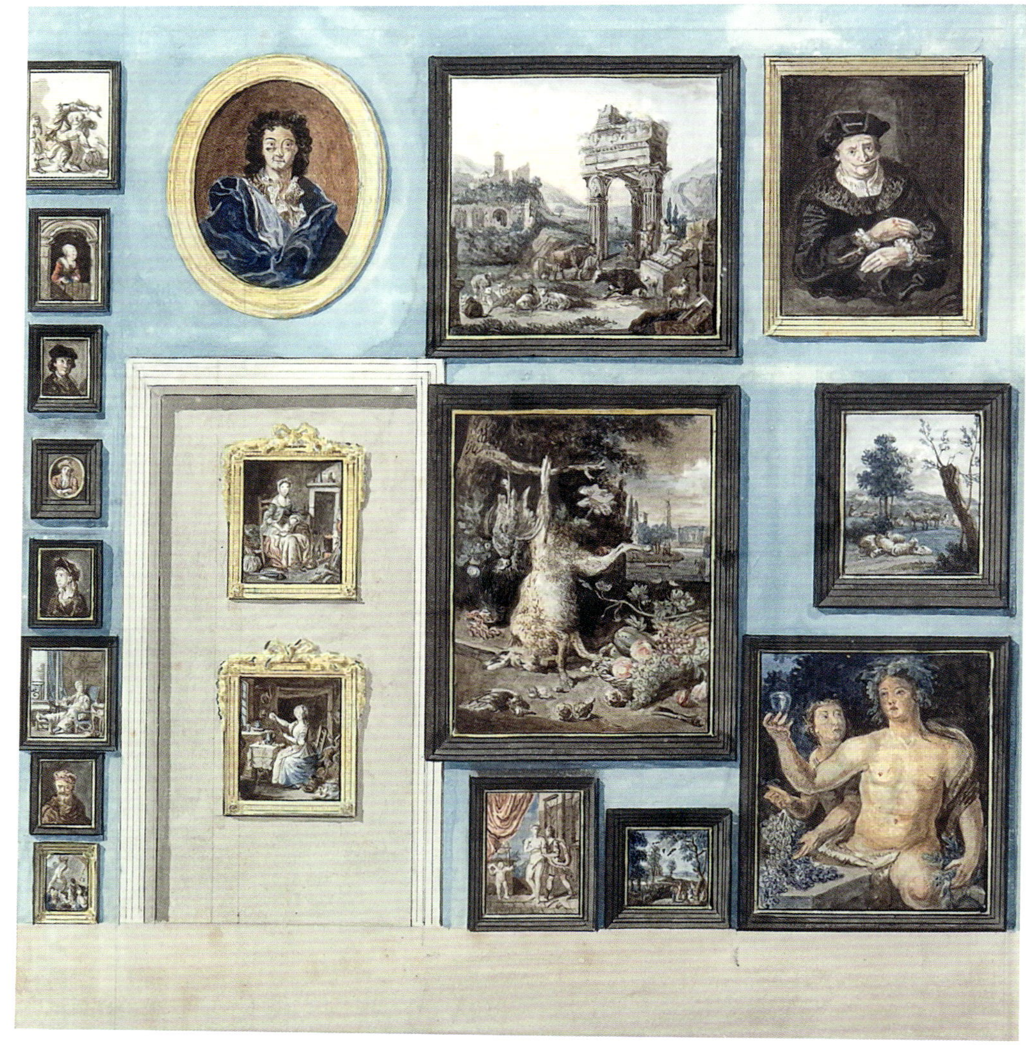

49.1

In eight watercolours, five of which are exhibited here, Christian Friedrich Wiegand captured the hanging of 218 paintings from the Winckler Collection in the garden house in front of the Grimma Gate in Leipzig. The important collection of the banker Gottfried Winckler (1731–1795) included works by Rembrandt, Ter Brugghen, Ruysch, Rubens, Jordaens, Boucher and Chardin, among others.[1] The Leipzig catalogue of 1768 lists ten paintings by Rembrandt, two of which are still regarded as authentic today, including *The Raising of Lazarus* (c. 1630–2, panel, 95 × 82 cm, Los Angeles County Museum of Art, inv. M.72.67.02; see fig. 7 on p. 76 and p. 254).[2] It hung in the collector's garden house and can be seen in one of the watercolours (cat. 49.2) on the left in the bottom row. Also on this wall (upper row, third from the left) was a painting by Rembrandt's student Willem Drost (*Old Peasant with Pipe and Other Figures*, Art Institute of Chicago, inv. 1987.285; only preserved as a fragment, there attributed to the German painter Johann Carl Loth).[3] Winckler also owned what was then thought to be a self-portrait by Rembrandt but is

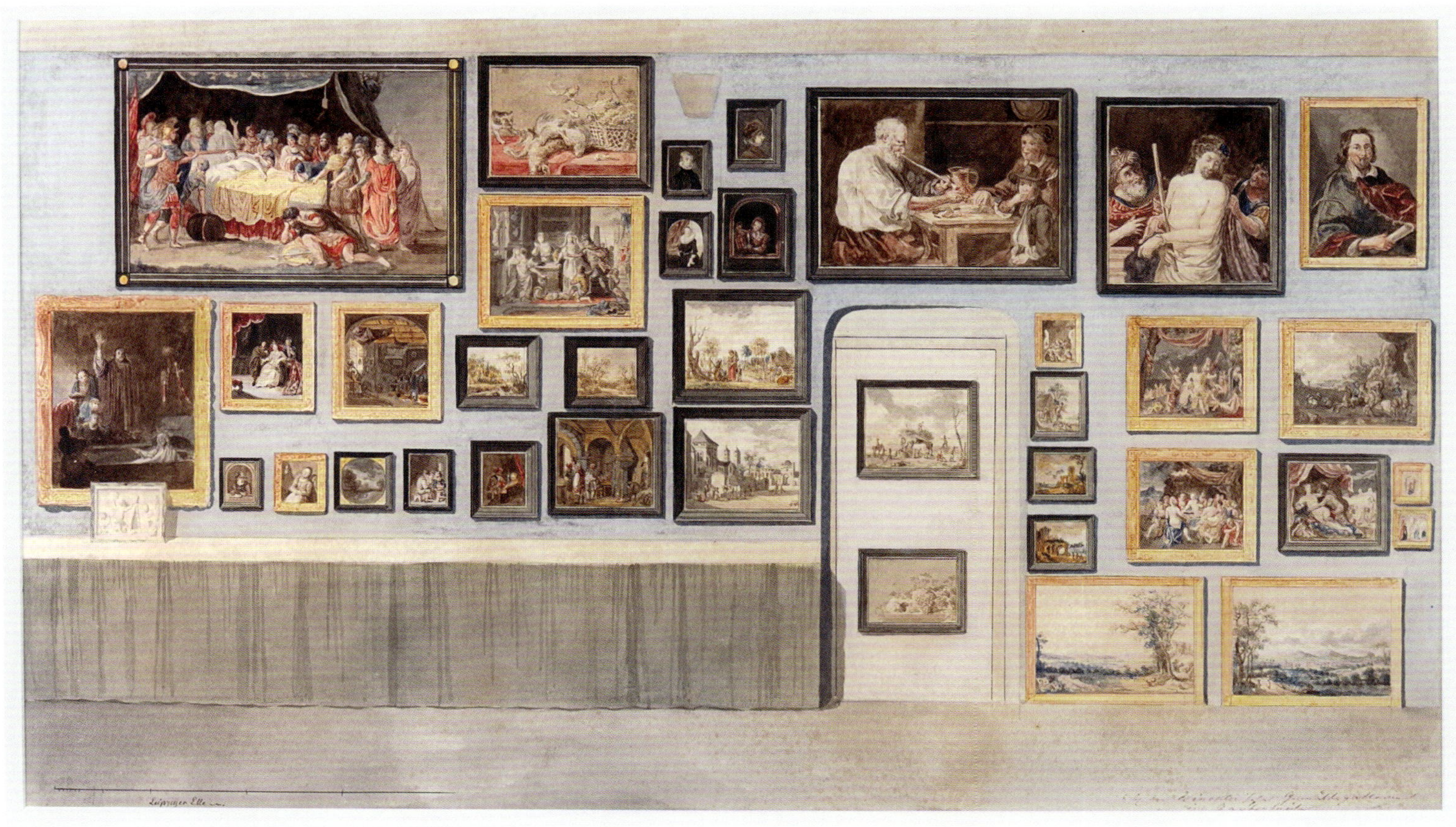

49.2

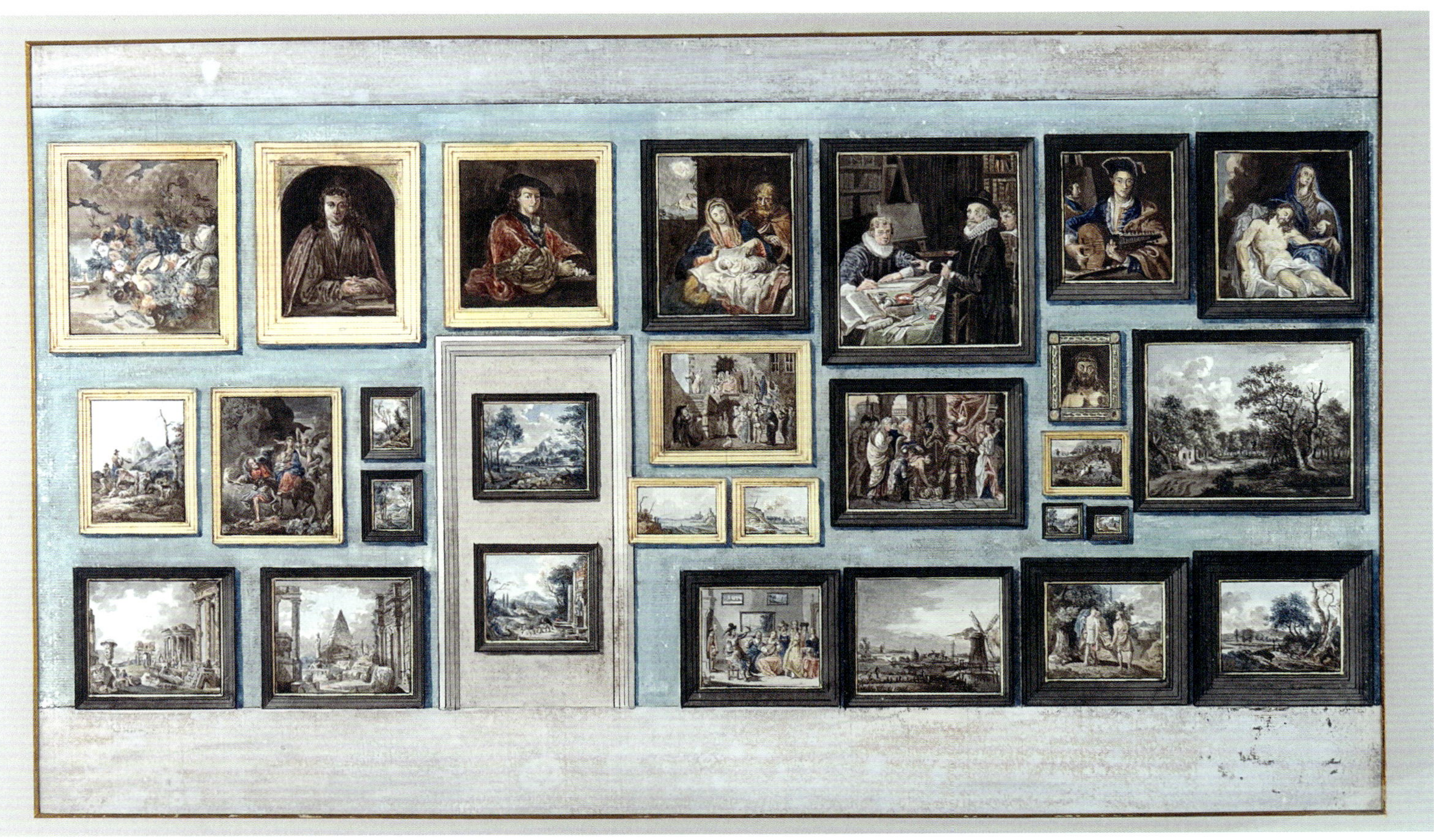

49.3

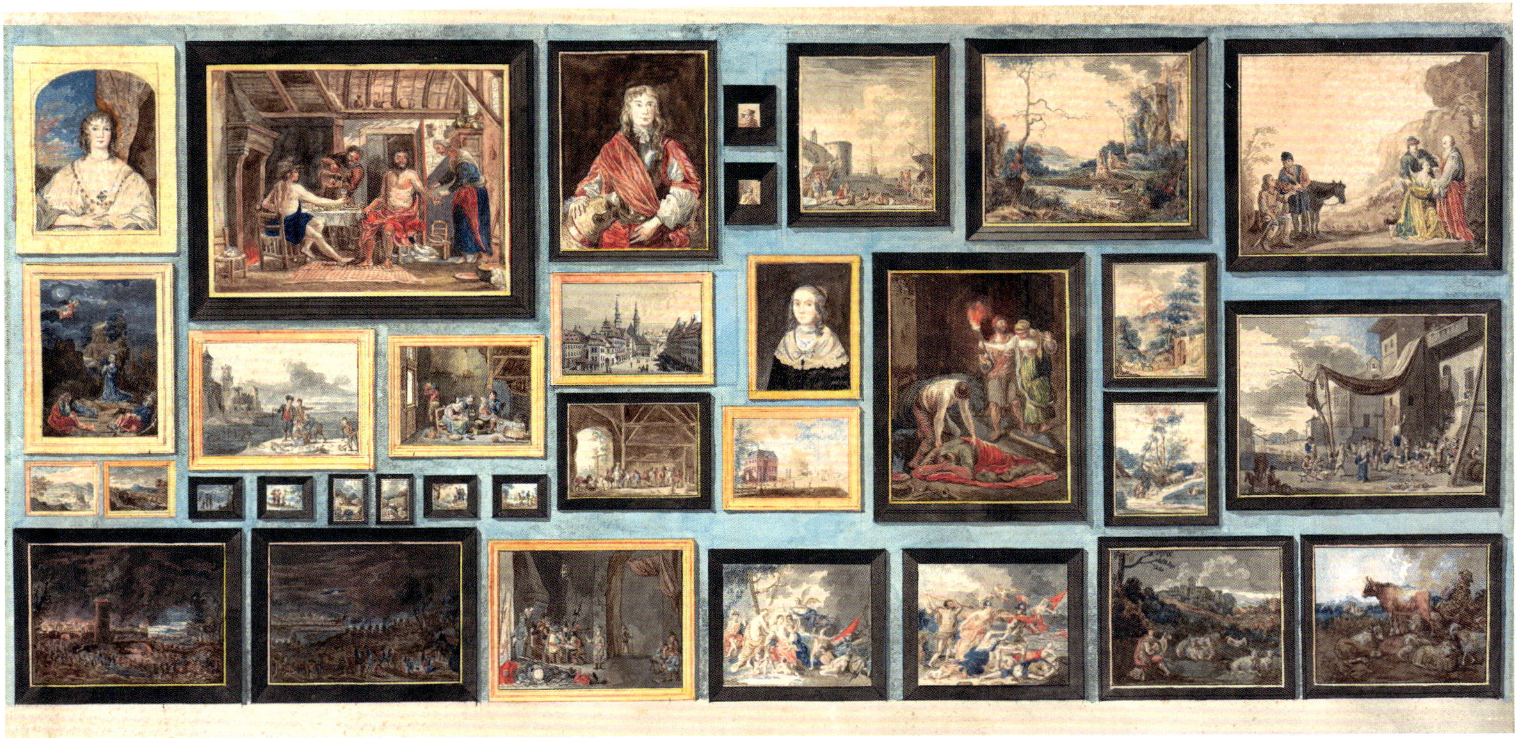

49.4

now considered to be the work of a follower (*Portrait of Rembrandt as a Young Man*, c. 1660 or later, panel, 21.9 × 16.5 cm, New York, The Metropolitan Museum of Art, inv. 53.13, fig. p. 78).[4] The small tronie also hung in the garden house in a vertical row of small pictures and is reproduced in one of the watercolours (cat. 49.1, left, third picture from the top). The large tronie of an old woman reading the Bible (cat. 41.2), now attributed to Abraham van Dijck, was also thought to be by Rembrandt. However, it did not hang in the garden house, but in Winckler's townhouse on Katharinenstraße, where it narrowly escaped destruction during the Battle of the Nations in October 1813.[5]

Following the dissolution of the Winckler Collection, later Leipzig collectors acquired important individual paintings or groups of paintings from it. Most notable among them was Maximilian Speck von Sternburg (1776–1856), who acquired more than 70 paintings, 27 of which ended up in the Museum der bildenden Künste Leipzig.[6] Through later collectors, paintings from the Winckler Collection by artists from other schools also came to the MdbK, such as the *Portrait of David Hoyer with Lute* by Jan Kupetzky from the Speck von Sternburg collection and *The Birth of Adonis* by Giuseppe Maria Crespi, known as Lo Spagnuolo, from the Krug von Nidda collection. Both are illustrated in the exhibited watercolours (cats. 49.3, 49.5).

Winckler also collected contemporary art from Saxony; one of the watercolours (cat. 49.4) shows the 1767 painting *Saul with the Witch of Endor* by Adam Friedrich Oeser (Stadtgeschichtliches Museum Leipzig, inv. IV/16/1). The academy rector Oeser, who probably arranged this commission for his student Wiegand, used the collection as illustrative material for teaching purposes and made etchings after works then attributed to Rembrandt (cat. 18.3).

The precise reproduction of the miniatures is remarkable, with every effort made to document the individual paintings and their exact hanging in as much detail as possible. The watercolours bear witness to the desire to present the collection in an aesthetically pleasing yet objective manner. They were made without the addition of any writing or numbers – in other words, they are purely visual – but the recognisability of the works fulfils a similar function to the short descriptive texts in catalogues or gallery publications of the eighteenth century. It is possible that they were made when the collection was to be divided up among the heirs of Gottfried Winckler after around 1804.[7] The collection, which had grown to over 1,300 paintings, was sold at auction in 1819.[8] Due to the large number of paintings reproduced in the watercolours and the astonishing care in the depiction of their composition, colour and lighting, they represent a valuable, not yet fully researched source for Leipzig's illustrious collection history in the eighteenth century. JN

1 Gleisberg 2011–12; see the essay by Sven Pabstmann in this catalogue, pp. 74–81.
2 The second painting is *An Old Man in Rich Costume (The Old Rabbi)*, panel, 72.5 × 58.5 cm, Bedfordshire, Woburn Abbey, Duke of Bedford Collection, which was reattributed to Rembrandt only in 2012. The work is listed in the 1768 Leipzig catalogue as a painting by Ferdinand Bol (no. 282); see Gleisberg 2011–12, p. 188; https://www.codart.nl/museums/woburn-abbey-unveils-newly-authenticated-rembrandt-portrait-the-old-rabbi/.
3 Cf. Leipzig 1768, no. 322; Bikker 2005, no. 37.
4 New York 1995, vol. 2, no. 21; Gleisberg 2011–12, p. 188.
5 See cat. 41.2 in this catalogue.
6 Gleisberg 2011–12, p. 158.
7 Schulz 1937, pp. 70–4; Gleisberg 2011–12, pp. 148f.; Hommel 2018, pp. 143f.
8 Hommel 2018, pp. 149, 154, 159.

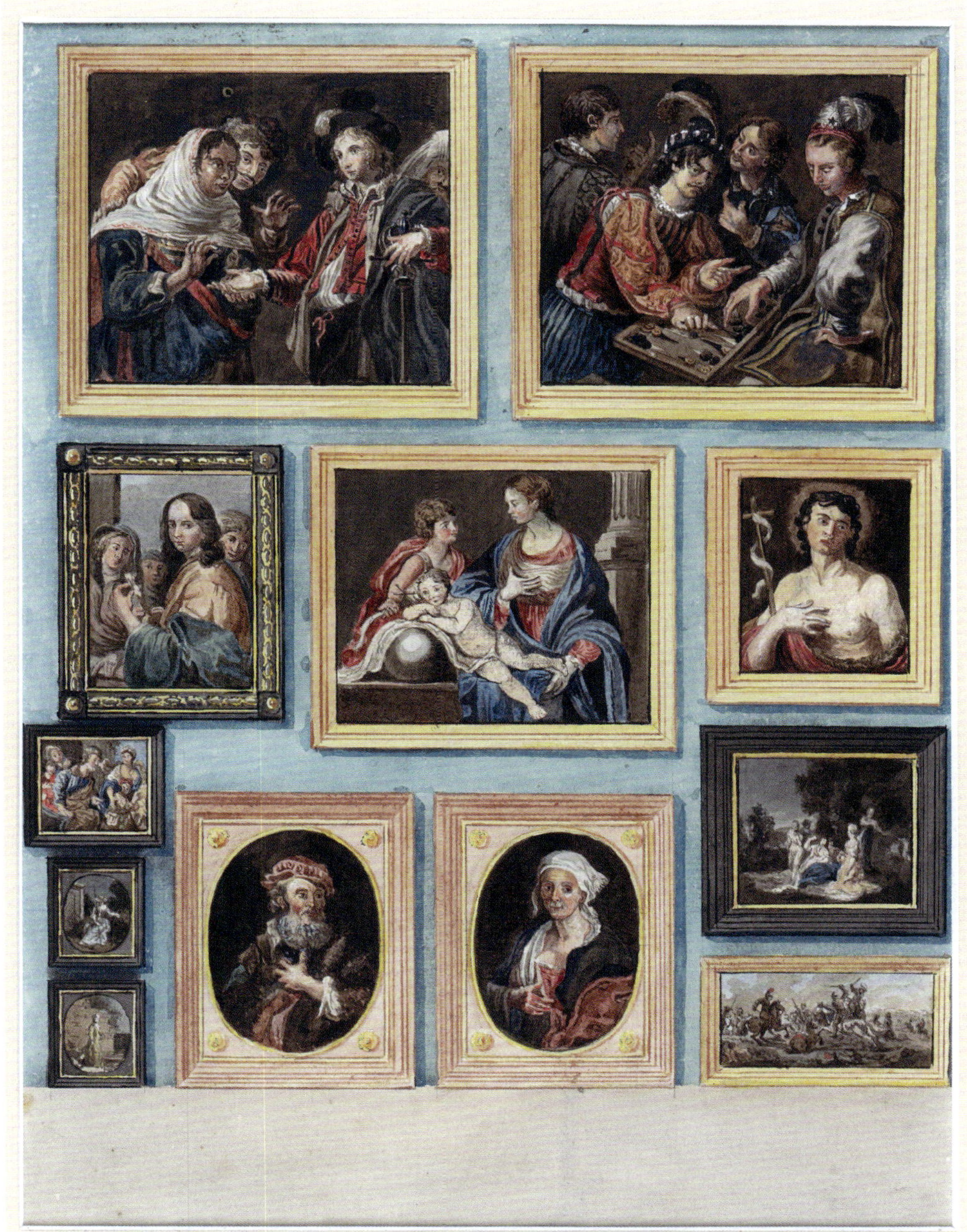

49.5

BIBLIOGRAPHY

Abu Dhabi 2019
Ducos, Blaise, and Lara Yeager-Crasselt, eds. *Rembrandt, Vermeer et le siècle d'or hollondais. Chefs-d'oeuvre de la collection Leiden et du musée du Louvre.* Abu Dhabi, 2019.

Adams 1984
Adams, Henry, 'If Not Rembrandt, Then His Cousin?', *The Art Bulletin* 66 (1984), pp. 427–41.

Albers 2008
Albers, Eckbert, *Erkenntnismomente und Erkenntnisprozesse bei Rembrandt.* Hildesheim, 2008.

Alpers 1988
Alpers, Svetlana, *Rembrandt's Enterprise: The Studio and the Market.* Chicago, 1988.

Altes 2006
Altes, Everhard Korthals, 'Der Kunsthandel mit Werken Rembrandts zur Zeit Wilhelms VIII. von Hessen-Kassel', in Kassel 2006, pp. 27–46.

Amsterdam 1972
Filedt Kok, Jan Piet, *Rembrandt: Etchings and Drawings in the Rembrandt House. A Catalogue.* Maarssen, 1972.

Amsterdam 1984
Schatborn, Peter, and Eva Ornstein-van Slooten, *Bij Rembrandt In De Leer / Rembrandt as Teacher.* Amsterdam, Museum Het Rembrandthuis. Amsterdam, 1984.

Amsterdam 1991
Tümpel, Astrid and Peter Schatborn, eds. *Pieter Lastman – leermaster van Rembrandt / the man who taught Rembrandt.* Amsterdam, Museum Het Rembrandthuis. Zwolle, 1991.

Amsterdam 1993
Bakker, Boudewijn, and Huigen Leeflang, *Nederland naar't leven. Landschapsprenten uit de Gouden Eeuw*, with essays by Ed de Heer, Nadine Orenstein and Jan Peeters. Amsterdam, Museum Het Rembrandthuis. Amsterdam, 1993.

Amsterdam 1996
Schuckman, Christiaan, Martin Royalton-Kisch and Erik Hinterding, *Rembrandt & Van Vliet, A Collaboration on Copper*, ed. Marlies Enklaar et al. Amsterdam, Museum Het Rembrandthuis – Rembrandt Information Centre. Amsterdam, 1996.

Amsterdam 1997
De Jongh, Eddy, and Ger Luijten, *Mirror of Everyday Life: Genre Prints in the Netherlands 1550–1700.* Amsterdam, Rijksmuseum. Ghent, 1997.

Amsterdam 1999
Van den Boogert, Bob, ed. *Rembrandt's Treasures*, with essays by Ben Broos, Roelof van Gelder and Jaap van der Veen. Amsterdam, Museum Het Rembrandthuis. Zwolle, 1999.

Amsterdam 2006
Bull, Duncan, ed. *Rembrandt-Caravaggio*, with essays by Taco Dibbits et al. Amsterdam, Rijksmuseum/Amsterdam, Van Gogh Museum. Zwolle, 2006.

Amsterdam 2011
Opstand als Opdracht. The Batavian Commissions. Flinck, Ovens, Lievens, Jordaens, De Groot, Bol, Rembrandt. Amsterdam, Koninklijk Paleis. Amsterdam, 2011.

Amsterdam 2014
Schatborn, Peter, and Leonore van Sloten, *Old Drawings, New Names: Rembrandt and his Contemporaries.* Amsterdam, Museum Het Rembrandthuis. Amsterdam, 2014.

Amsterdam 2015
De Witt, David, Leonore van Sloten and Jaap van der Veen, *Rembrandt's Late Pupils: Studying Under a Genius.* Amsterdam, Museum Het Rembrandthuis. Amsterdam, 2015.

Amsterdam 2016
Noorman, Judith, and David de Witt, eds. *Rembrandts naakte waarheid. Het tekenen van naaktmodellen in de Gouden Euuw.* Amsterdam, Museum Het Rembrandthuis. Amsterdam, 2016.

Amsterdam 2017
Ferdinand Bol en Govert Flinck. Rembrandts Meesterleerlingen. Amsterdam, Museum Het Rembrandthuis/Amsterdam Museum. Amsterdam, 2017.

Amsterdam 2019
DeWitt, Lloyd, et al., *Rembrandt's Social Network. Familie, Vrienden en Relaties.* Amsterdam, Museum Het Rembrandthuis. Zwolle, 2019.

Amsterdam 2024
Van Sloten, Leonore, Epco Runia and Nathalie Maciesza, eds. *Directed by Rembrandt: Rembrandt and the World of Theatre.* Amsterdam, Museum Het Rembrandthuis. Amsterdam, 2024.

Amsterdam/Groningen 1983
Blankert, Albert, et al., eds. *The Impact of a Genius: Rembrandt, his Pupils and Followers in the Seventeenth Century. Paintings from Museums and Private Collections.* Amsterdam, Waterman Galerie/Groningen, Groninger Museum. Amsterdam, 1983.

Amsterdam/London 2000
Hinterding, Erik, Ger Luijten and Martin Royalton-Kisch, eds. *Rembrandt: The Printmaker*. Amsterdam, Rijksmuseum/London, British Museum. London, 2000.

Amsterdam/Paris 1998
Bakker, Boudewijn, et al., *Landscapes of Rembrandt: His favourite walks*. Amsterdam, Gemeentearchief/Paris, Institut Néerlandais. Amsterdam, 1998.

Amsterdam/Washington 1981
Schatborn, Peter, ed. *Dutch Figure Drawings from the Seventeenth Century*. Amsterdam, Rijksmuseum/Washington, DC, National Gallery of Art. The Hague, 1981.

Amsterdam/Weimar 1999
Van den Boogert, Bob, et al., *Goethe & Rembrandt. Zeichnungen aus Weimar. Aus den graphischen Beständen der Kunstsammlungen zu Weimar, ergänzt durch Werke aus dem Goethe-Nationalmuseum*. Amsterdam, Museum Het Rembrandthuis. Amsterdam, 1999.

Antwerp/Dublin 2023
Van Hout, Nico, Lizzie Marx, Koen Bulckens, et al., *Turning Heads (Krasse Koppen)*. Antwerp, Koninklijke Museum voor Schone Kunsten/Dublin, National Gallery of Ireland. Antwerp, 2023.

Atkins 2012
Atkins, Christopher, *The Signature Style of Frans Hals: Painting, Subjectivity, and the Market in Early Modernity*. Amsterdam, 2012.

Baden 1797
Baden, Torkel, ed. *Briefe über die Kunst von und an Christian Ludwig von Hagedorn*. Leipzig, 1797.

Baer 2000
Baer, Ronni, 'The Life and Art of Gerrit Dou', in Washington/London/The Hague 2000, pp. 26–52.

Baldinucci 1845–7
Baldinucci, Filippo, *Notizie dei professori del disegno da Cimabue in qua*. 5 vols. Florence, 1845–7. Reprint Florence, 1974.

Basel/Potsdam 2020
Brinkmann, Bodo, et al., eds. *Rembrandts Orient. Westöstliche Begegnung in der niederländischen Kunst des 17. Jahrhunderts*. Basel, Kunstmuseum/Potsdam, Museum Barberini. Basel, 2020.

Bauch 1960
Bauch, Kurt, *Der frühe Rembrandt und seine Zeit. Studien zur geschichtlichen Bedeutung seines Frühstils*. Berlin, 1960.

Becker 1990
Becker, Peter Emil, *Sozialdarwinismus, Rassismus, Antisemitismus und Völkischer Gedanke*. Wege ins Dritte Reich, Part 2. Stuttgart, 1990.

Benesch 1973
Benesch, Otto, *The Drawings of Rembrandt*. 6 vols. 2nd rev. edn, ed. Eva Benesch. London, 1973.

Berlin 1956
Rembrandt. Gedächtnis-Ausstellung 1606–1669, Gemälde. Zeichnungen. Radierungen, foreword by Ernst Heinrich Zimmermann, catalogue by Hans Möhle and Fedja Anzelewsky. Berlin, Gemäldegalerie Dahlem. Berlin, 1956.

Berlin 1975
Beschreibendes Verzeichnis der Gemälde. Berlin, Gemäldegalerie. Berlin, 1975.

Berlin 2006
Bevers, Holm, *Rembrandt. Die Zeichnungen im Berliner Kupferstichkabinett. Kritischer Katalog*. Staatliche Museen zu Berlin, Kupferstichkabinett. Ostfildern, 2006.

Berlin 2009
Bevers, Holm, et al., eds. *Rembrandt – Wissenschaft auf der Suche*. Jahrbuch der Berliner Museen, Beiheft, vol. 51. Berlin, 2009.

Berlin 2018
Bevers, Holm, *Zeichnungen der Rembrandtschule im Berliner Kupferstichkabinett. Kritischer Katalog*, with an essay by Georg Josef Dietz and Antje Lenz. Staatliche Museen zu Berlin, Kupferstichkabinett. Dresden, 2018.

Berlin/Amsterdam 2006
Rembrandt. Genie auf der Suche. Staatliche Museen zu Berlin, Gemäldegalerie/Amsterdam, Museum Het Rembrandthuis. Cologne, 2006.

Berlin/Amsterdam/London 1991
Bevers, Holm, Peter Schatborn and Barbara Welzel, eds. *Rembrandt. Der Meister und seine Werkstatt. Zeichnungen und Radierungen*. Berlin, Kupferstichkabinett SMPK im Alten Museum/Amsterdam, Rijksmuseum/London, The National Gallery. Berlin, 1991.

Bevers 2010
Bevers, Holm, 'Early, Rembrandtesque Drawings by Gerbrand van den Eeckhout', *Master Drawings* 48, 1 (Spring 2010), pp. 39–72.

Bevers 2022
Bevers, Holm, review of Peter Schatborn and Erik Hinterding, *Rembrandt: The Complete Drawings and Etchings*, in *Master Drawings* 60, 2 (2022), pp. 249–64.

Bewer 1891
Bewer, Max, *Rembrandt und Bismarck*. Dresden 1891.

Biesboer 2001
Biesboer, Pieter, *Collections of Paintings in Haarlem. 1572–1745*, ed. Carol Togneri. Los Angeles, 2001.

Bikker 2005
Bikker, Jonathan, *Willem Drost (1633–1659): A Rembrandt Pupil in Amsterdam and Venice*. New Haven, 2005.

Bikker 2019
Bikker, Jonathan, *Biografie aan een Rebel*. Amsterdam, 2019.

Binstock 1999
Binstock, Benjamin, 'Rembrandt's Paint', *Res: Anthropology and Aesthetics* 36 (1999), pp. 138–65.

Birkmeyer 1949
Birkmeyer, Karl M. 'Observations on the Tour of Berlin Masterpieces', *College Art Journal* 9, 1 (1949), pp. 19–24.

Blankert 1982
Blankert, Albert, *Ferdinand Bol (1616–1680): Rembrandt's Pupil*. Doornspijk, 1982.

Blankert 1997
Blankert, Albert, 'Rembrandt's Impact', in Melbourne/Canberra 1997, pp. 202–12.

Blöss 2023
Blöss, Willy, *Rembrandt. Der Mann ohne Goldhelm*. Aachen, 2023.

Bode 1890
Bode, Wilhelm, 'Rembrandt als Erzieher, von einem Deutschen', *Preußische Jahrbücher* LXV (March 1890), pp. 301–14.

Bode 1891
Bode, Wilhelm, 'Das Bildnis von Rembrandts Bruder Adriaen im Mauritshuis', *Oud Holland* 9 (1891), pp. 1–6.

Bode 1909
Bode, Wilhelm von, *Great Masters of Dutch and Flemish Painting*. London, 1909.

Bode 1930
Bode, Wilhelm von, *Mein Leben*. 2 vols. Berlin, 1930.

Bode/Groot 1897–1905
Bode, Wilhelm von, and Cornelis Hofstede de Groot, *Rembrandt. Beschreibendes Verzeichnis seiner Gemälde mit heliographischen Nachbildungen. Geschichte seines Lebens und seiner Kunst*. 8 vols. Paris, 1897–1905.

Borenius 1944
Borenius, Tancred, *Rembrandt*. London, 1944.

Boston/Chicago 2003
Ackley, Clifford S., ed. *Rembrandt's Journey: Painter, Draftsman, Etcher*, with Ronni Baer, Thomas E. Rassieur and William W. Robinson. Boston, Museum of Fine Arts/ Art Institute of Chicago. Boston, 2003.

Braunschweig 2004
Büttner, Nils, and Ulrich Heinen, with Birgit Franke, *Peter Paul Rubens. Barocke Leidenschaften*. Braunschweig, Herzog Anton Ulrich-Museum. Munich, 2004.

Braunschweig 2006
Döring, Thomas, *Aus Rembrandts Kreis. Die Zeichnungen des Braunschweiger Kupferstichkabinetts*, with Gisela Bungarten and Christiane Pagel. Braunschweig, Herzog Anton Ulrich-Museum, Kunstmuseum des Landes Niedersachsen. Passau, 2006.

Bredius 1898–9
Bredius, Abraham, 'Kritische Bemerkungen zur Amsterdamer Rembrandt-Ausstellung', *Zeitschrift für Bildende Kunst*, n. s., 10 (1898–9), pp. 161–8, 191–8.

Bredius/Gerson 1969
Bredius, Abraham, *Rembrandt: The Complete Edition of the Paintings*, rev. Horst Gerson. London, 1969.

Bremen 2000
Röver-Kann, Anne, ed. *Rembrandt, oder nicht? Zeichnungen von Rembrandt und seinem Kreis aus den Hamburger und Bremer Kupferstichkabinetten*. Kunsthalle Bremen. Ostfildern-Ruit, 2000.

Broos 1981–2
Broos, Ben, review of Walter L. Strauss and Marjon van der Meulen, *The Rembrandt Documents*, in *Simiolus* 12 (1981–2), pp. 245–62.

Broos 1983
Broos, Ben, 'Fame Shared is Fame Doubled', in Amsterdam/Groningen 1983, pp. 35–58.

Broos 2012
Broos, Ben, 'Een onbekend "Zelfportret" van de jonge Samuel van Hoogstraten', *Oud Holland* 125 (2012), pp. 180–92.

Broos 2013
Broos, Ben, 'The Young Samuel van Hoogstraten, Corrected by Rembrandt', in *The Universal Art of Samuel van Hoogstraten (1627–1678), Painter, Writer, and Courtier*, ed. Thijs Weststeijn, pp. 75–95. Amsterdam, 2013.

Brown 1979
Brown, Christopher, *Rembrandt*. 2 vols. Milan, 1979.

Brown 1981
Brown, Christopher, *Carel Fabritius: Complete Edition with a Catalogue Raisonné*. Oxford, 1981.

Brusati 1995
Brusati, Celeste, *Artifice and Illusion: The Art and Writing of Samuel van Hoogstraten*. Chicago, 1995.

Bruyn 1983
Bruyn, Josua, 'On Rembrandt's Use of Studio-Props and Model Drawing during the 1630s', in *Essays in Northern European Art presented to Egbert Haverkamp-Begemann on his Sixtieth Birthday*, ed. Anne-Marie Logan, pp. 52–60. Doornspijk, 1983.

Bruyn 1987
Bruyn, Josua, review of Werner Sumowski, *Gemälde der Rembrandt-Schüler*, vol. 2, G. van den Eeckhout–I. de Joudreville, in *Oud Holland* 101 (1987), pp. 222–34.

Bruyn 1989
Bruyn, Josua, 'Studio Practice and Studio Production', in Corpus 1982–2015, vol. 3, 1989, pp. 12–50.

Bruyn 1991
Bruyn, Josua, 'Rembrandts Werkstatt: Funktion & Produktion', in Berlin/Amsterdam/London 1991, pp. 68–89.

Bulckens/Hout 2023
Bulckens, Koen, and Nico van Hout, 'Tronies. Een introductie to hun kenmerken en oorsprong', in *Krasse Koppen: Rubens, Rembrandt en Vermeer*, pp. 11–23. Antwerp, Koninklijk Museum voor Schone Kunsten/ Dublin, National Gallery of Ireland. Veurne, 2023.

Busche 2015
Busche, Ernst A., 'Der Mann mit dem Goldhelm. Neue Erkenntnisse zur Provenienz des Gemäldes', *Jahrbuch der Berliner Museen* 57 (2015), pp. 99–106.

Chapman 1990
Chapman, H. Perry, *Rembrandt's Self-Portraits. A Study in Seventeenth-Century Identity*. Princeton, 1990.

Chicago 1969
Rembrandt After Three Hundred Years: An Exhibition of Rembrandt and His Followers. Art Institute of Chicago, 1969.

Claus 2010
Claus, Horst, 'Rembrandt – Almost by Himself. The Use of Paintings in Hans Steinhoff's Film Biography "Rembrandt" (1942)', in *Strategien der Filmanalyse – reloaded. Festschrift für Klaus Kanzog*, ed. Michael Schaudig, pp. 277–87. Munich, 2010.

Coburg 1975
Maedebach, Heino, and Minni Maedebach, eds. *Meisterwerke europäischer Graphik 15.–18. Jh. aus dem Besitz des Kupferstichkabinettes Coburg. Ausstellung zur 200-Jahrfeier des Coburger Kupferstichkabinettes*. Coburg, 1975.

Moffitt 1984
Moffitt, John F., 'Who is the Old Man in a Golden Helmet?' *The Art Bulletin* 66, 3 (1984), pp. 417–27.

Molen 2015
Molen, Tom van der, 'Das Leben von Govert Flinck', in *Govert Flinck – Reflecting History. Mit einer künstlerischen Intervention von Ori Gersht*, pp. 11–21. Museum Kurhaus Kleve – Ewald Mataré-Collection. Kleve, 2015.

Moltke 1965
Moltke, Joachim Wolfgang von, *Govaert Flinck (1615–1660)*. Amsterdam, 1965.

Moltke 1994
Moltke, Joachim Wolfgang von, *Arent de Gelder, Dordrecht 1645–1727*. Doornspijk, 1994.

Montias 1982
Montias, John Michael, *Artists and Artisans in Delft: A Socio-Economic Study of the Seventeenth Century*. Princeton, 1982.

Montias 1987
Montias, John Michael, 'Cost and Value in Seventeenth-Century Dutch Art', *Art History* 10 (1987), pp. 455–66.

Montias 1988
Montias, John Michael, 'Art Dealers in the Seventeenth-Century Netherlands', *Simiolus* 18 (1988), pp. 244–56.

Montias 2002
Montias, John Michael, *Art at Auction in Seventeenth-Century Amsterdam*. Amsterdam, 2002.

Moroz 1993
Moroz, Vadim, and Monika Solomina Peretz-Moroz, *Der 'Mann mit dem Goldhelm'. Und doch Rembrandt. Ein Diskussionsbeitrag zur Belebung des Rembrandt-Streits*. Berlin, 1993.

Müller-Hofstede 1929
Müller-Hofstede, Cornelius, 'Studien zu Lastman und Rembrandt', *Jahrbuch der Preußischen Kunstsammlungen* 50 (1929), pp. 45–83.

Münster/Amsterdam/Jerusalem 1994
Tümpel, Christian, ed. *Im Lichte Rembrandts. Das Alte Testament im Goldenen Zeitalter der niederländischen Kunst*, with Gerlinde Beer. Münster, Westfälisches Landesmuseum für Kunst und Kunstgeschichte. Zwolle, 1994.

Munich 2003
Vignau-Wilberg, Thea, ed. *Rembrandt-Zeichnungen in Munich / The Munich Rembrandt Drawings. Symposion zur Ausstellung Rembrandt auf Papier, Werk und Wirkung*. Munich, Staatliche Graphische Sammlung. Munich, 2003.

Munich 2014
Hirschfelder, Dagmar, and León Krempel, eds. *Tronies. Das Gesicht in der Frühen Neuzeit, Beiträge zu einem internationalen Symposion zur Ausstellung 'Tronie – Marlene Dumas und die Alten Meister'*. Munich, Haus der Kunst. Berlin, 2014.

Munich/Amsterdam 2001
Vignau-Wilberg, Thea, *Rembrandt auf Papier. Werk und Wirkung / Rembrandt and his Followers. Drawings from Munich*, with essay by Peter Schatborn. Munich, Staatliche Graphische Sammlungen/ Amsterdam, Museum Het Rembrandthuis. Munich, 2001.

Nadler 2022
Nadler, Steven, *The Portraitist: Frans Hals and His World*. Chicago, 2022.

Neidhardt 2005
Neidhardt, Uta, 'Rembrandts Werke im augusteischen Dresden. Geschichte ihrer Erwerbung und Rezeption', *Dresdener Kunstblätter* 4 (2005), pp. 241–9.

Neidhardt 2006
Neidhardt, Uta, 'Rembrandts "Ganymed" – fremd und vertraut', in Dresden 2006, pp. 7–19.

Neumann 1902
Neumann, Carl, *Rembrandt*. 2 vols. Berlin, 1902.

Nevitt 1998
Nevitt, Rodney, Jr., 'Rembrandt's Hidden Lovers', *Nederlands Kunsthistorisch Jaarboek* 48 (1998), pp. 162–91.

New York 1995
Liedtke, Walter, et al., eds. *Rembrandt / Not Rembrandt in the Metropolitan Museum of Art: Aspects of Connoisseurship*, vol. 2: *Paintings, Drawings and Prints: Art-Historical Perspectives*. New York, Metropolitan Museum of Art. New York, 1995.

New York 2007
Liedtke, Walter, *Dutch Paintings in the Metropolitan Museum of Art*, New York. 2 vols. New Haven, 2007.

New York 2016
Bevers, Holm, and Per Rumberg, *Rembrandt's First Masterpiece*. New York, The Morgan Library & Museum. New York, 2016.

New York/London 2001
Liedtke, Walter, with Michiel C. Plomp and Axel Rüger, *Vermeer and the Delft School*, with essays by Reinier Baarsen et al. New York, The Metropolitan Museum of Art/ London, The National Gallery. New Haven, 2001.

NH
The New Hollstein: Dutch and Flemish Etchings, Engravings and Woodcuts, 1450–1700. Rembrandt, compiled by Erik Hinterding and Jaco Rutgers, ed. Ger Luijten. 7 vols. Oudekerk aan den IJssel, 2013.

Nicolaisen 2013
Nicolaisen, Jan, '"gemoet" – Anmerkungen zur Beschreibung des "inneren Menschen" in der holländischen Malerei des 17. Jahrhunderts', in *Ad fontes! Niederländische Kunst des 17. Jahrhunderts in Quellen*, ed. Claudia Frietzsche, Karin Leonhard and Gregor J. M. Weber, pp. 281–304. Petersberg, 2013.

Nicolaisen 2014
Nicolaisen, Jan, 'Theatralische Identitäten? Zu zwei Tronies von Jan Lievens im Museum der bildenden Künste Leipzig', in Munich 2014, pp. 89–96.

Nuremberg 1995
Tacke, Andreas, *Die Gemälde des 17. Jahrhunderts im Germanischen Nationalmuseum*. Nuremberg, 1995.

Nystad 1999
Nystad, Saam. 'Der Goldhelm', *Jahrbuch der Berliner Museen*, n. s., 41 (1999), pp. 245–50.

Ottawa/Frankfurt 2021
Dickey, Stephanie S., and Jochen Sander, eds. *Nennt mich Rembrandt! Durchbruch in Amsterdam*. Ottawa, National Gallery of Canada/Frankfurt a. M., Städel Museum. Munich, 2021.

Pächt 1991
Pächt, Otto, *Rembrandt*, ed. Edwin Lachnit. Munich, 1991.

Paris 2009
Foucart, Jacques, *Catalogue des peintures flamandes et hollandaises du musée du Louvre*, ed. Musée du Louvre, département des Peintures. Paris, 2009.

Paris 2016
Starcky, Emmanuel, et al., *Rembrandt intime*. Paris, Musée Jacquemart-André. Brussels, 2016.

Partsch 2018
Partsch, Susanna, *Schau mir in die Augen, Dürer!* Munich, 2018.

Pels 1681
Pels, Andries, *Gebruik en misbruik des tooneels*. Amsterdam 1681.

Pieh 1986
Pieh, Gerhard, 'Die Restaurierung', in Kelch 1986, pp. 28–37.

Pieh 1987
Pieh, Gerhard, 'Die Restaurierung des "Mann mit dem Goldhelm"', *Maltechnik. Internationale Zeitschrift für Farb- und Maltechniken, Restaurierung und Museumsfragen* (January 1987), pp. 9–34.

Postma 1988
Postma, Hugo J., 'De Amsterdamse verzamelaar Herman Becker (ca. 1617–1678). Nieuwe gegevens over een geldschieter van Rembrandt', *Oud Holland* 102 (1988), pp. 1–21.

Raupp 1984
Raupp, Hans-Joachim, *Untersuchungen zu Künstlerbildnis und Künstlerdarstellung in den Niederlanden im 17. Jahrhundert*. Hildesheim, 1984.

Rebel 1981
Rebel, Ernst, *Faksimile und Mimesis. Studien zur deutschen Reproduktionsgraphik des 18. Jahrhunderts*. Mittenwald, 1981.

Renard 1927
Renard, Edmund, *Clemens August Kurfürst von Köln. Ein Rheinischer Mäzen und Weidmann des 18. Jahrhunderts*. Bielefeld, 1927.

Rifkin 1969
Rifkin, Benjamin A., 'Rembrandt and His Circle, Part I', *Art News* 68 (1969), pp. 26–7.

Roberts 1976
Roberts, Keith, '"Art in Seventeenth Century Holland" at the National Gallery', *Burlington Magazine* 118 (1976), pp. 781–5.

Robinson 1996
Robinson, W. W., *The Early Works of Nicolaes Maes, 1635–1661*, Diss. Harvard University. Cambridge, Mass., 1996.

Roodenburg/Dickey 2010
Roodenburg, Herman, and Stephanie S. Dickey, eds. *The Passions in the Arts of the Early Modern Netherlands*. Zwolle, 2010.

Roscam Abbing 1993
Roscam Abbing, Michiel, with Peter Thissen, *De schilder & schrijver Samuel van Hoogstraten, 1627–1678. Eigentijdse bronnen & œuvre van gesigneerde schilderijen*. Leiden, 1993.

Roscam Abbing 1999
Roscam Abbing, Michiel, *Rembrandt toont sijn konst. Bijdragen over Rembrandt-documenten uit de periode 1648–1756*. Leiden, 1999.

Rosenberg 1948
Rosenberg, Jakob, *Rembrandt: Life and Work*. New York, 1948.

Rotterdam 1988
Giltaij, Jeroen, *The Drawings by Rembrandt and his School*. Rotterdam, Museum Boijmans Van Beuningen. Rotterdam, 1988.

Rotterdam 2006
Elen, Albert J., *Rembrandt in Rotterdam. Drawings of Rembrandt and his Circle in the Museum Boijmans Van Beuningen*, ed. Hanneke de Man. Rotterdam, 2006.

Röver 1986
Röver, Anne, *In Rembrandts Manier. Kopie, Nachahmung und Aneignung in den graphischen Künsten des 18. Jahrhunderts*. Bremen, 1986.

Sandrart 1675
Sandrart, Joachim von, *Teutsche Academie der edlen Bau-, Bild- und Mahlerey-Künste. Leben der berühmten Maler, Bildhauer und Baumeister*. Nuremberg 1675. Reprint Munich, 1925.

Savoy/Sissis 2013
Savoy, Bénédicte, and Philippa Sissis, eds. *Die Berliner Museumsinsel. Impressionen internationaler Besucher (1830–1990). Eine Anthologie*. Vienna, 2013.

Scallen 2004
Scallen, Catherine B., *Rembrandt, Reputation, and the Practice of Connoisseurship*. Amsterdam, 2004.

Schama 2000
Schama, Simon, *Rembrandts Augen*. Berlin, 2000.

Schatborn 1985
Schatborn, Peter, *Tekeningen van Rembrandt. Zijn onbekende leerlingen en navolgers / Drawings by Rembrandt. His Anonymous Pupils and Followers*. Catalogus van de Nederlandse tekeningen in het Rijksprentenkabinet, Rijksmuseum Amsterdam, 4. The Hague, 1985.

Schatborn 1986
Schatborn, Peter, review of J. Bruyn, B. Haak, S. H. Levie, P. J. J. van Thiel and E. van de Wetering, *Foundation Rembrandt Research Project. A Corpus of Rembrandt-Paintings*, vol. 1: *1625–1631*, The Hague, 1982, in *Oud Holland* 100 (1986), pp. 55–63.

Schatborn 1991
Schatborn, Peter, '"Papierenkunst" van Rembrandt en Lievens', in Leiden 1991, pp. 60–79.

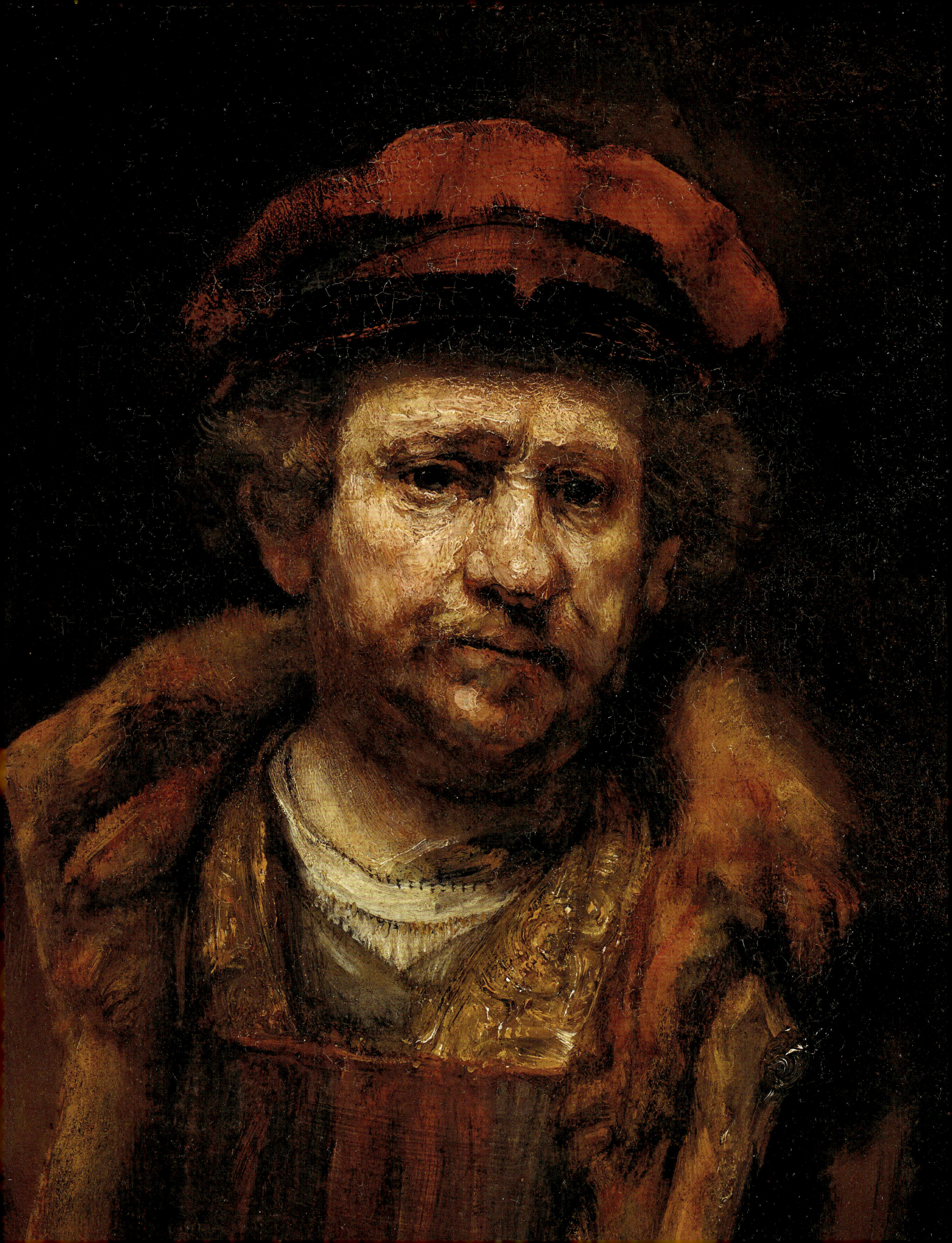

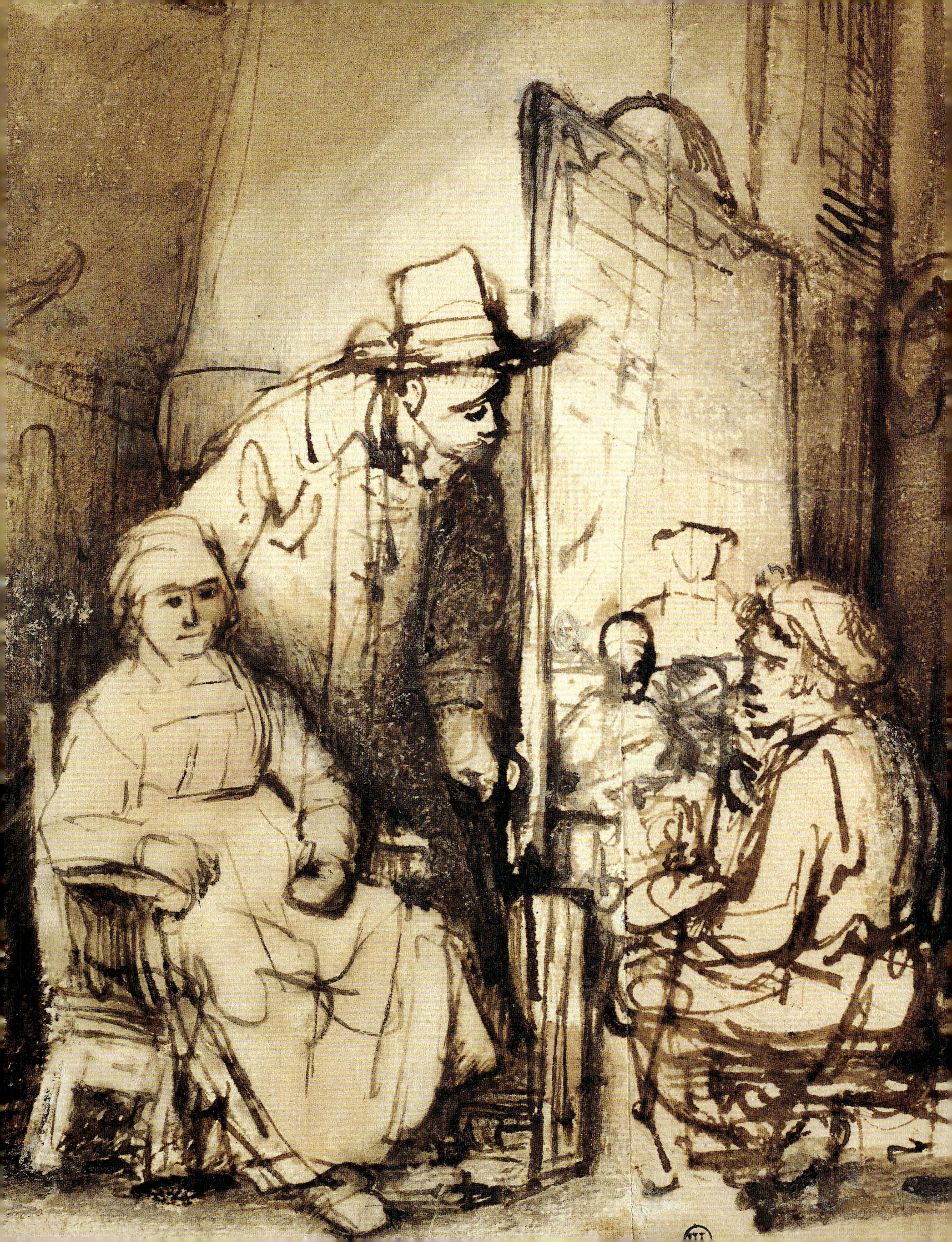